Julie's Favorites

Cooking with a little help from my Family and Friends

Copyright 2020 LENKK PRESS
Recipes collected and compiled by Julie Royce
Assistant Editor: Ezra Elitzur
Cover: Bob Royce
Photos courtesy of Pixabay Free Images

All Rights Reserved

Recipes

I've collected and culled and collated.
I've chopped, and I've peeled,
and I've grated.
Some quite nutritious,
some merely delicious,
these recipes come highly rated.

A special thanks to Bob Royce, Ezra Elitzur, Jes Phillips, and Diane Herron.

FORWARD

For me, home cooking always made a house feel like a home—the delicious smell of cookies fresh from the oven after school, or the aroma of a pot roast calling us to the dinner table.

My recipe drawer had become a mess. I would remember a recipe but knew that finding it would mean shuffling through a morass of loose papers that hadn't been alphabetized or sorted. I hadn't even discarded those that produced dismal failures. For someone who is a tad obsessive compulsive, the situation was maddening.

It seemed time to type my treasure trove, create a book, and restore order. I would make a hard cover version for my grandchildren. Ezra, especially, wanted a copy. He also offered input along the way. The job often afforded me happy memories: Chicken dinners at my Grandma Bertha's on Sunday afternoons, special birthday cakes from my Aunt Edith, and homemade bread with jam the nights I spent at my Grandma Emma's. I thought back to the Thanksgiving celebrations when my mother served turkey, mashed potatoes, stuffing, and lemon pie. When we couldn't swallow another bite, we retired to the living room to watch the Lions lose again. Comfort food and love. After my husband Bob's heart surgery, I added a few healthy dishes or healthier versions of old favorites.

As I sorted, I was reminded of Pete Seeger's *Turn, Turn, Turn*, suggesting there is a time and a place for everything. I have actually grown fond of black bean burgers and salad with lemon and olive oil (that great healthy fat). But there are also times when nothing but Caramel Pecan Pie with whipped cream and a side of Godiva bonbons will do. And even though Bob and I strive to eat healthier, you may notice a weighting towards sweets, particularly cookies and caramel.

This book is a compilation of eclectic recipes I have gathered over nearly sixty years of cooking. They came from family and friends and neighbors. I found some in books sold at church or other group fundraisers. Some leaped from magazine pages flaunting epicurean delights too tempting to ignore. These are my favorites.

To everyone who sent or gave me recipes over the years, I say thanks. To everyone who likes to eat, I say, enjoy. I hope you find something that makes your taste buds tingle.

Remember, as Harriet Van Horne said, "Cooking is like love. It should be entered into with abandon or not at all."

Or, as Australian Chef Skye Gyngell pointed out, "Cooking is not about being the best or most perfect cook, but rather it is about sharing the table with family and friends."

Wishing you many happy cooking experiences.
Julie

Contents

Appetizers, Dips, and Snacks 3

Beverages 32

Breads, Rolls, Muffins, and Waffles 45

Cakes and Frostings 85

Casseroles, Stews, and One Dish Meals 130

Cookies, Brownies, and Candy 146

Desserts 196

Eggs, Cheese, and Brunch 220

Italian, Mexican, Asian, and other Ethnic Dishes 238

Main Dishes: Beef, Fish, Pork, and Poultry 265

Pies 315

Sandwiches and Soups 384

Salads and Sides 384

Index 445

Appetizers, Dips, and Snacks

"Hors D'oeuvres: A ham sandwich cut into forty pieces." **Jack Benny**

"Appetizers are the little things you keep eating until you lose your appetite." **Joe Moore**

"I believe that I was a dog in a past life. That's the only thing that would explain why I like to snack on Purina Dog Chow." **Dean Koontz**

Artichoke and Crab Dip

<u>Ingredients:</u>

1 8 oz pkg cream cheese, softened
1 cup mayonnaise (not salad dressing)
1 clove garlic, pressed
1 (14 oz) can artichoke hearts in water, drained and chopped
1 ½ cups cooked crabmeat (you can use canned but get a high quality)
¾ cup freshly grated parmesan cheese
1/3 cup chopped green onion
1/3 cup chopped red bell pepper
1 tsp ground cayenne pepper
½ cup dry bread crumbs
2 tsp chopped green onion, or to taste
2 tsp chopped red bell pepper, or to taste

<u>Directions:</u>
1. Preheat oven to 350.
2. Combine cream cheese and mayonnaise in a large bowl and stir until smooth; stir in garlic. Gently stir in artichoke hearts, crab, parmesan cheese, green onion, red bell pepper, and cayenne pepper. Transfer to oven proof casserole dish and top with bread crumbs.
3. Bake in preheated oven until crumb topping is golden brown and dip is hot, about 30 minutes. Garnish with remaining green onion and red bell pepper.

<u>Notes:</u>
You can also use crushed corn flakes with a dash of butter for the topping.

Asparagus Roll-Ups

<u>Ingredients:</u>

12 slices of white bread, crust removed
8 slices bacon, cooked, drained, and crumbled
24 thin fresh asparagus spears, half cooked
¼ cup butter, melted
¼ cup freshly grated parmesan cheese
8 oz tub of cream cheese with chives

<u>Directions:</u>
1. Flatten bread with rolling pin.
2. Combine cream cheese and bacon. Spread on bread and cover up to the edges. Place 2 asparagus spears on each slice of bread and roll tightly. Place seam-side down on greased cookie sheet.
3. Mix parmesan cheese with melted butter and brush tops of asparagus rolls.
4. Bake at 400 for 12 minutes.

<u>Notes:</u>
This recipe is a bit labor intensive. I make the asparagus roll ups and freeze them so all I have to do is brush with butter/parmesan mixture and bake. If you freeze these roll-ups, make sure you don't put the rolls too tightly together (or they'll stick when you try to thaw them), and put waxed paper between layers.

Banh Mi Bruschetta

Ingredients:
24 (½-inch) slices from baguette-style French bread
1/3 cup mayonnaise
2 tbsp soy sauce
6 oz thinly sliced ham
1 English cucumber, sliced or shredded
2 carrots, shredded
½ cup coarsely chopped fresh cilantro
thin jalapeno pepper slices (optional)
lime wedges (optional)

Directions:
1. Preheat broiler. Spread mayonnaise on one side of each bread slice and arrange, spread side up, on a baking sheet. Broil 4 to 5 inches from the heat for 1 minute or just until starting to toast. Remove from oven; gently brush with soy sauce. Return to oven and broil 1 minute more.
2. Top bread slices with ham, cucumber, carrots, and cilantro. Add jalapeno slices and serve with lime wedges.

Bay Scallops and Shrimp Ceviche

Ingredients:

8 oz calamari steak
1 pound scallops
1 pound shrimp
1 cup fresh lime juice
½ cup mango
½ cup jicama
4 avocadoes
3 tbsp Roma tomato
4 tsp Serrano chili
½ cup grilled corn
4 tsp cilantro
blue corn chips

Directions:
1. In large bowl, chop seafood, cover with lime juice, stir and let sit for one hour. (The lime juice cooks the seafood.)
2. While seafood is 'cooking' grill corn on the cob and slice off the kernels.
3. Dice mango, 3 avocadoes, jicama, and tomato into small pieces. Finely dice chili. Add to seafood. Dice cilantro and add. Spoon mixture into glass tumblers.
4. Cut remaining avocado into slices, and put a slice on each serving.
5. Serve with blue corn chips and hot sauce. Serves 8.

Notes:

Jicama is a tuber vegetable. You might be able to substitute ¼ cup each of celery and water chestnuts if you absolutely can't find it in your grocery store. My son, Jes Phillips, got me this recipe from Nordstrom's restaurant when he worked there. It makes an excellent appetizer in smaller portions or a meal itself in larger amounts. Great for eating while sitting in the back yard on a hot summer day. Grab an ice-cold beer and you are all set.

Best Chicken Appetizer Ever

Ingredients:

2-3 boneless skinless chicken breasts
1 cup pineapple juice
½ cup brown sugar
1/3 cup soy sauce
¼ tsp liquid smoke
1 inch of fresh ginger, grated fine
1 tbsp fresh garlic, grated fine
2 tsp sesame seeds
skewers

Directions:
1. Soak wooden skewers in water for at least a half an hour. If the chicken is fresh, place on a baking sheet and put it in the freezer for 15-20 minutes to slightly firm it so that it will be easier to slice. If it is frozen, slightly thaw it for the same reason.
2. Slice the chicken across the grain in about ¼-inch slices. They can be different lengths, that is ok.
3. Mix all of the other ingredients except for the sesame seeds in a large bowl.
4. Place the chicken in the mixture and stir to coat the chicken pieces. Place the bowl in the refrigerator for at least 30 minutes but up to 6 hours. 6 hours is best.
5. Place each piece of chicken on a wooden skewer in a zig zag fashion and sprinkle with the sesame seeds.
6. Broil in the oven flipping them once to get both sides cooked. (5-7 minutes each side or to desired degree of doneness.)

Filet Mignon Towers

Ingredients:

1 8 oz (4 x 4-inch) piece beef tenderloin (filet mignon)
salt and pepper to taste
6 oz (2/3 cup) cream cheese
2 tsp fresh lemon juice
½ tsp sugar
2 tbsp finely chopped fresh basil
1 8-inch cucumber sliced into 32 quarter inch rounds
3 tbsp salsa, drained

Directions:
1. Season beef with salt and pepper and grill over medium heat until medium rare, 4 to 5 minutes per side. Cut beef into 8 equal size pieces, then slice each piece into 4 slices.
2. Combine cream cheese, lemon juice, sugar, basil, and salsa in a bowl. Using a spatula transfer mixture into a large Ziplock bag. Twist bag until mixture is forced into one corner of bag. Use scissors to snip off the corner of the bag.
3. Arrange steak slices on cucumber rounds.
4. Pipe 1 tsp cream cheese mixture onto each round.

Notes:
The original recipe called for diced tomato and onion not salsa. Cream cheese was piped onto steak and then sprinkled with diced onion and tomato. My feeble attempts always ended up with none of the tomato or onion staying on the cream cheese. I found it easier to buy a quality homemade salsa, drain and mix it with the cream cheese, and simply spoon it onto the steak. I thought it looked better and was simpler.

Grilled Marinated Shrimp

<u>Ingredients:</u>

1 cup olive oil
¼ cup chopped fresh parsley
1 lemon, juiced
2 tbsp hot sauce
3 cloves of garlic, minced
1 tbsp tomato paste
2 tsp dried oregano
1 tsp salt
1 tsp black pepper
2 pounds fresh, raw shrimp, cleaned and deveined, tail left on
wooden skewers (soaked in water for half hour prior to use)

<u>Directions:</u>
1. In bowl, mix oil, parsley, lemon juice, hot sauce, garlic, tomato paste, oregano, salt and pepper. Reserve a small amount for basting. Put remainder of sauce in large plastic bag and add shrimp. Seal, refrigerate, and marinate for two hours.
2. Preheat grill to medium-low. Thread shrimp onto skewers piercing once near head and once near tale. (Thread several shrimp on each skewer.) Discard marinade sauce.
3. Lightly oil grill grate. Grill skewers 5 minutes, flip and grill other side an additional five minutes, or until shrimp are opaque. Brush frequently with reserved marinade.

<u>Notes:</u>
We enjoyed this delicious dish at a Mardi Gras party hosted by our friends, Heidi and Mike Landry. Heidi provided me with the recipe.

Healthy Chimichurri Shrimp Appetizer

<u>Ingredients:</u>

2 cup fresh parsley
2 cup fresh cilantro
2 garlic cloves peeled
2 tsp sriracha sauce or other favorite hot sauce
¼ cup olive oil + more for cooking shrimp
1 tbsp lemon juice
1 tsp onion powder
½ tsp salt and more to taste
¼ tsp pepper
2 pounds fresh or frozen large shrimp thawed and peeled

<u>Directions:</u>

1. Add fresh parsley and cilantro to a blender or food processor. Pulse for a couple of seconds until the herbs are finely chopped.
2. Add all other ingredients except shrimp and pulse again until you have a well combined sauce. Add extra oil if necessary. Check the seasoning and add extra salt, hot sauce, or lemon juice to taste. Set aside the chimichurri sauce.
3. Heat about 2 tsp olive oil in a large nonstick skillet over medium-high heat. Once hot, add shrimp and season with a pinch of salt and pepper. Cook shrimp about 3 minutes, then flip and add about a tbsp chimichurri sauce to the top of each shrimp. Continue to cook, stirring shrimp around for about 2-3 minutes more until shrimp are thoroughly cooked. Once they are pink on both sides, remove them from the skillet to a large plate lined with a paper towel.
4. After all shrimp are cooked, transfer to a serving dish and serve with toothpicks, warm or at room temperature.

<u>Notes:</u>
Shrimp cook quickly and are easy to overcook so watch them closely. I find it easier and more attractive to spread the chimichurri sauce on a serving platter (instead of on shrimp as they are cooking), place the shrimp on top of sauce, and then sprinkle additional fresh parsley over the shrimp.

Individual Spicy Greek Layered Cups

Ingredients:

1 cup tzatziki sauce
1 tsp minced garlic
1 cup minced red onion
1 cup roasted red peppers (packed in water), chopped
12 tbsp spicy or regular hummus
1 cup diced cucumber
1 cup chopped plum tomato
10 large Kalamata olive, chopped
4 tbsp crumbled feta and ¼ cup fresh mint leaves for garnish

Directions:
1. Combine tzatziki with garlic in a small bowl.
2. Line up eight 9 ½ oz plastic cups or glasses. In each, layer 2 tbsp tzatziki mixture, 2 tbsp onion, 2 tbsp pepper, 1 ½ tbsp hummus, 2 tbsp cucumber, 2 tbsp tomato, 1 tbsp olives, and ½ tbsp feta; garnish with mint. Refrigerate until ready to serve.

Notes:

This appetizer recipe came from my friend, Susan Jurkiewicz, who served it at a social function she hosted. Everyone loved it, and she thought I might like the recipe. These cups can be served with pita bread cut into small pieces or are equally appreciated as individual salads on a buffet table.

Mushroom Croustades

<u>Toasted Cup Ingredients:</u>

24 slices thin white bread
2 tbsp soft butter

<u>Toasted Cup Directions:</u>

1. Cut out 3-inch circles of bread with a cookie cutter. Roll flat. Brush circles with melted butter.
2. Carefully fit circles of bread into 2 (12 cups each) mini muffin pans, butter side down, pressing gently to make little cups.
3. Bake at 400 for 8 to 10 minutes or until lightly brown.

<u>Filling Ingredients:</u>

4 tbsp butter
½ tsp salt
3 tbsp finely chopped shallots
1/8 tsp cayenne
½ pound mushrooms, finely chopped
1 tbsp chopped parsley
2 tbsp flour
1 cup heavy cream
1 clove garlic, crushed
1½ tbsp chopped chives
½ tsp fresh squeezed lemon juice

<u>Filling Directions:</u>

1. In heavy skillet, melt butter. Add chopped shallots, stir and cook 4 minutes, then stir in chopped mushrooms. Cook about 10 to 15 minutes, stirring occasionally.
2. Remove from heat and stir in flour. Mix well and stir in heavy cream. Bring to boil. Simmer 2 minutes. Remove from heat. Stir in herbs and other ingredients. Cool sauce and store in refrigerator until needed. This sauce may be made up to two days ahead of time.

<u>Topping Ingredients:</u>

6 slices bacon (optional), fried crisp, drained, and crumbled
2 tbsp freshly grated parmesan cheese
dots of butter
(Recipe continued on next page.)

Baking and Assembly:
1. When ready to bake, fill the toasted cups with mushroom mixture, put small amount of parmesan cheese and a dot of butter on each filled cup. Sprinkle with crumbled bacon.
2. Bake at 350 for 10 minutes. If you prefer tops browner, you can put under broiler for one additional minute.

Notes:
This recipe is not difficult, but it is time consuming. It helps to make the cups and bake them as much as a day ahead of time. Likewise, the filling can be made ahead of time and the bacon fried and crumbled beforehand. Then you just have to assemble. This is one of my family's favorites, so I have always considered it worth the effort.

I got the recipe from a church fund-raising recipe book that I bought from a friend, Linda Danko, at her low-key, casual wedding. The recipe lasted longer than the marriage.

Mushroom and Ricotta Bruschetta

<u>Ingredients:</u>

1 cup ricotta cheese
1 egg
1 lemon, zested
½ tsp salt and pinch freshly ground black pepper, or to taste
1 pinch red pepper flakes, or to taste
4 slices French bread, toasted
2 tbsp olive oil, divided
1 tbsp butter
16 large white mushrooms, sliced
¼ cup green onions, chopped
¼ cup Marsala wine
½ cup chicken broth
2 tsp lemon juice
2 tbsp chopped Italian parsley
1 tbsp butter

<u>Directions:</u>

1. Preheat oven to 425.
2. Mix ricotta, egg, lemon zest, ½ tsp salt, black pepper, and red pepper flakes in a bowl until smooth.
3. Place toasted bread slices on a baking sheet. Sprinkle with 1 tbsp olive oil and evenly divide ricotta mixture atop 4 bread slices.
4. Bake in the preheated oven until cheese is browned, about 12 minutes.
5. Heat butter and 1 tbsp olive oil in a large skillet over medium-high heat; cook and stir mushrooms in mixture until browned, 5 to 6 minutes.
6. Add green onions; cook and stir until softened, 2 to 3 minutes. Stir marsala wine into mixture and cook until reduced by half, about 1 minute. Reduce heat to medium-low. Add chicken stock and lemon juice to skillet; cook until liquid has evaporated. Reduce heat to low. Stir in parsley and butter. Season with salt and black pepper to taste.
7. Spoon mushroom mixture equally atop 4 slices of ricotta-topped bread slices.

<u>Note:</u>

My sister-in-law, Andrea Beach, introduced me to bruschetta as an appetizer when we made it for political fundraiser she was hosting in Grand Haven, Michigan.

Nine Mayonnaise Based Dips

1. **Hot Artichoke Dip** »» Stir the following until well-mixed: ½ cup mayonnaise, ½ cup sour cream, 1 can (14 oz) artichokes hearts (drained and chopped), 1/3 cup freshly grated parmesan cheese, ½ tsp hot sauce. Spoon into small casserole dish and bake 30 minutes at 350 or until bubbly.

2. **Bacon Horseradish Dip** »» Stir the following until well-mixed: 1 cup mayonnaise, 1 cup sour cream, ¼ cup real bacon bits (bacon fried, drained, and crumbled), ¼ cup prepared horseradish. Cover and chill.

3. **Hot Cheddar Bean Dip** »» Stir the following until well mixed: ½ cup mayonnaise, 16 oz pinto beans, drained and mashed, 1 cup shredded cheddar cheese, 4 oz chopped green chilies, ¼ tsp hot pepper sauce. Spoon into small ovenproof dish. Bake at 350 or until bubbly.

4. **Hot Crab Dip** »» Beat 3 oz softened cream cheese until smooth. Stir in ½ cup mayonnaise, 16 oz drained crabmeat, ¼ cup minced onion, 1 tbsp lemon juice, and 1/8 tsp hot pepper sauce. Spoon into small ovenproof dish. Bake at 350 or until bubbly.

5. **Cucumber Dill Dip** »» Beat 8 oz softened cream cheese until smooth. Stir in and mix the following: 1 cup mayonnaise, 2 medium cucumbers, peeled, seeded, and chopped, 2 tbsp sliced green onion, 1 tbsp lemon juice, 2 tsp snipped fresh dill or ½ tsp dried dill weed, ½ tsp hot pepper sauce. Cover and chill.

(More dips on next page.)

6. **French Onion Dip** »» Stir ½ cup mayonnaise, 2 cups sour cream, 1 package (1.9 oz) dried onion soup mix. Mix well. Cover and chill.

7. **Ginger Lime Fruit Dip** »» Stir until well mixed: ½ cup mayonnaise, ½ cup sour cream, 2 tsp grated lime peel, 1 tbsp fresh lime juice, 3 tbsp honey (less if you like it less sweet), ½ tsp ground ginger.

8. **Guacamole Dip** »» Stir ½ cup mayonnaise, 1 large avocado, peeled and mashed, 1 small tomato, chopped, ¼ cup minced onion, ¼ cup drained and chopped green chilies, 1 tbsp lemon juice, and ½ tsp salt. Cover and chill.

9. **Shrimp Louis Dip** »» Stir the following until well mixed: 1 cup mayonnaise, 1 cup sour cream, 1/3 cup finely chopped green pepper, ¼ cup chili sauce, 1 tbsp prepared horseradish, ¼ tsp salt, 2 cups finely chopped, cooked shrimp.
Notes:
Make sure you use mayonnaise NOT salad dressing or Miracle Whip. Serve with vegetables (or fruit for Ginger Lime Fruit Dip), chips, or crackers.

Nuts and Bolts

Ingredients:

6 tbsp butter, melted
2 tsp celery salt
2 tsp garlic powder
4 tsp Worcestershire sauce
2 cups Cheerios
2 cups Wheat Chex
2 cups Rice Chex
1 to 2 cans small mixed nuts
2 to 4 cups straight, small pretzels

Directions:
1. Mix first four ingredients on a cookie sheet with sides.
2. Add remaining ingredients.
3. Bake in an oven at 250 degrees for one hour. Stir every 15 minutes.

Note:
This recipe came from my cousin, Barb Albrecht.

Salmon Log

<u>Ingredients:</u>

1 pound red salmon (remove bones and skin)
8 oz cream cheese, room temperature
1 tbsp lemon juice
1 tbsp horseradish
¼ tbsp liquid smoke
3 tbsp finely chopped fresh parsley
½ cup finely chopped pecans

<u>Directions:</u>
1. Poach salmon and cool. Mix cream cheese, salmon, lemon juice, horseradish, and liquid smoke. Refrigerate overnight.
2. Shape into a log and roll log in parsley and pecans.
3. Serve with crackers.

<u>Notes:</u>
Many years ago, I received this recipe from my cousin, Linda Dawson Cutler, in a collection of salmon recipes she sent to me. The next time I distinctly remember it being served was when my daughter's mother-in-law (Shlomit Elitzur) served it at the party she hosted to celebrate my daughter's marriage to her son. I have made it many times, including one occasion when my cousin, Marilyn, and her husband, Chuck, joined us for dinner at my mother's house in Port Sanilac, Michigan. It's a tried and true (and easy) recipe. I prefer to use fresh poached salmon, but in a pinch have used canned.

Salmon Spread with Herbed Crostini

Ingredients:

10 oz salmon, skin removed
4 tbsp olive oil, divided
2 tbsp chopped chives
1 tbsp lime juice
1 tbsp chopped capers
1 shallot, peeled and sliced
1 clove garlic, minced
¼ jalapeno pepper, minced
salt and pepper to taste
16 baguette slices
1 tsp dried thyme
1 tsp chopped parsley
¼ tsp garlic powder

Directions:
1. Preheat oven to 350. Place salmon on a foil-lined baking sheet and bake for 15 minutes. Let cool.
2. Pulse cooled salmon in a food processor until chopped. Place salmon in a medium bowl with 2 tbsp oil, chives, lime juice, capers, shallot, garlic, and jalapeño. Stir well, then season with salt and pepper.
3. Place remaining 2 tbsp oil, thyme, parsley and garlic powder in a resealable plastic bag. Add crostini slices and toss to coat. Bake for 12 minutes or until golden brown.
4. Serve salmon mixture with crostini.

Notes:
If you are going to serve immediately, you can spread the salmon on the crostini. If it may sit for a while, leave it in a small bowl with a knife that allows guests to spread their own. This recipe came from Raley's grocery store and is similar to the salmon log included on the prior page in this book. The prior recipe uses poached salmon, this one uses broiled, and the spices are slightly different. Depending on your mood, either one works as a nice appetizer.

Shrimp Salsa

Ingredients:

½ pound shrimp, grilled and chopped
2 Roma (plum) tomatoes, diced
½ red onion, diced
¼ cup minced cilantro
¼ cup fresh lime juice
1 tsp salt
1 tsp freshly ground black pepper
1 clove garlic, minced
chopped jalapeño, optional

Directions:

1. Stir the shrimp, tomatoes, onion, cilantro, lime juice, salt, pepper, and garlic together in a large glass bowl. Cover with plastic wrap and refrigerate until the flavors combine, at least 1 hour. Serve cold.

Notes:

Make sure you don't overcook the shrimp. In fact, some chefs allow the lime juice to do the 'cooking.' I prefer to grill it with olive oil, but leave it slightly undercooked.

Spicy Nuts

<u>Ingredients:</u>

8 oz pecan halves
8 oz whole almonds
1 tsp kosher salt
½ tsp Aleppo
1½ tsp honey
2 tbsp olive oil

<u>Directions:</u>
1. Preheat the oven to 350. Line a sheet pan with parchment paper.
2. Combine the salt, pepper, and honey in a bowl. Whisk in the olive oil. Toss with the nuts until fully coated. Place on the parchment lined sheet pan in a single layer.
3. Place pan in the oven and set a timer for 5 minutes. Remove pan from the oven and turn the nuts over, then put back in the oven and roast for another 5 minutes.
4. Remove from the oven and move the nuts to a clean sheet pan to cool. When cool, store in an airtight container.

<u>Notes:</u>

Our neighbor, Gail Leyba Ng, gave us a container of these delicious spicy nuts in a box of Christmas goodies last year. Next year I will try making them for friends. You can substitute 4 parts sweet paprika to 1 part cayenne in place of the Aleppo. And, if you want spicier nuts, just add more cayenne. Bet you can't eat just one!!

Spicy Shrimp

Ingredients:

1 pound shrimp
1 tbsp butter
1 tbsp olive oil
2 tbsp sweet chili sauce
1 tbsp Worcestershire
1 tsp smoked paprika
1 tsp chili powder
1 tsp liquid smoke
1 tsp hot sauce
1 tsp dried oregano
4 cloves garlic
½ lemon, juiced
salt and pepper to taste
parsley

Directions:
1. Peel and devein shrimp.
2. Mix remaining ingredients except for parsley. Simmer for 5-10 minutes.
3. Let sauce cool. Add shrimp and toss so all is covered.
4. Put in oven-proof serving dish and place in refrigerator for 30 minutes or up to a half day.
5. Remove from refrigerator, place in oven preheated to 400, and bake for 8 to 10 minutes. Watch the shrimp for doneness. Time needed depends on size of the shrimp.
6. Sprinkle with parsley and serve with crusty French bread baguette slices.

Spinach and Ham Dip

Ingredients:

2 pkg frozen chopped spinach
2 (8 oz each) pkg cream cheese
1 tbsp freshly squeezed lemon juice
½ pound finely chopped, thin-sliced deli ham
1 tbsp butter
8 dashes hot sauce (or to taste)
freshly ground salt and pepper to taste
Tostitos or other chips for dipping

Directions:
1. Cook chopped spinach in small amount of water according to package directions. Drain.
2. Add cream cheese, chopped ham, and other ingredients. Cook over very low heat until cream cheese melts and you can stir all ingredients together. Serve hot with Tostitos.

Notes:
I usually add a tbsp horseradish because we like it a bit zestier. This was one of the recipes my children loved when they lived at home. I liked it because it was reasonably healthy. I would sometimes use the leftovers on top of baked potatoes. Along with a small salad, it made a simple meal. Now that it is just Bob and me, I often cut this recipe in half.

Stuffed Portobello Mushrooms Caps

Ingredients:

Portobello mushrooms, stems and fluffy stuff removed
(large if for a side or main dish, smaller for appetizer)
balsamic vinegar
1 can marinated artichokes and roasted bell peppers,
OR
chopped tomato and fresh chopped basil
grated mozzarella
bread crumbs

Directions
1. Place mushrooms, open or cup side up, in baking dish, or rimmed cookie sheet.
2. Drizzle with balsamic vinegar.
3. Chop the marinated artichokes and roasted bell peppers. (alternatively, you can use chopped tomato and fresh basil.)
4. Sprinkle with breadcrumbs and top with mozzarella cheese.
5. Bake at 425 for 15 to 20 minutes, or until tender.

Notes:

This recipe came from my neighbor, Gail Leyba Ng. She served it at her Super Bowl 50 party.

Taco Dip

<u>Ingredients:</u>

1 cup sour cream
1½ cups mayonnaise
2 packages taco seasoning mix
2 (16 oz each) cans refried beans
1 tomato, chopped
1 bunch green onions, chopped
1 can black olives, sliced
8 oz cheddar cheese
grated lettuce
taco chips

<u>Directions:</u>

1. Combine sour cream, mayonnaise, refried beans, and taco seasoning mix in a large bowl. Stir until smooth. Place in pie plate or quiche pan.
2. Top with cheese. Garnish with tomatoes, shredded lettuce, green onions, and black olives.
3. Serve with taco chips.

<u>Notes:</u>

This recipe comes from my cousin, Judy Albrecht. She uses fat free sour cream and mayonnaise and likes it that way. I have used reduced fat, and that works for me.

Thai Fried Wonton Wrapped Shrimp

Ingredients:
  12 raw large shrimp, peeled and cleaned, deveined, tails attached
  12 wonton wrappers
  egg wash (1 egg + 2 tbsp of water, beaten)
  1 shredded carrot
  2 green onions, very narrowly sliced or shredded
  ½ cup low-sodium soy sauce
  salt and pepper
  neutral oil for frying
  Thai Sweet Chili Sauce

Directions:
1. Put raw shrimp in a small bowl. Add carrot and onion, and sprinkle with salt and pepper, then add soy sauce. Cover and refrigerate for 10-30 minutes. If you marinate too long, they'll be too salty.
2. Remove from refrigerator, drain soy, and rinse carrot, onion, and shrimp and pat dry.
3. In order to get the shrimp to lie as flat as possible, cut a slit down the belly (the inside of the curl).
4. Place 1 wonton wrapper on a work surface. Brush a light layer of egg wash over the wonton.

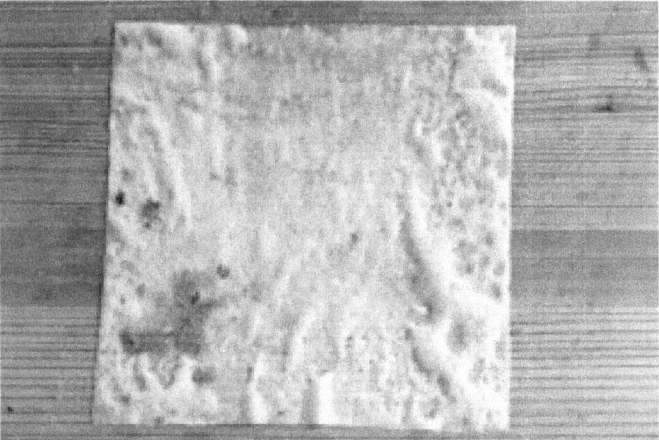

5. Place a shrimp about 1/3 of the way from the bottom of the wonton, with the tail hanging off the end of the wrapper. Add a piece of carrot and a piece of onion.

(Recipe continued next page.)

6. Fold the wrapper in half over the shrimp, like it's between the pages of a book.

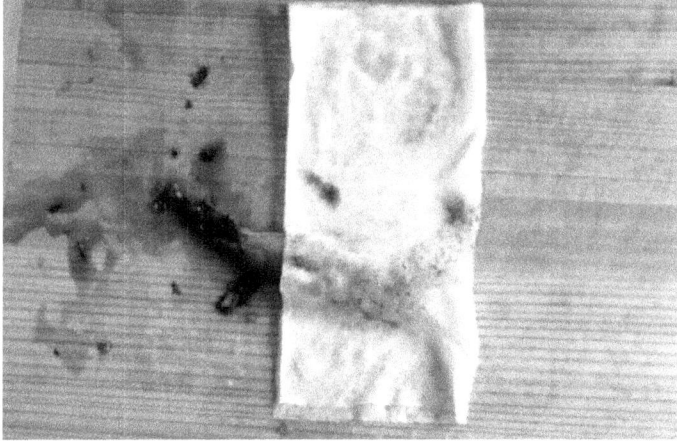

7. Roll the wrapper around the shrimp to wrap it up tightly.
8. Heat oil in large frying pan over medium until hot. Fry shrimp until golden brown. Serve with sweet chili sauce.

<u>Notes</u>:
My friend Linh Nguyen first introduced me to wonton wrapped shrimp. I'll never do them as beautifully as she does, but my family loves them.

Tuna Pâté

Ingredients:
  2 (10-oz) cans solid albacore tuna packed in olive oil, drained
  2 sticks unsalted butter, at room temperature
  1/3 cup heavy cream
  finely grated zest of one lemon
  ¼ cup fresh lemon juice
  ¼ tsp cayenne
  6 anchovy filets, drained and chopped
  3 tbsp capers, rinsed and drained, plus 2 tbsp minced capers
  freshly ground salt and pepper
  ¼ cup finely chopped fresh parsley
  ¼ cup finely chopped celery
  small toasts or crostini or crackers for serving

Directions:
1. Line a 7½x3½-inch loaf pan with plastic wrap, leaving plenty of overhang. Mix on low speed of mixer the tuna, butter, cream, lemon juice and zest, cayenne, anchovies, and the 3 tbsp of capers. Season with salt and pepper. Continue mixing until smooth. (You can use a food processor, if you prefer.) Scrape the puree into the loaf pan and smooth the top. Cover with the overhanging piece of plastic wrap and refrigerate until firm, at least 8 hours or overnight.
2. In a small bowl, stir the remaining 2 tbsp minced capers with the parsley and celery and set aside. Unwrap and unmold the pate onto a serving dish and sprinkle the parsley mixture over the top. Serve chilled with toast rounds or crackers.

Notes:
I make sure I cover the entire loaf pan tightly with aluminum foil before refrigerating so the taste and smell don't affect other foods in the refrigerator. I like this recipe because it's a fairly easy do-ahead.

Twice Baked New Potato Skins

Ingredients:

1½ pounds small red potatoes
½ pound bacon, fried, drained, and crumbled
2 tbsp olive oil plus more for browning tops of potato shells
1 cup shredded Monterey Jack cheese
½ cup sour cream
1 (3 oz) package cream cheese, softened
1/3 cup minced green onions
1 tsp dried basil
1 garlic clove, minced
½ tsp salt
½ tsp pepper
½ cup shredded cheddar cheese

Directions:
1. Pierce potatoes and rub skins with oil. Place in a baking pan. Bake, uncovered at 400 for 50 minutes or until tender. Allow to cool to touch.
2. While potatoes are baking, fry bacon until crisp. Crumble into pieces.
3. In mixing bowl, combine Monterey Jack, sour cream, cream cheese, onions, basil, garlic, salt, and pepper.
4. Cut potatoes in half. Carefully scoop out pulp, leaving a thin shell.
5. Add pulp to the cheese mixture and mash; stir in bacon.
6. Place shells, open end down, in heated olive oil and brown. Drain or pat grease with paper towel. Upright the shells and stuff with cheese/potato mixture and sprinkle with remaining shredded cheddar cheese.
7. Broil for 7-8 minutes or until heated through.

Notes:

I've been known to skip the olive oil and fry the potato skins open side down in the bacon grease before stuffing them. It's perfectly unhealthy, but the taste is almost worth it.

For a dinner side dish, I substitute full sized potatoes and use this as an accompaniment to a main entrée (See side dishes in this book).

Vegetable Pizza

<u>Ingredients:</u>

2 pkg Pillsbury Crescent Rolls
1 large (8 oz) + one small pkg (3 oz) Philadelphia Cream Cheese
½ cup mayonnaise
1 pkg dry Hidden Valley seasoning
fresh veggies, chopped fine
1 cup shredded cheddar cheese

<u>Directions:</u>

1. Spread Pillsbury Crescent Rolls flat on cookie sheet. Bake at 375 for 8 to 12 minutes or until brown. Cool.
2. Beat softened cream cheese, mayonnaise, seasoning until smooth. Spread over baked rolls.
3. Sprinkle veggies over cream cheese. (good choices are broccoli, cauliflower, tomatoes, mushrooms, green peppers, and onions).
4. Top with cheddar cheese.
5. Spread a piece of waxed paper over top of pizza and press veggies into place.
6. Cover with foil and refrigerate at least two hours before cutting and serving.

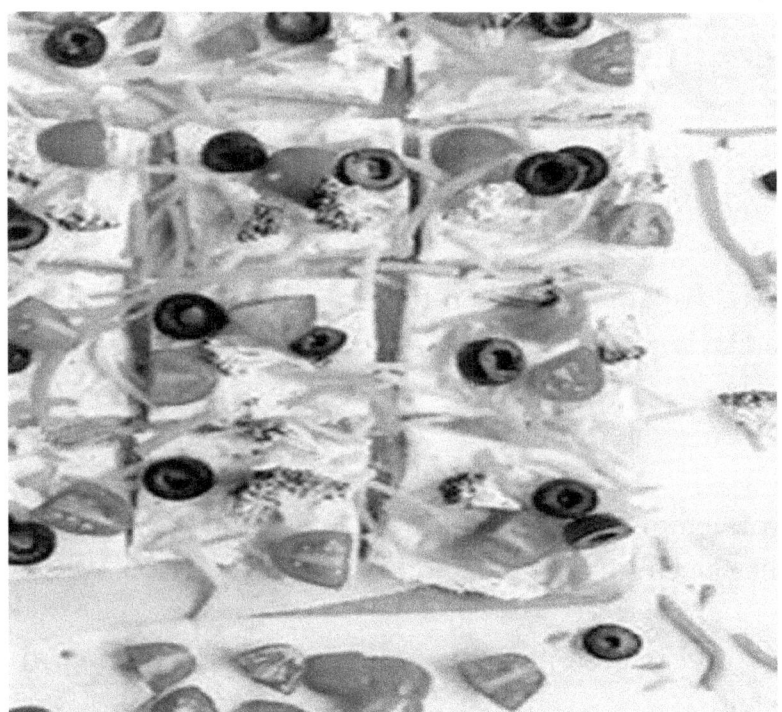

<u>Notes:</u>
I got this recipe from two of my cousins (Barb Albrecht and Judy Albrecht). Good way to get kids to eat veggies, and also makes an easy appetizer for a party since it's made ahead.

Beverages

"Show me how you drink, and I'll show you who you are." **Emile Peynaud**

"There comes a time in every woman's life when the only thing that will help is a glass of champagne." **Bette Davis**

"Write drunk. Edit sober." **Ernest Hemingway**

"I believe that if life gives you lemons, you should make lemonade . . . And try to find somebody whose life has given them vodka, and have a party." **Ron White**

"A woman is like a tea bag - you can't tell how strong she is until you put her in hot water." **Eleanor Roosevelt**

Almond Joy

<u>Ingredients:</u>

1 oz rum
1 oz amaretto
6 oz hot chocolate
whipped cream topping

<u>Directions:</u>
1. Mix first three ingredients by stirring well.
2. Using a can of whipping cream, spray a topping.

<u>Note:</u>
This is the Lone Eagle Grille's favorite winter cocktail.

~ ~ ~

Apple Pie Yuletide Spirits

<u>Ingredients:</u>

3 oz whiskey
2 oz honey syrup (recipe below)
1 drop vanilla extract
sparkling apple cider
apple rounds for garnish
cinnamon sticks for garnish

<u>Directions:</u>
1. Fill shaker or jar with handful of ice.
2. Add whiskey, syrup, and vanilla to shaker and shake vigorously. Pour into glass and top off with sparkling cider. Garnish with apple rounds and cinnamon sticks.

<u>Honey Syrup:</u> Combine 1 cup honey and one cup of water in medium saucepan. Over medium-high heat, bring to a boil. Continue cooking until reduced to about ¾ cup. Cool. Can be stored in airtight, refrigerated contained for up to one week.

~ ~ ~

Chalet View Lodge Cognac and Champagne

<u>Ingredients:</u>

2 oz cognac
2 oz freshly squeezed orange juice
1 oz fresh lemon juice (Recipe continued on next page)

1 tsp caster or superfine sugar
champagne
orange twist, to garnish

Directions:
1. Mix the cognac, citrus juices, and sugar until sugar dissolves.
2. Pour into a sparkling wine flute, top with champagne and garnish with a twist of orange peel.

~ ~ ~

Cranberry Margaritas

Ingredients:

½ cup cranberry juice
¾ cup lime juice
¾ cup tequila
½ cup triple sec or other orange flavored liquor
half slices lime for garnish and salt for glass

Directions:
1. Run a half lime around the rim of glass and dip in coarse salt.
2. Pour first four items over crushed ice in prepared margarita glass and stir.
3. Garnish with lime.

~ ~ ~

Dirty Snowman

Ingredients:

8 oz hot chocolate
1.5 oz Absolute Vanilla
1 oz Baileys
1 oz Frangelico
whipped cream

Directions:
1. Make your favorite hot chocolate.
2. Add next three ingredients and stir well.
3. Top with whipped cream.

Note:
This is the adult version of hot chocolate served at Northstar-at-Tahoe resort.

~ ~ ~

El Nino Anejo

<u>Ingredients:</u>

6 oz hot apple cider
1½ oz anejo (or other) tequila
1 oz apple brandy
whipped cream
nutmeg and cinnamon stick for garnish

<u>Directions:</u>
1. In a glass mug, combine hot cider, tequila and brandy.
2. Top with a mountain of whipped cream.
3. Sprinkle with nutmeg and add a cinnamon stick garnish.

<u>Note:</u>
I used a can of spray whipped cream.

~ ~ ~

Green Magic Punch or Orange Monster Punch

<u>Ingredients:</u> **(Green Magic)**

4 large cans of concentrated lemonade
4 cans water
½ gallon green sherbet
fifth of dry gin

<u>Ingredients:</u> **(Orange Monster)**

4 large cans concentrated orange juice
4 cans water
½ gallon orange sherbet
fifth of vodka

<u>Directions:</u>
1. For either of these punches, mix in a punch bowl: Concentrate, water, and liquor, stirring well.
2. Add sherbet on top. Do not stir. Sherbet will melt and keep punch cold.

<u>Note:</u>
These recipes came from my cousin, Barb Albrecht' who warns they are 'magic' and 'monster' because they can sneak up on you.

Green Tea Sangria

Ingredients:

1 bottle white wine
1½ cups strong green tea
½ cup sugar
½ cup lime juice
lime slices
mixed melon balls

Directions:
1. Mix first four ingredients in a large pitcher and stir well until sugar dissolves.
2. Add fruit and ice and serve.

Note:
Originally iced tea was made with green tea, not black, and it often included a shot of alcohol.

~ ~ ~

Hot Apple Pie Cocktail

Ingredients:

1¼ oz Tuaca liqueur
8 oz hot, spiced apple cider
whipped cream
sprinkle of nutmeg

Directions:
1. Mix cider and liqueur and stir well.
2. Top with whipped cream and sprinkle of nutmeg.

Notes:
From the Beacon restaurant, this is a drink that tastes like a slice of apple pie.

~ ~ ~

Honey Deuce Delight

Ingredients:

1½ oz vodka
2 oz lemonade
½ oz Raspberry Liqueur (like Chambord)
frozen melon balls

Directions: (next page.)

1. Fill a highball or double old-fashioned glass with crushed ice. Add vodka and fill the cup with lemonade to a half inch below the rim.
2. Drizzle premium raspberry-flavored liqueur over the top. Garnish with skewered honeydew balls.

Note:
Signature drink of the U.S. Open.

~ ~ ~

Julie's Easy Margaritas for a Crowd

Ingredients:
1 (12 oz) can frozen limeade concentrate
12 oz cold water
12 oz silver tequila
6 oz orange-flavored liqueur (such as Triple Sec)
6 oz pomegranate juice
1 (12-oz) bottle of Mexican lager such as Corona, chilled
lime wedges and coarse salt

Directions:
1. Scoop frozen limeade concentrate into a large pitcher. Using empty limeade can as a measure, pour one can of cold water, 1 can silver tequila, ½ can of Triple Sec, and ½ can of pomegranate juice over limeade and mix well.
2. Pour beer into pitcher and stir well.
3. Run a lime wedge around edges of margarita glasses and dip in coarse salt. Serve with additional lime wedges.

Notes:
I found a recipe for margaritas with beer, but it seemed something was missing. I played around and decided the pomegranate made a favorable improvement.

~ ~ ~

Long Bay Iced Tea

Ingredients:

1 oz vodka
1 oz tequila
1 oz white rum
1 oz gin
½ oz Chambord
1 oz freshly squeezed orange juice (Recipe continued on next page.)

1 oz freshly squeezed grapefruit juice

Directions:
Mix all ingredients in a martini shaker and add ice. Shake several times, then strain into a highball glass filled with ice. Garnish with an orange slice.

Notes:
At a backyard party, I multiplied all ingredients by 8 and made this by the pitcher. Be careful, it's potent.

~ ~ ~

Moscato Strawberry Lemonade

Ingredients:

1 bottle pink Moscato
6 cups lemonade
¼ cup strawberry vodka
frozen strawberry slices and lemon slices

Directions
1. Mix all ingredients in large punch bowl. Enjoy.

~ ~ ~

Moscow Mule

Ingredients: (per serving)

2 oz vodka
1 oz honey ginger syrup or simple syrup
1 oz Rose's lime juice
4 to 6 oz Ginger Beer
lime pieces

Directions:
1. Use copper mugs. Fill with ice.
2. Pour vodka over ice.
3. Add honey ginger or simple syrup. Double amount for sweeter drink.
4. Add Rose's lime juice. Stir and top with Ginger Beer.
5. Squeeze juice from a lime piece and drop lime into drink.
6. Rub rim of copper cup with freshly cut ginger and/or lime.

Notes:
Our friends, Jan and Chris Kinzel, hosted a Dogs and Mules party. We ate hotdogs with all the trimmings and drank delicious mules that Chris created.

Party Rum Punch

<u>Ingredients:</u>

fifth of rum
1-quart cranberry juice, chilled
8 oz orange juice, chilled
1 oz lime juice
1½ oz lemon juice
2 large bottles ginger ale, chilled
extra citrus fruit, frozen cranberries for garnish, and ice for bowl

<u>Directions:</u>
1. In punchbowl, combine rum and fruit juices.
2. Add ice and gently stir in chilled ginger ale.
3. Garnish by floating orange, lemon, and lime slices on top.

~ ~ ~

Peach Ginger Bellini

<u>Ingredients:</u>

For the ginger simple syrup »»

¼ cup sliced fresh ginger, with skin
2 cups granulated sugar
2 cups cold water

For the peach puree »»

10 oz semi-frozen peaches
½ cup ginger simple syrup

To serve »»

Champagne and ice

<u>Directions:</u>
1. Make simple syrup: Grate and peel the ginger. Add it together with the sugar and cold water in a saucepan. Bring to a boil and stir until sugar dissolves. Cover and let steep for 15 minutes. Strain and discard ginger pieces. Set simple syrup aside.
2. In a blender, add frozen peaches and ginger simple syrup. Blend until completely pureed, then place in refrigerator to cool.
3. To serve: Add ice cubes to a cocktail shaker and fill half way with peach puree. Top with champagne shake vigorously to combine. Pour into champagne glasses.

Notes:
I wanted to make this for a party, but was hesitant to put champagne in a shaker and shake. I also didn't want the hassle of the shaker for each drink. Instead I made the simple syrup and combined it with the ice cubes and peach puree in a pitcher. I stirred and refrigerated it. At the party I made the drinks one at a time, pouring the mixture from the pitcher into glasses and adding champagne. The guests seemed to approve.

~ ~ ~

Perfect Pear Punch

Ingredients:

9 oz vodka
3 oz pear liqueur
4½ oz fresh lemon juice
4½ oz honey syrup (3 parts honey to 1-part hot water)
1½ oz allspice dram
6 oz sparkling wine
6 oz seltzer or sparkling water
garnishes: fresh lemon slices, whole cloves,
fresh pear slices, cinnamon.

Directions:
1. Place a large block of ice in a punch bowl.
2. In a pitcher, mix vodka, pear liqueur, lemon juice, honey syrup, and allspice dram. Add it to the punch bowl.
3. Add sparkling wine and seltzer, stirring well.
4. Stud lemon slices with a few cloves each.
5. Garnish punch bowl with the lemon slices, pear slices, and grated cinnamon.

~ ~ ~

Pina Colada Slush

Ingredients:

1 large can of pineapple juice
(Recipe continued on next page.)

1 (12-oz) can cream of coconut
1 (12-oz) can of rum
diet or regular 7-up.

Directions:
1. Mix all ingredients except 7-up in a freezer container.
2. When ready to serve, scoop 3 heaping tbsp of frozen slush into glasses and fill glasses with 7-up.

~ ~ ~

Raspberry and Citrus Martini

Ingredients:
Simple syrup »»

1 cup water
1 cup sugar

Other Ingredients »»

pint raspberries
orange liqueur (like Cointreau)
grapefruit juice
lime juice
vodka

Directions: (for one drink)
1. In a small saucepan bring 1 cup sugar and 1 cup water to a boil; simmer until the sugar is dissolved. Remove from heat and let the simple syrup cool.
2. In a shaker muddle 3 raspberries and ¾ oz simple syrup. Add ¾ oz orange liqueur, ¾ oz grapefruit juice, ¾ oz lime juice, 2 oz vodka and ice.
3. Shake and strain into a martini glass. Garnish with a raspberry.

~ ~ ~

Raspberry Ginger Cocktail Syrup

Ingredients:

1½ pounds raspberries
2 cups sugar
2 tbsp peeled, grated fresh ginger
pinch of salt
¼ cup cider vinegar

Directions:

(Recipe continued on next page)

1. Mash raspberries, sugar, ginger, and salt until mostly smooth.
2. Refrigerate 1 to 2 days.
3. Strain into bowl and discard solids.
4. Add vinegar. Makes about 2 cups.

Notes:

Can be refrigerated up to 6 months. Good mixed with vodka or gin. Add seltzer for non-alcoholic drink.

~ ~ ~

Red Velvet Punch
(Alcoholic or Non-Alcoholic)

Ingredients:

8 cups cranberry juice cocktail
1 (6 oz) can frozen orange juice concentrate
1 (6 oz) can frozen pineapple juice concentrate
1 (6 oz) can frozen lemonade concentrate
2 cups brandy
2 bottles chilled champagne

Or

eliminate last two ingredients and instead, add:
1 bottle sparkling grape juice
2 quarts chilled ginger ale

Directions:
1. Mix all ingredients in a large punch bowl, stir well, and add ice.

Notes:

You can add 4 bananas that you have blended on liquify until very smooth. I make an ice block using a Jell-O mold, filling it with a mixture of the juices. This way the punch doesn't get watered down during the party.

Slush

Ingredients:

1 12 oz can frozen lemonade
2 cups sugar
4 tea bags (black)
2 cups apricot brandy
1 (12 oz) can orange juice concentrate
7 cups water
2 cups boiling water
1 cup vodka

Directions:
1. Bring sugar and 7 cups water to a boil and cool.
2. Put tea bags in 2 cups boiling water, steep, and cool. Remove tea bags.
3. Mix all ingredients including cooled sugar/water and tea.
4. Freeze in containers. Serve mixed with 7 Up.

Notes:
My mother, Bonnie Albrecht, often had a version of this in her freezer.

~ ~ ~

Slushie Gin and Tonic

Ingredients:

2 oz gin
4 oz tonic water
1 scoop Haagen Dazs Zesty Lemon Sorbet
lemon zest
lime zest
lemon slice and lime slices for garnish
orange peel, for garnish

Directions:
1. Build the drink by pouring gin and tonic water over ice in a stemless wine glass. Add a scoop of the sorbet, and grate the lemon and lime zest on top.
2. Garnish with lemon, lime, and orange slices.

Notes:
I quadruple the amounts and make it in a pitcher for a crowd. It's a refreshing summer drink that I make pretty weak (adding more tonic and sorbet).

Sparkling Sage Grapefruit Cocktail

Ingredients:
Cocktail »»

3 oz vodka
7 oz chilled brut style sparkling wine
4 oz freshly squeezed ruby red grapefruit
2 oz elderflower liqueur
1 ½ oz sage honey syrup (see below)
garnish: sprigs of fresh sage, half-moon slices ruby red grapefruit

Sage honey syrup »»

¾ cup orange blossom honey
1 cup water
10 fresh sage leaves'

Directions:
1. Make sage honey syrup by combining honey and water in small saucepan and bring to a boil over medium-high heat. Remove syrup from heat and add sage leaves. Let steep for 20 minutes. Strain syrup and cool before using. Can be made up to 2 weeks ahead.
2. Combine vodka, sparkling wine, grapefruit juice, elderflower liqueur, and honey syrup in a pitcher and stir.
3. Fill four serving glasses with ice. Add garnish and serve.

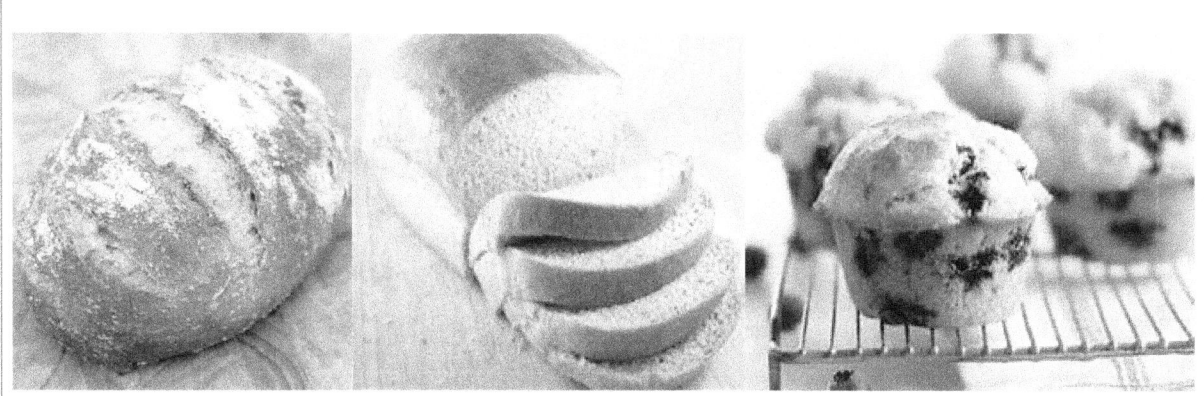

Breads, Rolls, Muffins, and Waffles

"Life is not worth living if I cannot have pasta or bread again." **Monica Seles**

"I judge a restaurant by the bread and by the coffee." **Burt Lancaster**

"A waffle is like a pancake with a syrup trap." **Mitch Hedberg**

Almond-Cherry Filled Braids

Ingredients:
1 (17.3 oz) pkg frozen puff pastry sheets, thawed (2 sheets)
1 (8-oz) can almond paste
¼ cup sugar
1 egg, separated
½ cup cherry or raspberry preserves
1 tbsp water
¼ cup sliced almonds
coarse granulated sugar

Directions:
1. Line 2 large baking sheets with parchment paper. Unfold pastry sheets; place 1 pastry sheet on each prepared baking sheet. Pinch seams together. Set aside.
2. For almond filling: in a medium bowl beat almond paste, sugar, and egg white with electric mixer on medium until combined. Spread half the filling in a 3-inch wide strip lengthwise down the center of each pastry sheet, leaving a ½-inch space on each end. Spread preserves over almond filling.
3. Using kitchen shears or a sharp knife, make 3-inch-long cuts at 1-inch intervals right up to the filling in pastry on each side of the filling. Starting at one end, alternately fold opposite strips of dough at an angle over the filling, overlapping ends of strips in middle. Press down gently on strips to seal. Repeat cutting and folding with remaining pastry.
4. Beat egg yolk with the water. Brush over braids. Sprinkle with almonds and coarse sugar. Cover lightly with plastic wrap and let stand for 20 minutes. Remove and discard plastic wrap.
5. In oven preheated to 375, bake 1 braid at a time, for 30-35 minutes or until tops and bottoms are golden brown. Cool braids on a wire rack about 15 minutes before cutting each braid into 6 slices. Serve warm. Makes 12 servings.

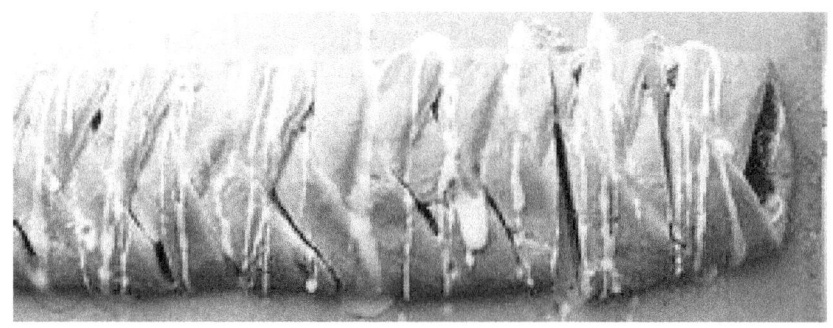

Bacon Ranch Bread Bites

<u>Ingredients:</u>

1 loaf frozen bread dough, thawed
2 tsp oil
1 cup shredded mozzarella cheese
1 pkg (1 oz) ranch salad dressing mix
1 pkg. (12 oz) center cut bacon, fried, drained, and crumbled

<u>Directions:</u>

1. Roll bread dough into ½ inch thick rectangle on a lightly floured surface; brush with oil. Cut dough with sharp knife into 1 x 1-inch pieces.
2. Toss bread dough pieces, cheese, salad dressing mix, and bacon in large bowl. Place on ungreased cooked sheet; shape into an oval loaf. Or you can use a greased baking dish. Let rise in warm place until double in size.
3. Bake in preheated 350-degree oven 20 to 30 min. or until golden brown. Cool 10 minutes. Remove from pan to wire rack; cool completely.

Banana-Blueberry Muffins

<u>Ingredients:</u>

3 cups all-purpose flour
1 cup sugar
1 tbsp baking powder
½ tsp baking soda
2 large eggs
¾ cup milk
¾ cup butter, melted
1 large banana, mashed (about ¾ cup)
1 tsp vanilla extract
2 cups fresh blueberries
1 cup walnuts

<u>Directions:</u>

1. Preheat oven to 375. Grease 18 muffin cups or line with paper cupcake liners; set aside.
2. Combine flour, sugar, baking powder, and baking soda in large bowl; set aside.
3. Beat eggs, milk, butter, banana, and vanilla in medium bowl with wire whisk until smooth. Stir egg mixture into flour mixture with wooden spoon, just until combined.
4. Gently fold in blueberries. Evenly spoon batter into prepared pans.
5. Bake 20 minutes or until toothpick inserted in centers comes out clean. Cool on wire rack 10 minutes. Remove from pans and cool.

Banana Bread

<u>Ingredients:</u>

½ cup butter
1 cup sugar
2 eggs
½ tsp salt
½ tsp baking soda
¼ tsp baking powder
1 cup mashed bananas (use very ripe bananas)
2 cups flour
½ cup chopped nuts

<u>Directions:</u>
1. On low speed of mixer, cream butter and sugar. Add 1 egg at a time, mixing on low after each.
2. Add flour, salt, baking soda, baking powder, and bananas (I use three because I don't mind if I have more than one cup). Add nuts.
3. Pour into a loaf pan which has been greased on the bottom.
4. Bake 55 minutes at 350 degrees.

<u>Notes:</u>
I always have trouble getting banana bread out of the pan without it sticking. To resolve this problem, I cut an eight-inch piece of waxed paper and run it from side to side of the pan with about an inch left over the top of the pan. I use the overhanging pieces to lift the loaf out of the pan. The paper peels off easily.

Banana Bread (No-fat version)

<u>Ingredients:</u>

1½ cups all-purpose flour
¾ cup white sugar
1¼ tsp baking powder
½ tsp baking soda
½ tsp ground cinnamon
2 eggs (1 whole egg and one egg white)
1 cup banana, (I use 3 very ripe, mashed bananas)
¼ cup applesauce

<u>Directions:</u>
1. Preheat oven to 350. Lightly grease an 8x4-inch loaf pan.
2. In a large bowl, stir together flour, sugar, baking powder, baking soda, and cinnamon. Add eggs, bananas, and applesauce. Stir until just combined. Pour batter into prepared pan.
3. Bake in preheated oven for 50-55 minutes, until a toothpick inserted into center of loaf comes out clean. Turn onto a wire rack and allow to cool before slicing.

<u>Notes:</u>
The original recipe called for 2 egg whites, but I liked it better with one whole egg and 1 egg white. I also sprinkle a bit of brown sugar on top of loaf before baking, but then I like sweets. I add 1/3 cup chopped walnuts or pecans. I also line the pan with an 8-inch piece of waxed paper run from side to side before pouring in the batter. It peels off the baked loaf with no problem and makes the bread easier to get out of the pan.

Banana Bread (with yogurt and toasted walnut)

Ingredients:

1½ cups all-purpose flour
½ cup whole-wheat flour
1½ tsp baking powder
¼ tsp baking soda
½ tsp salt
1 cup mashed, ripe bananas (about 3 medium)
¾ cup sugar
1 egg
2 egg whites
1/3 cup yogurt (can use buttermilk)
¼ cup canola oil
1/3 cup chopped toasted walnuts

Directions:
1. Preheat oven to 350. Coat an 8x4-inch loaf pan with cooking spray.
2. Combine flours, baking powder, baking soda, and salt in a large bowl. Stir well.
3. Combine banana, sugar, egg, egg whites, yogurt and oil; beat with a mixer at medium speed until blended. Add flour mixture; beat at low speed just until evenly blended. Stir in walnuts. Pour batter into pan.
4. Bake 60 minutes or until a wooden toothpick inserted in the center comes out clean. Cool in pan on wire rack 15 minutes. Remove from pan and finish cooling on rack before slicing.

Notes:
This is a healthy version of banana bread and the whole wheat flour and toasted nuts give it a rich flavor. In addition to spraying the loaf pan with cooking spray, I add an 8-inch wide strip of waxed paper run from side to side to make removal easier.

Banana Nut Waffles

<u>Ingredients:</u>

2 medium bananas (very ripe)
2 cups buttermilk
1 tsp vanilla extract
1 cup chopped walnuts
5 tbsp butter, melted
2 cups flour
¼ cup sugar
½ tsp salt
2 tsp baking powder
2 eggs, divided

<u>Directions:</u>
1. Spray waffle iron with non-stick cooking spray. Preheat the waffle iron.
2. Heat the chopped walnuts over medium heat in a skillet to toast (about five minutes, but be careful not to burn). Place toasted walnuts in a dish and set aside.
3. In a medium bowl, mix baking powder, salt, and flour.
4. In a separate bowl, thoroughly whisk the egg whites.
5. In a third bowl, use an electric mixer to blend sugar, butter, vanilla, buttermilk, bananas, walnuts, and egg yolks. Add to dry ingredients and mix.
6. Gently fold in egg whites.
7. Pour by cupful onto waffle iron (amount depends on size of waffle iron) and bake.

Blueberry Muffins

Ingredients:

2 eggs
½ cup vegetable oil
1 cup buttermilk
2 cups flour
1 cup granulated sugar
1 tbsp baking powder
1 tsp salt
1 tsp baking soda
1½ cup fresh blueberries

Directions:
1. Mix eggs, oil, and buttermilk.
2. Add flour and stir.
3. Add other dry ingredients and mix well.
4. Gently fold in blueberries.
5. Pour batter into muffin tins that have been lined with paper liners.
6. Bake at 400 for 15 minutes.

Notes:

My mother, Bonnie Albrecht, always made the best blueberry muffins. I think this was her recipe, but I had no name written on it. Any way you look at it, these are good. I often put ¼ cup of the flour in a plastic bag and then add blueberries to dust them. It keeps them from running.

Bran Muffins

<u>Ingredients:</u>

½ cup Crisco
1 cup boiling water
1½ tsp baking soda
½ tsp baking powder
1 pint buttermilk
1½ cups sugar
2 eggs
2 cups Nabisco 100% bran
1½ tsp salt
1 cup all bran
2½ cups flour

<u>Directions:</u>
1. Melt Crisco in boiling water.
2. Mix soda in a large bowl with buttermilk.
3. Mix in all remaining ingredients including Crisco/water.
4. Mix well and pour into lined cupcake tins. Each cup should be about 2/3 full.
5. Bake at 400 for 20 minutes. If you have to do it in batches, keep batter refrigerated between batches. Do not stir again.

Cheddar-Corn Bread Rolls

<u>Ingredients:</u>

1 (16-oz) pkg hot roll mix
1 cup (4-oz) shredded cheddar, Monterey Jack,
or Monterey Jack with jalapeno peppers
1/3 cup corneal
1¼ cups hot water
2 tbsp olive oil
1 egg, lightly beaten
milk for brushing dough
additional cornmeal

<u>Directions:</u>
1. Preheat oven to 375. In a large bowl, stir together the flour from the hot roll mix, the contents of the yeast packet, the cheese, and the 1/3 cup cornmeal. Add the hot water, oil, and eggs. Stir until combined.
2. Turn dough onto a well-floured surface. Knead dough for 5 minutes or until smooth and elastic. Cover and let rest 5 minutes. Lightly grease a 13x9x2-inch baking pan; set aside.
3. Divide dough into 15 pieces. Shape each piece into a ball by pulling and tucking the dough underneath. Arrange dough balls in prepared pan. Cover and let rise in a warm place 20 minutes.
4. Brush dough with milk and sprinkle with additional corn meal. Bake for 20-22 minutes until golden.
<u>Note</u>
These are great with chili or good sliced in half as slider buns.

Coffee Cake with Apple Pie Filling

Ingredients:

Cake »»

3 eggs
1 banana, cut into chunks
1 (18.25 oz) pkg yellow cake mix
1 (15.25 oz) can apple pie filling

Marbled Spice »»

¾ cup brown sugar
½ cup flaked coconut
½ cup chopped pecans
1 tbsp ground cinnamon

Icing »»

¾ cup confectioners' sugar
5 tsp milk

Directions:

1. Preheat oven to 350. Grease a 9x13-inch baking dish.
2. Beat eggs and banana together in a bowl until smooth. Add cake mix and apple pie filling to eggs; beat until batter is combined. Pour batter into prepared baking dish.
3. Stir brown sugar, coconut, pecans, and cinnamon together in a bowl; sprinkle over batter in the baking dish. Swirl coconut mixture into batter using a knife or toothpick.
4. Bake in the preheated oven until a toothpick inserted in the center of the cake comes out clean, about 60 minutes.
5. Whisk confectioners' sugar and milk together in a bowl until icing is smooth. Drizzle icing over the top of the hot cake. Cool cake in the baking dish to room temperature, cover the dish with plastic wrap, and refrigerate until cold.

Notes:

This recipe came to me from Linda Dawson Cutler, and she got it from the Sanilac County Medical Facility recipe book. Over the years, I've found some great recipes in church and other books created for fundraisers.

Corn Fritters with Roasted Peppers, Cilantro, and Feta

Ingredients:

2 cups fresh corn kernels stripped from the cob
½ cup roasted red peppers, diced
1 cup cilantro, chopped and extra for garnish
2 tsp cumin
2 green onions, chopped
salt and freshly ground black pepper to taste
pinch of dried chili flakes
4 large eggs, beaten
1 cup semolina flour
½ cup feta, crumbled
2 tbsp olive oil
fresh lime, cut in wedges

Directions:

1. Mix corn, roasted peppers, cilantro (reserving some for garnish), cumin, green onion, salt, chili flakes, and pepper in a large bowl.
2. In a separate bowl, beat the two eggs. Mix into the corn mixture and stir in the semolina. Crumble the feta into the mixture and carefully stir until all ingredients are incorporated.
3. Heat the olive oil in a large frying pan over medium-high heat. Drop by 3 tbsp amounts of the batter into the pan. Leave space between fritters. Cook slowly and flip once the fritters becomes crisp and golden, around 2 to 3 minutes. Once cooked through, (about an additional 1 to 2 minutes), remove from heat and place on a large plate. Cover with foil to keep warm and repeat with remaining batter until all fritters are cooked. Garnish with cilantro and lime wedges.

Notes:

We had these delicious fritters at a brunch hosted by Minna Dubin and Ben Elitzur.
To roast the peppers, I washed, diced, and coated them lightly with olive oil, then baked on cookie sheet at 350 until tender.

Dad's Favorite Crumb Coffee Cake

Ingredients:

1 tbsp lemon juice
1 cup milk (minus 1 tbsp)
1 tsp baking soda
1 tsp baking powder
1½ cups brown sugar
1 cup sifted flour
½ cup butter, softened
1 tsp cinnamon
1 tsp nutmeg
½ tsp salt
½ cup chopped walnuts

Directions:
1. Mix lemon juice, milk, and soda. Set aside.
2. Mix sugar, flour, baking powder, butter, cinnamon, nutmeg, and salt in another bowl. Reserve ½ cup for topping. Add remainder to liquid ingredients.
3. Add walnuts. Pour batter into a greased 8x8 pan.
4. Sprinkle reserved topping of crumb mixture over the top.
5. Bake at 350 for 25-30 minutes or until toothpick comes out clean.

Note:
This recipe came from my cousin, Linda Dawson Cutler, who called it Dad's Favorite Crumb Coffee Cake because her father loved it.

French Toast (Make ahead, Baked, and Stuffed)

<u>Ingredients:</u>

1 container (8-oz) whipped cream cheese, at room temperature
1/3 cup chopped pecans
¼ cup packed light brown sugar
2 tbsp maple syrup
1¾ tsp ground cinnamon, divided
2 cups milk
5 eggs
¼ cup + 2 tbsp granulated sugar
½ tsp vanilla extract
1 loaf (16-oz) challah, egg bread, or thick cut raisin bread cut into ¾-inch slices
confectioners' sugar

<u>Directions:</u>

1. Combine cheese, pecans, brown sugar, syrup, and ¼ tsp cinnamon and set aside.
2. Whisk together milk, eggs, ¼ cup granulated sugar, and vanilla.
3. Reserve 2 bread slices. Spread one side of each remaining bread slice with cheese mixture; layer at an angle in 13x9-inch baking dish, cheese side up, ending with reserved plain bread slices.
4. Pour milk mixture evenly over slices. Cover dish with plastic wrap; refrigerate overnight.
5. Preheat oven to 350. Remove plastic wrap. Combine remaining granulated sugar with cinnamon; sprinkle over slices.
6. Bake 20-25 minutes or until golden and egg mixture is set. Sprinkle with confectioners' sugar just before serving.

<u>Notes:</u>

This is a great do-ahead recipe that simplifies breakfast on special mornings. I cut the bread slices at an angle before putting them into baking dish. My brother and sister-in-law make it as their special treat on Christmas.

French Toast Italiano

<u>Ingredients:</u>

4 1-inch thick slices day old Italian Bread.
2 eggs
¼ cup milk
¼ cup orange juice
1 tbsp honey
1½ tbsp butter
½ cup crushed cornflakes
additional honey

<u>Directions:</u>
1. Arrange bread in a shallow dish. In a small bowl, beat eggs, milk, orange juice, and honey with a wire whisk. Pour over bread. Turn each slice to coat well.
2. Cover and refrigerate several hours or overnight.
3. Preheat oven to 475 degrees. Melt butter in 8-inch square baking dish.
4. Remove bread slices from egg mixture, letting excess drip off.
Dip each slice in crushed cornflakes to coat both sides.
5. Melt butter in a baking dish. Arrange toast in a single layer over the hot butter.
6. Bake, turning once, about 8 minutes on each side, until golden brown. Serve with additional honey or syrup.

George Cramer's Holiday Buttermilk Waffles

Ingredients:

2 cups all-purpose flour
½ tsp salt
1 tbsp sugar
2 eggs, separated
¼ tsp baking soda
1½ tsp double acting baking powder
1¾ cups buttermilk
6 tbsp butter, melted and cooled
½ tsp vanilla extract

Directions:
1. Separate eggs. Beat egg whites, then mix with sugar.
2. Combine remaining dry ingredients and then mix in buttermilk and egg yolks. Stir in butter and vanilla.
3. Gently fold in egg white/sugar mixture. Do not over mix or beat.
4. Preheat waffle iron and spray with cooking spray. Pour batter onto waffle iron and bake. Makes 4 to 6 waffles.

Strawberry Waffle Topping

Ingredients:

2 cups strawberries, washed, stemmed, and sliced
1/3 cup sugar
1/3 cup water
1 tbsp cornstarch
1 tsp vanilla

Directions:
Mix first four ingredients in pan and bring to a boil. Remove from heat and add vanilla.

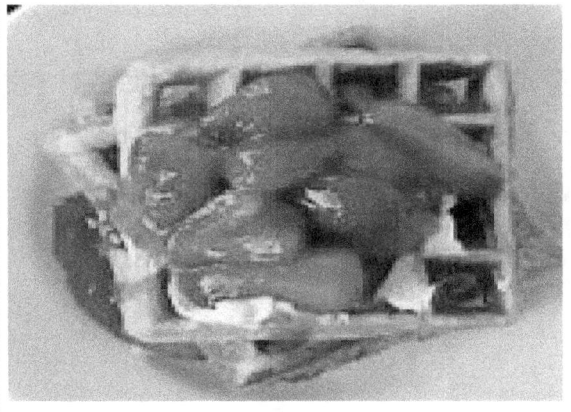

Notes:
George Cramer is my writing buddy. He says this recipe can be doubled or tripled for larger crowds. On one occasion, he even lent us his restaurant quality waffle maker to use at a brunch. He was willing to help in any way he could to make our attempt at these waffles perfect.

Healthy Blueberry Bran Muffins

<u>Ingredients:</u>

1 cup all-bran cereal
½ cup skim milk
1¼ cups all-purpose flour
2½ tsp baking powder
½ tsp salt
½ tsp cinnamon
1 tbsp canola oil
½ cup natural apple juice
½ cup natural applesauce
1/3 cup molasses
1/3 cup granulated sugar
1 whole egg (or egg substitute) and 1 egg white
½ cup blueberries dusted with ¼ cup flour

<u>Directions:</u>

1. Preheat oven to 400. Line a 12-cup muffin pan with paper liners or spray with cooking spray.
2. In a small bowl, add skim milk to bran. Let soak 5 minutes.
3. In a large bowl, mix flour, baking powder, salt, and cinnamon.
4. In a separate bowl, blend oil, apple juice, apple sauce, molasses, and sugar. Mix well. Add bran mixture. Mix well.
5. Add egg and egg white. Mix well.
6. Fold in dusted blueberries.
7. Add applesauce mixture to flour mixture. Mix until moistened.
8. Fill muffin cups ¾ full.
9. Bake 20 to 25 minutes.

Honey Gingerbread

<u>Ingredients:</u>

1½ cups all-purpose flour
1 tsp baking soda
1 tsp ground cinnamon
½ tsp salt
½ tsp ground allspice
¼ tsp ground ginger
1/3 tsp ground cloves
½ cup unsalted butter, room temperature
½ cup sugar
½ cup minced, drained ginger stem in syrup
2 eggs
½ cup buttermilk
whipped cream for garnish
reserved chopped, drained, stem ginger in syrup for garnish

<u>Directions:</u>
1. Preheat oven to 350. Butter 8-inch square glass baking dish.
2. Sift flour, baking soda, cinnamon, salt, allspice, ginger, and cloves into a medium bowl.
3. Using electric mixer, beat butter and sugar in a large bowl until light and fluffy.
4. Mix in honey and ¼ cup minced ginger. Beat in eggs.
5. Mix in dry ingredients alternately with buttermilk, beginning and ending with dry ingredients.
6. Spread batter in prepared dish. Bake until gingerbread begins to pull away from sides of dish and is springy to touch (about 50 minutes). Cool in pan on rack.
7. Serve warm or at room temperature. Cut into squares and top with whipped cream and chopped ginger.

Kaiser Rolls from Frozen Bread Dough

<u>Ingredients:</u>

12 Rhodes Yeast Texas rolls, thawed but still cold
1 egg, beaten
sesame or poppy seeds, if desired

<u>Directions:</u>

1. Combine two rolls and roll into a 14 to 16-inch rope. Tie each rope into a loose overhand knot. Bring one end of the dough over the top and tuck down into the middle. Bring the other end of the dough through the center, going the opposite way.
2. Place on a large sprayed baking sheet. If desired, brush with egg and sprinkle with sesame or poppy seeds. Cover with sprayed plastic wrap and let rise until double in size.
3. Remove wrap and bake at 350°F 15-20 minutes.

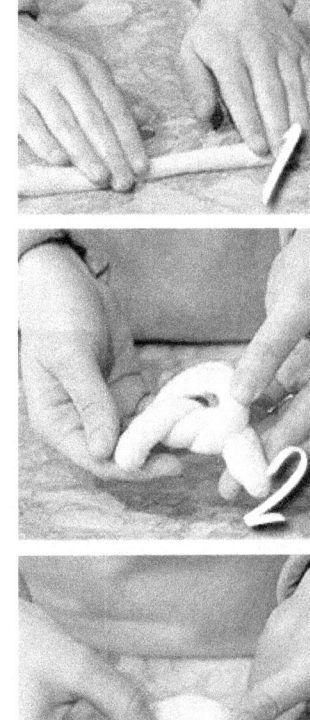

Oat-Zucchini Bread

<u>Ingredients:</u>

1¼ cups oatmeal
3 cups flour
3 tsp baking powder
2 tsp ground cinnamon
¼ tsp cloves
¼ tsp nutmeg
2 tbsp grated orange peel
1/3 tsp salt
2/3 cup sugar
2 tsp vanilla
2 tbsp vegetable oil
1 cup applesauce
3 cups grated zucchini

<u>Directions:</u>
1. Mix oatmeal, flour, baking powder, cinnamon, cloves, nutmeg, orange peel, salt, and sugar.
2. Beat eggs, sugar, vanilla, oil, applesauce, and zucchini.
3. Add dry ingredients and blend.
4. Turn into 2 greased and floured loaf pans.
5. Bake in preheated 350 oven for 1 hour. Makes 2 loaves.

<u>Note:</u>
I use an 8-inch piece of waxed paper to line bottom and long sides of baking dish so bread will come out easier.

Peachy Bran Muffins

<u>Ingredients:</u>

2 cups all-purpose flour
3 tsp baking powder
1 tsp ground cinnamon
¼ tsp ground nutmeg
2½ cups crunchy raisin bran cereal
1½ cups milk
½ cup (one stick) butter, melted
1 cup white granulated sugar
pinch salt
2 eggs
1 tsp vanilla extract
1 (16 oz) pkg frozen sliced peaches with no sugar added
1 cup nuts, pecans or walnuts (optional)

<u>Directions:</u>

1. Whisk together to flour, baking powder, ground cinnamon, and nutmeg in a large bowl and set aside.
2. Combine the raisin bran and milk in a bowl and let set until cereal is soft, about 10 minutes.
3. Add the melted butter, sugar, salt, eggs, and vanilla extract into the cereal mixture and stir.
4. Pour the cereal mixture into the dry ingredients and stir.
5. Thaw the sliced peaches about 2 minutes in the microwave. (Just enough that you can cut them with a knife into smaller, bite-sized pieces.) Fold in peaches and nuts.
6. Spray a regular 12 cup muffin pan with cooking spray or line with paper cups. Fill cups ¾ full. Bake in preheated oven at 400 for 25 to 30 minutes until brown on top.

Pear, Ginger, and Walnut Muffins

<u>Ingredients:</u>

2 cups all-purpose flour
¾ cup sugar
2 tsp baking soda
½ tsp salt
¼ tsp ground cinnamon
2 beaten eggs
½ cup cooking oil
2 tbsp milk
1 tsp grated gingerroot
2 medium pears (1½ cups chopped)
¾ cup chopped walnuts
½ cup raisins

<u>Directions:</u>

1. In a large mixing bowl combine flour, sugar, baking soda, salt, and cinnamon. Make a well in the center.
2. Combine eggs, oil, milk, and gingerroot; add all at once to center of flour mixture. Stir just until moistened.
3. Peel, core, and finely chop pears. You need about 1½ cups. Fold pears, walnuts, and raisins into the batter.
4. Lightly grease muffin cups or line with paper baking cups; fill each ¾ full.
5. Bake in a 350 oven for 20-25 minutes or until toothpick inserted near center comes out clean. Remove from pan. Makes 18 muffins. Best served warm.

Pecan Caramel Rolls

<u>Ingredients:</u>

1 loaf frozen bread dough, thawed as directed
4 tbsp butter, melted
¼ cup brown sugar
2 tsp water
2 tbsp light corn syrup
½ cup pecan halves
1 tsp cinnamon
¼ cup brown sugar

<u>Directions:</u>

1. Let dough rise until doubled in size.
2. Combine 3 tbsp of the melted butter, ¼ cup brown sugar, water, and syrup. Spread in a 10 x 8-inch or 9 x 9-inch pan. Sprinkle with pecans.
3. After bread has risen, roll into a 16x12-inch rectangle. Brush with remaining tbsp butter and sprinkle with remaining ¼ cup brown sugar and cinnamon.
4. Roll up, starting with 16-inch side. Pinch edges to seal. Cut into 15 or 16 pieces.
5. Place pieces in pan and cover loosely with waxed paper and let rise in warm place 30 to 60 minutes.
6. Bake at 350 degrees for 25-30 minutes. Cool 1 minute. Loosen edges and turn out onto plate to cool.

<u>Notes:</u>

I use non-stick aluminum foil to cover so if the rolls rise too high they still won't stick. This is Noah's and Ezra's (my grandsons) favorite. But they prefer it without pecans. We roll out the dough, sit it in a warm place, go for a long walk, and then bake the rolls when we get back.

Pecan Rolls

Ingredients:

4 oz pecans, chopped
2 loaves frozen bread dough, mostly thawed, but not allowed to rise
1 stick melted butter
1 cup brown sugar
1 to 2 tsp cinnamon
1 tsp milk
1 large box cook and serve butterscotch pudding (6 serving size)

Directions:

1 Grease a 13x9-inch baking pan. Spread pecans on bottom of pan.
2. Cut mostly-thawed frozen bread dough into small pieces.
3. Melt butter in microwave or on stovetop. Add brown sugar, milk, pudding mix (uncooked), and cinnamon. Pour this mixture over the bread.
4. Let rise 1 to 1½ hours. After the dough has risen, bake at 350 for ½ hour.
5. Serve warm.

Notes:

I use 8 oz chopped pecans. It may seem obvious, but I'll mention it anyway: Although you are using cook and serve pudding, **you do not cook it**. A version of this recipe was sent to me by my cousin, Linda Dawson Cutler. It called for one

loaf of bread, and it was made in a Bundt pan. The critical difference was that instead of describing it as one box of butterscotch cook and serve pudding, the recipe read one box of butterscotch pudding, cooked. The first time I tried this recipe, I actually prepared the pudding (milk and all). I had a feeling something wasn't right. When I inverted the Bundt pan, I had goo all over the kitchen island, dripping down the kitchen cabinets, and onto the floor. These rolls can be refrigerated overnight after step 3. Allow to rise 2 hours before baking.

Pistachio Coffee Cake

Ingredients:

½ cup white sugar
½ brown sugar
2 tsp cinnamon
¾ cup chopped nuts
1 pkg yellow cake mix
1 pkg pistachio pudding mix
4 eggs
¼ cup vegetable oil
¼ cup water
1 cup sour cream

Directions:
1. Mix first four ingredients together and set aside.
2. Mix cake mix, pudding mix, eggs, vegetable oil, water, and sour cream with a wooden spoon until ingredients are combined and batter is smooth.
3. Pour half of the batter over bottom of a greased 13x9x2 pan.
4. Sprinkle half of the sugar mixture over the batter. Repeat layers.
5. Bake in 400-degree oven for 35 minutes or until it tests done.

Notes:
This recipe came from my Aunt Edith Dawson. In our family, she had a reputation for making fabulous cakes, desserts, and other baking treats.

Poppy Seed Muffins

<u>Ingredients:</u>

2 cups all-purpose flour
1 tbsp poppy seed
½ tsp salt
1/3 tsp baking soda
1 cup sugar
½ cup unsalted butter
2 eggs
1 tsp vanilla
1 tsp finely grated lemon peel
1 cup plain yogurt

<u>Directions:</u>
1. Grease 18 muffin cups or line with paper cups.
2. Combine flour, poppy seed, salt, and baking soda.
3. In a large mixing bowl, beat sugar, vanilla, and lemon peel.
4. Add the flour mixture and yogurt alternately to the beaten mixture, beating after each addition until combined.
5. Fill prepared muffin cups 2/3 full. Sprinkle with additional sugar if desired.
6. Bake in a 375 oven for 20 minutes or until golden brown.

Pull Apart Bacon Cheese Wreath

<u>Ingredients:</u>

3 tbsp butter flavor Crisco
1 jar (5-oz) cheese spread with bacon
1 pkg (20-count) refrigerated flaky biscuits
4 slices bacon, cooked crisp, drained, and crumbled
2 tbsp chopped fresh parsley

<u>Directions:</u>

1. Preheat oven to 450. Cut a 12-inch square of non-stick aluminum foil and press on bottom and sides of a 9-inch round cake pan. Place inverted 3½ inch custard cup in center of pan. Spray Pam on foil and custard cup. Set aside.
2. Melt butter flavored Crisco and cheese spread in small saucepan on low heat (mixture may appear curdled). Remove from heat and stir vigorously until smooth and creamy. Spread to cover bottom of pan around custard cup.
3. Cut each biscuit into quarters and fit pieces into pan around custard cup to form a wreath.
4. Bake at 450 for 14 minutes (top will be brown).
5. Turn over onto serving platter. Remove foil and custard cup. Sprinkle with crumbled bacon and parsley. Serve warm.

<u>Note:</u>
This is a good holiday brunch recipe that I found in my mother, Bonnie Albrecht's recipe box when she moved out of her house.

Pumpkin Oatmeal Muffins

Ingredients:

4 eggs or 8 egg whites
1½ cups sugar
¾ cup unsweetened apple sauce
¾ cup vegetable oil
1 (16-oz) can pumpkin
1½ cups whole wheat flour
½ tsp ginger
1 tbsp cinnamon
½ tsp cloves
½ tsp salt
2 tsp baking powder
2 tsp baking soda
½ cup quick cooking oatmeal

Directions:
1. Beat eggs slightly.
2. Add sugar, apple sauce, oil, and pumpkin; beat thoroughly.
3. Combine dry ingredients in a separate bowl. Add to pumpkin mixture and mix until smooth.
4. Fill paper-lined or Pam sprayed muffin cups ¾ full.
5. Sprinkle tops with brown sugar if desired.
6. Bake at 350 for 15-20 minutes. Makes 2 dozen.

Notes:
I use a large bowl and after first two steps I just add all dry ingredients and mix. It saves cleaning one bowl.

Raisin Nut Bread

Ingredients:

1 cup raisins
1 cup water
1 beaten egg
¾ cup sugar
½ tsp vanilla
1½ cups sifted flour
1 tsp baking powder
¼ tsp baking soda
¼ tsp salt
½ cup chopped walnuts

Directions:
1. In saucepan, combine raisins and water, bringing to a boil. Remove from heat, cool to room temperature.
2. Mix together egg, sugar, and vanilla. Stir in raisin mixture.
3. Sift together flour, baking powder, baking soda and salt. Add to egg-raisin mixture, beating well.
4. Stir in nuts. Pour into 2 greased and floured 16 oz fruit or vegetable cans. Bake in 350-degree oven 50 to 60 minutes. Makes 2 loaves.

Notes:
I use 4 small bread pans. The recipe came from my cousin, Jean Ann Albrecht Wendt, who said she used to give these as gifts during the holidays.

Raspberry Royale Muffins

<u>Ingredients:</u>

1 cup sugar
½ cup butter
2 eggs
2 cups flour
2 tsp baking powder
½ tsp salt
½ cup milk
1 tsp vanilla
2½ cups fresh or frozen raspberries

Topping »»

1 tbsp sugar
¼ tsp cinnamon

<u>Directions:</u>
1. Cream together sugar and butter (do not use melted butter or the muffins will be flat). Add eggs and mix well.
2. Sift together the flour, baking powder, and salt. Add dry ingredients to the butter and egg mixture. Add milk and vanilla and stir the batter until dry ingredients are moistened. Gently fold in the raspberries. If using frozen berries, do not fully thaw before adding to the mix.
3. Line muffin tins with paper muffin cups or spray nonstick muffin tins with cooking spray.
4. Fill cups ¾ full with batter. Top with the cinnamon-sugar mixture.
5. Bake at 350 for 25-30 minutes. Muffins are done when a toothpick inserted in the center comes out clean.

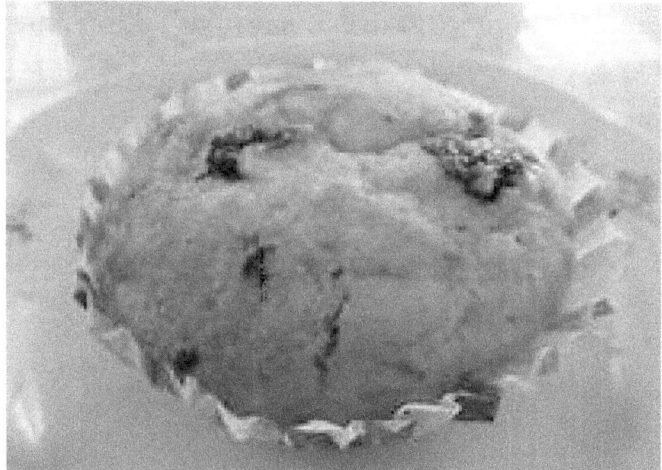

<u>Notes:</u>
This recipe came from Linda Dawson Cutler who says it is her favorite muffin recipe, but she sometime has to break the berries into two pieces if they are large. She uses 2 (6 oz) containers of fresh raspberries.

Raw Apple Bread

Ingredients:

½ cup butter
1 cup sugar
2 eggs
2 cups flour
½ tsp salt
½ tsp baking soda
1 tsp baking powder
2 tbsp buttermilk or milk soured with a few drops vinegar
½ cup walnuts or pecans (optional)
1 cup apples, peeled, cored, and chopped
1 tsp vanilla extract

Directions:
1. Cream butter, add sugar slowly. Beat until light and lemon colored.
2. Beat in eggs.
3. Sift flour, salt, baking soda, and baking powder.
4. Alternate adding dry ingredients and buttermilk to the butter/sugar mixture.
5. Add nuts, apples and vanilla.
6. Spoon batter into a greased loaf pan.
7. Bake in preheated 350-degree oven for 50 to 60 minutes or until loaf pulls away slightly from sides of pan.
8. Cool for about 5 minutes then turn out on a rack and finish cooling.

Notes:
Keeps well and is better the second day. The recipe came from my cousin, Barb Albrecht.

Red Lobster Cheddar Biscuits

Ingredients:

2 cups all-purpose flour
1 cup shredded sharp Cheddar cheese
1 tbsp baking powder
1 tsp salt
½ tsp garlic powder
2/3 cup milk
1/3 cup butter, softened
1 large egg
Pam
2 tbsp melted butter
¼ tsp garlic powder
¼ tsp onion powder
½ tsp parsley flakes
¼ tsp salt

Directions:
1. Preheat oven to 400. Line baking sheet with parchment and spray with Pam.
2. Combine flour, Cheddar cheese, baking powder, salt, and garlic powder in a bowl.
3. Combine milk, 1/3 cup butter, and egg in a separate bowl. Mix into the flour mixture until chunky; be careful not to over-mix the batter.
4. Drop batter by ¼ cups onto the prepared baking sheet.
5. Mix remaining ingredients: 2 tbsp melted butter, ¼ tsp garlic powder, ¼ tsp onion powder, ½ tsp parsley flakes, and ¼ tsp salt in small bowl. Set aside.
6. Bake biscuits in the preheated oven for 10 minutes. Brush with reserved melted butter and continue baking until golden brown, about 5 minutes more.

Notes:
Bob and I often ate so many of these at Red Lobster that we were too full for dinner!! It gave us great leftovers though. I now make these along with the Easy One-Hour Salmon Dinner p. 285 in this book.

Scones with Clotted Cream

Ingredients:

1¾ cups all-purpose flour
4 tsp baking powder
¼ cup white sugar
1/8 tsp salt
5 tbsp unsalted butter
½ cup dried currants or raisins
½ cup milk
¼ cup sour cream
1 egg
1 tbsp milk

Directions:
1. Preheat oven to 400.
2. Sift flour, baking powder, sugar, and salt into a large bowl. Cut in butter using pastry blender or rubbing between your fingers until it is in pea sized lumps. Stir in currants or raisins.
3. Mix together ½ cup milk and sour cream in small bowl. Pour all at once into dry ingredients and stir gently until well blended. Overworking the dough results in terrible scones!!
4. With floured hands, pat scone dough into balls 2 to 3 inches across, depending on what size you want. Place onto a greased baking sheet, and flatten slightly. Let the scones barely touch each other.
5. Whisk together the egg and 1 tbsp milk. Brush the tops of the scones with the egg wash. Let them rest for about 10 minutes.
6. Bake for 10-15 minutes in preheated oven, until the tops are golden brown, not deep brown. Break each scone apart, or slice in half.
7. Serve with butter or clotted cream and a selection of jams.

Clotted Cream

Ingredients:

2 cups heavy cream

Directions:
1. Cook cream over double boiler over simmering water until reduced by about half.

(Recipe continued on next page.)

2. It should be the consistency of butter, with a golden 'crust' on top.
3. Transfer, including crust, to a bowl.
4. Cover and let stand 2 hours, then refrigerate at least 12 hours.
5. Stir crust into cream before serving.
6. Keep unused portions refrigerated, tightly covered, for up to 4 days.

Notes:

I used to make scones for tea parties with my granddaughters. I think it is easier (and probably every bit as good, if not better) to buy clotted cream.

Sour Cream Coffee Cake

Ingredients:

Cake »»

¾ cup melted butter
1 cup sour cream
2 eggs
1 cup white sugar
2 cups flour
1 tsp vanilla
1 tsp baking powder
1 tsp baking soda
¼ tsp salt

Topping »»

1/3 cup brown sugar
2 tsp butter
¼ cup white sugar
1 tsp cinnamon
¾ cup chopped nuts

Directions:

1. Mix all cake ingredients together.
2. In a separate bowl, mix topping butter and sugar together and then add cinnamon and nuts.
3. Spread a layer of batter in a greased tube pan.
4. Sprinkle with a thin layer of topping, then another layer of batter until all ingredients are used.
5. Bake for 45 minutes to an hour at 350.

Notes:

This recipe came from my Aunt Dorothy Albrecht. She was known to be the baker on the Albrecht side of the family.

Toasted Garlic Bread

<u>Ingredients:</u>

1 pound loaf Italian bread
6 tbsp butter, softened
2 tsp extra virgin olive oil
3 cloves garlic, crushed
1 tsp dried oregano
salt and pepper to taste
1 cup shredded mozzarella cheese

<u>Directions:</u>
1. Preheat broiler.
2. Cut the bread into slices 1 to 2-inches thick.
3. In a small bowl, mix butter, olive oil, garlic, oregano, salt, and pepper. Spread the mixture evenly on the bread slices.
4. On a baking sheet, arrange the slices evenly and broil 5 minutes, or until slightly brown. Check frequently so they do not burn.
5. Remove from broiler. Top with cheese, and return to broiler 2 to 3 minutes, until cheese is slightly brown and melted. Serve immediately.

Waffle S'mores

Ingredients:

6 oz semisweet chocolate chips
½ heavy cream
1 egg
1¼ cups milk
2 cups cinnamon graham cracker waffle pancake mix
2 jars marshmallow cream (7 oz each)

Directions:

1. Put cream in a glass bowl and microwave until boiling hot. Remove from microwave, add chocolate chips, and whisk until smooth. Let the chocolate ganache cool until spreadable.

2. Using the egg, milk, and waffle mix, prepare the batter according to the package instructions. Preheat a waffle maker and cook the waffles according to instructions. If you cannot find graham cracker cinnamon waffle mix (Williams-Sonoma carries it), I have used my own substitution and added a half tsp of cinnamon and a tsp of sugar.

3. To assemble the s'mores: spread the chocolate ganache over the top of the waffles, dividing evenly. For each waffle, spread about ½ cup marshmallow cream over the ganache. Using a kitchen torch according to the manufacturer's instructions, toast the marshmallow cream until golden brown. Serve immediately. Makes about 6 s'mores.

Note:
I don't have a kitchen torch so I just put it under the broiler for a minute.

Whole-Grain Berry Pancakes

<u>Ingredients:</u>

¼ cup old-fashioned oats (oatmeal)
¾ cup buttermilk
½ cup whole wheat flour
1 tsp baking powder
¼ tsp baking soda
½ tsp pumpkin pie spice
1/8 tsp salt
1 large egg
1 tbsp canola oil
2 tsp vanilla

<u>Directions:</u>
1. Soak oats in buttermilk for 20 minutes.
2. In large bowl, whisk flour, baking powder, baking soda, pumpkin pie spice, and salt.
3. Whisk egg, oil, and vanilla into oat mixture until just combined.
4. Heat 12-inch nonstick skillet on medium. Working in batches, pour batter by ¼ cupful onto hot skillet. Cook until tops are bubbly and edges look dry. Turn; cook until undersides are golden.
5. Serve with walnuts, strawberries, blueberries, and/or pureed raspberries.
Serves 4.

<u>Notes:</u>
I serve with honey drizzled over the pancakes or with warm maple syrup. I also spray pan with Pam or other non-stick spray.

Zucchini-Chocolate Chip Muffins

<u>Ingredients:</u>

1½ cups flour
¾ cup sugar
1 tsp baking soda
1 tsp cinnamon
½ tsp salt

1 egg
½ cup oil
½ cup milk
1 tbsp lemon juice
1 tsp vanilla

1 cup shredded zucchini
1/3 cup miniature chocolate chips
¼ cup chopped nuts, if desired.

<u>Directions:</u>
1. Mix first five ingredients together.
2. Add next five ingredients and beat well.
3. Add zucchini, chocolate chips, and nuts.
4. Fill paper lined muffin cups 2/3 full.
5. Bake at 350 for 20 to 25 minutes. Makes 12 to 15 muffins.

<u>Notes:</u>
This recipe came from my cousin, Marilyn Albrecht Tackaberry. Marilyn learned her mother's (Dorothy Albrecht) baking secrets.

Cakes

"Cake is happiness! If you know the way of the cake, you know the way of happiness! If you have a cake in front of you, you should not look any further for joy!" **C. Joy Bell**

"You know you're getting old when you get that one candle on the cake. It's like, 'See if you can blow this out.'" **Jerry Seinfeld**

"Cupcakes are love with icing on top." **Anonymous**

"Happiness is knowing there's a cake in the oven." **Anonymous**

"A party without cake is just a meeting." **Julia Child**

Apple Pie Cake with Rum Butter Sauce

Ingredients:

Cake »»

¼ cup butter, softened
1 cup sugar
1 egg
1 cup all-purpose flour
1 tsp salt
1 tsp ground cinnamon
2 tbsp hot water
1 tsp vanilla
3 cups diced, peeled Ida Red or Granny Smith apples
½ cup chopped pecans

Rum Butter Sauce »»

½ cup firmly packed brown sugar
½ cup white sugar
½ cup (1 stick) butter, softened
½ cup whipping cream
2 tbsp rum

Whipping Cream »»

1 pint whipping cream
1/3 cup brown sugar
1 tsp vanilla

Directions for cake:

1. Cream butter. Add sugar. Add egg.
2. Combine dry ingredients and mix well. Add dry ingredients to creamed mixture. Beat on low until smooth. Stir in water and vanilla. Add apples and nuts.
3. Spoon into greased/floured 9-inch pie pan. Bake at 350 degrees for 45 minutes.

Directions for Rum Butter Sauce:

1. Combine all ingredients except rum in a saucepan and mix well. Bring to a boil. Cook 1 minute. Stir in rum.

Directions for whipped cream:

1. Beat cream until it stands in peaks. Add sugar and vanilla and mix well.
2. Serve each slice of apple pie cake with rum butter sauce drizzled over it, and add a dollop of the whipped cream.

Apple Sheet Cake

Ingredients:

Pastry »»

    3 cups all-purpose flour
    1½ tsp baking powder
    1 tsp salt
    ½ cup shortening
    1 cup milk

Apple Filling »»

    3 pounds apples—peeled, cored and sliced
    1 cup white sugar
    1 tsp ground cinnamon
    2 tbsp all-purpose flour
    ½ cup butter

Frosting »»

    2½ cups confectioners' sugar
    3 tbsp milk
    1/3 cup butter, softened
    ½ tsp vanilla extract

Directions:

1. Preheat oven to 400. In a large bowl, combine 3 cups flour, baking powder, and salt. Cut in shortening to the consistency of coarse crumbs. Stir in 1 cup cold milk slowly until completely blended. Separate dough into two balls. Roll out one ball of dough to fit a 15x10-inch pan with some dough extending over the edge of the pan.
2. In a large bowl, combine sliced apples, sugar, cinnamon, and 2 tbsp flour. Place filling in an even layer over prepared crust. Thinly slice ½ cup butter and evenly distribute over the apples. Roll out the remaining dough and place over the apple filling. Seal edges and prick the top all over with a fork.
3. Bake in the preheated oven for 30 minutes. Cool 5 minutes.
4. Mix frosting ingredients, beat until smooth, and spread over cake. It was tough to decide if this was a cake or a pie!

Best Ever Banana Cake with Cream Cheese Frosting

<u>Ingredients:</u>
    1½ cups bananas, mashed, ripe (I use five small or four large bananas)
    2 teas lemon juice
    3 cups flour
    1½ teas baking soda
    ¼ teas salt
    ¾ cup butter, softened
    2 1/8 cups sugar
    3 large eggs
    2 teas vanilla
    1½ cups buttermilk

<u>Frosting:</u>

    ½ cup butter, softened
    1 (8 oz) pkg cream cheese, softened
    1 teas vanilla
    3½ cups confectioners' sugar
    chopped walnuts or pecans for garnish

<u>Directions:</u>
1. Preheat oven to 275°F. (That is not a mistake. Cake will rise fine.) Grease and flour a 9x13-inch pan.
2. In a small bowl, mix mashed banana with the lemon juice; set aside.
3. In a medium bowl, mix flour, baking soda, and salt; set aside.
4. In a large bowl, cream ¾ cup butter and 2 1/8 cups sugar until light and fluffy.
5. Beat in eggs, one at a time, then stir in 2 teas vanilla.
6. Beat in the flour mixture alternately with the buttermilk.
7. Stir in banana mixture.
8. Pour batter into prepared pan and bake in preheated oven for one hour or until toothpick inserted in center comes out clean. Remove from oven. Place directly into the freezer for 45 minutes. This will make the cake very moist.
9. For the frosting, cream the butter and cream cheese until smooth. Beat in 1 teas vanilla.
10. Add confectioners' sugar and beat on low speed until combined, then on high speed until frosting is smooth. Spread on cooled cake. Sprinkle chopped walnuts over top of the frosting, if desired.

Banana Dump Cake

<u>Ingredients:</u>

1 cup milk
1 tbsp vinegar
½ cup butter, softened
2 cups sugar
1 cup banana, mashed
2 eggs
2 cups flour
1 tsp baking soda
1 tsp baking powder

<u>Directions:</u>
1. Add vinegar to milk to sour the milk. Let sit 10 minutes.
2. Dump margarine or butter, sugar, eggs, and banana in a bowl and mix. Dump in remaining ingredients, including the soured milk. Mix well.
3. Pour into a greased 9x13-inch pan. Bake at 350 for 35 minutes.

<u>Notes:</u>
This recipe came from my cousin, Judy Albrecht. She says this cake is her family's favorite. It is very moist so she doesn't frost it, but sprinkles with powdered sugar. I like a cream cheese frosting on top. I also sometimes add walnuts.

Best White Cake Recipe

Ingredients:

2¾ cups cake flour
1 tbsp baking powder
¾ tsp salt
1 cup buttermilk, room temperature
2 tsp vanilla extract
1 cup unsalted butter, softened to room temperature
1¾ cups granulated sugar
5 large egg whites, room temperature

For the **vanilla buttercream frosting:**

1½ cups unsalted butter, softened to room temperature
4½ cups powdered sugar
3 tbsp cream
1 tbsp vanilla extract
1/8 tsp salt

Directions:
1. Preheat oven to 350. Spray two 9-inch cake pans with nonstick cooking spray, line the bottom of the pans with parchment paper, and set aside.
2. In a large mixing bowl, whisk together the cake flour, baking powder, and salt. Set aside.
3. Combine buttermilk and vanilla extract in a measuring cup and stir until well combined. Set aside.
4. In a large mixing bowl using an electric mixer, cream together the butter and sugar for about 4 to 5 minutes or until light and fluffy.
5. On low speed, add the dry ingredients to the creamed butter and sugar in three additions, alternating with the buttermilk mixture (begin and end with the dry ingredients). Mix in each addition until just combined, making sure not to over mix.
6. In a separate clean mixing bowl, beat the egg whites to stiff peaks. Gently fold half of the egg whites into the batter, then fold in the remaining egg whites until just combined.
7. Pour the cake batter into the prepared cake pans and spread around into one even layer. Gently tap the cake pans on the counter to release any air bubbles.
8. Bake at 350 for 28-32 minutes or until a toothpick inserted into the center of
(Recipe continued on next page.)

the cake comes out clean. Remove from the oven, allow to cool in the pan for about 20 minutes, then remove the cakes from the pans and transfer to a wire rack to cool completely.

To make the **Vanilla Buttercream Frosting:**
1. In a large bowl using an electric mixer, beat the butter on medium speed until smooth.
2. Add the powdered sugar one cup at a time, making sure to mix well after each addition, stopping to scrape down the sides of the bowl as needed.
3. Add the cream, vanilla extract, and salt and mix on medium speed until fully combined, making sure to scrape down the sides of the bowl.

To assemble the cake:
Level the tops of each cake with a knife or cake leveler. Place one of the cakes on a cake stand, top with a layer of frosting, and smooth it out into one even layer. Place the second layer on top, then use the remaining frosting to frost the top and sides of the cake.

Boston Cream Pie

<u>Ingredients:</u>
Cake »»　　　　　　　　2½ cups cake flour, sifted
　　　　　　　　　　　　1½ cups sugar
　　　　　　　　　　　　1½ tsp baking powder
　　　　　　　　　　　　1 tsp salt
　　　　　　　　　　　　¾ cup butter, softened
　　　　　　　　　　　　¾ cup milk
　　　　　　　　　　　　3 eggs, unbeaten
　　　　　　　　　　　　1 tsp vanilla

<u>Directions:</u>
1. Preheat oven to 350. Sift flour and measure amount needed into large bowl. Add sugar, baking powder, and salt.
2. Add butter and ½ cup of the milk. Beat two minutes at medium speed. Add eggs, vanilla, and remainder of milk. Beat one minute longer.
3. Pour batter into two cake pans or pie pans. Bake 30 to 35 minutes.

Pastry Cream Filling

<u>Ingredients:</u>

　　　　　　　　　　　3 cups milk
　　　　　　　　　　　¾ cup sugar
　　　　　　　　　　　2 tbsp butter
　　　　　　　　　　　¼ tsp salt
　　　　　　　　　　　1 cup milk
　　　　　　　　　　　2 tbsp cornstarch
　　　　　　　　　　　2 egg yolks
　　　　　　　　　　　1 tsp vanilla

<u>Directions:</u>
1. Mix 3 cups milk, sugar, butter, and salt together in a pan. Bring to boil over low heat stirring constantly. Dissolve cornstarch in remaining 1 cup milk. Mix egg yolks and vanilla into cornstarch/milk mixture and add to boiling mixture, reduce heat and simmer 2 minutes, stirring constantly. Pour into pan, cover with waxed paper, and chill until set.

Bavarian Cream Filling

<u>Ingredients:</u> (Recipe continued on next page.)

1-quart pastry cream
1/3 oz plain gelatin
¼ cup boiling water
¾ cup whipping cream, whipped

Directions:
1. Dissolve gelatin into boiling water.
2. Mix gelatin mixture quickly into pastry cream. Mix until blended with no lumps.
3. Fold whipped cream into above mixture.

Chocolate Frosting

Ingredients:

4 oz bitter chocolate
4 oz butter
3 cups confectioners' sugar
½ cup heavy cream
1 tsp vanilla

Directions:
1. Melt chocolate and butter together. Cool. Mix in powdered sugar, vanilla, and cream.

Assembly:
Slice each cake into two layers. Place the bottom layer back into pan. Top with a thick coating of Bavarian Cream filling (about 2 cups). Place other half of cake on top. Cover the top with chocolate frosting. Repeat procedure with other cake. Cut into wedges and serve. Makes two cakes.

Note:
This recipe comes from the Lawyers' Club at the University of Michigan where it was a favorite.

Brownie Cupcakes

<u>Ingredients:</u>

1 cup butter
½ cup chocolate chips
1½ cups nuts, chopped
1 1/3 cups all-purpose flour
¼ tsp salt
1½ cups sugar
4 eggs, beaten
1 tsp vanilla

<u>Directions:</u>

1. Arrange 21 paper cup liners in cupcake tins. Melt butter and chocolate chips over very low heat, stirring. Stir in chopped nuts, (walnuts, almonds, or pecans). Set aside.
2. Sift together into a large bowl: all-purpose flour, salt, and sugar.
3. Add eggs and vanilla. Stir in chocolate mixture. Mix well.
4. Fill cups about 2/3 full and bake at 325 for 25-30 minutes. Cool. Leave plain, sprinkle with confections' sugar, or frost.

<u>Notes:</u>

This recipe comes from my cousin, Jean Ann Albrecht Wendt. She prefers to use pecans as the nuts because they give more flavor. This was a treat for her children to take to school on their birthdays. Of course, her children are now all grown up, and I wonder if she still makes them.

Carrot Cake with Cream Cheese Frosting

<u>Ingredients:</u>

4 eggs
1¼ cups vegetable oil
2 cups white sugar
2 tsp vanilla extract
2 cups all-purpose flour
2 tsp baking soda
2 tsp baking powder
½ tsp salt
2 tsp ground cinnamon
3 cups grated carrots
1 cup chopped pecans

<u>Cream Cheese Frosting:</u>

½ cup butter, softened
8 oz cream cheese, softened
4 cups confectioners' sugar
1 tsp vanilla extract
1 cup chopped pecans

<u>Directions:</u>

1. Preheat oven to 350. Grease and flour a 9x13-inch pan. In a large bowl, beat together eggs, oil, white sugar, and 2 tsp vanilla.
2. Mix in flour, baking soda, baking powder, salt, and cinnamon. Stir in carrots. Fold in pecans. Pour into prepared pan.
3. Bake in the preheated oven for 40 to 50 minutes, or until a toothpick inserted into the center of the cake comes out clean. Let cool in pan for 10 minutes, then turn out onto a wire rack and cool.
4. To Make Frosting: In a medium bowl, combine butter, cream cheese, confectioners' sugar, and 1 tsp vanilla. Beat until the mixture is smooth and creamy. Stir in chopped pecans. Frost the cooled cake.

<u>Notes:</u>

You can add ½ to ¾ cup of raisins to cake batter if desired. I prefer not to have raisins in my carrot cake.

Carrot Cake with Orange Glaze

<u>Ingredients:</u>

Cake »»

1¼ cups cooking oil
2 cups white sugar
2 cups sifted flour
2 tsp baking powder
1 tsp baking soda
2 tsp cinnamon
1 tsp salt
4 eggs
3 cups grated raw carrots
1 cup finely chopped pecans or walnuts

Glaze »»

¼ cup cornstarch
½ tsp salt
1 tsp fresh lemon juice
2 tsp grated orange peel
1 cup fresh orange juice
1 cup white sugar
2 tbsp butter

<u>Directions:</u>

Cake »»

1. Combine oil and sugar in a large bowl. Mix well.
2. Sift together dry ingredients. Add dry ingredients alternately with eggs (one egg at a time) into the sugar/oil mixture. Mix well after each addition.
3. Add carrots and mix well. Add nuts.
4. Pour into lightly greased 10-inch tube pan and bake in slow oven (325 degrees) about an hour and 20 minutes.
5. Cool in pan, upright. Remove from pan.

Glaze »»

1. Combine sugar and cornstarch in a pan. Add juices slowly and stir until smooth. Add remaining ingredients.

(Recipe continued next page.)

2. Cook over low heat until thick and glossy. Cool and spread on cake. If a heavier glaze is desired, you can double recipe.

Assembly »»

Split cake into 3 layers horizontally and spread orange glaze between layers and on top and sides.

Notes:

This recipe came from my Aunt Edith Dawson who got it from a former co-worker. Edie's grandson, Steve Cutler, always liked this cake. He called it the carrot cake with a hole in the middle. Aunt Edie sent the recipe with instructions that the original recipe for orange glaze seemed too little, doubling it seemed too much, and increasing it by 1 ½ seemed just right.

Chocolate Ice Box Cake

<u>Ingredients:</u>

3 (12 oz each) pound cakes
2 (8 oz) bars Bakers semi-sweet chocolate
6 tbsp water
6 tbsp sugar
8 eggs, separated
vanilla extract
1 quart heavy cream, whipped
confectioners' sugar

<u>Directions:</u>
1. Melt chocolate with sugar and water in double boiler. When melted, add slightly beaten egg yolks. Cook until smooth (3 to 5 minutes). Cool.
2. Fold in egg whites which have been beaten stiff.
3. Fold in half of whipped cream.
4. Line springform pan with thin slices of pound cake.
5. Put 1/3 of the chocolate mixture on cake. Repeat twice and end with the cake on top.
6. Refrigerate 12-24 hours. Remove sides of pan. Place cake on dish, remove bottom and ice with 1 pint of heavy cream, whipped and sweetened to taste with vanilla and confections' sugar.

Flourless Chocolate Cake
(Gluten-Free)

Ingredients:

6 tbsp unsalted butter, plus more for pan
8 oz bittersweet or semisweet chocolate, finely chopped
6 large eggs, separated
½ cup granulated sugar
confectioners' sugar for dusting
sweetened whipped cream to garnish

Directions:
1. Preheat the oven to 275 with the rack in the center. Butter the bottom and sides of a 9-inch springform pan. Set aside.
2. Place butter and chocolate in a large heatproof bowl and microwave in 30-second increments, stirring each time, until chocolate is completely melted. Let cool slightly. Whisk in egg yolks.
3. In a large bowl, beat egg whites until soft peaks form. Gradually add granulated sugar, and continue beating until glossy stiff peaks form. Whisk ¼ of the egg whites into the chocolate mixture; then gently fold in remaining egg whites.
4. Pour batter into the prepared pan, and smooth the top with a rubber spatula. Bake until the cake pulls away from the sides of the pan and is set in the center, 45 to 50 minutes. Cool completely on a wire rack; remove sides of pan. Serve at room temperature, dusted with confectioners' sugar. Top with whipped cream, if desired.

Notes:
This is a great recipe for friends who have a gluten sensitivity. I sometimes place a lace paper doily on the cooled cake and sift confectioners' sugar over the top. When I remove doily, I have a lovely lacy design. I serve with fresh raspberries on the side. Sometimes I make a chocolate ganache and pour over the top of the cake while it is still warm in the pan. **Ganache**: 1 cup heavy cream slowly brought to a boil in small saucepan, add 9 oz chopped bittersweet chocolate and stir until melted, and add 1 tbsp dark rum (optional).

Fresh Apple Cake

<u>Ingredients:</u>
Cake »»

    1½ cups oil
    2 cups white sugar
    3 eggs, beaten
    1 tsp vanilla
    3 cups flour
    1 tsp salt
    1 tsp baking soda
    1 tsp cinnamon
    3 cups peeled and chopped apples
    1 cup nuts, chopped

Filling/frosting »»

    1 stick butter
    2½ tbsp flour
    ½ cup milk
    1 cup sweet coconut
    3 cups confectioners' sugar
    1 tsp vanilla

<u>Directions:</u>
Cake »»
1. Mix oil, sugar, eggs, and vanilla.
2. Sift flour, soda, salt, and cinnamon. Add to liquid mixture and stir well.
3. Add apples and nuts. Mixture will be thick.
4. Bake in a 9x13 greased pan at 350 for 45 minutes or until the cake tests done when lightly touched.

Topping »»
Melt butter, add 2½ tbsp flour, ½ cup milk, and coconut. Boil 1 minute. Stir in confectioners' sugar and 1 tsp vanilla. Pour over cake.

<u>Note:</u>
This recipe came from my Aunt Edith Dawson who believed this cake was one of her best.

Fresh Orange Cake

<u>Ingredients:</u>

1 cup brown sugar
2/3 cup shortening or butter
2 eggs
1 cup raisins
1 orange
2 cups flour
1 cup sour milk or buttermilk
1 tsp baking soda
chopped nuts (walnuts or pecans)
½ cup confectioners' sugar

<u>Directions:</u>

1. Spray a tube or Bundt pan with cooking spray. Juice the orange and save the juice for the topping. Grind the orange rind with the raisins. Add the orange rind and raisins to the sugar. Blend with milk and add remaining ingredients, beating very thoroughly.

2. Bake in 350-degree oven for one hour or until cake tests done. Remove cake by inverting onto plate and top while still warm with glaze made from orange juice mixed with confectioners' sugar.

<u>Note:</u>

My Aunt Edith Dawson's mother used to make this cake for her, and my aunt passed the recipe on to me.

Frozen Chocolate Cake

<u>Ingredients:</u>

cocoa and butter for dusting pans
¾ cup chocolate liqueur
4 tbsp butter
6 oz semi-sweet chocolate pieces
4 large eggs
1/3 cup flour, sifted
1 pint of fresh raspberries or strawberries washed and stemmed
½ cup heavy cream, whipped
1/3 cup chocolate liqueur

<u>Directions:</u>

1. Preheat oven to 425. Butter an 8-inch springform pan and line the bottom with a round of waxed paper. Butter again and dust the pan with cocoa. Shake out excess cocoa.
2. In the top of a double boiler, combine the first amount of liqueur, chocolate pieces and butter. Heat over hot water until the chocolate is melted and stir until smooth.
3. Place the eggs in a large heat-proof bowl. Put the bowl over a pot of very hot water and heat the eggs, stirring until warm to the touch (about 1 minute). Remove from the heat and beat with an electric mixer at high speed until very light and tripled in volume, about 5 minutes.
4. Pour the chocolate mixture into the eggs and stir in the flour. Fold together until uniform in color, and pour into the prepared pan.
5. Bake until the center is just set, about 15 minutes. Cool, wrap in foil and freeze for at least 8 hours.
6. About 20 minutes before serving, remove cake from freezer. Frost the cake with whipped cream. Arrange the strawberries, pointed ends up, on top of the whipped cream and drizzle liqueur over the berries. Serve immediately.

Ghirardelli Individual Chocolate Lava Cakes

Ingredients:

Center »»
- ½ Ghirardelli (2 oz) 60% Cacao Bittersweet Chocolate Baking Bar
- ¼ cup heavy cream

Cake »»
- non-stick cooking spray
- 1 Ghirardelli (4 oz) 60% Cacao Bittersweet Chocolate Baking Bar
- 8 tbsp (1 stick) unsalted butter
- 2 whole eggs
- 2 egg yolks
- 1/3 cup sugar
- ½ tsp vanilla extract
- ¼ cup cake flour
- raspberries and whipped cream for garnish

Directions:

1. Center: melt chocolate and cream in double boiler. Whisk gently to blend. Refrigerate about 2 hours or until firm. Form into 6 balls; refrigerate until needed.
2. Cake: heat oven to 400. Spray 6 4-oz ramekins or custard cups with cooking spray. Melt chocolate and butter in double boiler; whisk gently to blend. With an electric mixer, whisk eggs, yolks, sugar, and vanilla on high speed about 5 minutes or until thick and light.
3. Fold melted chocolate mixture and flour into egg mixture just until combined. Spoon cake batter into ramekins. Place a chocolate ball in the middle of each ramekin.
4. Bake about 15 minutes or until cake is firm to touch. Let it sit out of the oven for about 5 minutes. Run a small, sharp knife around the inside of each ramekin, place a plate on top, invert, and remove ramekin.
5. Garnish with raspberries and a dollop of whipped cream.

Hawaiian Carrot Cake

Ingredients:

2 cups sifted flour
2 tsp baking soda
1 tsp salt
2 tsp cinnamon
2 cups granulated sugar
1½ cups cooking oil
4 eggs
1 jar (7 oz each) junior baby carrots
1 can (8 oz) crushed pineapple, drained
½ cup chopped walnuts or pecans

1 stick butter, softened
1 pkg (8 oz) cream cheese, softened
1 tsp vanilla
1 box (16 oz) confectioners' sugar

Directions:

1. In a large bowl, sift flour, baking soda, salt, and cinnamon together. Add granulated sugar. Add oil, eggs, and carrots. Mix together. Add pineapple and nuts.
2. Pour into 8½x13-inch pan prepared with cooking spray and a light dusting of flour. Bake in a 350 oven for 55 minutes.
3. For icing: Beat butter and cream cheese. Add vanilla and confectioners' sugar and beat again. Pour over cooled cake and spread with spatula.

Note:

The pineapple makes the difference in this carrot cake.

Hummingbird Cake

<u>Ingredients:</u>

3 cups all-purpose flour, plus more for pans
2 cups granulated sugar
1 tsp salt
1 tsp baking soda
1 tsp ground cinnamon
3 large eggs, beaten
1½ cups vegetable oil
1½ tsp vanilla extract
1 (8-oz) can crushed pineapple in juice, undrained
2 cups chopped ripe bananas (about 3 bananas)
1 cup chopped pecans, toasted
vegetable shortening

Cream Cheese Frosting:

2 (8-oz) pkg. cream cheese, softened
1 cup salted butter or margarine, softened
2 (16-oz) pkg. powdered sugar
2 tsp vanilla extract
¾ cup pecan halves, toasted (optional)

<u>Directions:</u>

1. Prepare the Cake Layers: Preheat oven to 350. Whisk together flour, sugar, salt, baking soda, and cinnamon in a large bowl; add eggs and oil, stirring just until dry ingredients are moistened. Stir in vanilla, pineapple, bananas, and toasted pecans.
2. Divide batter evenly among 3 well-greased (with shortening) and floured 9-inch round cake pans.
3. Bake in preheated oven until a wooden toothpick inserted in center comes out clean, 25 to 30 minutes. Cool in pans on wire racks 10 minutes. Remove from pans to wire racks, and cool completely, about 1 hour.
4. Prepare the Cream Cheese Frosting: Beat cream cheese and butter with an electric mixer on medium-low speed until smooth. Gradually add powdered sugar, beating at low speed until blended after each addition. Stir in vanilla. Increase speed to medium-high, and beat until fluffy, 1 to 2 minutes. Spread frosting on first layer, cover with second layer and frost top.

Ice Cream Cake (Baskin Robbins Style)

Ingredients:
 3 quarts ice cream (your choice, but should be flavors that go well with chocolate)
 2½ cups roughly crushed chocolate (or other) cookies*
 2 cups chocolate fudge sauce
 1 quart heavy whipping cream
 2 tbsp powdered sugar
 1 tsp vanilla extract
 sprinkles (optional)
 Magic Shell sauce (optional)
 maraschino cherries (optional)
 9-or 10-inch springform pan, chilled in the freezer overnight

Directions:
1. A few minutes before you are ready to start making your ice cream cake, set one quart of ice cream out on your counter to soften (5-15 minutes). You want the ice cream to be spreadable.

(Recipe continued next page.)

2. Spread the ice cream in the pan (bottom and a thin layer up the sides).
3. Pulse cookies in a food processor until they're broken into large crumbs. *Baskin-Robbins ice cream cake uses chocolate wafer cookies, but you can use any crunchy cookie: chocolate chip cookies, Biscotti cookies, or Oreo cookies including with the cream filling. All work well. Spread half of the cookie mixture over the ice cream. Slightly press the crumbs into the ice cream on the bottom of the pan.
4. Put the pan back in the freezer for an hour to re-harden the ice cream.
5. Soften the second flavor of ice cream. When the ice cream is spreadable, pack it into the pan on top of the now frozen first layer. Top with the other half of the cookie crumbs. Lightly push the crumbs into the ice cream. Warm the hot fudge until it is pourable, but don't let it get hot. Pour over crumbs. Freeze ice-cream cake for at least four hours or overnight, until firm.
6. Soften the third quart of ice cream. Spread it onto the cookie crumb/chocolate fudge layer and smooth the top of the cookie cake with a spatula. Freeze for at least four hours.
7. Run a butter knife along the inside of the springform pan and remove the outer ring. If the cake is too soft, return it to the freezer until hardened.
8. Whip the heavy cream and add confectioners' sugar, vanilla, and a drop or two of cake coloring if desired. Spread on the outside of the cake with a spatula and top with sprinkles, magic shell and/or cherries. Freeze uncovered for an hour. Then cover with plastic wrap and freeze until you are ready to serve. You can write on the cake with melted chocolate if you want to use a birthday (or other) greeting. You can keep in the freezer for a month before serving, so this is the ultimate do-ahead dessert.

Notes:
My grandson, Kohler, wanted one of these cakes for his birthday. He only recently told me this, and this year he got one. Of course, by this time he was eating healthy. At least I tried. I'm afraid my version looked nothing like this one.

Italian Cream Cake

Ingredients:
Cake »»

    1 stick butter, (8 tbsp)
    ½ cup shortening
    2 cups sugar
    5 egg yolks
    2 cups flour
    1 tsp baking soda
    1 cup buttermilk
    1 small can (about 3 oz) sweet, flaked coconut, about 1 1/3 C
    5 egg whites, stiffly beaten
    1 tsp vanilla extract
    1 cup chopped pecans or walnuts

Frosting »»

    1 pkg cream cheese, softened (8 oz)
    1 box confectioners' sugar (1 pound)
    ½ (4 tbsp) stick butter, softened
    1 tsp vanilla
    1/3 cup chopped pecans or walnuts

Directions:
1. Cream butter and shortening; add sugar. Add egg yolks and beat well.
2. Combine baking soda and flour; add to creamed mixture alternately with buttermilk. Stir in vanilla. Add coconut and nuts.
3. Fold in beaten egg whites.
4. Pour into 3 greased and floured cake pans; bake at 350 for 15 to 30 minutes.
5. Frosting: beat cream cheese until smooth; stir in confectioners' sugar. Add vanilla and beat until smooth. Spread on cake layers; sprinkle top with nuts.

Macadamia Fudge Torte

<u>Ingredients:</u>

Filling »»

    1/3 cup sweetened condensed milk
    ½ cup semi-sweet chocolate chips

Cake »»

    1 pkg Pillsbury Moist Supreme Devil's Food Cake Mix
    1½ tsp cinnamon
    1/3 cup oil
    1 (16-oz) can sliced pears in light syrup, drained
    2 eggs
    1/3 cup chopped macadamia nuts or pecans
    1 tsp water

Sauce »»

    1 (12.25 oz) jar Smucker's Caramel Ice Cream Topping
    3 tbsp milk
    Serve with Vanilla Ice Cream or whipped cream

<u>Directions:</u>

1. Heat oven to 350. Spray 9 or 10-inch springform pan with nonstick cooking spray.
2. In small saucepan, combine filling ingredients. Cook over medium-low heat until chocolate is melted, stirring occasionally.
3. In large bowl, combine cake mix, cinnamon, and oil; blend at low speed for 20 to 30 seconds or until crumbly. (Mixture will be dry.)
4. Place pears in blender or food processor, cover and blend until smooth.
5. In large bowl, combine 2½ cups of the cake mix mixture, pureed pears and eggs. Beat at low speed until moistened. Beat 2 minutes at medium speed. Spread batter evenly in sprayed pan.
6. Drop filling by spoonfuls over batter.
7. Stir nuts and water into remaining cake mix mixture. Sprinkle over filling.
8. Bake at 350 for 45 to 50 minutes or until top springs back when touched lightly in center. Cool 10 minutes. Remove sides of pan. Cool 1½ hours or until completely cooled.
9. In small saucepan, combine sauce ingredients. Cook over medium-low heat for 3 to 4 minutes or until well blended, stirring occasionally.

    (Recipe continued next page.)

10. To serve: Spoon 1½ tbsp warm sauce onto each serving plate, top with wedge of torte and scoop of ice cream. If desired, garnish with chocolate curls and/or fresh raspberries.

Notes:

For a recipe using a cake mix, this may look complicated. Having made it many times, I can say it really isn't all that difficult, it just looks that way at first glance. I heat the sweetened condensed milk in the microwave (don't overheat, it should be hot but not boiling) and then take it from the microwave and stir in chocolate pieces until melted.

I also use my own caramel sauce recipe, but you can use caramel ice cream topping.

This was my daughter's favorite dessert when she was in high school and before she decided she doesn't really like chocolate. Can she be my daughter?

Milky Way Cake

Ingredients:

Cake »»

8 Milky Way bars
2 sticks butter, softened
2 cups sugar
4 eggs
2½ cups all-purpose flour
½ tsp baking soda
1¼ cups buttermilk
1 cup chopped pecans

Icing »»

2½ cups sugar
1 stick butter
1 cup evaporated milk
6 oz semi-sweet chocolate chips
1 cup marshmallow cream

Directions:

Cake »»

1. Melt Milky Way bars in microwave or over double boiler. Add 1 stick of butter and set aside.
2. Cream sugar and 1 stick of butter and beat until fluffy. Add eggs to creamed sugar mixture and beat after each one.
3. Mix flour and baking soda and add alternately with buttermilk.
4. Add melted candy/butter mixture. Add pecans.
5. Bake at 325 degrees for 1 hour and 10 minutes in a tube pan sprayed with Pam. Cake should spring back when done.

Icing »»

Combine sugar and milk and cook to soft ball stage. Add chocolate chips, marshmallow cream, and butter. Stir until melted and spread over cake.

Mini-Bundt Cakes (from boxed mixes)

<u>Ingredients:</u> (for basic recipe)

6 eggs, lightly whisked
½ cup vegetable oil
2 boxes cake mix
1 large box instant pudding mix

<u>Directions:</u>

1. Spray the mini-Bundt pan wells with cooking spray and for each recipe below fill the cups to ¾ full of batter.
2. Bake all cakes at 350 about 25 minutes or until the top springs back at your touch. Let sit 5 minutes after removing from oven, then turn pan upside down onto a sheet of parchment paper lightly sprayed with cooking oil.
3. For variations, follow directions below:

Chocolate Chip Cherry Cake: Use Fudge brownie mixes in place of the cake mixes and add 2 cans cherry pie filling and only 4 eggs.

Red Velvet Mini-Cakes: Use red velvet cake mixes, chocolate pudding mix, powdered sugar to sprinkle on top.

Vanilla Nutmeg Sherry Pound Cake: Use yellow cake mixes, vanilla pudding mix, ½ cup crème sherry, 2 tsp ground nutmeg. Frost with vanilla cream frosting, 1 tbsp in center of each cake.

Lemony Mini-Bundt Cake: Lemon cake mixes, lemon pie filling, ½ jar Dickenson's lemon curd. Frosting: Vanilla butter cream frosting (homemade or canned) and the other ½ of lemon curd mixed together and placed 1 tbsp in center of each cake.

Strawberry Mini-Bundt Cake: Strawberry cake mixes, 1 cup strawberry jam, 1 tsp almond extract. Frosting: Butter cream (homemade or canned, mixed with ¾ cup strawberry jam. 1 tbsp in center of each cake.

Carrot Mini-Bundt Cakes: Carrot cake mixes, vanilla or butterscotch pudding mix

(you can add ½ cup pumpkin puree), 2 tbsp water. Frost with a cream cheese frosting mixed with 1 tbsp pumpkin pie spice.

Chocolate Peanut Butter Swirl Bundt Cakes: Chocolate fudge cake mixes, chocolate pudding mix, 1 cup creamy peanut butter, 2 tbsp water. Frost with chocolate frosting (homemade or canned) mixed with 1 cup whipped cinnamon honey peanut butter, 1 tbsp placed in center of each cake.

Mom's Florida Cake

<u>Ingredients:</u>
Cake »»

      2 cups flour
      2 cups sugar
      2 eggs
      1 tsp maple extract
      2 tsp baking soda
      1 large (No.2 ½) can crushed pineapple and juice
      1 cup of chopped walnuts

Frosting »»

      1 stick butter, softened
      2 cups confectioners' sugar
      2 tsp maple extract
      8 oz creamed cheese, softened

<u>Directions:</u>
1. Beat all cake ingredients except crushed walnuts. Add the walnuts last.
2. Bake in a greased 9x13-inch cake pan at 350 for 45 minutes or until cake springs back when touched.
3. Mix all frosting ingredients until no lumps, and frost cake after it has cooled.

<u>Notes:</u>

This recipe floated around Florida among snowbirds. It originally called for vanilla flavoring, but one day when my mom, Bonnie Albrecht, was out of vanilla, she substituted maple extract. Everyone seemed to like the change and from then on, she always used the maple extract.

Pumpkin Roll

Ingredients:

3 eggs, beaten
1 cup white sugar
½ tsp ground cinnamon
⅔ cup pumpkin puree
¾ cup all-purpose flour
1 tsp baking soda
2 tbsp butter, softened
8 oz cream cheese, softened
1 cup confectioners' sugar
¼ tsp vanilla extract
confectioners' sugar for dusting

Directions:
1. Preheat oven to 375. Butter or grease one 10x15-inch jelly roll pan, lined with parchment,
2. In a mixing bowl, blend together eggs, sugar, cinnamon, and pumpkin. In a separate bowl, mix together flour and baking soda. Add to pumpkin mixture and blend until smooth. Evenly spread the mixture in prepared jelly roll pan.
3. Bake 15 to 25 minutes in the preheated oven. Remove from oven and allow to cool enough to handle. Remove parchment.
4. Remove cake from pan and place on tea towel (cotton, not terry cloth). Roll up the cake by rolling a towel inside cake and place seam side down to cool.
5. Prepare the frosting by blending together the butter, cream cheese, confectioners' sugar, and vanilla.
6. When cake is cooled, unroll and spread with cream cheese filling. Roll up again without towel. Wrap with plastic wrap and refrigerate until ready to serve. Sprinkle top with confectioners' sugar and slice into 8-10 servings.

Rhubarb-Upside Down Cake

Ingredients:

> 5 cups rhubarb, washed, peeled, and cut into small pieces
> 1 cup sugar
> 1 (3 oz) pkg strawberry Jell-O
> 3 cups mini marshmallows
> 1 pkg white cake mix

Directions:
1. Mix rhubarb, sugar, and Jell-O and place in greased 9x13-inch pan.
2. Cover with marshmallows.
3. Mix cake mix according to box directions and pour over rhubarb and marshmallow mixture.
4. Bake at 350 for 50-60 minutes. Remove from oven, cover with platter slightly larger than cake pan and invert.
5. Serve warm, topped with whipped cream.

Notes:
This recipe came from my cousin, Judy Albrecht. I found trying to find a large enough platter and then invert such a large cake was difficult, so I bake in two smaller round pans.

Self-Filled Cup Cakes

Ingredients:

1 pkg chocolate cake mix
1 (8 oz) pkg cream cheese, softened
1 1/3 cups sugar
1 egg
dash of salt
1 (6 oz) pkg mini-chocolate chips

Directions:
1. Mix cake according to package directions. Line cupcake tin with paper baking cups and fill cups 2/3 full of batter.
2. Cream the cheese with the sugar. Beat in the egg and salt. Stir in the chocolate pieces. Drop one rounded tsp cheese mixture into each cup.
3. Bake as package directs for the cupcakes. Frost as desired. Makes 30 cupcakes.

Notes:
Aunt Edith Dawson used to make these to take to a medical facility for her brother, Ralph, on his birthday. She spelled out HAPPY BIRTHDAY RALPH with one letter on each cupcake.

Strawberry Shortcake with Basil Whipped Cream

Ingredients:

Basil Whipped Cream »»
- ¼ cup packed fresh basil leaves
- 1 cup heavy cream
- 3 tbsp confectioners' sugar

Shortcake »»
- 1 cup unbleached all-purpose flour
- ¾ cup sugar
- 1 tsp baking powder
- ½ tsp salt
- 4 tbsp unsalted butter, melted
- 1 large egg, beaten
- ½ cup whole milk
- 1 tsp vanilla extract

Rosy Strawberry filling »»
- 1 pound (reserve five pretty ones) fresh strawberries, hulled, washed, and diced
- 2 tsp rosewater
- ½ cup granulated sugar
- fresh basil or other herb leaves for garnish

Directions:

1. Prepare the whipped cream: Combine the basil leaves and cream in a saucepan over medium-high heat. Heat until bubbles form around the perimeter. Remove from heat, cover and let infuse for 30 minutes. Strain out the basil leaves and refrigerate the flavored cream until ready to whip.

2. Preheat the oven to 375. Grease an 8-inch cake pan. Line with parchment paper or waxed paper circle, butter the paper and dust pan with flour. Tap out excess.

(Recipe continued on next page.)

3. Prepare the cake: Whisk the dry ingredients together in a medium bowl. Whisk in the remaining wet ingredients until almost smooth. Pour batter into pan.
4. Bake for 22 to 25 minutes or until an inserted toothpick comes out clean. Cool the cake in the pan on a wire rack for 10 minutes, then remove from pan to cool completely on the rack.
5. Prepare the strawberry filling: (Don't forget to set aside 5 strawberries for garnish). Dice remaining strawberries and combine with sugar and rosewater.
6. Assemble: Cut the cake in half horizontally using a serrated knife. Spread the bottom layer, cut side up, with strawberry filling. Top with remaining layer, cut side down.
7. Whip the basil-infused cream until soft peaks form. Add confectioners' sugar and vanilla and beat until incorporated. For serving: Cut cake into eight pieces. Dollop whipped cream on each slice and garnish with whole strawberries and fresh basil.

<u>Note:</u>

To make rose water using fresh flowers is much simpler than you may think! All you need are washed petals from two roses and 2 cups distilled water. Add a splash of vodka to help preserve the water if you would like. Simmer for 20 to 30 minutes until petals are pale.

Texas Sheet Cake (Original Chocolate)

<u>Ingredients:</u>

2 cups all-purpose flour
2 cups white sugar
1 tsp baking soda
½ tsp salt
½ cup sour cream
2 eggs
1 cup butter
1 cup water
5 tbsp unsweetened cocoa powder

<u>Icing:</u>

6 tbsp milk
5 tbsp unsweetened cocoa powder
½ cup butter
4 cups confectioners' sugar
1 tsp vanilla extract
1 cup chopped walnuts (optional)

<u>Directions:</u> (For the cake)
1. Preheat oven to 350 degrees. Grease and flour a 10x15x1-inch pan.
2. Combine the flour, sugar, baking soda, and salt. Beat in the sour cream and eggs. Set aside.
3. Melt the butter on low in a saucepan, add the water and 5 tbsp cocoa. Bring mixture to a boil then remove from heat. Allow to cool slightly, then stir cocoa mixture into the egg mixture, mixing until blended.
4. Pour batter into prepared pan. Bake in the preheated oven for 20 minutes, or until a toothpick inserted into the center comes out clean.

<u>Directions:</u> (For the icing)
In a large saucepan, combine the milk, 5 tbsp cocoa and ½ cup butter. Bring to a boil, then remove from heat. Stir in the confectioners' sugar and vanilla, then fold in the nuts, mixing until blended. Spread frosting over warm cake.

<u>Note:</u>
This is a no-fail, easy sheet cake that is great for large groups.

Texas Sheet Cake (Peanut Butter Version)

Ingredients:

Cake »»

2 cups all-purpose flour
2 cups white sugar
½ tsp baking soda
¼ tsp salt
1 cup water
¾ cup butter or margarine, softened
½ cup peanut butter
¼ cup vegetable oil
2 eggs
½ cup buttermilk
1 tsp vanilla extract
2/3 cup white sugar

Frosting »»

1/3 cup evaporated milk
1 tbsp butter or margarine
1/3 cup chunky peanut butter
1/3 cup miniature marshmallows
½ tsp vanilla extract

Directions:
1. Preheat the oven to 350. Grease a 10x15xl-inch jellyroll pan.
2. In a large bowl, stir together flour, 2 cups sugar, baking soda, and salt. Set aside.
3. Combine the water and ¾ cup of butter in a saucepan, and bring to a boil. Remove from the heat and stir in ½ cup peanut butter and vegetable oil until well blended. Stir this mixture into the dry ingredients. Combine the eggs, buttermilk, and vanilla; stir into the peanut butter mixture until well blended.
4. Spread the batter evenly in the prepared pan. Bake for 18 to 26 minutes in the preheated oven, or until a toothpick inserted near the center comes out clean.

Frosting Directions:
1. While the cake bakes, place 2/3 cup sugar, evaporated milk, and butter in a saucepan. Bring to a boil, stirring constantly. Cook, stirring for 2 minutes.
2. Remove from heat and stir in the peanut butter, marshmallows, and vanilla until marshmallows are melted and the mixture is smooth.
3. Spoon the frosting over the warm cake and spread in an even layer. Allow to cool before cutting and serving.

Texas Sheet Cake (White Version)

<u>Ingredients:</u>

Cake »»

1 cup butter
1 cup water
2 cups all-purpose flour
2 cups white sugar
2 eggs
½ cup sour cream
1 tsp almond extract
½ tsp salt
1 tsp baking soda

Frosting »»

½ cup butter
¼ cup milk
4½ cups confectioners' sugar
½ tsp almond extract
1 cup chopped walnuts or pecans

<u>Directions:</u>

1. In a large saucepan, bring 1 cup butter and water to a boil. Remove from heat, and stir in flour, sugar, eggs, sour cream, 1 tsp almond extract, salt, and baking soda until smooth.
2. Pour batter into a greased 10x15x1-inch baking pan. Bake at 375 for 20 to 22 minutes, or until cake is golden brown and tests done. Cool for 20 minutes.
3. Combine ½ cup butter and milk in a saucepan; bring to a boil. Remove from heat. Mix in sugar and ½ tsp almond extract. Stir in nuts. Spread frosting over warm cake.

<u>Notes:</u>

This is my go-to recipe for white cake. It seemed every white cake I made was dry, but this one is always moist.

Texas Sheet Cake (Oatmeal Version)

Ingredients:

1¼ cups boiling water
1 cup quick oats
1 stick butter
½ tsp salt
1 cup white sugar
1 cup brown sugar
2 eggs
1½ cups all-purpose flour
1 tsp cinnamon
1 tsp baking soda
1 tsp baking powder

Directions:
1. Stir oats into boiling water with butter and salt. Let stand while mixing other ingredients. Add oatmeal mixture.
2. Stir well and bake in a greased and floured 10x15x1-inch baking pan at 350 degrees for 35-40 minutes.

Sauce for Oatmeal Sheet Cake

Ingredients:

½ cup buttermilk
1 cup sugar
1 stick butter
½ tsp baking soda
½ tsp vanilla

Directions:
1. Boil first four ingredients in 2-quart pan for two minutes. Remove from heat. Add vanilla and pour immediately over cake.

~ ~ ~

Texas Sheet Cake (Pumpkin Version)

Ingredients:

1 (15 oz) can canned pumpkin puree
2 cups white sugar
1 cup vegetable oil
(Recipe continued on next page)

4 eggs
2 cups all-purpose flour
2 tsp baking soda
1 tsp ground cinnamon
½ tsp salt
1 (3 oz) pkg cream cheese, softened
5 tbsp butter, softened
1 tsp vanilla extract
1¾ cups confectioners' sugar
3 tsp milk
1 cup chopped walnuts

Directions:
1. In a mixing bowl, beat pumpkin, 2 cups white sugar, and oil. Add eggs, and mix well.
2. In another bowl, combine flour, baking soda, cinnamon and salt. Add these dry ingredients to the pumpkin mixture, and beat until well blended.
3. Pour batter into a greased 15x10x1-inch baking pan.
Bake at 350 degrees for 25 to 30 minutes, or until cake tests done. Cool.
4. In a mixing bowl, beat the cream cheese, butter or margarine, and vanilla until smooth. Gradually add 1¾ cups confectioners' sugar, and mix well. Add milk until frosting reaches desired spreading consistency. Frost cake, and sprinkle with nuts.

~ ~ ~ ~ ~ ~ ~ ~ ~ ~ ~ ~ ~ ~ ~ ~ ~ ~ ~ ~

Notes:
Sheet cakes are easy and great for a crowd. They now come in many versions, so you have plenty of choices.

Waldorf Astoria Red Cake

Ingredients:

Cake »»

½ cup shortening
1½ cups sugar
2 eggs
3 tbsp cocoa
5 drops red food coloring
2½ cups all-purpose flour
¾ tsp salt
1 cup buttermilk
1 tsp vanilla
1 tsp baking powder
1 tbsp vinegar

Waldorf Astoria Frosting »»

5 tbsp flour
1 cup milk
1 cup butter, softened
1 cup sugar
1 tsp vanilla

Directions:

Cake »»

1. Cream together shortening, sugar, and eggs until light and fluffy. Make paste of cocoa and red food coloring and a few drops of water. Add this paste to creamed mixture.
2. Sift flour and salt together. Mix buttermilk and vanilla. Add flour and buttermilk mixtures alternately to creamed mixture.
3. Blend vinegar and baking soda together. Fold into cake mixture.
4. Bake in two 9-inch or three 8-inch, well-greased and floured, round pans at 350 for 25 to 30 minutes. (I line the pans with wax paper circles to avoid sticking.)

Waldorf Astoria Frosting »»

1. Cook flour and milk over medium heat until thick, stirring constantly. Cool completely (you can refrigerate until cold.)
2. Beat butter, sugar, and vanilla until creamy and fluffy; about 10-15 minutes. Do not under beat.
3. Gradually add cooled mixture, a little at a time and continue beating until the consistency of whipped cream. Spread on cooled cake.

Walnut Cake with Caramel Whipped Cream

<u>Ingredients:</u>

1 cup walnut halves or pieces
¾ cup unbleached all-purpose flour
1 cup sugar
1 medium orange
¼ tsp salt
7 eggs, separated
½ tsp cream of tartar
(Caramel Whipped Topping and Caramel Sauce recipes next page)

<u>Directions:</u>

1. Preheat oven to 350. In food processor or blender, combine walnuts and flour. Process until nuts are finely ground; set aside.
2. Set aside 2 tbsp of the sugar.
3. Finely shred peel from orange and juice the orange. In a large bowl combine the remaining sugar, 1 tsp of the orange peel, 1/3 cup of the orange juice, salt, and egg yolks. Beat on high with an electric mixer for 3 to 5 minutes or until very thick and pale.
4. In another large bowl, beat the egg whites and cream of tartar until soft peaks form when beaters are lifted. Gradually beat in the 2 tbsp reserved sugar until egg whites are stiff but not dry.
5. Spoon a quarter of the egg whites over yolk mixture. Add nut mixture. Fold together with a large rubber spatula. Add remaining egg whites and fold to combine. Scrape batter into an ungreased 10-inch tube pan with removable bottom; spread evenly in pan.
6. Bake 35 to 40 minutes or until cake is golden brown, springy to the touch, and toothpick inserted near center comes out clean. Cool cake upside down in pan by inverting cake pan over a bottle with a long neck.
7. By the time the cake is cool, most will have pulled away from the sides of pan; rap sides of pan sharply on counter to release any portion of cake that is still attached. Run a skewer or long spatula around the tube to detach; lift to remove cake. Slide a thin spatula around bottom of cake to detach bottom.
8. With serrated knife, cut cake into two layers. Fill between layers with Caramel whipped Cream. Serve with simple Caramel Sauce. Makes 12 servings.

(Caramel whipped topping and Caramel Sauce recipes on next pages.)

Caramel Whipped Cream

<u>Ingredients:</u>

½ cup water
1 cup sugar
1½ cups coarsely chopped walnuts or pecans
1 cup whipping cream

<u>Directions:</u>

1. Line baking sheet with foil or parchment paper; set aside.
2. Place water in a 2-quart saucepan. Pour sugar in a stream in center of pan to form a low mound. Don't stir; use your fingers to pat sugar mound down until it is entirely moistened. Any sugar touching the edges of the pan should be below the water line. Cover and cook over medium heat for a few minutes without stirring until sugar is dissolved and syrup looks clear.
3. Uncover and continue to cook without stirring until the syrup begins to color slightly. Swirl pan gently (rather than stirring) if syrup is coloring unevenly. Use a skewer to drop a bead of syrup on a plate from time to time. When a drop looks pale amber, add the nuts. Using a silicone spatula, gently turn nuts until they are completely coated with syrup.
4. Continue to cook, gently pushing nuts around if syrup is coloring unevenly, until a drop of syrup looks golden amber on the plate (about 30 minutes total). If syrup gets too dark, it will taste bitter. Immediately scrape mixture onto lined baking sheet and spread it out as well as you can.
5. While it is still warm, but cool enough to handle, break into pieces. Transfer to resealable plastic bag. Keep airtight until needed, so pieces will not become sticky.
6. When ready to use, break caramel into smaller pieces; chop medium fine or pulse in food processor. In a large chilled bowl, beat cream until it holds soft peaks. Fold in chopped caramel. Makes three cups.

Caramel Sauce

<u>Ingredients:</u>

1 cup granulated sugar
¼ cup water
1 tsp light-colored corn syrup
4 tbsp butter
(Recipe continued on next page.)

½ cup whipping or heavy cream
1 tbsp vanilla extract (or bourbon, rum, Grand Marnier, or a favorite liqueur)
½ to 1 tsp salt, optional and to taste

Directions:

1. In a medium to large saucepan (use a pan much larger than you think you'll need because the sauce will bubble vigorously at the end), add the sugar, water, corn syrup, and bring to a boil over high heat, whisking until sugar has dissolved.
2. Allow the mixture to boil for 5 to 12 minutes, or as necessary, for it to turn caramel-colored, at which point it will likely be smoking slightly.
The final stage where the mixture turns from pale amber to that perfect shade of caramel can go quickly, in less than 30 seconds, so keep a watchful eye and don't let it burn. Throughout the boiling time, you can swirl the pan gently every minute or two if necessary, but the less the sugary mixture gets on the sides of the pan, the better in preventing crystallization in the final sauce.
3. As soon as the sauce has turned caramel-colored, reduce the heat to low. Carefully and slowly, add the cream. Stand back because mixture will bubble up considerably.
4. Add the vanilla (or other flavoring) and salt. Stand back because mixture will bubble up again.
5. Whisk until sauce is smooth and combined, and let it boil another minute, which helps thicken it up. Transfer sauce to a 2-cup Pyrex measuring cup from which it will easily pour into a glass storage jar. Allow sauce to cool uncovered to room temperature; sauce thickens considerably as it cools. Sauce will keep in an airtight container at room temperature for at least a month or longer.

Notes:

This cake is a lot of work and not for the faint of heart. I use the caramel sauce recipe for an ice cream topping and for other desserts.

For a salted caramel sauce, I use 1 tsp coarse sea salt and add after the caramel is cooked.

Frosting

Maple-Walnut Topping

Ingredients:

1 cup maple (or maple flavored) syrup
2 tbsp butter
½ cup chopped walnuts
1/3 cup whipping cream
½ tsp vanilla

Directions:
1. Over medium heat, bring syrup to a boil and boil for 7 minutes. Remove from heat. Stir in butter until melted. Stir in chopped nuts, whipping cream, and vanilla.
2. Serve hot over pancakes, waffles, or French toast.

Marshmallow Frosting

Ingredients:

1 cup sugar
1 tsp cream of tartar
2 egg whites, unbeaten
1 dozen large marshmallows
¼ tsp salt
3 tbsp water
(Recipe continued on next page.)

Directions:
1. Cut marshmallows into pieces. Set aside. Place other ingredients in top of double boiler.
2. Cook and stir quickly until sugar dissolves and mixture turns white.
3. Remove from heat and add marshmallows.
4. When marshmallows become soft, place back over boiling water and beat until mixture stands in peaks.
5. Spread immediately on cake while still hot and then let cool.

Notes:
Marshmallows aren't my favorite sweet, but I used this recipe to top fat-free cakes for Bob after his heart surgery. If there is one thing that can be said for it, it contains no fat. I should keep in mind that my two grandsons love marshmallows. They drink hot cocoa just for the sticky white globs, so maybe I'll give this recipe another chance on a cake I bake just for them.

~ ~ ~

Whipped Chocolate Frosting

Ingredients:

2 cups confectioners' sugar
½ cup milk
¼ tsp salt
2 eggs
½ tsp vanilla
4 squares bitter chocolate
6 tbsp butter

Directions:
1. Place sugar, milk, eggs, salt, and vanilla in a bowl over ice water. Stir until eggs are broken.
2. Melt chocolate and butter together in microwave, checking every 30 seconds and stirring to avoid overcooking.
3. Add chocolate mixture while still warm to first mixture and beat until it holds its shape.

Casseroles, Stews, and One Dish Meals

"My mother really would make these dreadful concoctions. She prided herself on something called 'Everything Stew,' where she would take everything in the refrigerator, all the leftovers, and put them all together." **Ruth Reichl**

"I hate fussing about in the kitchen when I have people over to supper, so I make a rich beef stew cooked in wine with carrots, sundried tomato paste and chopped chorizo sausage." **Deborah Moggach**

"I refuse to believe that trading recipes is silly. Tuna Fish casserole is at least as real as corporate stock." **Barbara Grizzuti**

Authentic Fettuccine

<u>Ingredients:</u>

1 pound fettuccine
1 stick unsalted butter
4 oz (2 cups finely grated) Parmigiano-Reggiano

<u>Directions:</u>

1. Bring a soup pot of salted water to a boil. Add fettuccine and cook according to directions for al dente.
2. While noodles are cooking, cut butter into thin pats and transfer to a large, warmed platter.
3. Drain pasta, reserving 1½ cups pasta water. Place pasta over the butter on the platter.
4. Sprinkle grated cheese over the pasta and drizzle with 1/3 cup of the reserved pasta water.
5. Using a large spoon and fork, gently toss the pasta with the butter and cheese, lifting and swirling the noodles and adding more pasta water as necessary. The pasta water helps create the smooth sauce. Work in any melted butter or cheese that has pooled around the edge of the platter. Continue to mix the pasta until the cheese and butter have fully melted, and the noodles are coated, about 3 minutes.
6. The method in step 5 is the traditional way of making the sauce by coating the noodles. It can be quite a presentation if you are confident and want to do it at the table in front of your guests or to a crowd of guests huddled around your kitchen island (isn't that where all guests huddle?). This is the method used by chefs at fine dining establishments when they want to add a bit of drama to the meal. However, if you want a quicker preparation, bring ¾ cup of the reserved pasta water and the butter to a boil in a large skillet or soup pot from which you have removed and drained pasta. Then add the drained pasta back, sprinkle with cheese and toss with tongs over medium-low heat until the pasta is creamy and coated, about two minutes, and serve.

<u>Notes:</u>

You may be skeptical about this recipe when you see it only has three ingredients. My son, Jes Phillips, who is the culinary expert in our family, apparently wasn't fond of my creamy, gooey version. He introduced me to this purer and traditional recipe. It's wonderful. Without the cream and excess butter, the true taste of the dish shines.

Chicago-Style Deep Dish Pizza

<u>Ingredients:</u>

1 (1 pound) loaf frozen bread dough, thawed
1 pound bulk Italian sausage
2 cups shredded mozzarella cheese
8 oz sliced fresh mushrooms
1 small onion, chopped
2 tsp olive oil
1 (28-oz) can diced tomatoes, very well drained
¾ tsp dried oregano
½ tsp salt
¼ tsp fennel seed
¼ tsp garlic powder
½ cup freshly grated parmesan cheese (make sure it's fresh)

<u>Directions:</u>

1. Preheat the oven to 350. Press the dough into the bottom and up the sides of a greased 9x13-inch baking dish.
2. Crumble the sausage into a large skillet over medium-high heat. Cook and stir until evenly browned. Remove the sausage with a slotted spoon, and sprinkle over the dough crust. Sprinkle mozzarella cheese evenly over the sausage.
3. Add mushrooms and onion to the skillet; cook and stir until the onion is tender. Stir in the tomatoes, oregano, salt, fennel seed, and garlic powder. Spoon over the mozzarella cheese. Sprinkle parmesan cheese over the top.
4. Bake for 25 to 35 minutes in the preheated oven, or until crust is golden brown.

Chicken Pot Pie

<u>Ingredients:</u>

1 (10¾ can) condensed cream of mushroom, broccoli, onion, chicken, potato, or celery soup
1 (5 oz) can evaporated milk
1/3 cup fresh parsley, snipped or 1 tbsp dried
½ tsp dried rosemary or thyme, crushed
3 cups cubed cooked chicken, turkey, or beef
1 (10 oz) pkg frozen mixed vegetables with lima beans and corn
¾ cup instant mashed potato flakes
¾ cup all-purpose flour
¼ cup grated parmesan cheese
1/3 cup butter

<u>Directions:</u>
1. For the filling, combine soup, milk, parsley, and rosemary or thyme. Stir in the chicken, turkey, or beef. Stir in the vegetables.
2. Spoon into an 11x7x2 baking dish or 6 individual 10 oz casserole dishes. Set aside.
3. For the crust, stir together potato flakes, flour, and parmesan cheese. Cut in butter until mixture resembles coarse crumbs. Sprinkle ¼ cup cold water over mixture, 1 tbsp at a time, gently tossing with a fork until all is moistened. Form into a ball. On lightly floured board, roll and cut pastry to fit baking dish. Fit over casserole(s) and cut slits in the top.
4. Place on baking sheet and bake at 400 for 20 to 30 minutes or until hot and pastry is golden.

Creamy Fettuccine with Bacon

Ingredients:

8 oz bacon, chopped
2 cups frozen peas, thawed
1 cup shredded carrots
1 cup chopped fresh parsley
2 cups whipping cream
2 cups grated parmesan
1 pound fettuccine, freshly cooked

Directions:

1. Cook bacon in heavy large skillet over medium-high heat until crisp. Using a slotted spoon, transfer bacon to paper towel to drain. Pour off all but 1 tbsp fat from skillet.
2. Add carrots, peas, and parsley and sauté 1 minute.
3. Mix in cream and parmesan and simmer about 3 minutes until sauce thickens slightly.
4. Season to taste with salt and pepper.
5. Place fettuccine in large bowl, add cream mixture and toss well. Sprinkle with cooked bacon and serve.

Notes:

I often add cooked, warmed seafood to make this a **seafood fettuccine**. I use cooked scallops, crabmeat, shrimp, or some combination of those.

Ezra's and Noah's Favorite Tortilla Casserole

<u>Ingredients:</u>

1 tbsp olive, vegetable, or canola oil
1 onion, chopped
1 tsp ground cumin
1½ tsp chili powder
1 tsp minced garlic
1 can (14 oz) chopped tomatoes, drained, with 1/3 cup juice reserved
¼ cup tomato paste
2 cans (15.5 oz) white, black, or kidney beans (or mixture of two), rinsed and drained
kosher or coarse salt and freshly ground black pepper
1 can (15 oz) sweet corn kernels, drained, or 1½ cups frozen corn, thawed
1 can (15 oz) peas, drained, or 1½ cups frozen peas, thawed
3 cups coarsely chopped spinach
4 medium-size (8-inch) corn or flour tortillas
2 cups (8 oz) shredded Monterey Jack or cheddar cheese
chopped fresh cilantro (optional), for garnish
sour cream, salsa, and guacamole (optional) for serving

<u>Directions:</u>

1. Preheat the oven to 400. Spray 2 9-inch round cake pans, or baking dish with Pam.
2. Heat the oil in a large skillet over medium heat. Add the onion, cumin, chili powder, and garlic and cook until you can smell the spices and the onion is softened, about 3 minutes. Stir in the tomatoes with the 1/3 cup of reserved juice and the tomato paste, then stir in the beans. Season with salt and pepper to taste. Let the bean mixture simmer until everything is hot, about 3 minutes. Add the corn, peas, and spinach and stir until the spinach has wilted and everything is well blended and hot, about 3 minutes. Taste for seasoning, add salt and/or pepper as necessary.
3. Place 1 tortilla in the first prepared cake pan. Spread one eighth of the bean and vegetable mixture evenly over the tortilla, then sprinkle ¼ cup of the shredded cheese evenly over the top. Repeat with 3 more layers, ending with the last quarter of the bean mixture and then the last ¼ cup of shredded cheese.
4. Bake the tortilla casserole until it is hot throughout and the top is lightly browned, about 20 minutes. Let the casserole sit for about 5 minutes, then cut it into wedges using a sharp knife and serve it with a spatula or pie server. Sprinkle the top with cilantro, if desired, and serve with sour cream and/or salsa on the side. Add hot sauce as desired. Can be made a day ahead, covered, refrigerated, and reheated.

<u>Notes:</u>

My grandsons make this recipe with their Uncle Jes Phillips. Jes gave me the recipe.

Goulash

<u>Ingredients:</u>

2 pounds lean ground beef
2 large yellow onions, chopped
3 cloves garlic, chopped
3 cups water
2 (15 oz each) cans tomato sauce
2 (14.5 oz each) cans diced tomatoes
½ cup ketchup
3 tbsp soy sauce
2 tbsp Worcestershire
½ tsp white vinegar
dash or two of cayenne
2 tbsp dried Italian herb seasoning
3 bay leaves
1 tbsp seasoned salt, or to taste
2 cups elbow macaroni

<u>Directions:</u>

1. In a large Dutch oven, cook and stir the ground beef over medium-high heat, breaking the meat as it cooks, and the meat is no longer pink and has started to brown, about 10 minutes. Skim off excess fat, and stir in the onions and garlic. Cook and stir the meat mixture until the onions are translucent, about 20 more minutes.

2. Stir in water, tomato sauce, diced tomatoes, ketchup, soy sauce, Worcestershire sauce, vinegar, cayenne, Italian seasoning, bay leaves, and seasoned salt, and bring the mixture to a boil over medium heat. Reduce heat to low, cover, simmer 20 minutes, stirring occasionally.

3. Stir in the macaroni, cover, and simmer over low heat until the pasta is tender, about 25 minutes. Stir occasionally. Remove from heat, discard bay leaves and serve.

<u>Notes:</u>

In lieu of Italian seasoning, I add a mixture of rosemary, oregano, basil, thyme, and marjoram. If I have fresh herbs, I use those. Also, in the last ten minutes of cooking I often add a cup of frozen peas.

Hearty Beef Pot Pie with Cornmeal Cheese Crust

Ingredients:

1 pound boneless beef chuck, cut into ¼ inch pieces
1 tbsp cooking oil
1 large green pepper, chopped
1 medium onion, chopped
1 (8¾ or 7 oz) can whole kernel corn, drained
1 (7½ oz) can tomatoes
¼ cup tomato paste
1 or 2 fresh jalapeno peppers, seeded and chopped
1 tbsp chili powder
1 tsp sugar
¼ tsp salt

Cornmeal Crust:

1 cup all-purpose flour
½ cup yellow cornmeal
½ tsp salt
½ cup butter
¼ cup finely shredded cheddar

Directions:

1. Brown beef in hot oil. Remove with slotted spoon. Cook green pepper and onion in drippings until tender.
2. Add beef, corn, undrained tomatoes, tomato paste, jalapeno peppers, chili powder, sugar, 2/3 cup water, and ¼ tsp salt. Bring to boil, reduce heat. Cover and simmer 1 hour or until meat is tender.

Cornmeal-cheese crust:

1. Combine flour, cornmeal, and salt. Cut in butter and cheddar cheese until mixture resembles coarse crumbles. On lightly floured surface, roll dough for crust into 11x7-inch crust. Carefully place crust over beef in casserole dish. Flute crust against sides of dish. Cut slits in top for steam to escape.
2. Bake, uncovered, in 425 oven for 20 minutes. Sprinkle with remaining ¼ cup cheese. Let stand 5 minutes. Makes 6 servings.

Hearty Beef Stew (Slow cooker)

<u>Ingredients:</u>

1 boneless beef chuck roast (about 5 pounds), trimmed
and cut into 1½-inch cubes
salt and pepper
3 tbsp vegetable oil
4 onions, minced
1 (6 oz) can of tomato paste
2 cups low-sodium chicken or beef broth
3 tbsp soy sauce
1 pound carrots, peeled and cut into 1-inch pieces
1 pound parsnips, peeled and cut into 1-inch pieces
1 pound red potatoes, cut into 1-inch pieces
1½ tsp fresh thyme leaves
2 bay leaves
2 tbsp Minute tapioca
2 cups frozen peas, thawed

<u>Directions:</u>

1. Dry the beef with paper towels, then season with salt and pepper. Heat 1 tbsp of the oil in a large, nonstick skillet over medium-high heat, until just smoking. Add half of the beef and brown on all sides, about 8 minutes. Transfer to a slow-cooker and repeat with remaining beef.

2. Add 1 tbsp more of oil, the onions, and ¼ tsp salt to the empty skillet and cook until golden brown, about 6 minutes. Add the tomato paste and cook, stirring to coat the onions well, about 2 minutes. Add the broth and soy sauce, bring to a simmer and transfer to the slow cooker.

3. Season with salt and pepper to taste. Wrap the vegetables in a foil packet that will fit in the slow cooker. Add the bay leaves and tapioca to the slow cooker and stir; place the vegetable packet on top.

4. Cover and cook on low 10 to 11 hours (or on high for 6 to 7 hours). Transfer the vegetable packet to a plate. Discard the bay leaves. Carefully open the packet and stir the vegetables and juices into the stew. Add the remaining tsp of thyme and peas and let stand until heated through. 8 servings.

Lobster Mac and Cheese

Ingredients:

1 (16 oz) pkg elbow or corkscrew macaroni
1 (2 pounds) lobster, split
2 tbsp butter
1 small onion, diced
1 clove garlic, minced
1 shallot, chopped
10 black peppercorns
2 cups milk
5 tbsp butter
5 tbsp all-purpose flour
1 pound shredded Gruyere cheese
3 cups shredded cheddar cheese
1 cup grated Romano cheese
kosher salt and pepper to taste
3 tbsp Panko bread crumbs

Directions:
1. Fill a large pot with lightly salted water and bring to a rolling boil over high
(Recipe continued on the next page.)

heat. Once the water is boiling, stir in the macaroni, and return to a boil. Cook the pasta, uncovered, stirring occasionally, until the pasta has cooked through, but is still firm to the bite, about 8 minutes. Reserve 2 cups of the hot pasta water, then drain the pasta in a colander set in the sink, and rinse with cold water to cool and stop cooking. Set aside.

2. Return the reserved pasta water to the large pot, and place the lobster halves in the pot, cut-side up. Return the water to a boil, then reduce heat to medium-low, cover, and steam the lobster about 3 minutes, just until the meat firms and turns opaque. Remove the lobster and allow to cool for a few minutes, then remove the meat and cut into bite sized pieces. Reserve the shells.

3. Melt 2 tbsp of butter in a saucepan over medium heat. Stir in the onion and cook until the onion has softened and turned translucent, about 5 minutes; scrape the onions into a small bowl and set aside. Place the reserved lobster shells, garlic, shallots, peppercorns, and milk into the saucepan. Bring to a gentle simmer over medium heat, and cook for 20 minutes.

4. Preheat oven to 350. Melt 5 tbsp of butter in a saucepan over medium-low heat. Whisk in the flour, and stir until the mixture becomes paste-like and light golden brown, about 10 minutes. Remove lobster shells. Strain the milk through a mesh sieve. Gradually whisk the milk into the flour mixture, and bring to a simmer over medium heat. Cook and stir until the mixture is thick and smooth, 10 to 15 minutes.

5. Stir the Gruyere, cheddar, and Romano cheeses into the thickened milk mixture until melted and smooth. Season to taste with salt and pepper, then stir in the reserved lobster, onions, and macaroni. Pour the mixture into a 4-quart casserole or individual ramekins and smooth the top. Sprinkle evenly with the panko crumbs.

6. Bake in the preheated oven until the sauce is bubbly, and the top is golden brown, 8 to 12 minutes.

Notes:

This is high-falutin meets down-home cookin'. Jan Kinzel served a delicious version of Lobster Mac and Cheese at a brunch she hosted for Bob and me when we moved from Sorrento. I asked for the recipe because I loved the idea of Mac and Cheese with lobster and hers was delicious. Her instructions said to find a creamy Mac and Cheese, so I came up with the above. You can certainly simplify it with an easier version of mac and cheese. I prefer elbow macaroni.

Macaroni and Cheese

<u>Ingredients:</u>

1 tbsp vegetable oil
1 (16 oz) pkg elbow macaroni
9 tbsp butter
½ cup shredded Muenster cheese
½ cup mild shredded cheddar cheese
½ cup sharp shredded cheddar cheese
½ cup shredded Monterey Jack cheese
1½ cups half and half
8 oz cubed processed American cheese
2 eggs, beaten
¼ tsp salt
1/8 tsp ground black pepper
1 tbsp Dijon mustard

<u>Directions:</u>

1. Bring a large pot of lightly salted water to a boil. Add pasta and cook for 8 to 10 minutes or according to package directions until al dente; drain well and return to cooking pot.
2. In a small saucepan over medium heat, melt 8 tbsp butter; stir into macaroni.
3. In a large bowl, combine all cheeses EXCEPT American processed cheese; mix well.
4. Preheat oven to 350.
5. Add the half and half, 1½ cups of mixed cheeses, cubed processed American cheese, and eggs to macaroni; mix together and season with salt and pepper. Transfer to a lightly greased, deep 2½ quart casserole dish. Sprinkle with remaining ½ cup of cheese mixture and 1 tbsp of butter.
6. Bake in preheated oven for 35 minutes or until hot and bubbly around the edges. Serve hot.

Puttanesca Penne Pasta

<u>Ingredients:</u>

2 medium onions, chopped fine
6 garlic cloves, peeled, chopped fine
1 to 2 red chile, chopped fine
2 tbsp olive oil
1 cup fresh flat-leaf parsley, chopped fine
1 cup pitted black olives, chopped
5 tbsp capers
1 small can anchovies, packed in oil, drained, chopped fine
4 cans tomatoes, chopped
extra virgin olive oil, sugar to taste, salt and pepper to taste
16 oz penne pasta, cooked and drained

<u>Directions:</u>

1. Over medium-low heat, sauté the onions, garlic, and chile in olive oil until soft, about 10 to 15 minutes, stirring occasionally.
2. Add the parsley, canned tomatoes, and stir well. Add olives, capers, anchovies and sugar, salt and pepper to taste.
3. Let simmer over low heat, uncovered, stirring occasionally for about 45 minutes to an hour, until thick and reduced, and the color has darkened to a reddish-brown.
4. Test for flavors and adjust seasonings, add salt, pepper, and sugar as needed.
5. Cook the pasta according to the instructions on the package, drain, reserving some of the liquid, and then return to pan.
6. Ladle in a few helpings of the sauce at a time, stirring the mixture until all of the pasta has been generously coated. Serve remaining sauce on the side. This sauce is very thick, and if you want it a bit thinner, add a bit of the reserved pasta liquid.
7. Serve hot.

Quick Red Wine Chicken Stew

<u>Ingredients:</u>

2 pounds (about 8 medium) boneless, skinless chicken thighs
1 tbsp olive oil
salt and pepper
6 medium carrots, peeled and cut into small chunks
1 pkg (8 oz) baby Bella mushrooms
3 oz (6 thin slices) prosciutto minced
4 large garlic cloves, minced
1 tsp dried thyme leaves
1 tbsp all-purpose flour
1½ cups dry red wine
1½ cups chicken broth
2 pkg (9 oz each) frozen creamed pearl onions, not thawed
6 new potatoes, rinsed and halved
1 cup frozen peas

<u>Directions:</u>

1. Heat a large deep skillet over medium-high heat. Coat chicken thighs with the oil and sprinkle with salt and pepper. Add thighs to hot skillet. Cook until well browned, about 5 minutes. Turn and continue to cook until well browned on remaining side, about 3 minutes. Transfer to a medium bowl; set aside.
2. Add carrots to skillet (add additional oil if pan is dry); sauté until they start to brown, 2 to 3 minutes. Add mushrooms; cook stirring frequently and season lightly with additional salt and pepper, until carrots and mushrooms are well browned, about 3 minutes.
3. Stir in prosciutto, garlic, and thyme; cook until fragrant, about 2 minutes. Sprinkle in flour, then stir in wine and broth, along with creamed pearl onions. Bring to a simmer, breaking up pearl onions as they start to thaw.
4. Add chicken and potatoes; reduce heat to medium-low and simmer, partly covered, until potatoes are tender.
5. Stir in peas. Cover and let stand 5 minutes before serving. Serves 4.

Spicy Chicken Stew (Slow Cooker)

<u>Ingredients:</u>
2 baking potatoes (1½ pounds) peeled and cut into chunks (about 3 1/3 cups)
2 (10 oz) pkg frozen sweet corn (plain, no sauce or butter)
2 stalks celery, chopped
2 carrots, peeled and cut into chunks
1 onion, thickly sliced
2 cloves garlic, minced
2 (12.5 oz each) jars salsa
2 tsp kosher salt
1½ tsp ground cumin
1 tsp chili powder
½ tsp black pepper
2 skinless, boneless chicken breasts, halved (about 1 pound)
8 skinless boneless chicken thighs (about ¾ pound)
5 cups chicken broth
8 (6-inch) corn tortillas, cut into strips

<u>Directions:</u>
1. Place potatoes, corn, celery, carrots, onion, and garlic in slow cooker. Stir in salsa, salt, cumin, chili powder, and pepper. Distribute chicken evenly on top of vegetables and pour chicken broth over chicken. Cover slow cooker and cook stew on high for 4 hours.
2. Transfer chicken to a plate and shred with two forks into bite size chunks; return to slow cooker. Mix tortilla strips into the stew.

Tuna Casserole

<u>Ingredients:</u>

6 oz no yolk noodles (can use brown rice pasta for gluten free)
1 tbsp butter
1 medium onion, minced fine
3 tbsp flour (for gluten free use rice flour)
1¾ cups fat free chicken broth
1 cup 1% milk
1 oz sherry (optional)
10 oz sliced baby Bella mushrooms
1 cup frozen petite peas (thawed)
2 (5 oz) cans albacore tuna in water, drained
4 oz sharp cheddar (can used reduced fat)
butter flavored Pam cooking spray
2 tbsp parmesan cheese
2 tbsp whole wheat seasoned breadcrumbs

<u>Directions:</u>

1. Preheat oven to 375. Spray 9x12-inch casserole with Pam.
2. Cook noodles in salted water until al dente, or slightly undercooked by 2 minutes. Set aside.
3. Melt the butter in a large deep skillet. Add onions and cook on medium heat until soft, about 5 minutes. Add flour and pinch of salt. Stir well. Cook an additional 2 to 3 minutes on medium low heat.
4. Slowly whisk in the chicken broth until well combined, increasing heat to medium and whisking well for 30 seconds, then add the milk and bring to a boil. When boiling, add sherry, mushrooms, and petite peas, adjust salt and pepper to taste and simmer on medium, mixing occasionally until it thickens (about 7 to 9 minutes). Add drained tuna, stirring another minute.
5. Remove from heat. Add cheddar cheese and mix until it melts. Add the noodles to the sauce and mix well until evenly coated. Pour into casserole and top with parmesan cheese and breadcrumbs. Bake for 25 minutes. Place under a broiler a few minutes to get the crumbs crisp, but be careful not to burn.

Cookies, Brownies, and Candy

"Think what a better world it would be if we all, the whole world, had cookies and milk about three o'clock every afternoon and then lay down on our blankets for a nap." **Barbara Jordan**

"On more than one occasion, the camera has cut to me after a break and I'm still trying to swallow the last bite of cookie. Those of you who have thought to yourselves, 'That guy talks like he has marbles in his mouth,' should know that they are not marbles, but oatmeal cookies." **Lester Holt**

"There is nothing cozy as candy and a good book." **Betty McDonald**

Almond Cookies

<u>Ingredients:</u>
    2¼ cups blanched whole almonds (about 12 oz), plus 15 for garnishing
    2/3 cup sugar
    2 large egg whites, at room temperature
    ¼ tsp salt
    ½ tsp pure almond extract
    ¼ tsp pure vanilla extract
    15 candied cherries

<u>Directions:</u>
1. Arrange racks in upper and lower thirds of oven and preheat to 350. Lightly oil 2 large baking sheets, then line with parchment paper.
2. In a food processor or blender combine 2¼ cups almonds and 1/3 cup sugar. Process until finely ground, scraping down sides once or twice. Set aside. (If using a blender, you may have to do in two batches.)
3. With electric mixer beat egg whites and salt at high speed until soft peaks form. Reduce speed to medium and gradually sprinkle in remaining 1/3 cup sugar. Return speed to high and beat mixture until stiff, shiny peaks form. Gently fold in almond mixture and extracts.
4. Roll mixture into 1-inch balls, place 2 inches apart on baking sheets, and flatten slightly. Top each with a candied cherry or almond. Bake until cookies are golden, switching positions of pans halfway through (about 25 minutes). Cool on sheets 5 minutes, then transfer to racks to cool completely.
5. Cookies keep, wrapped, several days, or frozen, several weeks. Can be recrisped in warm oven.

<u>Notes:</u>
I first got a recipe for almond cookies from Shlomit Elitzur. I was looking for a cookie that had no fats and this one fit the bill.

Best Ever Oatmeal Cookie

Ingredients:

½ cup (1 stick) plus 6 tbsp butter, softened
¾ cup firmly packed brown sugar
½ cup granulated sugar
2 eggs
1 tsp vanilla
1½ cups all-purpose flour
1 tsp baking soda
1 tsp ground cinnamon
½ tsp salt (optional)
3 cups Quaker Oats (quick or old fashioned, uncooked)
1 cup raisins

Directions:

1. Heat oven to 350. In large bowl, beat butter and sugars on medium speed of electric mixer until creamy. Add eggs and vanilla; beat well.
2. Add combined flour, baking soda, cinnamon, and salt; mix well. Add oats and raisins; mix well.
3. Drop dough by tablespoons onto ungreased cookie sheets. Bake 8 to 10 minutes or until light golden brown. Cool 1 minute on cookie sheets; remove to wire rack. Cool completely. Store tightly covered.

Notes:

I don't remove to wire rack, but just let cookies cool on a piece of waxed paper. Bob and I used to start road trips with a big box of these cookies. He drove, I handed over the cookies when he requested them. This is the recipe on the Quaker Oatmeal box top where it is called the Vanishing Oatmeal Cookie.

Brickle Bars

<u>Ingredients:</u>

½ cup margarine or butter
2 squares (2 oz) unsweetened chocolate
1 cup sugar
2 eggs
1 tsp vanilla
¾ cup all-purpose flour
¾ cup almond brickle pieces
½ cup miniature semisweet chocolate pieces

<u>Directions:</u>

1. In a 2-quart saucepan, cook and stir butter and unsweetened chocolate over low heat until chocolate is melted. Stir.
2. Remove from heat; stir in sugar. Add eggs and vanilla and beat lightly with a wooden spoon until just combined (don't overbeat or bars will rise too high and then fall). Stir in flour.
3. Spread batter in a greased 8x8x2-inch baking pan.
4. Sprinkle almond brickle pieces and chocolate pieces over batter.
5. Bake in a 350-degree oven for 30 minutes.
6. Remove pan from oven and cool bars in the pan on a wire rack before cutting into pieces. Makes 16 bars.

Brownie Dress Ups

Follow recipe directions for boxed or homemade brownies, but make the following additions/changes:

1. **Brownie cupcakes with peanut butter cups:** Line 12 regular size muffin cups with foil baking cups. Spoon about ¼ cup batter into each cup. Press a bite-sized peanut butter cup into the center of each.
2. **M&M brownies:** Sprinkle ¾ cup M&M pieces over batter about 10 minutes before end of baking time.
3. **Caramel-coconut pecan brownies**: Bake and cool brownies; do not cut. Stir 20 caramels and 3 tbsp milk in a saucepan over medium-low heat until melted and smooth. (I use the microwave.) Spread caramel mixture over uncut brownies. Before caramel sets, sprinkle with 1 cup coarsely chopped pecans and ½ cup toasted coconut.
4. **Triple chocolate brownies:** Prepare a 9-inch baking pan by lining with non-stick foil and then spraying with cooking spray. Stir ½ cup white chocolate chips into batter; spread in pan, then sprinkle evenly with another ½ cup white chocolate chips. Bake. Cool, then drizzle with ¼ cup melted semisweet chocolate chips.
5. **Gingersnap macadamia nut brownies**: Stir 18 crumbled gingersnaps (1 ½ cups) into batter. Spread in prepared pan. Sprinkle with 1 cup coarsely chopped macadamia nuts.
6. **Raspberry-almond Viennese brownies**: Spread batter in prepared pan. Beat 3 oz room-temperature cream cheese, 2 tbsp each granulated sugar and softened butter, 1 large egg, 2 tbsp all-purpose flour and ½ tsp almond extract until smooth. Pour evenly over unbaked brownie batter. Drop small dollops of seedless red raspberry jam (about 1/3 cup altogether) over the top.
7. **Cream de menthe brownies**: Bake and cool brownies; do not cut. Cream de menthe layer: Beat ½ cup room temperature butter or margarine, 2 cups confectioners' sugar, and 2 tbsp green cream de menthe in a large bowl with electric mixer until smooth. Spread over brownies. Chocolate Glaze: Stir 1 cup semisweet chocolate chips and 6 tbsp butter in a saucepan over low heat until melted and smooth. Cool; pour over cream de menthe layer and spread evenly. Before glaze sets, sprinkle with coarsely chopped mint wafers.

(Recipes continued on next page.)

8. **Coffee brownies with mocha icing**: Dissolve 1 tbsp instant coffee granules in water used for batter. Bake brownies and cool. Dissolve 1 tbsp instant coffee granules in 3 tbsp water. Put in large bowl with ½ cup room temperature butter, 2 1/3 cups confectioners' sugar, and 1 tsp vanilla extract. Beat with electric mixer until smooth. Spread over uncut brownies.

9. **Rocky Road brownies**: Spread batter in prepared pan and bake about five minutes less than recipe calls for; Remove from oven, sprinkle with 1 cup miniature marshmallows and ½ cup semisweet chocolate chips. Bake an additional five minutes and allow to cool. Drizzle with chocolate syrup.

10. **Butterfinger Brownies**: Chop 24 bite sized Butterfingers and stir into batter before baking.

Calico Meringues

<u>Ingredients:</u>

2 egg whites
pinch of cream of tartar
½ cup sugar
¾ cup plain M&Ms

<u>Directions:</u>

1. Beat egg whites with cream of tartar in a small, deep bowl until foamy.
2. Gradually beat in sugar to make a stiff meringue.
3. Fold in M&Ms plain chocolate candies.
4. Grease and flour a large cookie sheet. (I use parchment paper.) Drop meringue mixture by teaspoon onto cookie sheet. Garnish each cookie with two M&Ms.
5. Bake in a slow 250-degree oven for 30 minutes or until cookies are firm to the touch, but still white.
6. Cool cookies on cookie sheet on wire rack. Remove from sheet with spatula.

<u>Notes:</u>
These cookies keep well in an air tight container. My cousin, Jean Ann Albrecht Wendt, says the recipe came from my great aunt, Louise Albrecht, who made the cookies without the M&Ms. After Bob's heart surgery, he went through a period of eating a lot of meringue cookies because they were fat-free.

Chewy Chocolate Cookies

<u>Ingredients:</u>

1¼ cups butter
2 cups sugar
2 eggs
2 tsp vanilla
2 cups flour
¾ cup cocoa
1 tsp baking soda
½ tsp salt
1 cup finely chopped nuts (optional)

<u>Directions:</u>
1. Cream butter with sugar in large bowl.
2. Add eggs and vanilla and blend well.
3. Combine flour, cocoa, baking soda, and salt. Blend into creamed mixture.
4. Stir in nuts.
5. Drop by teaspoon on ungreased cookie sheet. Bake at 350 for 8 to 9 minutes (Do not overbake.) The cookies will be soft. They will puff during baking and flatten upon cooling. Cool on cookie sheet until set, about one minute.

<u>Notes:</u>
This recipe came from my cousin, Linda Dawson Cutler. When Linda's sons, Steven and Jim, were little tikes, they asked their friend's mom for this recipe and took it home to Linda so she could make them the cookies. They taste like brownies, but in convenient cookie form.

Chocolate Brownie Cups

<u>Ingredients:</u>

½ cup all-purpose flour
¼ tsp baking powder
¼ tsp salt
6 tbsp butter
1½ tbsp corn syrup
½ cup cocoa, sifted
¾ cup lightly packed brown sugar
3 egg whites, slightly beaten
½ tsp vanilla extract
¼ tsp almond extract
3 tbsp slivered almonds
2 tbsp powdered sugar

<u>Directions:</u>

1. Preheat oven to 350. In small bowl stir together flour, baking powder, and salt; set aside.
2. Line two miniature cupcake pans (12 cupcakes each) with paper cups or lightly coat with non-stick spray; set aside.
3. In medium saucepan melt butter over low heat. Add corn syrup and cocoa and whisk until smooth. Add brown sugar and stir until melted and combined. Let mixture cool 10 minutes, then stir in egg whites and vanilla and almond extracts.
4. Gradually stir in flour mixture until batter is blended and smooth.
5. Fill mini cupcake pans 2/3 full of batter and sprinkle with almonds.
6. Bake until wooden toothpick inserted in center comes out barely clean (9 to 10 minutes). Remove from pans. Just before serving sift powdered sugar lightly over tops.

<u>Note:</u>
This is a recipe passed on to me from my Aunt Edith Dawson.

Chocolate Volcano Cookies

<u>Ingredients:</u>

1 pound confectioners' sugar
¾ cup unsweetened cocoa
½ tsp salt
4 large egg whites
1 tbsp vanilla extract
1½ cups semisweet or bittersweet chocolate chips

<u>Directions:</u>

1. Preheat oven to 350. Line 2 cookie sheets with parchment paper, lightly coat with nonstick cooking spray.
2. In large bowl, whisk confectioners' sugar, cocoa, and salt. Add egg whites and vanilla and beat with wooden spoon until smooth. Fold in chocolate chips. Set dough aside 5 minutes.
3. Drop dough by rounded tablespoonful, 2 inches apart, onto prepared cookie sheet. Bake 13 to 15 minutes or until set and crackly. Let cool on cookie sheets 3 minutes and then with spatula, carefully transfer to wire racks to cool completely.

Chocolate Whoopie Pie Cookies

<u>Ingredients:</u>

Cookies »»

1 pkg chocolate cake mix (regular size)
3 large eggs
½ cup canola oil
1 tsp vanilla extract

Filling »»

2/3 cup sugar
2 tbsp all-purpose flour
1/8 tsp salt
1 cup 2% milk
½ cup milk chocolate chips
2/3 cup shortening
1/3 cup butter, softened
¾ tsp vanilla extract

Garnish »»

1 cup miniature semisweet chocolate chips

<u>Directions:</u>

1. In a large bowl, combine the cake mix, eggs, oil, and vanilla; beat on low speed for 30 seconds. Beat on medium for 2 minutes (mixture will be sticky).
2. Drop by 2 tablespoonfuls, 2 inches apart onto greased baking sheets. Bake at 350 for 9-11 minutes or until edges are set. Cool for 2 minutes before removing to wire racks to cool completely.
3. For filling, in a small saucepan, combine the sugar, flour, and salt. Gradually add milk. Bring to a boil; cook and stir for 1-2 minutes or until thickened. Stir in chocolate chips until melted. Transfer to a small bowl; cover and refrigerate until chilled, about 1 hour.
4. In a large bowl, beat the shortening and butter until fluffy. Beat in chocolate mixture and vanilla.
5. Spread chocolate filling on the bottoms of half of the cookies, about 2 tbsp on each; top with remaining cookies. Roll sides in miniature chocolate chips for garnish. Store in the refrigerator. Yield: about 1 dozen.

Chocolet Cookies

<u>Ingredients:</u>

½ cup shortening
6 tbsp granulated sugar
6 tbsp brown sugar
1 egg, beaten
½ tsp baking soda
½ tsp salt
1 tbsp hot water
7 oz cocoa (slightly less than one cup)
1 tsp vanilla
1¾ cup flour
½ cup nuts optional

<u>Directions:</u>
1. Cream first six ingredients.
2. Mix hot water with cocoa and when blended add to first ingredients. Add nuts if desired.
3. Add vanilla, flour* and mix well.
4. Liberally grease a cookie sheet. Form dough into balls the size of quarters. Bake 10 to 12 minutes at 375. The cookies "crack" open when done.

<u>Notes:</u>

This recipe came from Sharron Dawson Beckwith who has the original handwritten version from my great grandmother, Cora Wiltsie. In fact, Sharron even kept Grandma's quaint spelling, i.e., dune for done, cooky for cookie. I changed the spelling (except for Chocolet) to make the recipe easier to read. Grandma's recipe only called for 1 1/8 cups flour, and Sharron uses closer to 1¾ cup. I've always gone closer to Sharron's measurement.

Chocolate Nut Toffee Bars

Ingredients:

1 cup margarine or butter, softened
1 cup confectioners' sugar
1¼ cups unsifted all-purpose flour
1/3 cup Hershey's cocoa
1 (14 oz) can sweetened condensed milk
2 tsp vanilla extract
1 cup (6 oz) semi-sweet chocolate chips
½ cup chopped nuts

Directions:
1. Preheat oven to 350. Reserve 2 tbsp margarine or butter. In large mixing bowl, beat remaining margarine or butter, and sugar until fluffy.
2. Add flour and cocoa; mix well. With floured hands, press into a greased 13 x 9-inch baking pan. Bake 15 minutes.
3. While the above is baking, in a medium saucepan, combine reserved margarine or butter and sweetened condensed milk. Cook and stir until mixture thickens slightly, about 15 minutes.
4. Remove from heat; stir in vanilla. Pour over crust when removed from oven. Bake 10-15 minutes longer or until golden brown.
5. Remove from oven; immediately top with chocolate chips. Let stand 1 minute; using a spatula, spread chocolate while warm. Top with nuts. Cool before cutting into bars.

Chocolate Oatmeal Sandwich Cookies

Ingredients:

2½ cups plus 2 tbsp margarine or butter, softened
1½ cup firmly packed brown sugar
1 cup granulated sugar
2 eggs
4 tsp vanilla extract
2½ cups unsifted all-purpose flour
½ cup Hershey's cocoa
2 tsp baking soda
1 tsp salt
6 cups oatmeal
1 (12 oz) pkg semi-sweet chocolate chips
1 (14 oz) can sweetened condensed milk

Directions:
1. Heat oven to 375. In a mixing bowl, beat butter and sugars until fluffy. Beat in eggs and 3 tsp vanilla.
2. Combine flour, cocoa, baking soda, and salt. Stir in oats.
3. Drop by tablespoon on ungreased baking sheets. Bake 10 minutes or until set. Cool.
4. In saucepan, combine chocolate chips, sweetened condensed milk, remaining two tbsp butter, and 1 tsp vanilla. Cook over medium heat until chips melt. (I do this in microwave.)
5. Immediately sandwich cookies together with chocolate/condensed milk mixture.

Notes:
You can omit cocoa and increase flour to 3 cups if you prefer less chocolate. If you don't want any chocolate, omit the cocoa/sweetened condensed milk mixture and put cookies together with marshmallow cream.

Chocolate Peanut Butter Pile Ups

Ingredients:

1 cup peanut butter
1 cup sugar
1 egg
1 (4 oz) bar sweet chocolate

Directions:

1. Mix sugar, egg, and peanut butter until well-blended. Pour into 10-inch square pan sprayed with cooking spray. Bake 20 minutes at 350.
2. Remove from oven and put chocolate over the cookies. Cover with aluminum foil and bake an additional 3 minutes.
3. Remove from oven, spread melted chocolate. Cool and cut into bars.

Notes:

This recipe came from Sharron Dawson Beckwith. It's a recipe I make for friends with gluten intolerance.

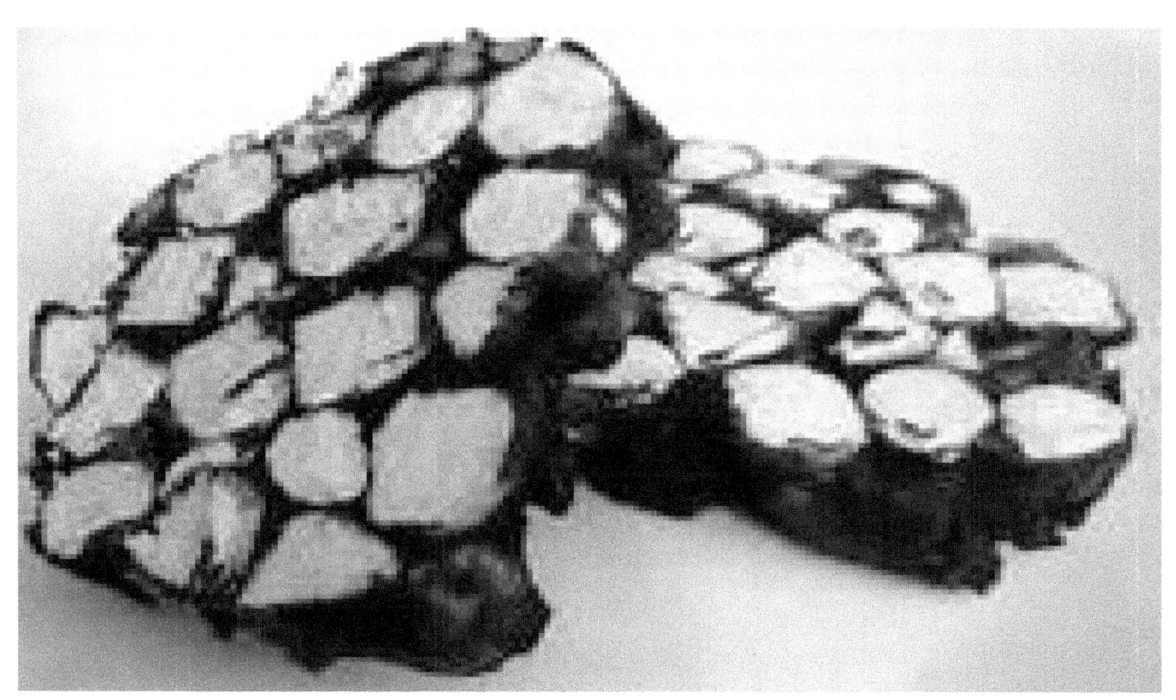

Church Windows

<u>Ingredients:</u>

1 stick butter
12 oz chocolate chips (semisweet or milk)
½ cup chopped nuts
1 pkg colored mini marshmallows
powdered sugar

<u>Directions:</u>
1. Melt together the butter and chocolate chips. Add nuts.
2. In large bowl, dump the marshmallows and then add above mixture to marshmallows.
3. Form mixture into a log. Roll up in doubled waxed paper and chill.
4. When ready to slice, remove from waxed paper and roll in confectioners' sugar.

<u>Notes:</u>

Honesty time: I am not fond of these cookies. My Grandma Bertha Dawson used to make them, and I would take one to be polite, but I have never liked the taste of marshmallows. Being fair, however, these are kind of pretty, and I now have two grandsons and a husband, all of whom adore marshmallows.

Clipper Chocolate Chip Cookies

<u>Ingredients:</u>

1 cup butter, softened
¾ cup sugar
¾ cup packed light brown sugar
1 tbsp vanilla
1 tbsp Tia Maria
1 tbsp Frangelico
2 eggs
1 tsp baking soda
½ tsp salt
2½ cups all-purpose flour
4 cups milk chocolate chips
1 cup walnut halves, chopped
½ cup pecan halves, chopped
½ cup macadamia nuts, chopped

<u>Directions:</u>

1. Cream butter, sugars, vanilla, Frangelico, and Tia Maria until light and fluffy. Add eggs; beat well.
2. Combine flour, baking soda, and salt. Gradually beat into creamed mixture.
3. Stir in chocolate chips and nuts. (I toast the nuts before adding.) Mix well.
4. Refrigerate dough overnight. Then drop by teaspoon onto an ungreased cookie sheet. Bake at 325 for 10 to 13 minutes or until golden brown.

<u>Notes:</u>

I first had these cookies on a cruise ship and decided they were my very favorite chocolate chip cookies. They are especially good warm. The ship's cookies were much larger than those made when you drop dough by a teaspoon. I often make giant cookies.

I sometimes spray a ramekin with cooking spray and press cookie dough in the bottom. After cookie is baked, I add vanilla ice cream and hot fudge sauce. It makes this more of a "dessert" rather than just a cookie. I do the same thing with oatmeal cookie dough and salted caramel ice cream with caramel topping, but you have to spray the ramekin well.

Crispy Snack Cookies

Ingredients:

½ tsp salt

2 eggs
1¾ cups granulated sugar
1½ cups shortening (Crisco)

1 tsp vanilla
1 cup plus 1 tbsp flour
1 cup plus 1 tbsp Quaker Oats
½ cup Rice Krispies
1 tsp baking soda
½ cup chopped nuts

Directions:
1. Mix all ingredients in a large bowl.
2. Preheat oven to 375. Form dough into small balls. Flatten down a little and space two inches apart. They spread out in the oven.

Notes:
My cousin, Sharron Dawson Beckwith shared this recipe she got from my great grandma, Cora Wiltsie. Grandma Wiltsie got the recipe from Steffon Bakery in Croswell, Michigan. The bakery is long since gone.

Death by Chocolate Cookie

<u>Ingredients:</u>

1 pkg Bakers Semi-Sweet chocolate (8 squares)
¾ cup firmly packed brown sugar
¼ cup (½ stick) butter, softened
2 eggs
1 tsp vanilla
½ cup flour
¼ tsp baking powder
1 pkg (8 squares) Bakers Semi Sweet baking chocolate or 1 ½ cups semi-sweet chocolate chunks
2 cups walnuts, chopped (optional)

<u>Directions:</u>

1. Preheat oven to 350. Microwave chocolate squares in large ovenproof bowl on high 2 minutes. Check at intervals to make sure chocolate doesn't overcook. Stir until chocolate is melted and smooth.
2. Stir in butter, eggs, and vanilla with wooden spoon until well blended. Stir in flour and baking powder. Stir in chopped chocolate and nuts. Drop by scant ¼ cupful onto ungreased cookie sheets.
3. Bake 13 to 14 minutes until cookies are puffed and feel set to the touch. Cool one minute on cookie sheet before removing to racks to cool completely.

<u>Note:</u>

If omitting nuts, increase flour to ¾ cup to avoid spreading.

Decadent Candy Bar Cookies

<u>Ingredients:</u>

¾ cup butter, softened
¾ cup confectioners' sugar
1 tsp vanilla
2 tbsp evaporated milk
¼ tsp salt
2 cups all-purpose flour

½ pound light colored caramel candies (I use Kraft)
¼ cup evaporated milk
¼ cup butter
1 cup confectioners' sugar
1 cup chopped pecans

6 oz pkg (1 cup semi-sweet chocolate pieces
1/3 cup evaporated milk
2 tbsp butter
½ cup confectioners' sugar
1 tsp vanilla

<u>Directions:</u>

1. Cream first amount of butter and confectioners' sugar. Add vanilla, evaporated milk, and salt. Mix well. Blend in flour. If necessary, chill for easier handling. Roll out dough, half at a time, on floured surface to a 12x8-inch rectangle. Trim sides. Cut into 3x1½-inch rectangles or 2-inch squares. Place on ungreased cookie sheets. Bake at 325 for 12 to 16 minutes until lightly browned. Cool.
2. Caramel filling: (2nd group of ingredients) combine candies and evaporated milk over double boiler until caramels melt, stirring occasionally. Remove from heat and stir in butter, confectioners' sugar and pecans. Spread 1 tsp of filling on each shortbread square.
3. Chocolate icing: Melt semisweet pieces with evaporated milk over low heat. Remove from heat. Stir in remaining butter, vanilla, and confectioners' sugar. Top squares with ½ tsp icing and a pecan.

Delicious Chocolate Dollops

<u>Ingredients:</u>

¾ cup unsalted butter (1½ sticks), melted
¾ cup brown sugar, packed
¼ cup granulated sugar
2 large eggs
2 tsp vanilla extract
1 (3.7 to 3.9 oz) pkg instant chocolate pudding mix
¼ cup unsweetened cocoa powder
2 cups all-purpose flour
2 tsp baking soda
1 cup semi-sweet chocolate chips
½ cup toffee bits

<u>Directions:</u>

1. Combine butter, sugars, egg, and vanilla. Mix until creamed and well-combined. Scrape sides of bowl and add pudding mix, cocoa, and mix well, until just combined. Scrape sides of bowl and add chocolate chips and toffee bits and mix until just combined.
2. Using a large cookie scoop, ¼ cup measure, or your fingers, form 15 to 18 cookies of equal size. Roll into balls and flatten slightly. Place on a tray covered with plastic wrap and chill for 2 to 3 hours or up to 4 days.
3. Preheat oven to 350. Line baking sheet with parchment paper or cooking spray. Place dough in mounds on baking sheet, space at least 2 inches apart (8 to 9 cookies per sheet).
4. Bake for 10-14 minutes or until edges are set (do not overbake) cookies will firm up as they cool. Cool on the sheet for 10 minutes before removing. Drizzle melted chocolate on top of cookies for decoration.

<u>Notes:</u>

This recipe was sent to me by Linda Dawson Cutler. It was created and submitted by Carol Kammer (Linda's sister-in-law) to a Bake-Off contest in Frankenmuth, Michigan, and took first prize in the cookie category.

Double Tree Chocolate Chip Cookies

Ingredients:

1½ cups unsalted butter
1½ cups white sugar
¾ cup packed brown sugar
4 eggs
3 cups all-purpose flour
¾ cup rolled oats
2½ tsp vanilla extract
1 teas lemon juice
¾ tsp baking soda
1 tsp salt
¼ tsp ground cinnamon
3 cups semisweet chocolate chips
1½ cups chopped walnuts

Directions:
1. With mixer, cream butter in large bowl. Add both sugars and beat on medium for 2 minutes. Add eggs one at a time, beating well after each addition. Add lemon juice and vanilla; mix well.
2. In a separate bowl, stir together dry ingredients. Add to creamed mixture and stir well to blend. Add chips and nuts; stir to combine.
3. Drop by quarter cup on parchment-lined baking pans, 2 to 3 inches apart. Bake at 350 degrees for 13 to 15 minutes or until lightly browned around the edges. Cool; remove from paper and cool completely on wire racks. Makes 36 cookies.

Notes:
We love the Double Tree Chocolate Chip Cookies. During the Shelter-in-Place and COVID-19 Virus, Doubletree graciously shared their recipe. The difference I see between this and most other chocolate chip cookie recipes is that they add ¾ cup oatmeal and a tsp of lemon juice. These are great cookies, and I may try milk chocolate chips next time because that's my family's preference.

Great Harvest Bread Company Chocolate Chip Cookies

Ingredients:

2 cups whole wheat flour
1 tsp baking powder
½ tsp baking soda
¼ tsp salt
2 cups brown sugar, packed
1 cup butter, softened
2 cups rolled oats
2 eggs
2 tbsp molasses
1 tbsp milk
1 (12-oz) pkg semisweet chocolate chips

Directions:
1. Preheat oven to 350. Combine flour, baking powder, baking soda, and salt; set aside.
2. Beat together brown sugar and butter until well combined. Add oats, eggs, molasses, and milk; beat well.
3. Add dry ingredients to beaten mixture; beat until blended. Stir in chocolate chips.
4. Using a ¼ cup measuring cup, scoop dough and drop about 3 inches apart onto ungreased cookie sheets. Bake 12 to 13 minutes, until just starting to brown around the outside. Cool 2 minutes on cookie sheets. Makes 24 giant cookies.

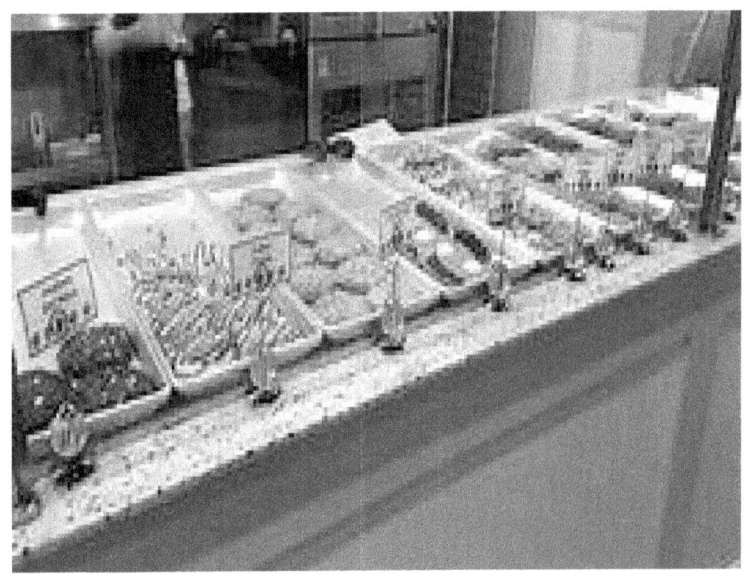

Notes:
These were a favorite of mine when I worked at the Accident Fund of Michigan. We had a Great Harvest Bread Company in Lansing at that time, and it was only a short walk from the office. Many a lunch hour found me standing in line and convincing myself that the short trek made up for the calories. 😊

Hermits

<u>Ingredients:</u>

1½ cups sugar
1 cup shortening
3 eggs
1 tsp baking soda
1 tsp cinnamon
1 tsp salt
1 tsp clove (or allspice)
1 cup chopped raisins
2½ cups flour

<u>Directions:</u>

1. Mix all ingredients and roll into balls. Drop onto lightly sprayed cookie sheet and press with fork.
2. Bake at 375 for 8 to 10 minutes.

<u>Notes:</u>

I got this recipe from my cousins, Linda Dawson Cutler and Sharron Dawson Beckwith. Linda attributed the recipe to our Grandma Bertha Dawson, and Sharron gave credit to our Great Grandma Cora Wiltsie. These were Linda's very favorite cookie. Grandma Bertha Dawson always kept a Tupperware container in her bottom cupboard, and as often as not, it was filled with hermits. Linda wondered why Grandma's hermit cookies were square. After Linda married and began baking on her own, she concluded Grandma maybe put them too close together on the cookie sheet. The other possibility was the flour to shortening ratio was off. My Aunt Edith used 3 cups of flour. At the bottom of the recipe Linda sent me, she had scrawled, "Grandma, forgive me, I love you," I thought then, and I still believe, Grandma Dawson would be thrilled that we are still talking about and remembering her love and her special cookies. I go with 3 cups of flour.

Lemon Bars with Shortbread Crust

<u>Ingredients:</u>
Crust »»

½ cup confectioners' sugar, sifted
1½ cups all-purpose flour
¾ cup (1½ stick) unsalted butter, softened
½ cup pine nuts (optional, and I toast them slightly)

Filling »»

½ cup all-purpose flour, sifted
2¼ cups sugar
1 cup + 2 tbsp freshly squeezed lemon juice
lemon zest from one small lemon
6 large whole eggs
1 large egg yolk
pinch of salt
additional confectioners' sugar to sift over tops

<u>Directions:</u>
1. Preheat oven to 350. Cream together softened butter, flour, and confectioners' sugar. Grease your hands with additional butter, or use a piece of waxed paper and press flour mixture into the bottom of a 9x13-inch pan, and ¾ inch up the sides. Bake 25 to 30 minute or until the crust is golden brown. Remove from oven.
2. While crust is baking, mix filling ingredients. Pour over baked crust, spreading evenly. Return to oven, reduce heat to 300 and bake 30 to 40 minutes until filling is set.
3. Allow to cool, refrigerate, and when completely cool, cut with a very sharp knife. Using a flour sifter, sift confectioners' sugar over the top of the cooled bars.

<u>Notes:</u>
For years I had made lemon bars, but this recipe comes from the famous Tartine Bakery in San Francisco. There is more filling, and the toasted pine nuts add a delightful taste to the crust. It's my favorite.

Lemon Shortbread Triangles

<u>Ingredients:</u>
Dough »»

¾ cup powdered sugar
1¼ cups butter, softened
2¾ cups flour
½ cup mixed nuts, finely chopped (I use a can of salted mixed nuts and chop them)
1 tsp ginger

Topping »»

1 cup mixed nuts, coarsely chopped
¾ cup white chocolate chip morsels

Glaze »»

1 cup powdered sugar
1 tsp grated lemon peel
4 tsp lemon juice

<u>Directions:</u>
1. Preheat oven to 325. Beat sugar and butter until fluffy. Add flour, finely chopped ½ cup nuts, and ginger. Mix until combined. Press dough onto a cookie sheet (I used a 10x15-inch) with a 1-inch edge.
2. Sprinkle with 1 cup coarsely chopped nuts and white chips and press lightly into dough.
3. Bake 25 minutes or until edges are golden. Remove from oven to a rack (leave in pan), cut into squares and then cut diagonally through the squares to make triangles. Cool completely.
4. Mix all ingredients for the glaze and drizzle over the triangles.

Meringue Topped Chocolate Coconut Nut Bars

Ingredients:

¾ cup butter, softened
½ cup white sugar
½ cup brown sugar, packed
4 egg yolks, (save whites for topping below)
2 cups flour
1 tsp vanilla
1 tsp baking powder
¼ tsp baking soda
¼ tsp salt

6 oz pkg chocolate chips (either milk or semisweet)
1 cup sweet coconut
¾ cup chopped nuts

4 egg whites
1 cup brown sugar

Directions:
1. Mix butter, sugars, egg yolks, flour, vanilla, baking powder, baking soda, and salt together and pack in lightly greased 12x18 rimmed cookie sheet.
2. Sprinkle crust with chocolate chips, coconut, and nuts.
3. Beat egg whites until fluffy. Add brown sugar. Spread over chips/coconut.
4. Bake in 325 or 350 oven for 35-45 minutes.

Notes:
Aunt Edith Dawson said to add meringue in small dabs; it is easier to spread. She cut a tray of bars to make 72 bars.

Mrs. Field's Chocolate Chip Oatmeal Cookies

(This recipe makes a lot of cookies, but you can freeze part of the dough for another time.)

Ingredients:

2 cups butter
2 cups granulated sugar
2 cups brown sugar
4 eggs
2 tsp vanilla
5 cups oatmeal
4 cups flour
2 tsp baking powder
2 tsp baking soda.
24 oz semi-sweet chocolate pieces
1 {8 oz) Hershey bar
3 cups chopped nuts.

Directions:
1. Cream butter and sugars. Add eggs and vanilla.
2. Put small amounts at a time of oatmeal into blender and blend until each amount is turned into a powder. Add remaining dry ingredients.
3. Add chocolate chips. Grate Hershey's bar. Add both chips and grated bar to above mixture. Add nuts.
4. Make golf ball sized balls and drop onto an ungreased cookie sheet. Bake at 375 for 6 minutes.

Peanut Butter Temptations

<u>Ingredients:</u>

½ cup butter
½ cup peanut butter
½ cup granulated sugar
½ cup brown sugar, packed
1 egg
½ tsp vanilla
1¼ cups all-purpose flour
¾ tsp baking soda
½ tsp salt
48 miniature Reese's peanut butter cups

<u>Directions:</u>
1. Cream butter, peanut butter, sugars, egg, and vanilla. Stir in dry ingredients until blended.
2. Roll dough into 1-inch balls. Press into 1½-inch muffin tins that are very lightly sprayed with cooking spray. (There is a lot of fat in this recipe, so don't add much cooking spray. I just find it's easier to get them from muffin tins if lightly sprayed.
3. Bake at 350 for 12 minutes. Remove from oven and immediately press one miniature peanut butter cup candy into each hot cookie crust. Allow to cool. Makes 4 dozen.

Pecan Toffee Bars with Browned Butter Icing

<u>Ingredients:</u>

Bars »»

1 cup (2 sticks) unsalted butter, softened
¼ cup firmly packed light brown sugar
½ cup granulated sugar
½ tsp salt
1 large egg yolk
2¼ cups all-purpose flour
2/3 cup milk chocolate English toffee bits (like Heath Bar Chips)
½ cup chopped pecans

Browned Butter Icing »»

2 tbsp butter
1 cup confectioners' sugar
½ tsp vanilla extract
2 to 3 tsp milk

<u>Directions:</u>

Bars»»

1. Heat oven to 350. Cream butter, sugars, salt, and egg yolk with an electric mixer until smooth. Gradually beat in flour. Mix in toffee bits.

2. Line a 13x19-inch baking pan with heavy duty aluminum foil. Press dough evenly into bottom of baking pan. Sprinkle with pecans and press lightly into dough. Bake until lightly browned, 20 to 22 minutes. Cool. Drizzle icing and cut into bars to serve.

Icing »»

1. Heat butter in small saucepan over low heat until browned (be careful not to burn).

2. Remove from heat. Stir in confectioners' sugar, vanilla extract, and enough milk to make a thin icing. Drizzle over Pecan Toffee Bars.

<u>Notes:</u>

I like this icing and often use it to drizzle over cake when I don't want a thick frosting. I double the ingredients, going light on milk for thinning, and use whatever flavoring I want, sometimes maple flavoring, sometimes almond, and sometimes I stick with the vanilla.

Rick's Spicy Molasses Cookies

<u>Ingredients:</u>

2 cups packed brown sugar
1½ cups Crisco
½ cup molasses
2 eggs
4 scant cups all-purpose flour
2 tsp cinnamon
1 tsp ginger
½ tsp cloves
½ tsp salt
4 tsp baking soda

<u>Directions:</u>
1. Combine all ingredients in a bowl. Mix and chill.
2. Roll into balls about the size of a walnut and roll in granulated sugar.
3. Bake at 350 for about 10 minutes. (They will be rather soft but their tops should begin to "crack.")

<u>Notes:</u>

These cookies are called *Rick's* because they are my brother's (Rick Albrecht) favorite, and while I don't consider him a cook or a baker to any great extent, he does make these cookies. They are also my daughter Courtney's favorite, and she's passed on her love of them to her sons, my grandsons, Ezra and Noah.

Sand Art Brownies

<u>Ingredients:</u>

1 cup flour
½ cup cocoa
¾ cup packed brown sugar
2/3 cup granulated sugar
½ tsp salt
½ cup chocolate chips
½ cup white chocolate chips
¼ cup chopped nuts

<u>Directions:</u>
Place ingredients, layer by layer, carefully into a 1-quart jar. Cap with a pretty lid. Tie with a bow and add a card with the following directions for preparation:

> **TO BAKE: Mix contents of jar with 1 tsp vanilla, 3 eggs, and ½ cup oil. Pour into a greased 9x9-inch baking pan. Bake at 350 for 30-35 minutes.**

<u>Note:</u>
This gift suggestion was sent to me by my cousin, Sharron Dawson Beckwith.

Saucepan Candied Fruit Bars

<u>Ingredients:</u>

3 cups flour
½ tsp baking soda
½ tsp salt
1 cup butter
1½ cups sugar
2 eggs
2 tsp vanilla
¼ cup orange juice
1 pound container mixed candied fruit
½ to 1 cup chopped nuts

1 cup powdered sugar
4 tsp orange juice

<u>Directions:</u>
1. Mix the flour, soda, and salt. Set aside.
2. In medium saucepan over low heat, melt butter. Remove from heat and add sugar, eggs, and vanilla. Mix well.
3. Add flour mixture and orange juice and mix. Stir in candied fruit and nuts.
4. Spread in a greased 15½x10½x1-inch jelly roll pan. Bake in preheated 350 oven for 25 minutes or until golden brown.
5. Make a smooth paste with the 1 cup powdered sugar and 4 tsp orange juice. Blend until smooth. While cookies are still warm, brush with orange glaze.
6. Cool completely in pan on rack. Cut into 1x2-inch bars. Makes 75.

Shortbread Cookies

<u>Ingredients:</u>

1 cup butter or margarine
1 cup packed brown sugar
1 egg yolk
1 tsp vanilla
¼ tsp salt
2 cups flour
1 (12 oz) bag chocolate chips (milk or semisweet)
¾ cup chopped nuts

<u>Directions:</u>
1. Mix butter or margarine, brown sugar, egg yolk, vanilla, salt, and flour together. Press into a 10½x15½x1-inch jelly roll pan.
2. Bake at 350 degrees for 20 minutes.
3. Remove from oven and sprinkle with chocolate chips. Spread melted chocolate evenly and sprinkle with chopped nuts.
4. Using very sharp knife, cut while bars are still warm.

<u>Note:</u>
Another of my Aunt Edith Dawson's shared recipes.

Skillet Cookies

<u>Ingredients:</u>

½ cup butter
¾ cup sugar
1 cup chopped dates
3 egg yolks
2 cups Rice Krispies
½ cup chopped nuts
1 tsp vanilla
sweetened shredded coconut

<u>Directions:</u>
1. Melt butter in large skillet. Mix in egg yolks, sugar, and dates. Cook over medium heat 10 minutes. Stir to keep from burning. Remove from heat.
2. Add Rice Krispies, nuts, and vanilla.
3. Mix well and form into balls while still warm and roll balls in coconut.

<u>Note:</u>
Grandma Bertha Dawson's recipe, given to me by my cousin, Sharron Dawson Beckwith.

Sugar Cookies

<u>Ingredients:</u>

1 cup unsalted butter
1 cup granulated white sugar
1 tsp vanilla extract
½ tsp almond extract
1 egg
2 tsp baking powder
½ tsp salt
3 cups all-purpose flour

<u>Directions:</u>
1. Preheat oven to 350. Cream butter and sugar until smooth, at least 3 minutes
2. Beat in extracts and egg.
3. In a separate bowl combine baking powder and salt with flour and add a little at a time to the wet ingredients. The dough will be very stiff. If it becomes too stiff for your mixer, turn out the dough onto a countertop surface. Wet your hands and finish kneading the dough by hand.
4. DO NOT CHILL THE DOUGH. Divide into workable batches, roll out onto a floured surface and cut. You want these cookies to be on the thicker side (closer to ¼ inch rather than 1/8).
5. Bake at 350 for 6-8 minutes. Let cool on the cookie sheet until firm enough to transfer to a cooling rack.

Paint for Sugar Cookies

<u>Ingredients:</u>

1 cup confectioners' sugar
2 tsp milk
2 tsp light corn syrup
¼ tsp almond extract
assorted food coloring

<u>Directions:</u>
1. In a small bowl, stir together confectioners' sugar and milk until smooth. Beat in corn syrup, and almond extract until icing is smooth and glossy. If icing is too thick, add more corn syrup.
2. Divide into separate bowls and add enough food colorings to each to obtain desired intensity. Dip cookies or paint them with a kitchen baking brush.

Spicy Gingerbread Men

Ingredients:

½ cup butter
½ cup sugar
½ cup molasses
1 egg yolk
2 cups sifted all-purpose flour
½ tsp salt
½ tsp baking powder
½ tsp baking soda
½ tsp ground cinnamon
1 tsp ground cloves
1 tsp ginger
½ tsp ground nutmeg

Directions:

1. In a large bowl, cream together the butter and sugar until smooth. Stir in molasses and egg yolk. Combine: flour, salt, baking powder, baking soda, cinnamon, cloves, ginger, and nutmeg; blend into the molasses mixture until smooth. Cover and chill for at least one hour.
2. Preheat the oven to 350. On a lightly floured surface roll the dough out to ¼-inch thickness. Cut into desired shapes (gingerbread men, what else?) with cookie cutters. Place cookies 2 inches apart on ungreased cookie sheets.
3. Bake for 8 to 10 minutes until firm. Remove from cookie sheets to cool. Frost or decorate when cool.

Notes:

My grandsons had fun decorating, but not as much fun as they had eating. Noah was sneaking the dough, and thought 10 minutes was a ridiculously long time for a cookie to bake in the oven.

Roasted Hazelnut Shortbread Cookies

<u>Ingredients:</u>

2 cups (4 sticks) butter, room temperature
1¼ cups sugar
¼ cup light brown sugar
2 egg yolks
4 cups flour
1 tbsp salt
1 cup finely chopped, toasted hazelnuts
colored sugar sprinkles or frosting

<u>Directions:</u>

1. Using a beater, cream the butter and sugars until fluffy. Add the egg yolks and keep mixing until blended.
2. Sift together flour and salt. Add to butter mixture on low speed, until almost incorporated. Stir in hazelnuts and mix until just combined. Take care not to over mix the dough.
3. Divide dough into four portions. Flatten each portion and wrap in plastic wrap. Chill dough in refrigerator for at least 2 hours or overnight.
4. Preheat oven to 325. Take one portion of dough and place it on a piece of parchment paper. Lightly flour the top, and roll out to about ¼-inch thickness.
5. Punch out cookies using a round 1½-inch cutter. Place cookies on a parchment lined sheet, and garnish tops with a pinch of colored sugar.
6. Bake for 10 minutes, rotating sheet after five minutes, until cookies are golden brown around the edges. Repeat with rest of dough. Cool.

<u>Notes:</u>

This has become my favorite Christmas cookie. I cut the dough into a variety of shapes and then frost with butter frosting instead of using colored sugar sprinkles. I sometimes paint the cookies with the *Paint for Sugar Cookie* frosting, p. 181 in this book. The dough freezes well.

Thumbprint Cookies

Ingredients:

1½ cups butter, softened
1 cup packed light brown sugar
3 large eggs, separated
1 tbsp vanilla extract
3 cups all-purpose flour
1½ cups finely chopped pecans
buttercream frosting, Hershey's kisses, peanut or almond M&Ms, or jelly

Directions:

1. In a mixing bowl, beat butter, brown sugar, egg yolks, and vanilla until smooth and well blended. Stir in the flour just until blended. Cover and refrigerate for 30 to 45 minutes.
2. Preheat oven to 375. Whisk the eggs white or beat with a fork until slightly foamy.
3. Roll the dough into small balls, about ½-inch in diameter. Dip the balls into the slightly beaten egg white; roll in chopped pecans.
4. Place the cookie dough balls on ungreased baking sheets, leaving about 1 inch between each cookie.
5. With a thumb, press each cookie to make an indention in the center. If you are using Hershey's kisses, insert one into each indentation before baking. (If you are using frosting or jelly, fill indentations after step six.)
6. Bake the cookies for about 7 to 9 minutes, or just until light golden brown. Remove to a rack and let cool completely.

Notes:

My cousin Jean Ann Albrecht Wendt made these cookies and put a peanut M&M in the center. I usually fill the thumbprint indentations with colored buttercream frosting. You can get creative.

Top of the Stove Oatmeal Peanut Butter Clusters

<u>Ingredients:</u>

2 cups white sugar
½ cup milk
1 stick butter
pinch of salt
½ cup peanut butter
3 cups regular rolled oats
½ cup coconut (optional)
½ cup nuts, chopped
1 tsp vanilla

<u>Directions:</u>

1. In a medium sauce pan combine sugar, milk, butter, and salt. Bring to a boil, stirring occasionally. Boil one minute. Remove from heat. Add peanut butter and vanilla, stirring until smooth.
2. Add oatmeal, coconut, and nuts. Stir until well-mixed.
3. Drop by tablespoon onto waxed paper. Cool.

<u>Notes:</u>

This recipe came from my Aunt Edith Dawson. She used 1½ cups regular rolled oats and 1½ cups quick oats because she said it made the cookies chewier. Also, when she used chunky peanut butter, she omitted the nuts.

If you want chocolate oatmeal clusters, add 1/3 cup cocoa to sugar and milk mixture and boil 1½ minutes before proceeding with remainder of recipe.

Triple Treat Shortbread, Caramel, and Chocolate Cookies

Ingredients:

⅔ cup butter, softened
¼ cup white sugar
1¼ cups all-purpose flour
½ cup butter
½ cup packed light brown sugar
2 tbsp light corn syrup
½ cup sweetened condensed milk
1¼ cups milk chocolate chips

Directions:

1. Preheat oven to 350 degrees.
2. In a medium bowl, mix together 2/3 cup butter, white sugar, and flour until evenly crumbly. Press into a 9-inch square baking pan. Bake for 20 minutes.
3. In a 2-quart saucepan, combine ½ cup butter, brown sugar, corn syrup, and sweetened condensed milk. Bring to a boil. Continue to boil for 5 minutes. Remove from heat and beat vigorously with a wooden spoon for about 3 minutes. Pour over baked crust (warm or cool). Cool until it begins to firm.
4. Place chocolate in a microwave-safe bowl. Heat for 1 minute, then stir and continue to heat and stir at 20 second intervals until chocolate is melted and smooth. Pour chocolate over the caramel layer and spread evenly to cover completely. Chill. Cut into 1-inch squares. These need to be small because they are so rich. In fact, they are so rich they are sometimes called millionaire's bars.

Notes:

My daughter used to buy cookie bars similar to these for me from Bi-Rite Market in San Francisco. They were incredibly decadent. I decided to experiment and see if I could make them myself. With only minimal bragging, I think these are almost as good.

Walnut Crescent Cookies

<u>Ingredients:</u>

1 cup walnuts
¾ tsp ground cardamom
¾ cup plus ¼ cup confectioners' sugar (divided)
1 cup cold unsalted butter, cut into small pieces (2 sticks)
2 tsp pure vanilla extract
2 cups all-purpose flour
½ tsp Kosher salt
1/8 tsp ground cinnamon

<u>Directions:</u>

1. In food processor, pulse walnuts, cardamom, and ¾ cup confectioners' sugar until walnuts are finely ground. Add butter and process until smooth.
2. Mix in vanilla. Add flour and salt and pulse to combine. Shape into 1-inch-diameter logs, wrap in plastic, and refrigerate until firm, at least 1½ hrs.
3. Line baking sheets with parchment paper. Cut or pinch off 1-inch-thick pieces dough and roll into 3½-inch log with tapered ends, then bend into crescent shape. Repeat. Place crescents 1½ inches apart on prepared baking sheets. Freeze until firm, about 20 minutes.
4. Heat oven to 350. Bake, rotating sheets halfway through, until cookies are set and just barely turning golden brown around edges, 15 to 18 minutes. Let cool completely on baking sheets.
5. In bowl, combine cinnamon and remaining ¼ cup confectioners' sugar. Liberally dust cookies with cinnamon sugar before serving.

<u>Note:</u>
For me, these are the perfect Christmas cookie, definitely one of my favorites.

Candy and Other Sweet Confections

~ ~ ~

Caramel Apples

Ingredients:

8 large Granny Smith or other tart apples
8 wooden popsicle sticks for handles
1 cup (2 sticks) butter
2 cups packed brown sugar
1 cup light corn syrup
1 (14 oz) can sweetened condensed milk
2 tsp vanilla extract

Directions:

1. Bring a large saucepan of water to a boil. Dip apples in boiling water for a few seconds, then dry with paper towels to remove any wax from the peels. Set apples aside; when completely cool, insert a wooden popsicle stick firmly into the bottom of each apple for handle.

2. Line a baking sheet with parchment paper. Stir butter, brown sugar, corn syrup, and sweetened condensed milk together in a saucepan over medium-high heat. Bring to a boil, stirring constantly, and reduce heat to medium. Cook until a candy thermometer reads 248 degrees, 25 to 30 minutes; stir constantly to prevent burning. A teaspoon of the syrup, dropped into a glass of cold water, should form a firm ball. Remove caramel from heat and stir in vanilla.

(Recipe continued on next page.)

3. Working quickly, dip each apple into the hot caramel to completely coat the apple and ½ inch of handle. While still hot, sprinkle apples with any desired topping (finely chopped nuts, chocolate sprinkles). Let caramel apples cool on the parchment paper.

~ ~ ~

Caramel Corn

<u>Ingredients:</u>

2 cups brown sugar
½ cup light Karo syrup
2 sticks butter
½ tsp baking soda
1/3 tsp salt
18 cups popped popcorn
nuts of your choice

<u>Directions:</u>
1. Put popped popcorn on a large cookie sheet and spread evenly. Add any desired nuts.
2. Melt brown sugar, butter, syrup, salt, and soda in heavy 2-quart pan.
3. Increase heat and bring to a boil for five minutes or to soft boil stage.
4. Pour immediately over popcorn/nuts and stir.
5. Bake at 250 for one hour, stirring every 15 minutes. Pour onto waxed paper to cool.

Caramel Dip

Ingredients:

1 cup white sugar
1 cup brown sugar
1 stick butter
1/3 cup light Karo syrup
1 large can (12 oz) evaporated milk
1 tsp vanilla
apples, sliced for dipping

Directions:
1. Combine sugar, half of the evaporated milk, and butter in a heavy two-quart pan. Stir and bring to a boil over medium heat.
2. Reduce heat to low and boil for about 45 minutes, stirring occasionally.
3. Gradually add the other half of the evaporated milk, trying to do so slowly enough to not break the mixture's low boil.
4. Add Karo syrup and continue boiling an additional half hour, stirring occasionally.
5. Remove from heat and when slightly cooled, pour into a blender. Add vanilla and blend on medium for two minutes. Refrigerate until cool.

Notes:
This is not a recipe that you have to stand and stir constantly. You DO have to make sure it's a low boil so it doesn't boil over, and then stir every ten or fifteen minutes. I make it when I'm working on other things in the kitchen.

I used to make this when my children were in high school. I would always hide myself a small container in the back of the refrigerator under something they would never look for (like broccoli). Invariably they found my caramel, and all I got was an empty bowl. ☺ It's my version of caramel apples without the difficulty of trying to dip whole apples into a hot mixture and hope the apples don't fall off the flimsy sticks, the mixture doesn't cool too quickly, or that the caramel isn't too runny to stick. Much, much easier.

Caramels to Die For

Ingredients:

1 cup (2 sticks) butter
1 box (16-oz) brown sugar
1 cup light corn syrup
1 (14-oz) can sweetened condensed milk
1 tsp vanilla extract
sea salt, if desired

Directions:
1. Melt butter in a heavy saucepan. Add brown sugar and stir until thoroughly combined. Stir in corn syrup and mix well. Gradually add sweetened condensed milk, stirring constantly.
2. Cook and stir over medium heat until candy reaches firm ball stage (245 on candy thermometer) or about 12 to 15 minutes.
3. Pour into an 8x8-inch pan lined with non-stick aluminum foil and let set to harden.

Chocolate Bon Bon Pops

Ingredients:

18 chocolate sandwich cookies with cream filling (Oreos)
1½ cups pecans, toasted
2 tbsp Cointreau (or orange juice)
1 tbsp light corn syrup
2 tbsp unsweetened cocoa powder
20 lollipop sticks
1 (12-oz) pkg milk chocolate pieces
1 tbsp shortening

Directions:
1. In blender or food processor combine cookies and ¾ cup of the nuts; pulse until cookies are crushed. Add orange liqueur, corn syrup, and cocoa powder; process until combined. Add remaining nuts; pulse until coarsely chopped.
2. Line a large baking sheet with parchment paper. Shape cookie mixture in 1-inch balls. Place on baking sheet, insert a lollipop stick, and freeze for 30 minutes.
3. In a small saucepan combine chocolate pieces and shortening. Cook and stir over medium-low heat just until melted. Remove from heat. Dip pops into chocolate. Return to baking sheet. Loosely cover and refrigerate 1 hour or until chocolate is set.

Creamy Double Decker Fudge

<u>Ingredients:</u>

1 cup (6 oz) peanut butter chips
1 (14 oz) can sweetened condensed milk
1 tsp vanilla extract
1 cup (6 oz) semi-sweet chocolate pieces

<u>Directions:</u>
1. In a 2-cup glass measuring cup with handle, combine peanut butter chips and 2/3 cup sweetened condensed milk. Cook in microwave at 100% power for 1 to 1½ minutes, stirring after 1 minute, until chips are melted and mixture is smooth. Stir in ½ tsp vanilla. Spread evenly into foil-lined 8-inch square pan.
2. Repeat procedure for remaining sweetened condensed milk and chocolate chips, and when chips are melted, add remaining ½ tsp vanilla. Spread evenly over peanut butter layer.
3. Chill 2 hours or until firm. Turn onto cutting board. Peel off foil and cut into squares. Store, covered, in refrigerator.

~ ~ ~

English Toffee

<u>Ingredients:</u>

1 cup butter (NOT margarine)
1 cup sugar
3 tbsp water
1 tsp vanilla
2/3 cup ground almonds or pecans
4 (1.05 oz) Hershey bars

<u>Directions:</u>
1. Cook butter, sugar, water, and vanilla over medium heat, stirring constantly until golden brown. It may smoke but that's okay.
2. Put 1/3 cup nuts in 9x9-inch pan. Pour sugar mixture over nuts.
3. Place Hershey bars on top. Spread chocolate evenly when soft.
4. Sprinkle with remaining 1/3 cup nuts, and press into chocolate. When cool, break into pieces. (Hint: mark lines in toffee when hot. When cool, push knife into lines to cut.)

<u>Note:</u>
I got this recipe from Merry Rosenberg when we both were working for the Attorney General.

Hot Fudge Sauce

Ingredients:

4 (1 oz) squares unsweetened chocolate
1 stick butter
3 cups sugar
1 (12 oz) can evaporated milk

Directions:

1. Melt Chocolate and butter together over a double boiler, then add sugar, one cup at a time, until melted.
2. When hot to the touch (about ten minutes more), add evaporated milk.

3. Continue cooking, stirring occasionally, until thickened. Store in refrigerator and heat serving size portions in the microwave.

~ ~ ~

Peanut Butter Fudge

Ingredients:

4½ cups white sugar
1 large can evaporated milk
1 stick butter
4 oz marshmallow cream
one 18 oz jar peanut butter (plain or chunky)
1 tsp vanilla

Directions:

1. In heavy pan, mix sugar, milk, and butter. Boil 8 minutes or slightly longer, stirring constantly. It should come to soft ball stage on candy thermometer.
2. Remove from heat; add marshmallow cream, peanut butter, and vanilla.
3. Mix well and return to heat until mixture appears to thicken.
4. Pour into a buttered 9x13-inch pan and let set overnight.

Praline Crunch Party Mix

<u>Ingredients:</u>

4 cups rice Chex cereal
4 cups corn Chex cereal
2 cups wheat Chex
2 cups mini pretzels
2 cups pecan halves
1½ cups brown sugar
1½ cups light corn syrup
1½ cups (3 sticks) butter
3 teaspoons vanilla extract
1½ teaspoons baking soda

(I add cashews, salted dry roasted peanuts, and walnut halves to equal 2 cups nuts). I sometimes use 4 cups pretzels and omit Wheat Chex)

<u>Directions:</u>
1. Preheat oven to 250°F. Line two baking sheets with parchment paper.
2. In a large bowl, combine cereal, pretzels, and nuts.
3. In a medium saucepan over medium-high heat, combine brown sugar, corn syrup, and butter. Bring to a boil while stirring occasionally. Add baking soda. It will boil rapidly and expand so be careful. Use a larger pan than you think you'll need.
4. Remove from heat and stir in vanilla. Pour over cereal mixture and stir until evenly coated.
5. Spread mixture onto prepared pans and bake for 1 hour, tossing or stirring mixture every 20 minutes.
6. Pour onto wax or parchment paper to cool. Break into pieces.
<u>Note:</u> You can alter the cereal/pretzel and nuts to suit your taste. I often increase the ingredients for the brown sugar/corn syrup mixture by ¼ so I have more of the Praline taste.

Desserts

"Seize the moment. Just think of all those women on the Titanic who said, 'No, thank you,' to dessert that night. And for what!" **Erma Bombeck**

"If it's warm and chocolate it's nirvana for most people . . . but I can't give away prune desserts." **Claudia Fleming**

"I want to have a good body, but not as much as I want dessert." **Jason Love**

My two-cents about dessert: When you are stressed, you eat hot fudge sundaes, pecan pie, cookies by the dozen—even caramel sauce right out of the jar if nothing else is available. Why? Because stressed is desserts spelled backwards. So, you are destressing by eating desserts.

Almond Stuffed Chocolate Dipped Strawberries

<u>Ingredients:</u>

12 large strawberries, rinsed
¼ cup milk chocolate or semi-sweet chocolate chips
1 (3 oz) pkg cream cheese, softened
2 tbsp honey
¼ tsp almond extract
1 tbsp finely chopped almonds

<u>Directions:</u>
1. Using tip of a paring knife, cut berries in half, including through the leafy part. Using knife tip, cut out the center core.
2. Pat and dry berries on paper towels.
3. Place chocolate chips in a microwavable bowl and heat at 20 second intervals, stirring after each until chocolate is melted. Make sure you don't overcook.
4. Line a baking sheet with waxed paper. Holding each berry by the stem, dip halfway into the chocolate and place cut side down, on the waxed paper. Refrigerate chocolate covered berries for ten minutes.
5. In small bowl, beat cream cheese, honey, and almond extract. Spoon mixture into pastry bag fitted with small tip. Turn berries over and pipe onto cut and cored side of berry. Sprinkle with finely chopped almonds and arrange on serving dish.

<u>Note:</u>
This recipe came from my granddaughter, Kaelin Royce. We all loved it when she made them.

Apple Crisp

Ingredients:

4 pounds apples
1 tsp orange zest
1 tsp lemon zest
2 tbsp orange juice
2 tbsp lemon juice
½ cup sugar
¼ cup flour
1 tsp cinnamon
½ tsp nutmeg

Topping:

1½ cups flour
¾ cup granulated sugar
¾ cup light brown sugar, packed
1 cup oatmeal
1 cup butter, cold and cubed

Directions:

1. Preheat oven to 350. Peel and slice apples. Toss apples, both zests, both juices, ½ cup sugar, ¼ cup flour, cinnamon, and nutmeg. Mix until apples are coated. Pour into a 9x13-inch baking dish.

2. For topping: Combine 1½ cups flour, ¾ cup brown sugar, ¾ cup granulated sugar, 1 cup oatmeal, 1 cup (two sticks) cubed cold butter in a mixer and mix until crumbly.

3. Using your hands, crumble topping over the apple mixture. Make sure to cover all of the apples. Bake for 50 minutes.

Notes:

Apple crisp is my daughter's favorite dessert. I've made it and stuck a candle in the middle for her birthday. The only difference between what she wants and the above recipe is that I double the topping. And, of course, I serve it with vanilla ice cream.

Apple Turnovers

<u>Ingredients</u>:

½ cup Marzetti's Old Fashioned Caramel Dip
4 Granny Smith apples, peeled, cored, and diced into ½-inch pieces
2 tbsp unsalted butter
½ tsp ground cinnamon
1/3 cup sugar cookie, cake, or graham cracker crumbs
1 (17.3 oz) pkg prepared puff pastry, thawed
additional Marzetti's Old Fashioned Caramel Dip for drizzling

<u>Egg glaze</u>:

1 egg beaten with 1 tbsp water

<u>Directions</u>:

1. Preheat the oven to 400.
2. In a microwave safe bowl, combine apples, butter, and cinnamon and microwave for 3-4 minutes. The apples should be slightly tender. Microwave longer if necessary. Drain apples. Allow apples to cool. Toss with cookie crumbs and Marzetti Old Fashioned Caramel Dip.
3. Lightly dust a work surface with flour. Roll pastry sheet into a 10x10-inch square.
4. Cut into four squares. Lightly brush a ½-inch border around each square with cold water. Fill the center of each square with an equal amount of apple mixture.
5. Fold one corner over the fruit to the other corner to create a triangle. Press the dough together on both sides. Transfer to a baking sheet lined with parchment paper. With a fork, crimp the sides together. Repeat the process with remaining apples and dough.
6. Lightly brush turnovers with egg glaze. With a small knife, make vent in the top of each turnover.
7. Bake 18-22 minutes or until golden brown.
8. In a microwave safe container, microwave Marzetti Old Fashioned Caramel Dip for 10-30 seconds, stirring every 10 seconds. Transfer warm caramel to a resealable plastic bag. Snip the end of one of the corners of the bag and drizzle the top of turnovers with the warm caramel. Serve with ice cream or whipped cream.

<u>Note</u>:
I use Mrs. Richardson's Hot Caramel Ice Cream topping, warmed and drizzled over the turnovers.

Aunt Edie's Pineapple Cheesecake

Ingredients:
Crust »»

        8 oz graham crackers, crushed
        1 stick butter, softened
        3 tbsp brown sugar

Directions:
Mix together and press on bottom of a 9x13-inch pan. You can save out ¼ cup of mixture to sprinkle on top.

Filling »»

        1 pkg lemon Jell-O
        1 cup hot water
        1 large can Carnation milk
        1 (3 oz) pkg cream cheese
        1 cup sugar
        2 tsp vanilla
        1 can drained, crushed pineapple

Directions:
1. Mix together Jell-O and let stand to cool.
2. Pour Carnation milk in bowl and put in freezer until ice forms around the side. Whip until stiff. Add sugar and vanilla.
3. Add the cooled, but not set Jell-O, a little at a time to the cream cheese. Refrigerate until cold.
4. Add pineapple to the whipped milk mixture. When cream cheese mixture is cold add to the whipped milk mixture and pour into the pan. Sprinkle reserved crumbs on top. Refrigerate.

Notes:
This recipe originally came from Edith Dawson. Her daughter, Linda Dawson Cutler passed it on to me. Linda often put maraschino cherries on top.

Assorted Tiny Tarts

<u>Ingredients:</u> (Shells)

1 cup butter, softened
½ cup sugar
1 egg
1 tsp vanilla extract
2 cups flour

<u>Directions:</u>
1. Preheat oven to 325. Cream butter and sugar thoroughly. Beat in egg and vanilla, then stir in flour. Drop a rounded tsp of dough into each cup of mini muffin tin that has been sprayed with cooking spray. Press dough over bottom and up sides to form a cup.
2. Fill cups 2/3 full with choice of fillings below. Bake 25-30 minutes. Tarts should slip out easily when slightly cooled. Makes 42 tarts.

<u>Fillings:</u>
1. **Almond-Raspberry**: Divide ½ cup red raspberry preserves among pastries (about ½ tsp each). Beat together 2 eggs, 1 cup sugar, and 1 cup almond paste, crumbled. Spoon 2 level tsp of the almond mixture over preserves. Sprinkle with chopped sliced almonds. If desired, drizzle cooled, baked tarts with thinned red raspberry preserves.

2. **Cranberry-Nut**: Beat together 2 eggs, 1½ cup brown sugar, 2 tbsp melted butter, and 2 tsp vanilla extract. Stir in 2/3 cup finely chopped fresh cranberries and 6 tbsp chopped walnuts.

3. **Lemon Tarts**: ½ cup butter, 2 cups sugar, 4 eggs, 1 tbsp flour, 1/3 cup lemon juice, grated rind of one lemon. Beat all ingredients together.
(Additional mini tart recipes on next page.)

4. **Macaroon**: 3 eggs, ¾ cup sugar, 2 cups finely blanched almonds, 1 tsp vanilla, and optional candied cherries. Beat eggs with sugar, then beat in nuts and vanilla. Top with cherry if desired.

5. **Mini Pecan Pie Tarts**: 1 cup dark corn syrup, ¾ cup sugar, 3 tbsp softened butter, 3 lightly beaten eggs, 1 tsp vanilla, 1½ cups coarsely chopped pecans. Combine corn syrup, sugar, and butter in saucepan and bring to a boil. Pour over beaten eggs, mix well, and stir in vanilla and nuts. (For these, set oven to 350.)

6. **Pumpkin-Sour Cream**: Beat together 2 eggs, 1 cup canned pumpkin, 2/3 cup sugar, ½ cup dairy sour cream, 2 tbsp milk, and 1 tsp pumpkin pie spice. If desired, top cooled tarts with a dollop of whipped cream.

7. **Walnut Cups**: 1½ cups brown sugar, 2 tbsp softened butter, 2 eggs, 2 tsp vanilla extract, 1 tsp salt, 1 cup chopped walnuts. Mix first five ingredients and fill cups. Sprinkle with walnuts.

Note:
These are a bit time consuming, but made a day ahead, they are perfect for a buffet and providing guests a variety of choices.

Baklava

Ingredients:

1 (16 ounce) pkg phyllo dough
1 pound chopped walnuts
1 tsp ground cinnamon
1½ cups water
1½ cups white sugar
1½ tsp vanilla extract
¾ cup honey
1 cup butter, melted

Directions:
1. Preheat oven to 350. Butter the bottoms and sides of a 9x13-inch pan.
2. Remove phyllo dough from freezer and allow to thaw according to package instructions. (Phyllo dough is in the grocer's freezer section.)
3. Lightly roast the walnuts, then chop and toss with cinnamon. Set aside.
4. Make the sauce: Boil sugar and water until sugar is melted. Add vanilla and honey. Simmer for about 20 minutes. Allow to cool slightly and then put in refrigerator until you are ready for it.
5. Unroll thawed phyllo dough. Cut whole stack in half or to fit pan. Cover phyllo with a dampened cloth to keep it from drying out as you work. Place two sheets of dough in pan, using a pastry brush, butter thoroughly. Repeat until you have 8 sheets layered. Sprinkle 2-3 tbsp of nut mixture on top. Top with two sheets of dough, butter, nuts, layering as you go. The top layer should be about 6 - 8 sheets deep.
6. Using a sharp knife cut into diamond or square shapes all the way to the bottom of the pan. You may cut into 4 long rows the make diagonal cuts. Bake for about 50 minutes until baklava is golden and crisp.
7. Remove baklava from oven and immediately spoon cooled sauce over it. Let cool. Leave uncovered or it will get soggy.

Notes:
Baklava is my daughter's father-in-law, Moshe Elitzer's favorite. Since it freezes well, if you don't want all of it at one time, you can wrap tightly, put in a freezer container, and save for another occasion.

Caramel Cups

Ingredients:

8 oz cream cheese, softened
2 sticks butter, softened,
1¾ cups flour
½ cup confectioners' sugar
½ cup evaporated milk
1 bag (14-oz) Kraft light caramels
¼ cup butter,
½ cup Crisco, butter flavor
1/3 cup sugar
1/3 cup + 1 tbsp evaporated milk
2 tsp vanilla
chopped pecans or walnuts, if desired

Directions:

1. Mix first four ingredients together and form into two dozen balls. Place one ball into each cup of mini muffin pan. Form to cup shape. Bake at 350 for 15-20 minutes.

2. Mix ½ cup evaporated milk and caramels in microwavable bowl and cook until caramels have melted and can be stirred smooth. During cooking, remove from microwave every thirty seconds and stir. Do not overcook. Fill cooled cups with caramel.

3. Mix final five ingredients in order given, starting by beating butter, Crisco and sugar, then adding milk and vanilla. Frost cooled caramel cups. Sprinkle with chopped nuts, if desired.

Notes:

Of all of my Aunt Edith Dawson's recipes, this may be my very favorite. But I've gotten lazy, and I often use mini phyllo shells (in grocer's freezer section) that I crisp for three or four minutes in the oven. I fill them with caramel mixture and top with a squirt of whipped cream. It saves the labor intensive first and third steps of this recipe. The only downside is the tarts with mini phyllo shells must be eaten soon after being filled with caramel or they get soggy.

Cherry-Rhubarb Crunch

Ingredients:

1 tsp shortening or floured baking spray
1 cup rolled oats
1 cup packed brown sugar
1 cup all-purpose flour
¼ tsp salt
½ cup butter
4 cups diced rhubarb, cleaned; leaves and ends removed
1 cup sugar
2 cups cold water
1 tsp almond extract
1 can (21 oz) cherry pie filling
½ cup chopped walnuts

Directions:

1. Preheat oven to 350. Grease a 9x13-inch baking pan with shortening or baking spray.

2. In a large bowl, combine oats, brown sugar, flour, and salt. Stir well. Using a pastry cutter or fork, cut in the butter until crumbly. Pat 2 cups of the mixture into prepared pan. Set aside remaining crumb mixture. Cover the mixture in pan with rhubarb.

3. In a saucepan, combine sugar and cornstarch. Stir in cold water; cook over medium heat until mixture is thickened and clear (2 to 3 minutes). Stir in extract and cherry filling; spoon over rhubarb. Combine nuts with reserved crumb mixture, sprinkle over cherry layer. Bake 40 to 45 minutes. Serves 12.

Cream Puffs in a Pan

<u>Ingredients:</u>

½ cup butter
1 cup water
1 cup all-purpose flour
4 eggs
1 (8 oz) pkg cream cheese, at room temperature
3 cups milk
2 (3 oz) pkgs instant vanilla pudding mix
1 (16 oz) pkg frozen whipped topping, thawed
¼ cup chocolate syrup
1 cup sliced almonds (optional)

<u>Directions:</u>

1. Preheat oven to 400. Grease and flour a 9x13-inch pan.
2. In a saucepan or in the microwave, bring water and margarine to a boil. Mix in the flour, then beat in the eggs, one at a time. Spread mixture in the prepared pan; bake in preheated oven until puffed and golden, about 25 minutes. Press down any large bubbles with a wooden spoon. Cool cream puff before filling.
3. For the filling: Beat the cream cheese until fluffy. Stir in the milk and pudding mix. Beat until mixture is thick, then spread over cream puff. Top with whipped topping, drizzle with chocolate syrup, and sprinkle with almonds. Refrigerate 24 hours before serving.

<u>Note:</u>

This recipe was sent to me by Linda Dawson Cutler who found it in a Sanilac County Medical Facility collection of recipes.

Elegant Pear Dessert

<u>Ingredients:</u>

    4 ripe pears, preferably Bosc, with stems, washed and dried
    2 cups Riesling or other fruity white wine
    ¼ cup honey
    4 cinnamon sticks
    4 bay leaves
    4 strips orange zest

<u>Directions:</u>

1. Preheat oven to 400. Cut a thin slice off the bottom of each pear so they will stand upright. Remove core from bottom. Arrange the pears in an 8x8-inch baking dish. Whisk wine and honey until well blended and pour over the pears. Add cinnamon sticks, bay leaves, and orange zest to the wine mixture around the pears.
2. Roast the pears, basting every 15 minutes, until they are wrinkled and tender (45 minutes to 1 hour, depending upon the type of pear).
3. Use a slotted spoon to transfer the pears to shallow dessert bowls. Pour the wine mixture into a small saucepan; bring to a boil. Boil until slightly thickened, about 6 minutes. Drizzle over the pears and garnish with the cinnamon sticks, bay leaves, and orange zest. Serve warm, at room temperature, or chilled.

Fudgy Ice Cream Sandwiches

Ingredients:

½ cup (1 stick) butter
12 oz pkg semisweet or milk chocolate chips
1 can (14 oz) sweetened condensed milk
¼ tsp salt
1 cup flour
1 tbsp vanilla extract
your choice of ice cream flavors

Directions:
1. Preheat oven to 350. Line 2 cookie sheets with parchment paper.
2. In 4-quart saucepan, combine butter, chocolate chips, sweetened condensed milk, and salt. Cook on med-low, 5 to 6 minutes, or until chips are melted.
3. Remove from heat and stir in flour and vanilla until combined. With 1½-inch wide ice cream scoop, scoop dough onto cookie sheets, spacing 2 inches apart. Flatten slightly. Bake 8 to 10 minutes or until tops are dry but still soft when pressed. Cool on sheets on wire racks.
4. Sandwich a small scoop of slightly softened ice cream between two cookies and press together. Freeze in freezer bags until ready to serve.

Gingerbread with Lemon Curd

<u>Ingredients:</u>

2 lemons
½ cup sugar
2 tsp cornstarch
2 tbsp cold water
2 large egg yolks
3 tbsp butter (no substitutions), cut into small pieces
¼ cup reduced-fat or regular sour cream

2 cups all-purpose flour
½ cup sugar
2 tsp ground ginger
1 tsp ground cinnamon
½ tsp baking soda
½ tsp salt
1 cup light molasses
½ cup (1 stick) butter or margarine, cut into 8 pieces
¾ cup boiling water
1 tbsp fresh peeled ginger
1 large egg

<u>Directions:</u>

Lemon Curd »»
1. Juice lemons and measure 1/3 cup. Grate 1½ tsp of peel. Set aside.
2. In 2-quart saucepan, with wire whisk, combine sugar and cornstarch. Whisk in water and lemon juice until smooth. Whisk in 2 egg yolks. Cook on medium until mixture comes to a boil, whisking constantly. Reduce heat to low and simmer 1 minute or until thickened, whisking constantly.
3. Strain mixture through sieve set over medium bowl. Stir in butter and lemon peel until butter melts. Cool 10 minutes, then cover and refrigerate 20 minutes or until cold. Stir in sour cream. Refrigerate until needed.

Gingerbread »»
1. Preheat oven to 350. Grease and flour 9x9-inch metal baking pan.

(Recipe continued on next page.)

2. In large bowl, with wire whisk, combine flour, sugar, ground ginger, cinnamon, baking soda, and salt.

3. In small heatproof bowl, place molasses and butter. Add boiling water and grated ginger and stir until butter melts. Add molasses mixture and egg to flour mixture; whisk until blended. Pour batter into prepared pan. Bake 35-40 minutes or until toothpick inserted in center of gingerbread comes out clean. Cool in pan on wire rack 20 minutes to serve warm. Cut gingerbread into squares and spread with lemon curd.

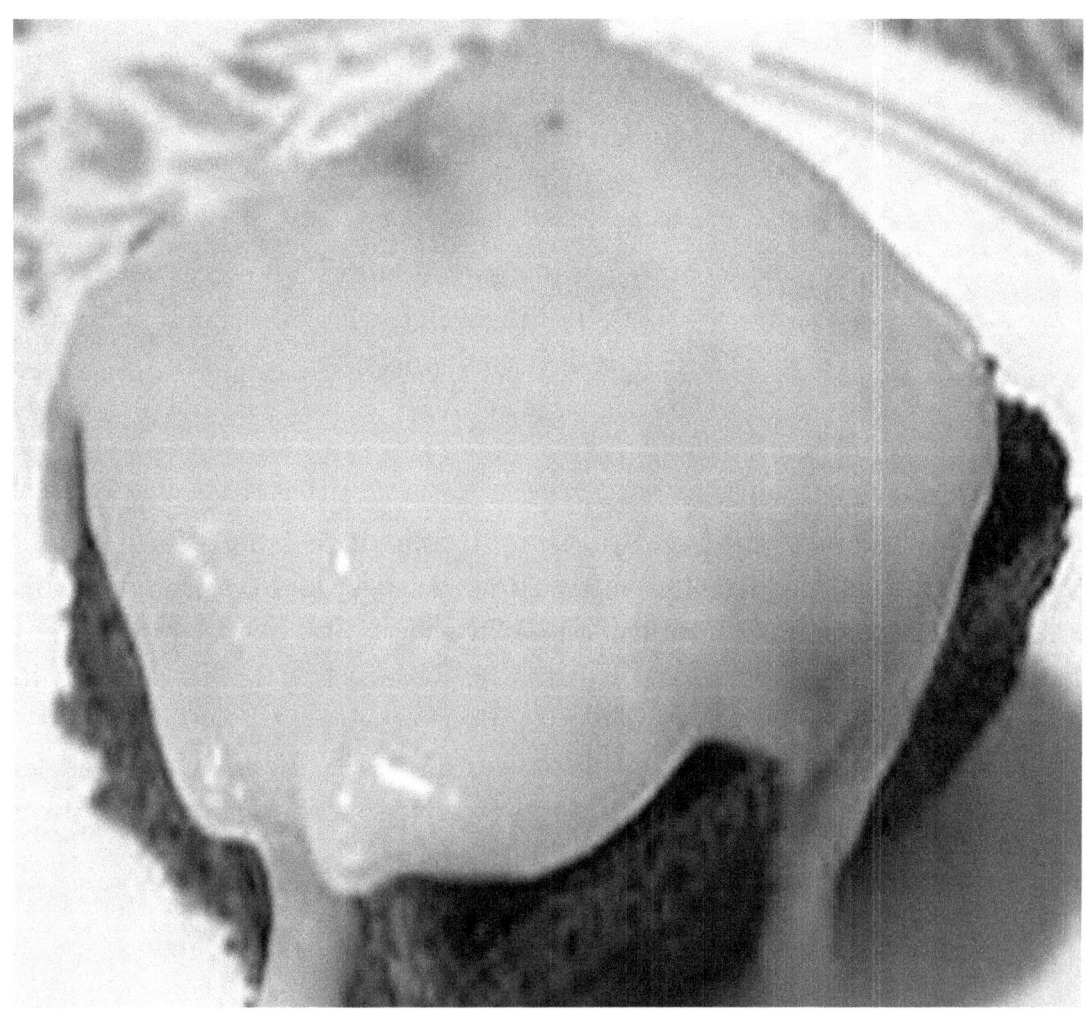

Gooey Chocolate Caramel Fantasy

<u>Ingredients:</u>

2 cups chocolate wafer crumbs
1/3 cup butter, melted
30 light caramels (like Kraft wrapped caramels)
½ cup caramel ice cream topping
½ cup whipping cream, divided
2 cups chopped pecans
¾ cup semisweet chocolate pieces

<u>Directions:</u>

1. In a medium mixing bowl, stir together chocolate wafer crumbs and melted butter. Press onto the bottom of a 9-inch springform pan. Bake at 350 for 10 minutes. Cool slightly on a wire rack.

2. Unwrap caramels. In a heavy medium saucepan, melt caramels and caramel ice cream topping over low heat, stirring often. Stir in ¼ cup of the whipping cream. Remove from heat, stir in nuts. Spread over crust. Cool; cover and chill for 1 hour.

3. In a heavy small saucepan, melt chocolate. Remove from heat, stir in remaining ¼ cup whipping cream. Drizzle or spread chocolate over caramel-pecan mixture. Cover and chill for at least 1 hour. Makes 12 servings.

<u>Notes:</u>
Chef Tom Kavanaugh at Kavanaugh's Resort and Restaurant near Brainerd, Minnesota, calls this a big candy bar on a plate, and he says you don't even have to unwrap it.

I toast my pecans before adding them to caramel mixture. I also melt caramels/heavy cream in microwave, and likewise for the chocolate/heavy cream, but I watch each carefully so I don't overcook.

Hot Fudge Ice Cream Puffs

Ingredients:

1 stick piecrust mix
2/3 cup boiling water
2 eggs
vanilla (or other) ice cream
hot fudge sauce (your own or recipe on page 194)
whipping cream
confectioners' sugar
chopped pecans

Directions:

1. In a medium saucepan, crumble pie crust mix into boiling water; cook and stir vigorously until pastry forms a ball and leaves sides of pan. Remove from heat. Cool for 10 minutes. Add eggs, one at a time, beating with a wooden spoon until smooth after each addition.

2. For each cream puff, spoon about ¼ cup mixture onto greased baking sheet. Bake in a 400-degree oven for 30-35 minutes or until puffs are dry and golden brown. Remove from baking sheet; cool on wire racks.

3. Cut off tops of puffs; remove excess webbing or insides.

4. In a small saucepan heat hot fudge sauce over low heat (or microwave in a small bowl).

5. To serve: put large scoop of ice cream onto bottom of each cream puff, add top of each cream puff; drizzle with hot fudge sauce and a dollop of whipped cream sweetened to taste with confectioners' sugar. Sprinkle with chopped nuts. Serves six.

Individual Bittersweet Chocolate Cheesecakes

<u>Ingredients:</u>
1 (8 oz) pkg cream cheese, softened at room temperature
1/3 cup sugar
4 oz chocolate (bittersweet or semisweet), chopped, divided, and melted
1 large egg

<u>Directions:</u>
1. Position a rack in the center of the oven and preheat to 300. Line 6 standard muffin tins with foil liners and lightly spray with cooking spray.
2. In a medium bowl, beat the cream cheese with an electric mixer on medium speed until very smooth, about 2 minutes. Add the sugar and 3 oz of melted chocolate. Beat on medium low speed until well blended, about 1 minute. Add the egg and mix until just incorporated. Spoon the batter into the muffin cups.
3. Bake until the centers of the cheesecakes barely jiggle when nudged (about 15 to 18 minutes). Set the muffin tin on a rack and let cool completely.
4. Cover and refrigerate until ready to serve or for up to 3 days (or freeze for up to 1 month). Just before serving, drizzle with remaining 1 oz melted chocolate (rewarmed, if necessary).

Mountain Dew Apple Dumplings

Ingredients:

2 large Granny Smith apples, peeled and cored
2 (10-oz) cans refrigerated crescent roll dough
1 cup butter
1½ cups white sugar
1 tsp ground cinnamon
1 (12 oz) can or bottle Mountain Dew

Directions:
1. Preheat the oven to 350. Grease a 9x13-inch baking dish.
2. Cut each apple into 8 wedges and set aside.
3. Separate the crescent roll dough into triangles. Roll each apple wedge in crescent roll dough starting at the smallest end. Pinch to seal and place in the baking dish.
4. Melt butter in a small saucepan and stir in the sugar and cinnamon. Pour over the apple dumplings. Pour Mountain Dew over the dumplings.
5. Bake for 35 to 45 minutes in the preheated oven, or until golden brown. Serve with ice cream or whipped cream with a dash of nutmeg.

Notes:
This recipe came from my son's godmother, Margie Lampel. I was an unbeliever when I first considered it. But several people insisted these were great, and they are pretty darned good.

Poached Pear in Puff Pastry

Ingredients:

4 small pears
4 cups water
2 cups sugar
1 cup honey
1 small lemon, halved
3 cinnamon sticks (3 inches)
6 to 8 whole cloves
1 vanilla bean or 1 tsp vanilla extract
1 sheet frozen puff pastry, thawed
1 large egg, lightly beaten

Directions:

1. Core pears from bottom, leaving stems intact. Peel pears; cut ¼ inch from the bottom of each to level if necessary.
2. In a large saucepan, combine the water, sugar, honey, lemon halves, cinnamon, and cloves.
3. Split vanilla bean and scrape seeds; add bean and seeds to sugar mixture. (If you are using vanilla extract, do not add it until just before you are ready to remove pears from the poaching liquid.) Bring to a boil. Reduce heat; place pears on their sides in saucepan and poach, uncovered, until almost tender, basting occasionally with poaching liquid, 16-20 minutes. Remove pears with a slotted spoon; cool slightly. Strain and reserve ½ cup poaching liquid; set aside.
4. Unfold puff pastry on a lightly floured surface. Cut into ½-inch-wide strips. Brush lightly with beaten egg. Starting at the bottom of a pear, wrap a pastry strip around pear, adding additional strips until pear is completely wrapped in pastry. Repeat with remaining pears and puff pastry.
5. Transfer to a parchment paper-lined 15x10x1-inch baking pan. Bake on a lower oven rack at 400 until golden brown, 25-30 minutes.
6. Meanwhile, bring reserved poaching liquid to a boil; cook until liquid is thick and syrupy, about 10 minutes. Place pears on dessert plates and drizzle with syrup. Serve warm.

Pretzel Salad

<u>Ingredients:</u>

1 (8 oz) pkg cream cheese, softened
½ cup white sugar
1 (8 oz) can crushed pineapple, drained
1 (8 oz) container frozen whipped topping
1 cup crushed pretzels
½ cup butter, melted
1/3 cup white sugar

<u>Directions:</u>

1. Mix cream cheese and ½ cup sugar together in a bowl; add pineapple and mix well. Fold whipped topping into pineapple mixture; refrigerate until chilled, about 30 minutes.
2. Preheat oven to 400. Line a baking sheet with a silicone mat or parchment paper.
3. Combine pretzels, butter, and 1/3 cup sugar in a bowl until evenly coated; spread onto the prepared baking sheet.
4. Bake in the preheated oven until pretzel mixture holds together like toffee, 6 to 8 minutes. Remove pan from oven and cool. Break pretzel mixture into pieces and mix into pineapple mixture just before serving.

<u>Notes:</u>

This recipe came from my cousin, Linda Dawson Cutler. Over the years, she has shared many, many of her recipes with me. Some came from her mother, the family baker, and some came from our grandmother and great grandmother.

It's hard to know if this is a side dish, salad, or dessert. I guess the message is to simply enjoy.

Raisin Pudding Cake with Caramel Sauce

<u>Ingredients:</u>

½ cup white sugar
1 cup flour
2 tsp baking powder
1 cup California raisins
½ cup milk
2 cups boiling water
1 cup packed brown sugar
3 tbsp butter

<u>Directions:</u>
1. Preheat oven to 350. Lightly grease a 2 quart, round, glass, casserole dish.
2. In a medium-size bowl, stir together white sugar, flour, and baking powder. Stir the raisins and milk into the flour mixture. Spread the thick lumpy batter into the greased dish, it evens out during the baking.
3. Bring 2 cups water to a boil in a one-quart saucepan and remove from heat. Stir 3 tbsp butter and one cup of brown sugar into the water until dissolved. Pour the watery mixture over the batter.
4. Bake on middle rack of oven for 30 minutes at 350 or until light brown on top with center of cake looking dry when poked with a fork. Handle carefully when removing from the oven because the caramel sauce will be hot and runny. Serve warm cake upside-down in bowls, topped with the caramel sauce. Serve with ice cream if desired.

<u>Notes:</u>
I found this recipe after having lost track of it for close to thirty years. It was like reconnecting with an old friend. As a teenager, I prepared family dinners because my mother worked outside the home. I made this for dessert at least once a week. Later in life, my mother lived with us and this was her favorite.

Raspberry Mocha Torte

Ingredients:

6 eggs, separated
¾ cup sugar, divided
1 cup all-purpose flour

Filling »»

1/3 cup sugar
3 eggs
2 egg yolks
1 tsp instant coffee granules
2 squares (1 oz each) semisweet chocolate, melted
1 tsp vanilla extract
1 cup butter, softened
½ cup raspberry jam

Directions:
1. In a large bowl, beat egg yolks and ½ cup sugar until thickened and lemon-colored. In a small bowl, beat the egg whites on medium speed until soft peaks form. Gradually beat in remaining sugar, 1 tbsp at a time, on high speed until stiff peaks form. Gently fold into egg yolk mixture alternately with the flour.
2. Divide the batter among three waxed paper-lined ungreased 9-inch round baking pans. Bake in preheated 350 oven for 15-20 minutes before removing from pans to wire racks. Remove waxed paper.
3. In a small saucepan, whisk the sugar, eggs, yolks, and coffee granules. Add chocolate. Cook over medium heat, stirring constantly, until mixture reaches 160 degrees and coats the back of a metal spoon. Remove from heat, stir in vanilla. Cool. In a small bowl, cream butter. Gradually beat in cooled chocolate mixture until smooth.
4. To assemble, place one cake layer on a serving plate, spread with half of the mocha filling. Top with another cake layer, spread with raspberry jam. Place remaining cake on top, spread with remaining mocha filling.
5. Refrigerate for 3 hours. Garnish with raspberries and mint if desired. Serves 10.

Rice Pudding

<u>Ingredients:</u>
>4¾ cups (or more) milk, divided (do not use low-fat or nonfat)
>2/3 cup medium or short grain white rice
>1/3 cup sugar
>2 tbsp (¼ stick) unsalted butter
>1 cinnamon stick
>pinch of salt
>1/3 cup golden raisins
>2 tsp vanilla extract
>2 large egg yolks

<u>Directions:</u>

1. Combine 4 cups milk, rice, sugar, butter, cinnamon stick, and salt in heavy large saucepan. Simmer over medium-low heat until rice is tender and mixture is creamy, stirring frequently, about 1 hour. Remove from heat. Discard cinnamon stick. Stir in raisins and vanilla.

2. Pour ¾ cup milk into heavy small saucepan. Bring to simmer. Whisk egg yolks in medium bowl to blend. Gradually whisk hot milk into beaten yolks. Return mixture to same saucepan. Stir over medium heat until thermometer registers 160, about 2 minutes (do not boil). Stir egg mixture into rice mixture.

3. Transfer rice pudding to large nonmetal bowl. Cover and chill until cold, about 30 minutes. Can be prepared 1 day ahead. Keep chilled.

4. Thin rice pudding with more milk, if desired. Spoon into bowls and serve.

<u>Notes:</u>

For Christmas one year, this was the dessert my grandson, Kohler, requested. Of course, it's one of the desserts I made. I don't think he really liked it. Maybe he preferred the baked, custardy type of rice pudding, but I prefer this.

Eggs, Cheese, and Brunch

"As everybody knows, there is only one infallible recipe for the perfect omelet: your own." **Elizabeth David**

"Pigs might make great pets, but they make better breakfast. I'll take one snuggled, with a side of scrambled eggs." **Jarod Kintz**

"An egg is always an adventure; the next one may be different." **Oscar Wilde**

"Cold omelet, like fish out of sea; does not improve with age." **Charlie Chan**

Baked Eggs on Puff Pastry

<u>Ingredients:</u>

1 sheet frozen puff pastry, thawed (½ of pkg)
non-stick cooking spray
1 small yellow onion, chopped
1 cup chopped bell pepper
1 cup asparagus pieces, (1-inch pieces)
2 tsp olive oil
1 tsp Italian seasoning
2 tbsp grated parmesan cheese
¼ tsp salt
2 tbsp shredded mozzarella cheese
4 eggs
¼ tsp crushed red pepper flakes
fresh oregano or basil as garnish

<u>Directions:</u>
1. Preheat oven to 400. Place thawed pastry sheet on lightly floured surface. Cut into 4 squares. Place squares on one side of large, shallow baking pan sprayed with non-stick cooking spray. Prick top of pastry squares all over with fork. Set aside.
2. Toss vegetables with oil. Sprinkle with Italian seasoning, parmesan cheese and salt; toss again to coat well. Spread vegetables on other side of pan next to the pastry squares. Bake 10 minutes or until puff pastry is lightly browned, and vegetables are partially cooked. Remove pan from oven.
3. Make an indentation with back of large spoon in center of each pastry square. Place vegetables evenly around indentations, making sure to cover edges of pastry squares. Sprinkle squares with mozzarella cheese. Break an egg into each indentation. Sprinkle with crushed red pepper.
4. Bake 10 to 15 minutes longer or until eggs are softly set.

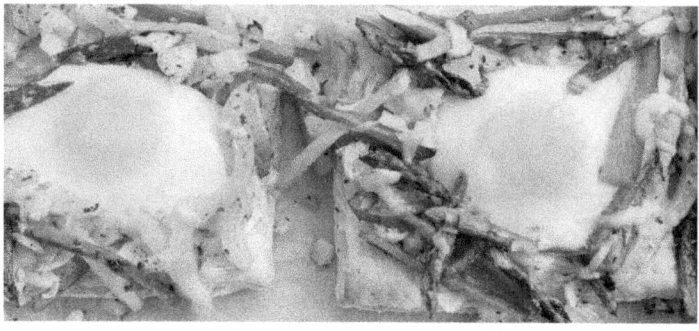

Baked Oatmeal

<u>Ingredients:</u>

½ cup oil
1 cup brown sugar
2 eggs
3 cups quick oats
1½ tsp baking powder
1 tsp salt
1 tsp cinnamon
1 cup milk

<u>Directions:</u>
1. Mix first three ingredients together. Add remaining ingredients and stir well.
2. Pour into buttered 9x5-inch pan (bread pan). Bake at 350 for 30 minutes. Serve warm with milk.

<u>Notes:</u>
This can be mixed together the night before and baked in the morning. The recipe came from my cousin Marilyn Albrecht Tackaberry. It may not be possible to make oatmeal over-the-top exciting, but it's good for you, and this is a convenient way to make it.

Breakfast Casserole

<u>Ingredients:</u>

24 oz bulk pork sausage
½ cup onion, chopped
1 cup red bell pepper, chopped
3 cups frozen hash brown potatoes
2 cups sharp cheddar cheese, grated, divided
1 cup Bisquick
2 cups milk
¼ tsp salt
¼ tsp pepper
4 large eggs

<u>Directions:</u>
1. Preheat oven to 400. Spray a 9x13-inch baking dish with nonstick cooking spray.
2. In a 12-inch skillet, cook sausage, onions, and red bell pepper over medium heat, stirring occasionally, until sausage is cooked through and there is no longer any pink. Drain any excess fat.
3. Add sausage mixture, hash brown potatoes, and 1½ cups cheese to the prepared baking dish and stir until ingredients are evenly combined.
4. In a medium mixing bowl, whisk together eggs, milk, salt, and pepper. Whisk in Bisquick and pour over sausage mixture.
5. Bake in preheated oven 40-45 minutes or until it is set in the center and a knife inserted into the center of casserole comes out clean.
6. Sprinkle with remaining cheese and bake until cheese is melted, about 5 minutes. Cool for 10 minutes before cutting. Serve six.

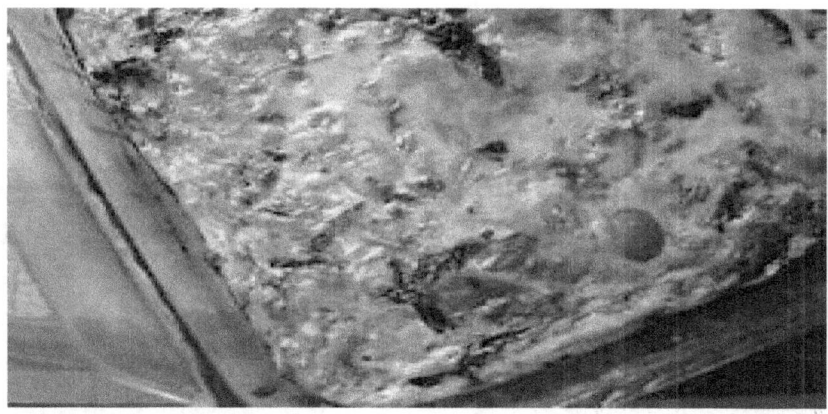

Breakfast Strudel

<u>Ingredients:</u>

1 box puff pastry
2 tbsp butter
1 cup frozen cubed hash brown potatoes
1 cup red, green or yellow bell pepper, seeded and diced
½ cup onion, diced
1 cup bacon, fried, drained, and crumbled
11 eggs
2 tbsp minced fresh chives
4 oz cream cheese, softened
salt and pepper to taste
1 egg + 1 tbsp water
Cheddar, Monterrey Jack, or Swiss cheese to sprinkle over top

<u>Directions:</u>

1. Preheat oven to 375. Thaw pastry according to package directions.
2. Melt butter in a large nonstick skillet over medium-high heat. Add potatoes and sauté five minutes. Stir in onion and pepper, sauté three minutes, then add bacon.
3. Whisk eggs and chives together. Add them to the pan and scramble just until set. Season with salt and pepper to taste; take off heat, stir in cream cheese until blended. Refrigerate eggs while working with the pastry.
4. Unfold a pastry sheet on a work surface that's been lightly dusted with flour. Roll pastry lengthwise to 12x10 inches, then transfer to a piece of parchment paper cut to fit and placed on a baking sheet. Trim pastry (see next page), fill with half the egg mixture, and braid. Repeat the process with remaining pastry and egg filling on a second baking sheet lined with parchment.
5. Combine the remaining egg and water; brush over top of strudels. Sprinkle with cheese and bake 30 minutes or until golden. Let cool five minutes before slicing. Makes two strudels. (Additional recipe diagrams and notes on next page.)

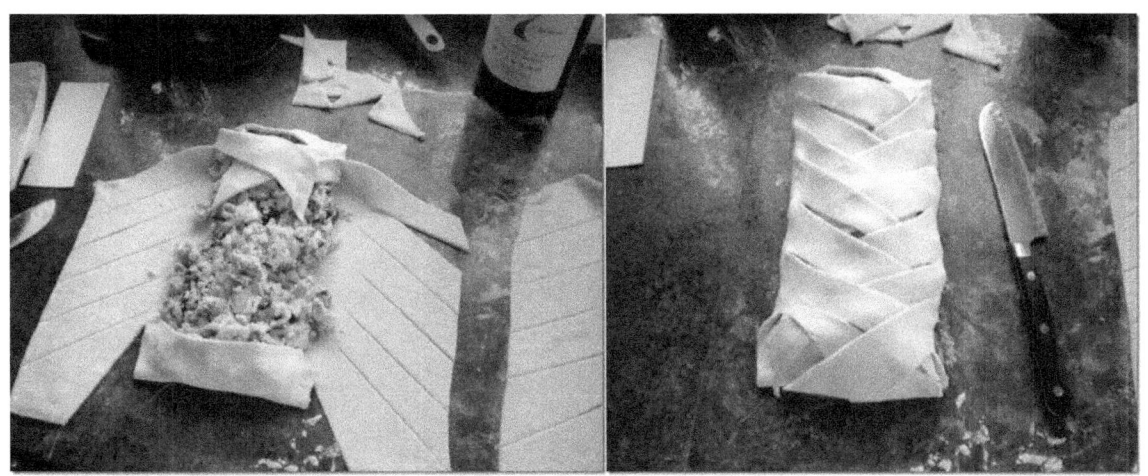

Notes:

This is an easy recipe to alter to suit your taste. I prefer crisp, crumbled bacon, but sausage or ham work equally well. If you don't like peppers, add well-dried spinach or mushrooms, or even canned, and well-dried artichokes. If hash browned potatoes aren't your thing, replace them with any of the mentioned veggies.

These bake up and look lovely at a brunch, and they aren't all that difficult. I often make the egg mixture the day before since it's supposed to be refrigerated while you are working with the pastry anyway. Just don't overcook the eggs. They should be set, but soft. Otherwise they'll be dry in the finished strudel. Twelve servings.

Cheesy Hash Brown Potato Casserole

Ingredients:

32 oz frozen shredded hash brown potatoes
2 cups sour cream
1 can cream of mushroom soup
2 cups sharp cheddar cheese
1 cup chopped onion
½ stick butter or margarine, melted
salt and pepper to taste

Directions:
1. Mix all ingredients together in large baking dish.
2. Bake at 375 for one hour. Casserole should be bubbling and slightly brown on top.

Notes:
I got this recipe from a co-worker and friend, Rose Houk, when we both worked for the Attorney General. It became one of my granddaughters' favorites when they visited our condo on Lake Huron.
Several family members have their own version of this recipe because it lends itself to changes. You can add ham or crisp-fried, crumbled bacon. You can add green, red, yellow, or orange peppers cut into small pieces and they'll add a bit of color. You can use cream of chicken soup instead of cream of mushroom, and you can choose a different type of shredded cheese. I like to mix ¾ cup of crushed cornflakes with a tbsp of melted butter and sprinkle over the top before baking.

Crustless Spinach and Mushroom Quiche
(Slow Cooker)

Ingredients:
- 1 (10 oz) pkg frozen, chopped spinach, thawed and well-drained
- 4 slices bacon
- 1 tbsp olive oil
- 2 cups coarsely chopped Portobello mushrooms
- ½ cup chopped red sweet pepper (1 small)
- 1½ cups (6 oz) shredded Gruyere or Swiss cheese
- 8 eggs
- 2 cups half and half
- 2 tbsp snipped fresh chives
- ½ tsp salt
- 1/3 tsp ground black pepper
- ½ cup packaged biscuit mix (like Bisquick)

Directions:

1. Spray a 3½ or 4-quart slow cooker with cooking spray. Using paper towels, press spinach to remove as much liquid as possible; set aside.

2. In a medium skillet, cook bacon until crisp; drain, crumble, and set aside. Discard drippings. In same skillet, heat oil over medium heat. Add mushrooms and sweet pepper, cook or stir until tender. Remove from heat and stir in spinach and cheese.

3. In a medium bowl, combine eggs, half and half, chives, salt, and pepper. Stir egg mixture into spinach mixture in skillet. Gently fold in biscuit mix. Pour egg mixture into prepared slow cooker. Sprinkle with bacon.

4. Cover and cook on low-heat setting for 4-5 hours or on high-heat setting for 2 to 2½ hours or until a knife inserted into center comes out clean. Turn off cooker and cool for 15-30 minutes before serving.

Note:
This recipe has timing versatility that makes it ideal for brunch.

Everything Glazed Bacon

Ingredients:

1 pound thick cut bacon
apricot preserves

Everything Seasoning »»

2½ tbsp poppy seeds
2 tbsp dried minced garlic
1½ tbsp dried minced onion
2½ tbsp sesame seeds

Directions:

1. Preheat oven to 400. Arrange bacon on rimmed cookie sheet lined with parchment. Bake 5 minutes, turn bacon, brush with apricot preserves, bake 5 additional minutes. Remove baking sheet, turn bacon again, and brush with apricot preserves. Return baking sheet to oven bake 4 more minutes or until crisp. Remove from oven.

2. Make Everything Seasoning by mixing all ingredients in small bowl. Sprinkle over bacon while bacon is still hot.

Note:
This is good as a side dish at a brunch, or chopped into small pieces for salads.

Festive French Toast

Ingredients:

3-4 Granny Smith apples, peeled, cored, thinly sliced
1 cup packed brown sugar
½ cup butter, melted
3¼ tsp cinnamon (divided)
½ cup dried cranberries
½ cup raisins
1 loaf of cinnamon swirl bread, cut into ¾-inch slices
6-7 large eggs (6 for drier toast)
1 2/3 cups milk
1 tbsp vanilla
confectioners' sugar

Directions:
1. In a large bowl, add sliced apples, brown sugar, butter, 1 tsp cinnamon, cranberries, and raisins; toss to coat apples well.
2. Mix together eggs, milk, vanilla, and remaining cinnamon until well-blended. Pour mixture over bread and apples, soaking bread completely. Cover and refrigerate 4-24 hours.
3. Preheat oven to 375. Cover with foil and bake for 40 minutes; uncover and bake 5 minutes or until golden. Remove from oven and let stand for 5 minutes.
4. Serve warm, fruit side up. Serve plain, with light syrup, or sprinkled with confectioners' sugar. Makes 12 servings.

Italian Brunch Torte

<u>Ingredients:</u>

2 tubes (8 oz each) refrigerated crescent rolls, divided
1 tsp olive oil
1 pkg (6 oz) fresh baby spinach
1 cup sliced fresh mushrooms
7 large eggs
1 cup grated parmesan cheese
2 tsp Italian seasoning
1/8 tsp pepper
½ pound thinly sliced deli ham
½ pound thinly sliced hard salami
½ pound sliced provolone cheese
2 jars (12 oz each) roasted sweet red peppers, drained, sliced and patted dry

<u>Directions:</u>

1. Preheat oven to 350. Place a greased 9-inch springform pan on a double thickness of heavy-duty foil (about 18 in. square). Securely wrap foil around pan. Unroll one tube of crescent dough and separate into triangles. Press onto bottom of prepared pan to form a crust, sealing seams well. Bake 10-15 minutes or until set.

2. Meanwhile, in a large skillet, heat oil over medium-high heat. Add spinach and mushrooms; cook and stir until mushrooms are tender. Drain on several layers of paper towels, blotting well. In a large bowl, whisk six eggs, parmesan cheese, Italian seasoning, and pepper.

3. Layer crust with half of each of the following: ham, salami, provolone cheese, red peppers and spinach mixture. Pour half of the egg mixture over top. Repeat layers; top with remaining egg mixture.

4. On a work surface, unroll and separate remaining crescent dough into triangles. Press together to form a circle and seal seams; place over filling. Whisk remaining egg; brush over dough.

5. Bake, uncovered, 1 to 1¼ hours (or until a thermometer reads 160), covering loosely with foil if needed to prevent overbrowning. Carefully loosen sides from pan with a knife; remove sides from pan. Let stand 20 minutes. Yield: 12 servings.

Joe's Special: A San Francisco Tradition

Ingredients:

1 pound ground beef, preferably ground sirloin
2 tbsp vegetable oil
1 medium-size onion, peeled and chopped
½ tsp marjoram or basil or your choice of spices
salt and pepper to taste
10 oz fresh spinach, washed, dried, and chopped
4 eggs, well beaten

Directions:
1. In a large skillet, heat the oil and sauté the onion until it is translucent and soft.
2. Add meat and seasonings and stir to break up meat while it cooks. Drain off excess fat.
3. Stir in spinach and cook until it wilts.
4. Stir in the beaten eggs, stirring and cooking until eggs are set. Makes 2 large servings or 4 smaller ones.

Notes:
This recipe was brought to my attention by a friend, Fred Kosanke, who I hadn't seen since high school. Fred asked if I'd ever had Joe's Special in San Francisco. The first Joe's Special scramble was served in the 1920s at Original Joe's in the Tenderloin District. After a fire, Original Joe's relocated to the North Beach neighborhood, and San Francisco mayor Ed Lee issued a proclamation calling the Joe's Special "famous." Today, many variations are offered locally, and they always include eggs, spinach, onion, and ground beef. The dish is served with ketchup on the side. The basic recipe is limited only by your imagination. Add Tabasco, Worcestershire, sautéed mushrooms, garlic, cumin, chili powder, or other spices of your choice. One recipe even calls for ¼ cup of red wine. Serve Joe's Special with San Francisco sour dough toast on the side, shut your eyes, and imagine you can see the Golden Gate Bridge.

Make-Ahead Eggs Benedict

Ingredients:

4 English Muffins, split and toasted
16 thin slices Canadian bacon
8 eggs
¼ cup butter
¼ cup all-purpose flour
1/8 tsp ground nutmeg
1 tsp paprika
1/8 tsp pepper
2 cups milk
2 cups shredded Swiss cheese
½ cup dry white wine
½ cup crushed cornflakes
1 tbsp butter or margarine

Directions:
1. In 13x9x2-inch baking dish arrange toasted muffins, cut side up. Place 2 thin bacon slices on each muffin half.
2. Half fill 10-inch skillet with water and bring to a boil. Break one egg into a small ramekin or other dish. Carefully slide egg into water. Repeat with the other eggs. Simmer, uncovered 3 minutes or until just set. Remove eggs with a slotted spoon. Repeat with remaining eggs. Place one egg on top of each muffin stack; set aside.
3. Sauce: In medium saucepan melt ¼ cup butter. Stir in flour, paprika, nutmeg, and pepper. Add milk all at once. Cook and stir until thickened and bubbly. Stir in cheese until melted. Stir in wine. Carefully spoon sauce over muffin/egg stacks.
4. Combine cornflakes and 1 tbsp butter; sprinkle over stacks.
5. Cover and chill overnight. In the morning, bake in a 375-degree oven, uncovered, for 20-25 minutes or until heated through. Makes 8 servings.

Notes:
I was skeptical of a "do-ahead" eggs benedict, but was pleasantly surprised. I had these at a brunch and even after they had set out for a couple hours, a guest took home the leftovers, and she insisted they were good reheated, and asked for the recipe.

Make-Ahead Savory Breakfast Bread Pudding

<u>Ingredients:</u>

6 oz thick-cut smoked bacon, diced, fried, and drained
1¼ cups chopped yellow onion
¾ cup chopped mixed red and green bell peppers
2¾ tsp Essence Spice (recipe on next page.)
4 large croissants (about 12 oz total), cut into 1-inch pieces
2 green onions, minced (about ¼ cup
6 oz grated medium yellow cheddar
7 large eggs
1¼ cups milk
¾ cup heavy cream
½ tsp salt, plus a pinch

<u>Directions:</u>

1. In a medium skillet cook the bacon over medium-high heat until crisp and the fat has rendered, 4-6 minutes. Remove bacon using a slotted spoon and transfer to a paper towel-lined plate to drain. Remove all but 1½ tbsp of the bacon drippings from the pan and reserve the drippings on the side. To the remaining drippings in the pan add onion, peppers, and ¾ tsp of the Essence and cook, stirring often, until soft and lightly caramelized, 4 to 6 minutes. Return the bacon to the pan and stir to combine.

2. Using a bit of the reserved bacon drippings, lightly grease a 1½ quart oval gratin dish, or other shallow baking dish of similar size. Add half of the croissant pieces to the dish, then spoon half of the vegetable-bacon mixture over the bread. Sprinkle with half of the green onions, and then top with half of the cheese. Repeat to form a second layer.

3. In a mixing bowl combine the eggs, milk, heavy cream, salt, and remaining 2 tsp of Essence and whisk to combine. Pour the egg-milk mixture slowly over the casserole so that it is evenly distributed. Cover with plastic wrap and refrigerate for at least 4 hours or up to overnight.

4. Preheat the oven to 325. Remove breakfast casserole from the refrigerator while the over is preheating. Remove the plastic wrap from the casserole and then cover with a piece of buttered aluminum foil, buttered side down. Bake for 30 minutes. Remove casserole from oven and remove the foil, then continue to bake, uncovered until casserole is puffed, set in the middle, and golden brown on top, (Recipe continued on next page.)

30-35 minutes longer. Remove from the oven and allow to sit for 10-15 minutes before serving.

Essence Spice:

<u>Ingredients:</u>

> 1 tbsp paprika
> 1 tbsp sea salt
> 1 tbsp garlic powder
> 1½ tsp onion powder
> 1½ tsp dried oregano
> 1½ tsp dried thyme
> 1 tsp freshly ground black pepper
> 1 tsp cayenne pepper (if you like it spicy, use more)

<u>Directions:</u>
In a small bowl, add all of the above ingredients and mix well to combine. Makes 1/3 cup which is more than needed for this recipe, but it is a good spice on meats or chicken. Keep in small, tightly-sealed glass jar.

Mini Breakfast Quiches with Potato Crust

<u>Ingredients:</u>
1 box (4.5 oz) Betty Crocker Seasoned Skillets traditional recipe potatoes
water and vegetable oil as called for on potato box
½ cup crumbled cooked bacon
½ cup shredded Swiss cheese (2 oz)
3 eggs
1 cup whipping (heavy) cream
cooking spray

<u>Directions:</u>
1. Heat oven to 350. Spray 12 regular-size muffin cups with cooking spray. Make sure you spray each cup thoroughly to avoid trouble removing from pan.
2. Make potatoes as directed on box. Divide potato mixture evenly among muffin cups, pressing in bottom and up side of each cup to form crust. Sprinkle bacon and cheese evenly in cups. In medium bowl, beat eggs and cream. Pour filling evenly in cups, about ¼ cup each.
3. Bake 25 to 30 minutes or until knife inserted in center comes out clean. Let stand 10 minutes before serving.

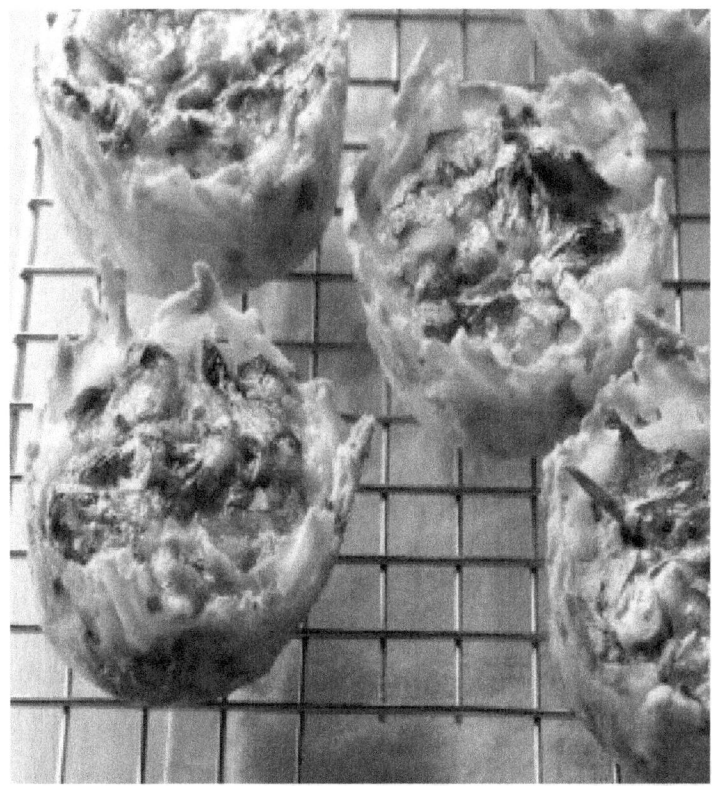

<u>Notes:</u>
My friend, Jan Kinzel, gave me a very similar recipe. I had a little problem getting the mini-quiches out of the pan. The next time I looked for the recipe, I couldn't find it. I went online and found this similar version except I remember Jan's used egg beaters.

This is a recipe that can be varied. A vegetarian version with spinach (dried well) or sautéed onions and mushrooms is awesome. Let your imagination or taste run wild.

Spicy Southwest Bacon-Sausage Bake

Ingredients:

1 pound bulk pork sausage
1 pound bacon, fried crisp, drained, and crumbled
1¼ cups shredded cheddar cheese
1¼ cups shredded Monterey Jack cheese
½ cup finely chopped green onion
1 (4 oz) can chopped green chili peppers
1 tbsp minced jalapeno pepper
12 eggs
1 tsp chili powder
1 tsp cumin
½ tsp salt
½ tsp pepper

Directions:

1. Preheat oven to 375. Lightly grease a 9x13-inch baking dish.
2. Place sausage in a large, deep skillet. Cook over medium-high heat until evenly browned. Drain and crumble. Cook and crumble bacon. Spread crumbled sausage and bacon onto bottom of baking dish. Sprinkle with cheeses, onion including some of the green, chili peppers, and jalapeno pepper.
3. In a medium bowl, mix eggs and chili powder, cumin, garlic powder, salt, and pepper. Pour over contents of baking dish.
4. Bake in preheated oven for 18-22 minutes or until a knife inserted into the center comes out clean. Cool for 10 minutes, then cut into squares. Serve with hot sauce.

Turkey Breakfast Pizza

<u>Ingredients:</u>

1 pound turkey breakfast sausage
1 pkg (8 oz) refrigerated crescent rolls
1 cup frozen hash brown potatoes, defrosted
1 cup cheddar cheese, shredded
5 medium eggs, beaten
¼ cup milk
½ tsp salt
¼ tsp pepper
2 tbsp parmesan cheese, grated

<u>Directions:</u>

1. Preheat oven to 375. In medium-sized skillet, over medium heat, sauté sausage 6 to 10 minutes or until no longer pink.
2. Unroll crescent rolls and separate dough. In 12-inch round pizza pan arrange crescent rolls with points toward the center. Press rolls over bottom and up the sides of the pan to form pizza crust, sealing perforations.
3. Top pizza crust with sausage, potatoes, and cheddar cheese.
4. In small bowl combine eggs, milk, salt, and pepper. Pour egg mixture very slowly over turkey and potato mixture. Top with parmesan cheese.
5. Bake 25 minutes. Slice into 8 wedges and serve hot.

Italian, Mexican, Asian, and other Ethnic Dishes

(Additional ethnic dishes are included in other sections as appetizers, brunch dishes, main dishes, salads, or soups.)

"My mind thinks thin, but my heart says I love a shrimp enchilada with a big side of refried beans. I believe that on a bad day, pasta or Mexican food makes the world okay."

"Life is too short, and I'm Italian. I'd much rather eat pasta and drink wine than be a size 0." **Sophia Bush**

"I love Chinese food. My favorite dish is number 27." **Clement Attlee**

Afghani Bolani (Potato and Green Onion Stuffed Flatbread)

Ingredients:
Dough »» (makes 6 Bolani)
>3 cups flour, plus extra for rolling
>1 tsp salt
>3 tbsp olive oil, divided
>¾ cup or more water

Potato Filling »»
>1 pound potatoes, peeled and boiled until fork tender
>1 packed cup roughly chopped cilantro (leaves and stems)
>½ packed cup roughly chopped green onions or leeks
>1 jalapeño, minced (optional)
>2 tbsp olive oil
>salt and freshly ground black pepper (be generous with salt and pepper)

Yogurt Sauce »»
>1 cup Greek yogurt
>1 clove garlic, minced
>½ tsp ground coriander seed (freshly ground is best)
>1 tsp dried dill
>salt

Directions:
Dough »»
1. Whisk the flour, salt, and 1 tbsp olive oil together in a large bowl. Set the remaining 2 tbsp of olive oil aside for brushing on the Bolani later.
2. Use a fork or your fingers to mix in ¾ cup of water. Begin to knead the dough, adding additional water, a splash at a time as needed, until it comes together. If your dough becomes sticky, add a dusting of flour. Continue kneading for about 8 minutes, until the dough is smooth and soft.
3. Cover with a lightly dampened towel, and set aside to rest for 20 minutes

Potato Filling »»
1. Lightly mash the potatoes so they are mostly smooth, with a few small chunks.
2. Using a food processor or a knife, pulse or finely mince the cilantro, green onions, and jalapeño together.

(Recipe continued on next page.)

3. In a large bowl, combine the cilantro mix with the potatoes, 2 tbsp olive oil, and salt and pepper to taste.

Putting the Bolani Together »»

1. Divide the dough into 6 equal pieces.
2. On a floured work surface, roll each piece into a thin round about 8 inches across. Keep covered under a slightly damp towel until ready to stuff. If you stack your dough rounds while working, be sure they are well dusted with flour, or they may stick together.
3. Spread a generous 1/3 cup of filling on half of each round, leaving a border along the edge for sealing. Fold the dough over, making a half-circle shape, and gently press the surface to remove any big air pockets. Press the edges together to seal. Set aside under a slightly damp towel until ready to fry.
4. Heat a 10-inch skillet or a griddle over medium heat. Generously brush one side of one Bolani with some of the reserved olive oil. Place oil side down on the hot skillet, and fry until golden brown. Brush the second (now top) side with oil, flip, and cook until golden brown and delicious. Set aside, lightly covered with foil or a towel to keep warm, and repeat with the remaining Bolani.
5. Serve hot, with yogurt sauce on the side. (Mix together all sauce ingredients.)

Notes:

To save time, you can make and refrigerate all the parts ahead of time. Just pull your dough out of the fridge to rest at room temperature for about 45 minutes before rolling it out and assembling.

These make a great appetizer if you use a pizza cutter and cut them each into three pieces. They can also be used whole as a side dish.

I have ordered Bolanis when I ate at the Oasis Mediterranean Grille in Pleasanton with our friends Susan and Joe Jurkiewicz, Gail Ng, and Violet Moore. They never disappoint me or my friends.

Asian Pork and Noodles

<u>Ingredients:</u>

2 (1 pound each) pork tenderloins
½ cup low-sodium soy sauce, divided
2 tbsp hoisin sauce
2 tbsp tomato sauce
2 tsp sugar
2 tsp grated peeled fresh ginger
4 garlic cloves, minced
6 tbsp seasoned rice vinegar
2 tsp dark sesame oil
8 cups hot cooked Chinese-style noodles (about 16 oz uncooked)
1 cup matchstick-cut carrots
¾ cup diagonally sliced green onions
¼ cup fresh cilantro leaves
1/3 cup chopped unsalted, dry-roasted cashews
additional fresh cilantro and lime wedges for garnish

<u>Directions:</u>

1. Place tenderloins in a 5-quart electric slow cooker. Combine 1 tbsp soy sauce and next 5 ingredients (through garlic); drizzle over tenderloins. Cover and cook on low for 3½ hours. Remove pork from slow cooker and place in a large bowl, reserving cooking liquid in slow cooker. Let pork stand 10 minutes.
2. Strain cooking liquid through sieve into a bowl. Cover and keep warm. Shred pork with 2 forks.
3. Return cooking liquid to slow cooker; stir in remaining 3 tbsp soy sauce, vinegar, and sesame oil. Cover and cook on high for 10 minutes. Turn slow cooker off. Add pork, cooked noodles, and next three ingredients (through cilantro leaves), tossing to coat. Spoon noodle mixture into bowls; sprinkle with nuts and chopped cilantro. Serve with lime wedges.

Crabmeat Quesadillas

Ingredients:

¾ cup (3 oz) shredded cheddar cheese
¾ cup (3 oz) shredded mozzarella cheese
¾ cup mayonnaise
1/3 cup sour cream
2 tbsp green onions, sliced
8 oz cooked crabmeat
2 tbsp mild green chilies, chopped and drained
10 (8-inch) flour tortillas
2 tbsp butter

Directions:
1. Heat oven to 375. In large bowl stir together all ingredients except tortillas and butter. Brush one side of tortillas with butter and place, buttered side down on cookie sheet. Spread cheese mixture evenly over one side of each tortilla and fold uncovered side over filled side and press together.
2. Bake for 10-15 minutes or until heated through. Cut each quesadilla into 3 wedges.
3. Serve with desired toppings: salsa, sour cream, guacamole.

Note:
I've used imitation crabmeat and it works, not quite as tasty, but if you can't get fresh crabmeat, it will still be delicious.

Gnocchi with Wild Mushrooms and Basil Cream

Ingredients:

1½ to 2 pounds frozen gnocchi (unless you want to make from scratch)
6 oz oyster mushrooms
6 oz baby Bella mushrooms, dark gills scraped off
4 oz shitake mushrooms, stems removed
1 tbsp olive oil and 1 tbsp butter
2 cloves garlic, peeled, chopped
½ pound frozen pearl onions or 1 medium sliced sweet onion
1/3 cup dry white wine
½ cup half and half, mixed with 1 tsp cornstarch
salt and pepper to taste
1 cup frozen peas
1 cup chiffonade of basil
½ cup shredded Italian blend cheese or parmesan cheese

Directions:

1. In a large pot of salted boiling water, cook the gnocchi according to package directions. Reserve 1 cup of the cooking water. Transfer gnocchi to a serving platter. Keep warm.
2. Rinse mushrooms and slice into ¼-inch thick pieces. Set aside. Heat olive oil and butter in a large skillet over medium-high heat. Add garlic and sauté 1 minute; do not brown.
3. Add onions and continue to sauté until they start to become tender and turn golden in color. Add the mushrooms. Cook until they release their juices and are tender, about 8 minutes.
4. Remove ingredients from the skillet and toss with the gnocchi.
5. To make the basil cream: In the now empty skillet, over medium heat, add the white wine. Deglaze by scraping up any browned bits on the bottom. Stir in the chicken broth and cook 1 minute. Slowly whisk in the half and half/cornstarch mixture over medium heat. Don't have the heat too high or it will curdle.
6. Season the sauce with salt and pepper to taste, and stir in the peas; cook 1 minute. Stir in the basil and cheese and heat through until the cheese melts. Pour the sauce over the gnocchi mixture and serve.

Grilled Asian Flank Steak

Ingredients:

¼ cup soy sauce
3 tbsp teriyaki sauce
3 tbsp rice wine vinegar
1 tbsp Asian garlic-chili sauce
1 tbsp minced fresh ginger
2 green onions, chopped
1½ pounds flank steak

Directions:
1. Mix all ingredients except steak in a large zip-top plastic freezer bag or shallow dish. Add steak and turn to coat. Seal or cover and chill 4 hours, turning occasionally.
2. Remove steak from marinade and discard marinade. Grill flank steak, covered with grill lid, over medium-high heat, 5-7 minutes on each side or to desired degree of doneness.
3. Let stand 10 minutes before slicing. Cut diagonally across the grain into thin strips. Makes 4-6 servings.

Note:
Good served with basmati rice and salad.

Hungarian Chicken Paprikash with Dumplings

<u>Ingredients:</u>

3 tbsp vegetable oil
1 tsp kosher salt and pepper to taste
1 Vidalia onion, chopped
2 cloves garlic, peeled and halved
1 large mixed pkg (about 10 pieces) boneless, skinless breast and thighs of chicken
2 tbsp sweet paprika
3 chicken bouillon cubes
3 cups water

1 pint sour cream
1 cup water
4 tbsp flour (or more to thicken if you like)
3 tsp Lawry's seasoning salt

4 eggs
3 cups water
6 cups all-purpose flour
1 tsp salt
parsley

<u>Directions:</u>

1. In 6-quart slow cooker, stir together onions, ½ tsp salt, and paprika. Spread mixture evenly over bottom of insert. Rub garlic halves over chicken, then sprinkle chicken with pepper and remaining ½ tsp salt.
2. In medium saucepan over moderately high heat, heat butter and oil until hot but not smoking. Add chicken pieces and brown, turning occasionally, until golden, about 6 minutes. Transfer to slow cooker (do not clean pan), layering chicken on top of onion mixture.
3. In same saucepan over high heat, bring stock to simmer, scraping up browned bits from bottom of pan. Pour over chicken in slow cooker, cover, and cook on low until chicken is tender, 5 to 6 hours.
4. When chicken is a half hour from being done, whip sour cream, water, and flour until very smooth. Add slowly to slow cooker and continue cooking until sour cream mixture is warmed through with chicken.

(Recipe continued on next page.)

5. After adding sour cream mixture to chicken, prepare dumplings.

<u>Directions for Dumplings:</u>

1. Bring a large pot of water to a boil. With a mixer combine eggs, water, flour, and salt. Mix together to form a soupy dough. Dip a tablespoon into the boiling water (so dough won't stick), then use it to take a scoop of dough and drop the into the boiling water. Repeat with remaining dough, one scoop full at a time.

2. Cook for about 7 minutes. The dough will rise to the surface when the dumplings are done. Drain and rinse. Place on large serving platter, cover with chicken and sour cream, and sprinkle with parsley.

<u>Notes:</u>
Chicken Paprikash is my granddaughter Lauren's favorite Hungarian dish. She loved it when she traveled to Hungary with her grandma, Marilyn Royce. So, when Lauren's sister, Kaelin, spent the summer with us, we tried this recipe. It may not be quite as good as the tasty dishes Lauren and Grandma Marilyn were served, but we decided it was a keeper.

Indian Chicken Stew

<u>Ingredients:</u>
- 2 pounds skinless, boneless chicken thighs, cut into 1-inch pieces
- 1 medium onion, chopped
- 3 cloves garlic, minced
- 5 tsp curry powder
- 2 tsp ground ginger
- ½ tsp salt
- ¼ tsp ground black pepper and/or cayenne pepper
- 2 (15 oz) cans garbanzo beans (chickpeas), rinsed and drained
- 2 (14.5 oz) cans diced tomatoes, undrained
- 1 cup chicken broth
- 1 bay leaf
- 2 tbsp lime juice
- 1 (9 oz) pkg fresh spinach
- hot cooked rice

<u>Directions:</u>
1. Lightly coat a 6-quart slow cooker with nonstick cooking spray or oil. Add chicken, onion, and garlic to the slow cooker. Add curry powder, ginger, salt, and pepper to the slow cooker. Toss to coat. Stir in drained beans, undrained tomatoes, broth, and bay leaf. Cover and cook on high setting 4 to 5 hours or low heat setting 8 to 10 hours.
2. Stir lime juice into cooked stew. Stir spinach leaves into stew and let stand 2 to 3 minutes to wilt. Serve with rice. Makes 8 servings

Lasagna with Four Cheeses and Meat Sauce

<u>Ingredients:</u>

2 cups fresh ricotta
8 oz grated provolone
8 oz grated mozzarella
8 oz grated Romano
1 egg
¼ cup milk
1 tbsp chiffonade of fresh basil
1 tbsp chopped garlic
salt and freshly ground black pepper
1 recipe of Meat Sauce, recipe follows
½ pound grated Parmigiano-Reggiano cheese
1 pkg dry lasagna noodles*

<u>Meat Sauce</u> »»

2 tbsp olive oil
1/3 pound ground beef
1/3 pound ground veal
1/3 pound ground pork
salt and freshly ground black pepper
2 cups finely chopped onions
½ cup finely chopped celery
½ cup finely chopped carrot
2 tbsp chopped garlic
(Recipe continued on next page.)

2 (28-ounce) can peeled, seeded and chopped tomatoes
1 small can tomato paste
4 cups beef stock or water
2 sprigs of fresh thyme
2 bay leaves
2 tsp dried oregano
2 tsp dried basil
pinch of crushed red pepper
2 oz Parmigiano-Reggiano cheese

Directions:
1. Make meat sauce: In a large nonreactive saucepan, over medium heat, add the oil. In a mixing bowl, combine the meat. Season with salt and pepper and mix well. When the oil is hot, add the meat and brown for 4 to 6 minutes. Add the onions, celery, and carrots. Season with salt and pepper. Cook for 4 to 5 minutes or until the vegetables are soft. Add the garlic and tomatoes. Season with salt and pepper. Continue to cook for 2 to 3 minutes.
2. Whisk the tomato paste with the stock and add to the tomatoes. Add the thyme, bay leaves, oregano, basil, and red pepper. Mix well. Bring the liquid to a boil, reduce the heat to medium and simmer for about 2 hours. Stir occasionally and add more liquid if needed. During the last 30 minutes of cooking, season with salt and pepper and stir in the Parmigiano-Reggiano.
3. Preheat oven to 350. In a mixing bowl, combine the ricotta, provolone, Mozzarella, Romano, egg, milk, basil, and garlic. Mix well. Season with salt and pepper.
4. To assemble, spread 2½ cups of the meat sauce on the bottom of a deep-dish lasagna pan. Sprinkle ¼ of the grated cheese over the sauce. Cover the cheese with ¼ of the dry noodles. * Spread ¼ of the cheese filling evenly over the noodles. Repeat the above process with the remaining ingredients, topping the lasagna with the remaining sauce. Place in the oven and bake until bubbly and golden, about 45 minutes to 1 hour. Remove from the oven and cool for 10 minutes before serving. Slice and serve.

Notes:
*I soak lasagna noodles for ten minutes in hot water. I've tried cooking them (too mushy), using them dry (sometimes too hard), and found that I like them best presoaked but not cooked. I usually double the recipe and freeze half. Also, I didn't like the way the provolone melted so I skip it and double the mozzarella.

Pesto

Ingredients:

2 cups fresh basil leaves, packed
3 garlic cloves, minced (about 3 tsp)
1/3 cup pine nuts (I toast mine slightly first)
½ cup extra virgin olive oil
¼ tsp salt, more to taste
1/8 tsp freshly ground black pepper, more to taste
½ cup freshly grated Romano or parmesan-Reggiano cheese (about 2 oz)

Directions:

1. Combine the basil, garlic, and pine nuts in a food processor and pulse until coarsely chopped. Add ½ cup of the oil and process until fully incorporated and smooth. Season with salt and pepper.
2. Add cheese and mix well.

Notes:

Can be frozen for up to three months, but if you freeze it, it's better to add cheese after removing from freezer and thawed for use. You'll want to add a bit more olive oil as well.

Ideas for Pesto use:

Pesto Cream Tortellini: Simmer 1 cup *heavy cream* with ¼ cup grated *parmesan*. Toss with 12 oz cooked *tortellini* and 2 cups steamed *broccoli*.

Pesto Quesadilla Sauce: Sauté ½ cup each sliced *scallions*, *mushrooms*, and *zucchini* with some pesto, add minced *jalapenos*, and *cilantro*. Brown a flour *tortilla* in a skillet with butter; top with the vegetables, shredded *muenster* and another tortilla. Flip and cook on other side.

Pesto Potato Salad: Cook 2 pounds quartered *new potatoes* in salted boiling water until tender, 10-15 minutes. Drain and cool slightly. Whisk 1 cup *mayonnaise*, 3 tbsp pesto, and the juice of 1 *lemon*. Toss with the potatoes and 2 cups diced *celery*.

Pesto Egg Salad: Whisk ¼ *mayonnaise*, 2 tbsp each pesto and *olive oil*, and 1 tbsp *lemon juice*. Fold in 8 chopped hard-boiled *eggs*, 1 cup chopped *celery*, and 2 tbsp minced *red onion*.

Pesto-Tomato Soup: Cook ¾ cup chopped *shallots* and some *fresh thyme* in a pot with *butter*. Add 1 large can *crushed tomatoes*, 1½ cups water, and ½ cup *cream*. Simmer 20 minutes. Puree, then stir in 3 tbsp pesto.

Quesadillas with Brie, Avocado, Eggs, & Fruit Salsa

Ingredients:

2 mangos (about 2 cups)
1/3 pineapple (about 2 cups)
½ cup green onion, minced
3-4 chipotles, canned in adobo, or to taste
½ cup chopped cilantro
2 to 3 tbsp brown sugar
½ tsp kosher or sea salt, to taste
12 flour tortillas
12 oz brie cheese
2 avocadoes
10-12 eggs, scrambled (don't overcook)
2 tbsp butter or oil

Directions:
1. To prepare salsa: Dice fruits. In a medium-sized bowl, combine fruits with green onion. Chop chipotles into small pieces and add along with sugar and chopped cilantro. Add salt. Taste and adjust seasonings.
2. Slice brie into 12 pieces. Cut avocado into thin slices. Set these aside while preparing the scrambled eggs.
3. When eggs are ready, assemble the quesadillas: On one side of the tortilla, place a large spoonful of the eggs, then a piece of brie cheese along with a slice or two of avocado. Fold over tortilla and press down. A toothpick can hold them closed temporarily. Quesadillas may be brushed with a little oil and cooked on a flat grill, sautéed in a large sauté pan, or placed under the broiler until lightly browned.
4. Garnish with fresh cilantro and serve with fruit salsa.

Notes:

This recipe came in a book given to me by my friend, Julie Rosas, who lives in Mexico. Of course, the recipe I most love from the book she sent is described as a *gringo* version and not very traditional although quite delicious. It is even better if you add 1 pound of cooked, chopped shrimp to the eggs after you've scrambled them.

Sali Par Edu

<u>Ingredients:</u>

3 eggs
2 tbsp olive oil
2 large potatoes
salt and pepper to taste

<u>Directions:</u>

1. Grate the potatoes and then boil until partially done. Drain and blot excess water from potatoes using paper towel.
2. Pour olive oil into a frying pan and heat oil on medium-high. Add potatoes and fry until brown on one side. Add salt and pepper. Flip potatoes.
3. Make three small indentations in the potatoes and break the eggs into the indentations on top of the flipped potatoes and cook (frying the now bottom side) until eggs are desired firmness.
4. Serve with baked beans and toast.

<u>Notes:</u>

I won't claim this is authentic. I modified the original recipe a bit. We had been walking in our neighborhood hills each morning for years, and most days we saw Mahandra. He was friendly and always stopped and chatted for a few minutes. One day, we invited him for coffee. Besides coffee, we had orange juice, bagels, and fruit. He ate a bagel but seemed uninterested in the fruit or orange juice. The next time we invited him, I wanted to try an Indian dish, but since I had little or no experience cooking Indian food, it had to be simple. This is a Parsi dish that looked easy enough for me to tackle. Mahandra seemed to enjoy it. I've made variations of this in the past without knowing its origin. What can be easier than potatoes and eggs? I've never tried serving it the traditional way with beans and toast, so maybe next time, I'll offer beans on the side. The last place I had beans for breakfast was a trip to Beijing where canned Pork and Beans were a morning staple.

Salsa Verde Enchiladas with Chicken and Kale

<u>Ingredients:</u>

2 tbsp olive oil, plus more for the dish
1 medium-large onion, chopped
5 oz pkg baby kale
2 cloves garlic, minced
½ tsp dried oregano
½ tsp ground cumin
½ tsp salt
⅛ tsp ground black pepper
4 oz cream cheese
¼ cup milk, plus more as needed
1 (16 oz) jar salsa verde, divided
3 cups (12 oz) cooked, shredded rotisserie chicken
4 oz sharp white cheddar cheese, shredded and divided
7 to 8 (8-inch) round soft flour tortillas
2 scallions, white and green parts, thinly sliced

<u>Directions:</u>
1. Preheat the oven to 400. Brush 9x13-inch casserole with olive oil.
2. Heat 2 tbsp olive oil in a large skillet over medium heat. Add onion and cook until softened, about 5 minutes, stirring occasionally. Add kale, cover the skillet, cook until wilted, about 1 to 2 minutes. Stir in garlic and cook 1 minute more, stirring constantly.
3. Add oregano, cumin, salt, black pepper, cream cheese, milk, and ½ cup salsa verde. Bring to a simmer, then add chicken and simmer 1 to 2 minutes, add milk to thin the sauce if needed. Turn off the heat and stir in 1/3 of the cheddar cheese.
4. Reserve ½ cup salsa verde. Spread remainder in oiled dish.
5. Wrap ½ cup of chicken filling in a tortilla and place seam-side-down in the prepared dish (you should get 7 to 8 tortillas). Spoon the reserved ½ cup salsa verde on top, and sprinkle with the reserved shredded cheddar cheese.
6. Bake uncovered until enchiladas start to brown and are warmed through, about 10 to 15 minutes. Sprinkle with scallions. Serve hot.

Slow Cooker Layered Huevos Rancheros

Ingredients:

16 eggs
1 cup half-and-half or milk
½ tsp salt
¼ tsp pepper
3 tbsp butter
1 can (10¾ oz) condensed Fiesta nacho cheese soup
2 tbsp chopped fresh chives
2/3 cup Old El Paso Thick 'n Chunky or other salsa
4 soft corn tortillas (6 inch), cut into ¾-inch strips
1 cup pinto beans (15-oz can), drained, rinsed
1 cup shredded sharp cheddar cheese (4 oz)
½ cup sour cream
4 medium green onions, sliced (¼ cup)

Directions:

1. In large bowl, beat eggs with whisk. Add half-and-half, salt, and pepper; beat well. In 12-inch nonstick skillet, melt butter over medium heat. Add egg mixture; cook about 7 minutes, scraping cooked eggs up from bottom of skillet occasionally, until mixture is firm but moist. Stir in soup and chives.
2. Spray 3-to-4-quart slow cooker with cooking spray. Spread 1/3 cup of the salsa in bottom of slow cooker. Carefully place half of the tortilla strips on salsa to within ½ inch of edge of slow cooker. Top with ½ cup of the beans, 3 cups of the egg mixture, and ½ cup of the cheese. Layer with remaining salsa, tortilla strips, beans, and egg mixture.
3. Cover; cook on high heat setting for 2 hours. Sprinkle with remaining ½ cup cheese. Cover; let stand until cheese is melted. Serve with sour cream and onions.

Note:

As written, this is a pretty unhealthy recipe, but it can be made less toxic by swapping the cheese, sour cream, and milk for their healthier low-fat versions.

Soft Tacos with Seafood and Vegetables

Ingredients:

6 tbsp corn oil
2 tbsp fresh lime juice
1½ tsp dried oregano
¾ tsp ground pepper
12 oz uncooked sea scallops, connective muscle removed
12 oz uncooked large shrimp, peeled, deveined
12 oz uncooked sea bass filets, cut into 1-inch pieces
16 (6-inch) flour tortillas
Mexican Vegetable Sauté (recipe and ingredients below)
Tomatillo Salsa (recipe and ingredients below)

Directions:

1. Combine oil, lime, oregano, and pepper in large bowl. Add seafood and toss to coat. Cover and refrigerate 4 hours. Preheat oven to 250 degrees.

2. Heat heavy large skillet over high heat. Add tortillas, one at a time and cook just until hot, turning once. Place on a plate and cover with foil. Transfer to oven to keep warm.

3. Heat remaining 2 tbsp oil in same skillet over medium-high heat. Add bass and cook 2 minutes. Turn bass, add scallops and shrimp. Cook until seafood is opaque, turning scallops and shrimp once, about 2 minutes.

4. Slightly overlap 2 warm flour tortillas on each plate. Place seafood down center of tortillas. Arrange Mexican Vegetable Sauté over seafood. Top with Chipotle Tomatillo Salsa. Fold tortillas over, or serve open face.

5. **Mexican Vegetable Sauté:** 3 tbsp *butter*, 1 large *carrot*, cut into matchstick-size strips, 1 large *zucchini*, cut into matchstick-size strips, 1 *onion*, thinly sliced, 1 red bell *pepper*, thinly sliced, 1 *chayote squash*, halved, seeded and cut into matchstick-size strips, ½ pound *jicama*, peeled and cut into matchstick–size strips and ¼ cup chopped fresh *cilantro*. **Directions:** Melt butter in heavy large skillet over medium heat. Add all vegetables (not cilantro) and sauté until crisp-tender, about 3 minutes. Mix in cilantro. Season with salt and pepper.

6. **Chipotle Tomatillo Salsa:** 3 *Chipotle chilies* from 1 (7 oz) can *chipotle chilies in adobo sauce*, rinsed and patted dry, 3 tsp *corn oil*, 1 pound *tomatillos*, husks removed,

(Recipe continued next page.)

1 small red *onion*, chopped, 1/3 cup chopped fresh *cilantro*, 1 tbsp *vinegar*, ½ tsp *dried oregano*. **Directions:** Puree chilies in blender. Transfer to large bowl. Heat 1 tsp oil in heavy large skillet over high heat. Add tomatillos and cook until brown on all sides, about 7 minutes. Transfer to work surface. Add 2 tsp oil to skillet. Add onion and sauté until tender, about 4 minutes. Add onion to chilies. Chop tomatillos; add to chili-onion mixture. Mix in cilantro, vinegar, and oregano. Season with salt and pepper. (Can be made two days ahead, covered, and kept in refrigerator. Bring to room temperature before serving.)

Notes:
I use fresh salsa from the grocery store to save time. It may not be as good, but then, how would I know? I also add a can of corn to the veggie mix.

Spaghetti Sauce with Meat

<u>Ingredients:</u>

2 pounds sweet Italian sausage
1½ pounds lean ground beef
1½ cups minced onion (one large or two medium)
2 bell pepper (can be red, yellow, or green)
16 oz mushrooms (preferably cremini or shitake)
4 cloves garlic, crushed
2 (28 ounce) cans crushed tomatoes
2 (12 oz) or 4 (6 oz) cans tomato paste
2 (13 oz) cans tomato sauce
1 cup water
1 cup Merlot
½ cup olive oil
4 tbsp white sugar (you can use less)
¼ tsp crushed red pepper
½ tsp fennel seed
2 tsp Italian seasoning (or fresh oregano, basil, and rosemary)
1 tsp salt
½ tsp ground black pepper

<u>Directions:</u>
1. In a large pot or Dutch oven over medium heat, cook the sausage and beef until browned. Add onion, peppers, and garlic and simmer until onions and pepper are soft. Add mushrooms and cook until soft. Drain and return to pot.
2. Stir in crushed tomatoes, tomato paste, tomato sauce, and water. Mix in sugar and season with basil, fennel seed, Italian seasoning, salt and pepper, and the fresh herbs. Reduce heat to low, cover, and simmer 1½ hours, stirring occasionally.

<u>Notes:</u>
I double this recipe which makes 32 servings and I freeze whatever I don't need. I simmer the sauce for three hours.

Sweet and Sour Chicken (Slow Cooker)

Ingredients:

1 cup chopped onion (about 1 medium)
1/3 cup sugar
1/3 cup ketchup
¼ cup orange juice
3 tbsp cornstarch
3 tbsp cider vinegar
2 tbsp lower-sodium soy sauce
1 tbsp grated peeled fresh ginger
1 pound skinless, boneless chicken thighs, cut into 1-inch pieces
2 (8 oz) cans pineapple chunks in juice, drained
1 large green bell pepper, cut into ¾-inch pieces
1 large red bell pepper, cut into ¾-inch pieces
3 cups hot cooked white rice

Directions:
1. Combine all ingredients except rice in a slow cooker. Cover and cook on low for 6 hours or on high for 4 hours. Serve over cooked rice.

Sweet and Sour Chicken (Stir-Fry)

<u>Ingredients:</u>

2 tbsp vegetable oil
2 boneless chicken breasts, sliced into strips
salt and pepper
½ cup chopped red pepper
4 tsp cornstarch, mixed with 4 tsp water
1 cup canned pineapple chunks, drained with ½ cup reserved juice
3 tbsp light brown sugar
3 tbsp rice wine vinegar
¼ cup chicken stock
½ cup chopped green pepper

<u>Directions:</u>
1. In a large non-stick skillet, heat oil over medium high heat. Season chicken strips and add to pan. Brown chicken and remove to plate.
2. Add red and green peppers and cook for 1 minute. Stir in pineapple chunks, juice, sugar, vinegar, and chicken stock and bring to a simmer. Simmer until sauce begins to reduce.
3. Stir in cornstarch mixture and bring liquid to a simmer. Stir in chicken strips and cook for 5 minutes. Serve over rice.

Taco Dip (Seven Layer)

<u>Ingredients:</u>

1 oz taco seasoning, (see recipe below or use prepackaged)
1 (16 oz) can refried beans
1 (8 oz) pkg cream cheese, softened
1 (16 oz) container sour cream
1 (16 oz) jar salsa
1 large tomato, chopped
1 green bell pepper, chopped
1 bunch chopped green onions
1 small head iceberg lettuce, shredded
1 (6 oz) can sliced black olives, drained
2 cups shredded cheddar cheese

<u>Directions:</u>

1. In a medium bowl, blend the taco seasoning (see below) and refried beans. Spread the mixture onto a large serving platter.
2. Beat the sour cream and cream cheese in a medium bowl. Spread over the refried beans.
3. Top the layers with salsa. Place a layer of chopped tomato, green bell pepper, green onions, and lettuce over the salsa, and top with cheddar cheese. Garnish with black olives.

Taco Seasoning

<u>Ingredients:</u>

1 tbsp chili powder
¼ tsp garlic powder
¼ tsp onion powder
¼ tsp crushed red pepper flakes
¼ tsp dried oregano
½ tsp paprika
1½ tsp ground cumin
1 tsp sea salt
1 tsp black pepper

<u>Directions:</u>

Mix all ingredients together. If you don't use all of it, save the remainder in a tightly sealed container.

Thai Green Curry with Chicken and Asparagus

<u>Ingredients:</u>

1½ pounds asparagus
4 boneless, skinless chicken breast halves, each about 6 oz
1 tsp sea salt, plus more, to taste
2 tbsp peanut or grapeseed oil
1 yellow onion, cut into 8 wedges
1 small red bell pepper, seeded, and cut into 1½-by-¼-inch strips
½-inch piece fresh ginger, peeled and minced
2 garlic cloves, minced
1 can (14 oz) unsweetened coconut milk
3 tbsp Thai green curry paste
1 cup low-sodium chicken broth or stock
2 tbsp Asian fish sauce
½ cup loosely packed small Thai basil leaves
1 lime, cut into 8 wedges

<u>Directions:</u>

1. Bring a saucepan of lightly salted water to a boil over high heat. While the water is heating, snap the tough stems off the asparagus spears and cut the spears into 2-inch lengths. Add the asparagus to the boiling water and cook just until crisp-tender, about 2 minutes. Drain well and rinse under cold running water until cool. Pat dry.

2. Cut the chicken breast halves across the grain on a slight diagonal into slices about ½ inch thick. Cut the slices vertically into strips about ½ inch wide. Season the chicken strips with the tsp salt.

3. Heat a very large frying pan over medium-high heat until hot. Pour in the oil and swirl the pan to coat it well. Add the onion and bell pepper and sauté until beginning to soften, about 3 minutes. Stir in the ginger and garlic and sauté until fragrant, about 30 seconds. Transfer the mixture to a plate.

4. Open the can of coconut milk (do not shake it) and scoop out 3 tbsp of the thick coconut cream on the top. Return the frying pan to medium-high heat, add the coconut cream and curry paste and stir well. Whisk in the remaining coconut cream and milk, the broth and fish sauce. Return the vegetable mixture to the pan, stir in the chicken strips and bring to a boil. Reduce the heat to medium-low and simmer briskly, stirring occasionally, until the sauce has reduced slightly and the

(Recipe continued on next page.)

vegetables are crisp-tender, about 5 minutes. Stir in the asparagus and cook until the chicken is opaque throughout and the asparagus is heated through, about 3 minutes. Adjust the seasoning with salt.

5. Scatter the basil over the curry. Divide the curry evenly among warmed bowls and serve immediately. Pass the lime wedges at the table. Serves 4 to 6.

Notes:

Recipe originally came from *Williams Sonoma New Flavors for Chicken* and was printed in the local Sunday paper when I was looking for something that was at least ostensibly healthy.

Veggie Lo Mein

<u>Ingredients:</u>

8 oz whole-grain spaghetti
10 oz frozen chopped broccoli
1½ cups frozen shelled edamame
2 cups shredded carrots
10 oz baby spinach
2 tbsp toasted sesame oil
1 large onion, thinly sliced
2 tsp fresh ginger, peeled and grated
¼ cup plus 1 tbsp lower-sodium soy sauce
2 tbsp balsamic vinegar
4 large eggs, well beaten

<u>Directions:</u>

1. Cook spaghetti in large pot of boiling water according to label directions. Two minutes before draining add broccoli, edamame, carrots, and spinach. Drain well. Set aside.
2. In same pot, heat sesame oil on medium-high. Add onion and cook 5 minutes. Add ginger, soy, and balsamic vinegar and cook 1 minute. Add eggs and cook 2 minutes without stirring.
3. Add noodle mixture; cook, tossing 2 minutes, or until heated through. Serves 4.

Vietnamese Chicken Noodle Soup

<u>Ingredients:</u>

2 cans (14½ oz each) reduced-sodium chicken broth
1½ pounds boneless, skinless chicken thighs, cut into bite-size pieces
1 cup shredded carrots
1 cup snow peas, thinly sliced
2 tbsp chopped fresh ginger
2 scallions, thinly sliced
1 tbsp reduced-sodium soy sauce
1 tbsp lime juice
2 tsp Asian hot sauce (such as Sriracha)
6 oz rice noodles (such as Thai Kitchen Stir-Fry Rice Noodles)
¼ cup mint leaves
¼ cup cilantro leaves

<u>Directions:</u>

1. In a large pot, bring chicken broth and 1½ cups water to a boil. Add chicken and simmer 3 minutes. Add carrots, snow peas, and ginger; simmer 3 minutes.
2. Stir in scallions, soy sauce, lime juice, and hot sauce.
3. Meanwhile, boil rice noodles for 6 minutes. Drain.
4. Divide cooked noodles among four bowls. Spoon an equal amount of soup into each bowl of noodles.
5. Sprinkle mint and cilantro over each dish and serve immediately.

Main Dishes: Beef, Fish, Pork, and Poultry

"You could probably get through life without knowing how to roast a chicken, but the question is, would you want to?" **Nigella Lawson**

"Beef is the soul of cooking." **Marie-Antoine Carême**

"Fish, to taste right, must swim three times—in water, in butter, and in wine." **Polish Proverb**

"For less than the cost of a Big Mac, fries, and a Coke, you can buy a loaf of fresh bread and some good cheese or roast beef, which you will enjoy much more." **Steve Albini**

~~~BEEF~~~

Beef Bourguignon

<u>Ingredients:</u>

5 pounds stewing beef
2 onions, chopped
1 cup beef broth or stock
½ cup full-bodied red wine
1 bay leaf
1 small can tomato sauce
1 tbsp tomato paste
5 carrots, cleaned and sliced
small basket of white mushrooms, cleaned and sliced
extra virgin olive oil
breadcrumbs or flour
salt and pepper (can use Creole seasoning for additional flavor)

<u>Directions:</u>
1. Dry beef, dust with breadcrumbs or flour and season with salt and pepper.
2. In a large non-stick frying pan, heat a little bit of olive oil. Sauté the beef in small batches and transfer to a big cast iron pot.
3. Sauté chopped onions in the same frying pan. Add to the pan the tomato paste, tomato sauce, beef broth, and wine. Pour over the beef. Add the bay leaf (and a pinch of herb de Provence or Creole seasoning, if desired). Add the carrots and mushrooms. Bring to boil on top of the stove.
4. Preheat oven to 350. Place covered pot in oven for 1 hour. Remove cover and continue cooking for 2 more hours, until beef is very soft. Check occasionally to make sure there is enough liquid, and if not, add more broth.

<u>Note:</u>

This is Shlomit Elitzur's recipe, and the dish tastes even better the second day, so you can refrigerate overnight, remove fat, reheat and sprinkle with parsley.

Beef Stroganoff

Ingredients:

2½ pounds beef tenderloin, well-trimmed, cut into strips
2 tbsp canola oil
8 tbsp (1 stick) butter
1/3 cup finely chopped shallots
1 pound small button mushrooms, cleaned and thickly sliced
1½ cups canned beef broth
3 tbsp Cognac
1½ cup sour cream or whipping cream
1 tbsp Dijon mustard
1 tbsp chopped fresh dill (optional)
12 oz wide egg noodles
1 tbsp paprika

Directions:

1. Pat meat dry with paper towels. Sprinkle with salt and pepper. Heat oil in heavy large skillet over high heat until very hot. Working in batches, add meat in single layer and cook just until brown on outside, about one minute per side. Set aside.
2. Melt 2 tbsp butter in same skillet over medium-high heat. Add chopped shallots and sauté until tender, scraping up browned bits, about two minutes. Add button mushrooms. Sprinkle with pepper and sauté until liquid evaporates, about 12 minutes. Add beef broth and Cognac. Simmer 14 minutes until thick enough to coat mushrooms.
3. Stir in sour cream and Dijon mustard. Add meat and any accumulated juices. Simmer over medium-low heat until meat is heated through but still medium-rare, about 2 minutes. Stir in chopped dill. Season to taste with salt and pepper.
4. Cook noodles according to directions. Drain. Transfer to bowl. Add the remaining 4 tbsp butter and toss to coat. Sprinkle with paprika. Divide among 6 plates and cover with stroganoff.

Notes:

Best thing we ever imported from Russia! Well, some might argue it comes second to vodka.

Best Ever Pot Roast

<u>Ingredients:</u>

1 (3 to 4 pounds) boneless chuck roast
salt, pepper, garlic powder to taste
flour for dredging
2 tbsp olive oil
1 cup thinly sliced onion wedges
3 cloves garlic, crushed
2 bay leaves
1 can cream of mushroom soup
1/3 cup red wine
2 tbsp Worcestershire sauce
1 tbsp beef bouillon granules
¾ cup water
small bag carrots, peeled
½ cup celery, chopped into ½-inch pieces

<u>Directions:</u>
1. Preheat oven to 350. Rub roast with salt, pepper, and garlic salt on both sides.
2. Heat oil in large skillet and dredge roast in flour. Brown the roast, searing on both sides. Place meat and bay leaves in a roaster pan. Add onions and garlic to skillet for 1 to 2 minutes to absorb leftover roast juice and then add to meat in roaster pan.
3. Place carrots and celery in roaster pan with meat and bay leaves.
4. Combine the soup, wine, Worcestershire sauce, and bouillon into a bowl. Pour over roast. Add water.
5. Cover pan with foil and bake for 3 to 3½ hours or until tender. Remove and discard the bay leaves.

<u>Note:</u>
I either serve with mashed potatoes, or I add peeled potatoes to the roaster pan along with the carrots and celery.

Lobster-Stuffed Beef Tenderloin with Béarnaise Sauce

Ingredients:

2 rock lobster tails
1 tbsp vegetable oil
¼ pound pancetta or bacon, chopped
½ cup chopped shallots
3 tbsp minced celery
2 tsp minced garlic
4 oz baby chanterelle mushrooms, stems trimmed and sliced
salt and freshly ground black pepper
2 tbsp minced green onions
2 tbsp dry white wine
1 tbsp chopped fresh parsley leaves
1 center-cut beef tenderloin, about 3½ pounds, trimmed and butterflied
Béarnaise Sauce recipe follows on next page

Directions:

1. Preheat the oven to 400.
2. Set up a large steamer. Place the lobster tails in the steamer and steam until just cooked through, about 6 minutes. Remove the lobster tails from the steamer. Cut along the underside of the shell and remove the tail meat whole. Set aside
3. In a large skillet, heat 1 tsp of the oil over medium-high heat. Add the pancetta and cook, stirring, until crisp and the fat is rendered, about 5 minutes. Remove with a slotted spoon. Drain off all but 2 tsp of fat from the pan. Add the shallots and cook, stirring, until soft, about 2 minutes. Add the garlic and cook, stirring, for 30 seconds.
4. Add the mushrooms and a pinch each of salt and pepper, and cook until the mushrooms give off their liquid, 3 to 4 minutes. Add the green onions and stir.
5. Add the wine, increase the heat, and cook until it has nearly all evaporated, 1 to 2 minutes. Add the parsley and stir. Remove from the heat, stir in the cooked pancetta, and let cool.
6. Spread the butterflied beef, cut side up, flat on a surface. Spread the pancetta-vegetable mixture in a line across the meat, about 2 inches from the top, leaving a ½-inch border on the sides. Lay the lobster on top of the mixture, going across the beef. Pull the top flap over the lobster and roll the meat over the stuffing, jellyroll fashion, and tuck in the ends. Tie with kitchen twine every 2 inches.

(Recipe continued on next page.)

7. Place in a large heavy roasting pan, rub on all sides with the remaining 2 tsp olive oil, and season lightly with salt and pepper. Place over medium-high heat and sear the meat on all sides, about 6 minutes. Place in the oven and roast to desired temperature, 30 to 35 minutes for medium-rare.

8. Transfer to a cutting board. Tent and let rest for 10 minutes before carving. Remove the kitchen twine and slice thickly. Place on a platter, surround with the asparagus, and drizzle with the Bearnaise Sauce. Serve immediately.

Béarnaise Sauce:

> 2 tbsp chopped shallots
> 4 sprigs fresh tarragon
> ¼ cup dry white wine
> ¼ cup dry vermouth
> 4 large egg yolks
> 1 cup (2 sticks) melted unsalted butter or clarified butter
> 1 tsp fresh lemon juice
> 2 tbsp chopped fresh tarragon leaves
> ½ tsp salt
> 1/8 tsp ground white pepper

Directions for sauce:

1. In a small saucepan, combine the shallots, tarragon, white wine, and vermouth. Bring to a boil and cook until reduced to 2 tbsp. Remove from the heat, strain, and cool.

2. In the top of a double boiler, or in a metal bowl fitted over a pot of barely simmering water, whisk the egg yolks and reduced wine until ribbons start to form. Whisking constantly, drizzle in the melted butter a bit at a time until all the butter is added and the mixture is thick. Remove from the heat.

3. Whisk in the lemon juice, chopped tarragon, salt, and pepper. Adjust the seasoning, to taste. Cover to keep warm until ready to serve. To serve, place in a decorative bowl with a small sauce ladle.

Notes:

This is not your everyday meal. But if you want memorable, you might give it a try. I've only made it once. This recipe book project brought it back to my attention, so maybe the next time I want fancy, I'll make it again.

Meatballs with Beef/Veal/Pork

<u>Ingredients:</u>

¾ cup plain bread crumbs
½ cup milk
2 tbsp olive oil
1 onion, diced
1 pound ground beef
1 pound ground pork
1 pound ground veal
2 eggs
¼ bunch fresh parsley, chopped
3 cloves garlic, crushed
2 tsp salt
1 tsp ground black pepper
½ tsp red pepper flakes
1 tsp dried Italian herb seasoning
2 tbsp grated Romano cheese

<u>Directions:</u>
1. Soak bread crumbs in milk in a small bowl for 20 minutes.
2. Heat olive oil in a skillet over medium heat. Cook and stir onions in hot oil until translucent, about 20 minutes.
3. Mix beef, veal, and pork together in a large bowl. Stir onions, bread crumb mixture, eggs, parsley, garlic, salt, black pepper, red pepper flakes, Italian herb seasoning, and Romano cheese into meat mixture with a rubber spatula until combined. Cover and refrigerate for about one hour.
4. Preheat an oven to 425.
5. Using wet hands, form meat mixture into balls about 1½ inches in diameter. Arrange into rimmed cookie sheet sprayed with cooking spray.
6. Bake in the preheated oven until browned and cooked through, 15 to 20 minutes.

<u>Note:</u>
Veal is more expensive and harder to find than the other two meats and your meatballs will still be perfect if you leave it out and use 1½ pounds each of pork and beef.

Meatballs

<u>Ingredients:</u>

3 pounds lean ground beef
2¼ cups crushed seasoned croutons
¾ cup chopped sweet onion
3 eggs, lightly beaten
6 cloves garlic, chopped
½ cup Worcestershire sauce
3 tbsp prepared yellow mustard
1 tbsp red pepper flakes
1 tbsp Cajun seasoning
1 tbsp extra virgin olive oil
2 tbsp butter

<u>Directions:</u>
1. In a large bowl, mix all ingredients by hand. Shape into meatballs, larger if you are using for spaghetti and meatballs or over rice, smaller if you will put in BBQ sauce or pineapple sauce for appetizer.
2. Heat olive oil and melt the butter in a skillet over medium heat. Place the meatballs in the skillet, and cook, turning constantly until browned and cooked.
<u>Notes:</u> I usually bake (in 350-degree oven, turning once) in a rimmed baking pan lined with non-stick aluminum foil. The meatballs seem to stay nicely shaped this way. This recipe makes a generous 12 servings of large meatballs or 24 cocktail meatballs.

Meatball Dress-Ups: (Using recipes from above or prior page)

Meatballs in Pineapple Sauce

<u>Ingredients:</u>

1 can (13.25 oz) pineapple chunks in juice
1 green bell pepper, sliced
½ cup brown sugar
2 tbsp cornstarch
2 tbsp soy sauce
2 tbsp lemon juice
(Recipe continued on next page.)

Directions:
1. Pour pineapple chunks with juice into a saucepan. Stir green bell pepper, brown sugar, cornstarch, soy sauce, and lemon juice through the pineapple chunks until sugar and cornstarch dissolve.
2. Bring the mixture to a boil; cook and stir until thickened, about 10 minutes.
3. Pour over cooked meatballs.
4. Good as an appetizer (with toothpicks) or over rice as a main course.

Meatballs in BBQ Sauce

Ingredients:

½ onion, minced
4 clove garlic, minced
¾ cup bourbon whiskey
½ tsp ground black pepper
½ tbsp salt
2 cups ketchup
½ cup tomato paste
½ cup cider vinegar
1 tbsp liquid smoke flavoring
¼ cup Worcestershire sauce
½ cup packed brown sugar
1/3 tsp hot pepper sauce, or to taste

Directions:
In a large skillet over medium-low heat, combine the onion, garlic, and whiskey and cook for 10 minutes or until onion is translucent. Mix in remaining ingredients, reduce heat and simmer for 20 minutes. Strain if you prefer smoother sauce.

Meatballs in Pesto

Directions: Add ½ cup pesto sauce (See Pesto Sauce, p. 250.) to meatball mixture before shaping into balls.

Meatballs in Pesto Cream

Directions: In a pan pour 1 cup chicken broth, ¼ cup pesto, and ½ cup cream. Add cooked meatballs to pan and simmer until warm. (See Pesto Sauce, p. 250.)

Meatloaf One

Ingredients:

1 tbsp olive oil
3 medium onions, chopped
2 tsp chopped fresh thyme leaves
2 tsp kosher salt
1 tsp freshly ground black pepper
¼ cup Worcestershire sauce
1/3 cup canned chicken stock or broth
1 tbsp tomato paste
3 pounds ground chuck or extra lean hamburger
2/3 cup Progresso plain dry bread crumbs
3 eggs, beaten
2/3 cup ketchup

Directions:
1. Preheat the oven to 325. Heat the olive oil in a medium sauté pan. Add the onions, thyme, salt, and pepper and cook over medium-low heat, stirring occasionally, for 8 to 10 minutes, until the onions are translucent but not brown.
2. Remove pan from heat and add the Worcestershire, chicken stock, and tomato paste. Cool slightly.
3. In a large bowl, combine the ground chuck, onion mixture, bread crumbs, and eggs. Mix lightly with a fork. Don't over mix or the meat loaf will be dense. Line a sheet pan with parchment paper. Shape meat mixture into two rectangular loaves and place on pan. Spread the ketchup evenly on top. Bake for 1 to 1¼ hours, until the meat loaf is cooked through.

Notes:
This is enough for two meat loaves, so I often freeze one. However, it is my grandson, Kohler's, favorite, so if we are having company, and I need more meatloaf, I make this into one large loaf. I have also used finely crumbled soda crackers or homemade breadcrumbs (bread crumbs lightly toasted), when I haven't had Progresso crumbs.

Meat Loaf Two

Ingredients:

1½ pounds lean ground beef
½ cup milk
2 eggs
1½ tsp salt
¼ tsp ground black pepper
1 (1 oz) pkg dry onion soup mix
¼ tsp ground ginger
¾ cup finely crushed saltine cracker crumbs

½ cup packed brown sugar
1 tbsp Worcestershire sauce
½ cup ketchup

Directions:
1. Preheat oven to 350. Lightly grease a 5x9-inch loaf pan. Mix first eight ingredients together and shape into a loaf. Put into prepared pan. Don't overmix.
2. Mix remaining three ingredients together and pour over top of meatloaf in pan.
3. Bake for at least one hour, until juices run clear. I usually bake closer to one and a half hours.

Meat Loaf Three (Italian)

Ingredients:

2 large eggs, lightly beaten
1 cup pizza sauce, divided
1 cup seasoned bread crumbs
1 medium onion, chopped
1 medium green pepper, chopped
1 tsp dried oregano
1 garlic clove, minced
½ tsp salt
¼ tsp pepper
2 pounds lean ground beef
1 pound bulk Italian sausage
½ pound sliced deli ham
2 cups (8-oz) shredded part-skim mozzarella cheese, divided
1 jar (6 oz) sliced mushrooms, drained

Directions:

1. Preheat oven to 375. In a large bowl, combine the eggs, ¾ cup pizza sauce, bread crumbs, onion, green pepper, oregano, garlic, salt, and pepper. Crumble beef and sausage over mixture and mix well, but don't overmix.
2. On a piece of parchment paper, pat beef mixture into a 12x10-inch rectangle. Layer the ham, 1½ cups cheese and mushrooms over beef mixture to within 1 inch of edges. Roll up jelly-roll style, starting with a short side and peeling parchment paper away as you roll. Seal seam and ends. Place seam side down in a greased 13x9-inch baking dish and brush with remaining pizza sauce.
3. Bake, uncovered, 1 hour. Sprinkle with remaining cheese. Bake an additional 15-20 minutes. Using two large spatulas, carefully transfer meat loaf to a serving platter.

Mississippi Pepperoncini Pot Roast

Ingredients:

1 (4 pounds) beef chuck roast
1 stick butter
5 pepperoncini peppers
1 (1 oz) packet dry ranch dressing mix
1 (1 oz) packet dry au jus mix

Directions:

1. Place roast in a slow cooker. Add two dry mixes, butter, pepperoncini peppers. **Do not add any liquids**.
2. Cook on low for 8 hours.

Notes:

I've tried many pot roast recipes because pot roast is one of my husband's favorites. He should go easy on beef for the sake of his heart, but every now and then, nothing but pot roast and mashed potatoes will satisfy his hunger for a home-cooked meal. Although I use different recipes depending upon my mood and what ingredients I have available, this may be my favorite. It is a simple recipe that is also good served with buttered noodles. I thicken the gravy with 2 tbsp cornstarch mixed in ½ cup cold water.

Helpful Hint: I recently learned a secret that made serving pot roast a lot easier. One of my complaints about pot roast was that it always looked so messy. You'd get it cooked to tender perfection, but it fell apart, and there seemed no way to make it look nice. The secret is to cook it the day before and put it in the refrigerator overnight. Cold, it slices beautifully and the juice separates so you can remove the fat layer before making gravy. Once you've sliced and arranged the pot roast, just put it in the microwave or a warm oven and reheat.

St. Louis BBQ Ribs

Ingredients:

¼ cup paprika
¼ cup packed light brown sugar
3 tbsp chili powder
3 tbsp granulated garlic
2 tbsp onion powder
2 tbsp kosher salt
1 tbsp freshly ground black pepper

2 (3 pound each) slabs St. Louis rib racks
1/3 cup yellow mustard
favorite BBQ Sauce

Directions:
1. Make a rub of the seven dry ingredients. Rinse and pat the rib slabs dry with paper towels. Brush meat with mustard and coat heavily with dry rub. Refrigerate overnight.
2. Set out two large sheets heavy-duty, non-stick foil. Place 1 rack on each sheet, meat side down. Fold foil to form sealed pouch. Place pouches in large roasting pan and bake in 350 oven for 2 hours. Check for tenderness.
3. When ribs are tender, remove to outdoor grill, preheated and hot. Baste with your favorite BBQ sauce and cook 10 minutes, then turn and baste other side for additional 10 minutes.

Stuffed Flank Steak

Ingredients:

½ cup olive oil
1/3 cup soy sauce
¼ cup balsamic vinegar
2 tbsp fresh lemon juice
½ tbsp Worcestershire sauce
1 tbsp Dijon mustard
2 cloves garlic, minced
½ tsp ground black pepper
2½ pounds flank steak, butterflied

Filling ingredients:

¼ tsp salt
1 clove garlic
¼ cup chopped onion
¼ cup dry bread crumbs
1 cup frozen chopped spinach, thawed and squeezed dry
½ cup crumbled feta cheese

Directions:
1. In a large resealable bag, combine first eight ingredients and squeeze the bag to blend well. Pierce the flank steak with a fork or knife, making slits about 1-inch apart. Place steak into the bag, and seal. Refrigerate overnight to marinate.
2. Preheat oven to 350.
3. Crush the remaining clove of garlic, sprinkle with salt to make paste. Remove steak from bag and discard marinade. Open the butterflied steak and spread the garlic paste over the top inside of the opened steak. Place layers of chopped onion, bread crumbs, spinach, and cheese over the garlic. Roll the steak up lengthwise, and secure with kitchen twine or toothpicks.
4. Place roll in shallow glass baking dish and bake uncovered for one hour, or until internal temperature is at least 145 degrees in the center. Let stand five minutes and then slice into 1-inch slices and serve.

Swiss Steak in Wine Sauce

Ingredients:

2 pounds beef round steak, cut 1-inch thick
2 tbsp all-purpose flour
2 tsp salt
2 tbsp canola oil
1 cup chopped onion
½ cup sliced carrot
2 tbsp chopped green peppers
1 (28 oz) can diced tomatoes
1 garlic clove, minced
1½ cups Burgundy wine
2 tsp sugar
½ cup frozen peas

Wine Sauce »

1½ cups reserved liquid
¼ cup cold water
2 tbsp all-purpose flour

Directions:

1. Trim fat from steak; cut meat into 6 equal pieces. Coat with mixture of flour, salt, and ¼ tsp pepper. Pound steak to ½-inch thickness using meat mallet. Brown meat in hot oil; drain. Place onion, carrot, and green pepper in crock pot. Place meat on top.
2. Combine undrained tomatoes, wine, garlic, and sugar. Pour over meat. Cover and cook on low heat setting for 8 to 10 hours. About a half hour before cooking time is up, add peas.
3. Transfer meat and vegetables to serving platter. Reserve 1½ cups of the cooking liquid for Wine Sauce.
4. Wine Sauce: (I double the ingredients for wine sauce.) Pour reserved liquid into saucepan. Blend ¼ cup cold water slowly into 2 tbsp flour; stir into liquid. Cook and stir until thickened and bubbly. Season to taste.

Teriyaki Beef Tenderloin

<u>Ingredients:</u>

1 cup sherry (or Progresso Beef Broth)
½ cup reduced-sodium soy sauce
1 envelope (1 oz) dry onion soup mix
½ cup packed brown sugar
1 beef tenderloin roast (2 pounds)
2 tbsp water

<u>Directions:</u>
1. In a large bowl, combine the sherry, soy sauce, soup mix, and brown sugar. Pour ¾ cup into a large resealable plastic bag; add tenderloin. Seal bag and turn to coat; refrigerate for 5 hours or overnight. Put remaining marinade in jar, cover tightly, and refrigerate.
2. Drain and discard marinade from tenderloin. Place meat on a rack in a shallow roasting pan. Bake, uncovered, at 425 for 45-50 minutes or until meat reaches desired doneness, basting often with 1/3 cup reserved marinade. Let stand for 10-15 minutes.
3. Meanwhile, in a small saucepan, bring water and remaining marinade to a rolling boil for 1 minute or until sauce is slightly reduced. Slice beef; serve with sauce. 8 servings.

~~~FISH~~~

Almond Crusted Salmon

Ingredients:

¼ cup almond meal
¼ cup Panko
¼ tsp ground coriander
1/8 tsp ground cumin
4 (6 oz) salmon filets, about 1-inch thick
2 tsp lemon juice
½ tsp kosher salt
¼ tsp freshly ground black pepper
cooking spray
4 lemon wedges

Directions:
1. Preheat oven to 500.
2. Combine first 4 ingredients in a shallow dish; set aside.
Brush tops and sides of fish with lemon juice; sprinkle with salt and pepper.
3. Working with one filet at a time, dredge top and sides in almond mixture; place skin side down on broiler pan coated with cooking spray. Sprinkle any remaining crumb mixture evenly over fish; press gently to adhere.
4. Bake for 15 minutes or until fish flakes easily when tested with a fork or until desired degree of doneness. Serve with lemon wedges.

Beer Battered Whitefish

<u>Ingredients:</u>

½ cup cornstarch
1½ tsp baking powder
¾ tsp salt
½ tsp Creole seasoning*
¼ tsp paprika
¼ tsp cayenne pepper
1 cup all-purpose flour, divided
½ cup 2% milk
1/3 cup beer
2 cups crushed unsalted saltines (about 40)
1½ pounds fresh or frozen whitefish
oil for deep-fat frying

<u>Directions:</u>

1. In a shallow bowl, combine the cornstarch, baking powder, salt, Creole seasoning, paprika, cayenne, and ½ cup flour. Stir in milk and beer until batter is smooth. Place finely crushed crackers and remaining flour in separate shallow bowls. Coat filets with flour, dip in batter, and then coat with crackers.
2. In an electric skillet or deep-fat fryer, heat oil to 375. Fry fish in batches for 2-3 minutes on each side or until golden brown. Drain on paper towels. Yield: 4 servings.

<u>Notes:</u>
*The following spices may be substituted for ½ tsp Creole seasoning: ¼ tsp ground cumin, and cayenne pepper to taste. I love Michigan whitefish, but you can substitute cod, tilapia, or other fish filets.

Couscous Crusted Salmon

<u>Ingredients:</u>

4 salmon filets (6 oz each)
salt
1 cup water
¾ cup couscous
¼ cup refrigerated pesto
¼ tsp cider vinegar
1/8 tsp pepper

<u>Directions:</u>
1. Preheat oven to 450.
2. Place salmon filets skin side down on foil-lined cookie sheet. Season with salt.
3. Heat water in 1-qt saucepan to boiling. Remove from heat; stir in couscous, pesto, cider vinegar, and pepper. Cover and let stand 5 minutes.
4. Mound ½ cup couscous mixture on top of each salmon filet, pressing into even layer.
5. Bake in upper third of oven 12 to 15 minutes or until salmon is just opaque throughout.

Easy One-Hour Salmon Dinner with Dill Sauce

<u>Ingredients:</u>

1½ pounds small, new red potatoes
6 medium carrots
4 (4 to 6 oz each) pieces of salmon
olive oil
salt and pepper to taste
2 tbsp honey
2 tbsp Dijon mustard
optional: fresh orange zest, thyme, rosemary,
herbs de Provence, basil, or sage

<u>Directions:</u>

1. Preheat oven to 425. Wash and dry new potatoes. Cut each potato in half. In a resealable food bag, place cut potatoes, about 2 tbsp olive oil and salt and pepper to taste. Make sure all potatoes are covered, adding additional olive oil if needed. Place potatoes, cut side down on one half of a baking sheet and put in preheated oven.

2. After placing potatoes in oven, peel carrots and cut each long carrot into three pieces, then cut each piece into strips about ¼ inch thick (like matchstick pieces, only slightly thicker). In same resealable food bag that you used for potatoes, add another 2 tbsp olive oil and more salt and pepper. Add carrots and make sure they are covered with olive oil.

3. When potatoes have been in the preheated 425 oven for ten minutes, add carrots to the other side of baking sheet and return the potatoes/carrots to the oven. (You can add a dash or two of sage or other spice to carrots.)

4. In same resealable food bag, add another measure of olive oil, salt, and pepper. Add salmon and make sure each piece is covered with olive oil.

5. When the carrots have been in the oven for 10 minutes (and potatoes in the oven for 20 minutes), place salmon pieces, skin side down, on a second baking sheet and place baking sheet on top oven rack above the veggies.

6. Bake everything for another ten minutes. During this baking period, mix the mustard with honey in a small bowl. After the additional ten minutes, brush salmon with honey-mustard and bake another five minutes. At this point I also sprinkle the carrots and potatoes with fresh herbs depending upon what I have available. Get creative, although I like fresh rosemary on the potatoes and fresh

(Recipe continued on next page.)

thyme on the carrots.

7. Remove everything from the oven. Serves 4, but amounts can be altered to accommodate additional servings.

Notes:
This is a recipe that is all about the timing. By watching the time and adding each new food at the right moment, you have a complete meal that is delicious and ready (prep included) in about an hour:

35 minutes prior to finish time, put potatoes in oven.
25 minutes prior to finish time, add carrots to baking sheet.
15 minutes prior to finish time, put salmon in oven.
5 minutes prior to finish time, baste salmon with honey-mustard.

Dill Sauce: (Can be made ahead)

Ingredients:

1/3 cup sour cream
1/3 cup mayonaise
¼ cup dry white wine
1 tbsp capers
1 tbsp finely chopped onion
1 tbsp caper brine
1 tsp lemon juice
1 tsp prepared horseradish
¾ tsp dried dill weed
¼ tsp garlic salt
ground black bepper to taste

Directions:
While the salmon bakes, stir all dill sauce ingredients together in a bowl. Serve with salmon.

Note:
I often make Red Lobster Cheese Biscuits (Recipe for Cheese Biscuits page 77) with this dinner.

Grilled Salmon with choice of three rubs

<u>Ingredients:</u>

8 skin on salmon filets (6 oz each), patted dry
olive oil
salt

<u>Choice of rubs:</u>
1. **Curry:** 2 tbsp finely grated orange peel, 4 tsp curry powder, 1 tsp black pepper.
2. **Herb:** ½ cup finely chopped fresh dill, ¼ cup finely chopped fresh tarragon, 1 tbsp finely grated lemon peel, 1 tbsp sugar.
3. **BBQ:** 3 tbsp brown sugar, 2 tsp paprika, 1 tsp garlic powder, 1 tsp onion powder, ½ tsp black pepper.

<u>Directions:</u>
1. Preheat grill to medium. Brush dried salmon filets with oil and sprinkle with salt. Coat flesh side with choice of three rubs above.
2. Push soaked skewers through salmon, lengthwise, (one or two pieces per skewer). Place skin side down on grill.
3. Cover; cook without turning over 14 minutes or until just opaque. With metal spatula, scrape filets from grill. If skin sticks to grate, remove filet only.

Honey Lime Tilapia

Ingredients:

¼ cup honey
3 tbsp lime juice
2 cloves garlic, minced
1 pound tilapia filets
salt and pepper to taste
1 butternut squash: peeled, seeded, and sliced
1 bunch fresh asparagus spears, trimmed, and chopped
poultry seasoning
½ cup mozzarella cheese

Directions:
1. In a large bowl, mix the honey, lime juice, and garlic. Season tilapia with salt and pepper, place in the bowl, and marinate one hour in the refrigerator.
2. Preheat oven to 350. Lightly grease a medium baking dish.
3. Arrange the squash and asparagus in the baking dish. Place tilapia on top of vegetables, and season with poultry seasoning. Discard remaining marinade.
4. Bake 20 minutes in the preheated oven, until vegetables are tender and fish is easily flaked. Sprinkle with mozzarella, and continue baking 5 minutes, or until cheese is lightly browned.

Note:
For a healthier version, I skip the mozzarella and sprinkle lightly with parmesan.

Little River Inn's Crab Pot Pie

<u>Ingredients:</u>

1 tbsp butter, for sautéing
1 yellow onion, diced
1 leek, diced
2 stalks celery, diced
2 tbsp flour
2 cups clam juice
1 russet potato, diced
zest from 1 lemon
1 tsp Old Bay seasoning
pinch of salt and white pepper
½ cup (1 stick) butter, browned
1 cup frozen peas
1 pound cleaned crab meat
pie dough (your preferred recipe for 10-inch double crust)
lightly beaten egg, to finish

<u>Directions:</u>
1. Heat oven to 400 degrees.
2. In a large skillet, melt 1 tbsp butter and sauté the onions, leeks, and celery over medium heat for 3 minutes.
3. Add flour and cook for 1 minute, using a whisk to incorporate the flour. Whisk in clam juice. Add potato and cook over medium heat, until potatoes are just tender, about 15 minutes.
4. Remove from heat and add lemon zest, Old Bay, salt, and pepper.
5. In a separate pan, melt the ½ cup butter over medium heat and cook until slightly browned. Add to potato mixture and let cool. (The recipe can be made ahead to this point.)
6. Add peas and crab meat; mix well. Divide into oven-proof baking dishes or individual-sized pie plates.
7. Divide dough into 8 pieces and shape into balls. Roll out circles and top each little pie with pastry, crimping, or fluting the edges. Brush the crust with lightly beaten egg. Bake for 25 minutes or until crust is golden. Serves 8.

Louisiana Barbecued Shrimp

<u>Ingredients:</u>

2-3 pounds unpeeled shrimp
1 loaf crusty fresh bread, for dipping

<u>Wet Ingredients:</u> »»

1 cup (2 sticks) butter
1/3 cup olive oil
4 cloves garlic, minced
1 tbsp fresh lemon juice

<u>Dry Herbs:</u> »»

4 bay leaves, crushed to a powder (or ¼ tsp powdered)
2 tsp dried rosemary, powdered with the bay leaves
½ tsp dried basil
½ tsp dried oregano
½ tsp cayenne
1 tbsp paprika
½ to 1 tsp freshly ground black pepper

<u>Directions:</u>

1. Combine all the dry herbs and mix well. Simmer wet ingredients for the sauce on the stovetop for 5 minutes.
2. Add the dry herbs, stirring for about 6-7 minutes. Use a large enough pot for the shrimp to fit in a single layer.
3. Add the shrimp and bring to boil. Lower heat, and cook 10 minutes or more, stirring and lifting, until all are pink. Do not overcook.
4. Turn off heat, cover pan, and let sit to absorb the flavors for about 15 minutes.
5. If you prefer, you can bake the shrimp in a 400-degree oven until cooked through. Don't overcook them, they just have to be very hot throughout—overcooking will toughen them, but the longer they sit in the sauce, the better they taste. Serve with hot fresh bread.

Mendocino's First Place Crab Cakes

<u>Ingredients:</u>

1 pound fresh crab meat
1 tsp unsalted butter
3 tbsp minced shallots
1 extra-large egg, beaten
finely grated zest of 1 lemon
¼ cup mayonnaise
1½ tbsp minced flat-leaf parsley
2 drops Tabasco sauce
¼ tsp freshly ground black pepper
¾ tsp sea salt
6 tbsp panko crumbs + 1½ cups for coating
safflower or other neutral oil for frying

<u>Directions:</u>

1. Put panko crumbs in food processor or blender and process until you have enough for 6 ground tbsp for mixing in the cakes and 1½ cups for coating. These crumbs will be very fine.
2. Coating: 1½ cups ground panko crumbs seasoned with ½ tsp each sea salt and freshly ground black pepper.
3. Rinse and pick over crab meat, discarding any pieces of shell or cartilage. Break up lumps (Some recipes say to leave big lumps, but this can cause the cakes to fall apart). Set aside.
4. In a small skillet set over low heat, melt butter and sauté shallots. Let cool.
5. Mix together the cooled shallots, egg, lemon zest, mayonnaise, parsley, Tabasco, pepper, salt, and 6 tbsp panko crumbs. Let sit 15 minutes, then mix thoroughly with crab.
6. Form into 8 patties, and dredge in the seasoned panko crumbs. Refrigerate on a tray for at least an hour.
7. When ready to cook, add oil to a large skillet so that the oil is about ¼-inch deep. Heat over medium high to high heat. When oil is hot, add crab cakes 4 at a time, don't crowd them. Cook on one side, then flip, until richly browned on both sides, drain briefly on paper towels and serve immediately with your favorite sauce.

Mustard Crusted Tilapia

<u>Ingredients:</u>

2 (6 oz each) fresh tilapia filets
1 tsp spicy brown mustard
1 tsp Worcestershire sauce
½ tsp lemon juice
¼ tsp garlic powder
¼ tsp dried oregano
½ tsp grated parmesan cheese
1 tsp fine Italian bread crumbs

<u>Directions:</u>

1. Preheat oven to 375. Spray a glass baking dish with cooking spray.
2. Place tilapia filets into prepared baking dish, and bake in preheated oven for 10 minutes. Meanwhile, stir together the mustard, Worcestershire sauce, lemon juice, garlic powder, oregano, and parmesan cheese.
3. When fish has cooked for 10 minutes, spread with herb paste, and sprinkle with bread crumbs. Continue baking for another 5 minutes until the topping is bubbly and golden. Makes 2 servings.

Pepper Jelly and Soy Glazed Salmon

Ingredients:
 2 pounds fresh or frozen skinless salmon filet, about 1 inch thick
 2/3 cup green jalapeno pepper jelly
 1/3 cup rice vinegar
 1/3 cup soy sauce
 3 green onions, sliced
 1 tbsp grated fresh ginger
 2 tsp toasted sesame oil
 3 cloves garlic, minced
 ¼ tsp crushed red pepper
 ¼ cup snipped fresh cilantro
 ¼ cup sliced fresh jalapeno or sliced green onions

Directions:
1. Thaw fish, if frozen. Rinse fish and pat dry. In saucepan, melt jelly over low heat remove from heat. Stir in next 7 ingredients. Place fish in shallow dish, pour mixture over fish. Cover and refrigerate 1 to 2 hours turning fish occasionally.
2. Remove fish from marinade, reserve marinade. For charcoal grill, arrange medium hot coals around edge of grill. Test for medium heat in center of grill. Place fish on greased piece of heavy-duty foil in center of grill. Cover your grill and cook 15-18 minutes or until fish flakes.
3. For gas grill adjust your grill for indirect cooking. Grill over medium heat as above. Bring reserved marinade to boiling. Reduce heat. Simmer uncovered 10-15 minutes or until reduced to ½ cup. Drizzle over fish , then sprinkle fish with cilantro, peppers, and onions.

Salmon Cakes with Ginger Sesame Sauce

<u>Ingredients:</u>

6 slices whole-wheat sandwich bread
2 (15 oz each) cans salmon, drained and picked over for skin/bones
2 large eggs, lightly beaten
5 scallions (white and green parts)
½ cup canned water chestnuts, drained and finely chopped
¼ cup finely chopped fresh cilantro
½ tsp freshly ground black pepper
3 tsp olive oil

<u>Ginger-Sesame Sauce:</u>

½ cup plain non-fat yogurt or 6 tbsp plain Greek-style non-fat yogurt
1 tbsp mayonnaise (not salad dressing)
1½ tbsp peeled and grated fresh ginger
1 tsp toasted sesame oil
1 tsp low-sodium soy sauce

<u>Directions:</u>

1. Remove crusts from the bread and discard, tear remaining bread into pieces and process in a food processor or blender until fine bread crumbs. In a large bowl, flake apart the salmon with fork. Add eggs and mix well. Finely chop 4 of the scallions and add to the bowl. Add the water chestnuts, cilantro, pepper, and bread crumbs. Mix well and shape into 12 patties.

2. In large non-stick skillet, heat 1½ tsp of the oil over medium heat. Add 6 patties and cook 5 minutes on each side. Transfer the cooked patties to a plate and cover with aluminum foil. Add remaining 1½ tsp oil and repeat. Serve cakes with sauce and garnish with scallion.

3. **Ginger-Sesame sauce:**

If using regular yogurt, place the yogurt in a strainer lined with a paper towel. Set the strainer over a bowl and let drain and thicken for 30 minutes. Place the drained or Greek-style yogurt in a small bowl. Add mayonnaise, ginger, sesame oil, and soy sauce and whisk until smooth. Serve with salmon cakes.

Seared Scallops with Wine Sauce

Ingredients:

1 pound large sea scallops
kosher salt
freshly ground black pepper
1 tbsp extra-virgin olive oil
2 tbsp butter, cut into pieces
lemon wedges, for serving

For Pan Sauce:

¼ cup dry white wine or chicken stock
2 tbsp salted butter
1 clove garlic, minced
1 medium shallot, finely diced
2 tbsp freshly chopped parsley
salt and pepper to taste

Directions:

1. In large skillet over medium-high heat, melt butter with oil. Rinse scallops well and blot dry with paper towels, then season generously with salt and pepper. When the pan is just starting to smoke, add scallops.

2. Cook, undisturbed, until bottom has developed a golden crust, 2 to 3 minutes. Flip and cook until golden on other side, 2 to 3 minutes more. Transfer to paper towels.

3. For Pan Sauce: into the same skillet, add butter and melt. Add wine and deglaze, scraping any browned bits that have formed as the scallops cooked. Add shallot and garlic to the wine, stirring constantly. Cook about 3 minutes until the shallots have become tender and translucent.

4. To serve: Place sauce on platter and then arrange scallops on top. Add lemon wedges in case anyone wants them. Sprinkle with parsley.

Note:

This was my grandson Kohler's birthday dinner request this past year.

Tilapia with Tomato and Artichoke Sauce

<u>Ingredients:</u>

1 tbsp cooking oil
4 cloves garlic, minced
½ cup red wine
2½ cups canned crushed tomatoes in thick puree
1¼ tsp dried rosemary
1¼ tsp salt
½ tsp fresh ground black pepper
1½ cups chopped drained and rinsed artichoke hearts
2 tbsp chopped parsley or basil

<u>Directions:</u>

1. In a large, deep frying pan, heat the oil over moderately low heat. Add the garlic and cook, stirring, until fragrant, about 1 minute. Stir in the wine, tomatoes, rosemary, ¾ tsp of the salt, and ¼ tsp of the pepper. Bring to a simmer and continue simmering, covered, for 10 minutes.

2. Sprinkle the filets with the remaining ½ tsp salt and ¼ tsp pepper. Nestle the fish in the sauce, bring back to a simmer, and continue simmering gently, covered, until just done, about 6 minutes for ½-inch-thick filets.

3. Carefully remove the fish from the pan. Stir the artichoke hearts and parsley into the sauce and cook until warmed through, about 2 minutes. Stir in any accumulated juices from the fish. Spoon the sauce over the tilapia.

<u>Note:</u>
Cod, haddock, grouper, and Chilean sea bass filets all work well in this recipe.

~~~PORK~~~

Panko Crusted Pork Tenderloin with Dijon Cream Sauce

<u>Ingredients:</u>

3½ to 4 pounds pork tenderloin
2½ cups buttermilk
3 tbsp Dijon mustard
3 tbsp brown sugar
1 tbsp kosher salt
3 cups Panko breadcrumbs
3 tbsp olive oil
1½ tsp kosher salt
¾ tsp freshly ground black pepper
3 tbsp butter
1 large shallot, minced (about 3-6 tbsp)
1 large clove garlic, minced (about 1 tbsp)
3 cups cream
1½ tsp Dijon mustard
¾ tsp kosher salt and a pinch of black pepper
6 tbsp finely chopped fresh parsley

(Recipe continued on next page.

Directions:
1. Combine the marinade ingredients (buttermilk, Dijon mustard, brown sugar, salt) in a medium bowl. Add the pork tenderloin to the marinade. Cover with plastic wrap and refrigerate for at least one hour, or up to overnight. Remove the pork tenderloin from the refrigerator an hour before you intend to cook it.
2. Heat a thick-bottomed sauté pan on medium high heat. Add the Panko breadcrumbs to the pan. Lower the heat to medium and slowly toast the Panko breadcrumbs until golden brown. Remove from heat. Stir the olive oil, salt, and pepper into the Panko breadcrumbs until they are well coated.
3. Preheat the oven to 375. Line a roasting pan with aluminum foil and place a baking rack or roasting rack over it. Place the toasted Panko in a shallow bowl for dredging. Remove the pork tenderloin from the buttermilk marinade and place it in the bowl of breadcrumbs. Dredge the tenderloin in the breadcrumbs, pressing the tenderloin firmly into the crumbs as you roll it to help the crumbs adhere.
4. Place the breaded tenderloin on the baking rack and bake at 375 for 30 to 40 minutes, until the internal temperature is 145°F, meaning the cooked pork will be a little pink. Remove the pork from the oven when done and let rest on the rack for 10 to 15 minutes while you make the sauce.
5. To make the sauce, melt a tbsp of butter in a shallow saucepan. Add the minced shallots and cook on medium heat until softened, about 3 to 4 minutes. Add the minced garlic and cook a minute more. Add one cup cream, the mustard, salt, and pepper to the shallots. Stir to combine and let come to a simmer. Simmer gently until slightly thickened, 2 to 3 minutes. Stir in 1 tbsp of chopped parsley. Set aside until ready to serve. (If you need to reheat the sauce to serve and it has thickened up, loosen it with a little water while you reheat.)
6. Gently transfer the pork tenderloin to a cutting board and slice into ½-inch thick medallions. Place sauce on a serving platter and place the pork medallions on top of the sauce. Sprinkle everything with chopped parsley.

Note:
This is Bob's favorite pork tenderloin recipe; it is a company-worthy recipe but time consuming. For a terrific husband, it's worth the effort.

Chili Pork Tenderloin Rubbed with Apricot-Ginger Glaze

Ingredients:

2 (1 pound) pork tenderloins, trimmed

Spice Rub »»

1 tbsp chili powder
1 tbsp garlic powder
½ tbsp sugar
1 tsp salt
½ tsp ground black pepper

Glaze »»

1½ cups apricot preserves
½ cup barbecue sauce
1 tsp grated ginger
½ tsp garlic powder
½ tsp hot sauce
1 tbsp chopped cilantro
1 lime, juiced

Directions:

1. Place chili powder, garlic powder, sugar, salt, and pepper in a jar; shake to blend. Rub spice mixture onto pork tenderloins. Cover tenderloins and refrigerate for 2 to 24 hours.
2. Prior to grilling, melt apricot preserves in saucepan over medium heat. Remove pan from the heat and stir in remaining glaze ingredients. Place half of the glaze in a serving bowl and hold for serving with meat.
3. Prepare grill at medium-high heat. Grill pork tenderloins for 15-20 minutes, or until the internal temperature of the pork reaches 145 degrees.
4. When approximately 4 minutes of cook time remains, brush the pork tenderloins with the apricot glaze remaining in the pan. Cook for 2 minutes, turn the pork tenderloins and brush glaze on other side.

Pulled Pork (Slow Cooker or Oven)

<u>Ingredients:</u>

5 to 6½ pounds bone-in pork shoulder blade roast
3 tbsp Dijon-style mustard
½ cup packed dark brown sugar
3 tbsp kosher salt
2 tbsp smoked paprika
1 tbsp chili powder
½ tsp freshly ground black pepper
½ tsp garlic powder
½ cup apple cider vinegar (if using slow cooker method)
serve with pickles, onion slices, coleslaw, and BBQ sauce (recipe next page)

<u>Directions:</u>

1. Trim excess fat from pork, leaving fat cap about ¼-inch thick. Pat pork dry with paper towels. Place on a large piece of plastic wrap. Spread mustard on all sides of pork. In a small bowl stir together brown sugar, salt, paprika, chili powder, black pepper, and garlic powder. Coat all sides of pork with spice mixture. Wrap the pork tightly in the plastic wrap. Place on a tray and chill for at least 1 hour or overnight.

2. <u>Slow Cooker</u>: (for oven method, skip to step 3.) Unwrap roast and place in a 6-quart slow cooker. Add apple cider vinegar. Cover; cook on low-heat setting for 10 to 12 hours or on high-heat setting for 5 to 6 hours. Remove meat from cooker, strain cooking juices. When cool enough to handle, use 2 forks to pull the pork apart, removing fat as you pull. Drizzle with 1 cup of cooking juices and 2 cups of BBQ sauce (modify amounts of each to reach desired moistness and taste).

3. <u>Oven method:</u> Preheat oven to 325. Line a shallow roasting pan with foil. Place a rack in the pan. Unwrap pork and place on the rack. Roast, uncovered, for 4 hours. Wrap roast with a double thickness of foil and return to the rack. Roast for 2 hours more or until an instant-read thermometer inserted in meat registers at least 190 degrees F. Remove from oven. Let roast stand for 30 minutes to 1 hour (this allows the "bark" or "crust" to soften). Unwrap. Using 2 forks, pull the pork apart, removing any large pockets of fat as you pull.

4. Lightly butter both sides of 12 hamburger buns and toast under broiler. Put a scoop of pulled pork on bottom side of each bun, cover with top. Serve with suggested accompaniments. Serves 12.

(Recipe for BBQ Sauce next page)

Pulled Pork BBQ Sauce

<u>Ingredients:</u>

1½ cups ketchup
¾ cup packed brown sugar
½ cup apple cider vinegar
½ cup honey
1/3 cup soy sauce
1½ tsp ground ginger
1 tsp salt
¾ tsp ground mustard
½ tsp garlic powder
¼ tsp pepper
½ tsp liquid smoke

<u>Directions:</u>

1. Mix all ingredients in medium saucepan. Stir well. Cook over low heat for five minutes. Makes 2½ cups.

<u>Notes:</u>
I prefer the slow cooker method because I think the meat is moister and making the pulled pork is less work. I often cook overnight on low. This recipe uses bone-in pork shoulder roast which is arguably more flavorful than boneless pork loin, but pork loin is leaner and less messy so I often use loin. The BBQ sauce is also good on chicken or beef.

~~~Poultry~~~
Baked Chicken with Honey Mustard Sauce

<u>Ingredients:</u>

4 boneless chicken breasts with skin
juice from two fresh lemons
1½ cups chicken broth
2½ tbsp honey
2 tbsp Dijon mustard
¼ cup sliced dried apricots
2 tbsp coarsely chopped walnuts
1 tbsp chopped parsley
4 bunches fresh spinach
salt and pepper to taste

<u>Directions:</u>
1. Place the chicken breasts skin side down in slow cooker. Mix lemon juice and chicken broth and pour over chicken. Cook on medium four hours or until tender, but still moist. Remove from cooker and place on serving dish. Cover with sauce (Step two).
2. Sauce: For honey-mustard sauce, combine broth-lemon juice from slow cooker with honey in a small saucepan. Whisk together and bring to a boil on high heat. Once it comes to a boil, simmer for about 20 minutes. You want it to be reduced to a little less than half the volume you start with to thicken and intensify flavor.
3. Add apricots and cook on high for another 5 minutes. When sauce is done, add chopped walnuts, parsley, salt, and pepper. Serve over cooked spinach or other cooked greens, or add 1 pound of new potatoes, halved, and bake potatoes with chicken. Serves 4.

<u>Note:</u>
I use boneless, skinless, chicken thighs.

Cashew Chicken

Ingredients:
- 2 pounds boneless skinless chicken breasts (about 4 pieces)
- 3 tbsp cornstarch
- ½ tsp black pepper
- 1 tbsp canola oil
- ½ cup reduced sodium soy sauce
- 4 tbsp rice wine vinegar
- 4 tbsp ketchup
- 2 tbsp sweet chili sauce
- 2 tbsp packed brown sugar
- 2 garlic cloves, minced
- 1 tsp grated fresh ginger
- ¼ tsp red pepper flakes
- 1 cup dry roasted, salted cashews

Directions:
1. Combine cornstarch and pepper in resealable food storage bag. Add chicken. Shake to coat with cornstarch mixture.
2. Heat oil in skillet over medium-high heat. Brown chicken about 2 minutes on each side. Place chicken in slow cooker.
3. Combine soy sauce, vinegar, ketchup, sweet chili sauce, brown sugar, garlic, ginger, and pepper flakes in small bowl; pour over chicken.
4. Cook on low for 3 to 4 hours.
5. Add cashews after chicken has cooked. (I usually add five minutes before I remove from crock-pot so they are hot, but don't get too soft.
6. Serve over rice. Makes 4-6 servings.

Notes:
This recipe is one of Bob's favorites, but there never seems to be enough sauce so I double the sauce ingredients. I also often use boneless, skinless chicken thighs because they are more tender.

Catalina Cranberry Chicken

Ingredients:

4-6 skinless, boneless chicken breasts or 6-8 thighs
1 pkg Lipton Onion Soup Mix
16 oz can whole cranberry sauce
10 oz bottle Catalina dressing

Directions:
1. Combine the soup, salad dressing, and cranberry sauce. Add chicken, cover, and let stand for 30 minutes, turning once.
2. Bake at 350 for 1½ hours in a covered dish. Turn the chicken half way through the cooking time.
3. Serve over rice or with baked potatoes and asparagus.

Note:
If I'm going to be gone for a half day, I put all ingredients in a slow cooker and set on low for 4 hours. I skip the step about letting it stand.

Chicken with Couscous Patties

<u>Ingredients:</u>

4 large boneless and skinless chicken thighs
1½ tsp lemon peel
2 tsp fresh oregano
4 tsp olive oil
1/8 tsp each salt and pepper
6 slices lemon
1¼ cups chicken broth
3 green onions
1 cup couscous
⅓ cup grated parmesan
2 tbsp bread crumbs
1 large egg
1 tsp chopped oregano
1/8 tsp each salt and pepper
2 tbsp bread crumbs

<u>Directions:</u>
1. Toss chicken thighs in jelly-roll pan with lemon peel, 2 tsp fresh oregano, 2 tsp olive oil, 1/8 tsp each salt and pepper, and 6 lemon slices.
2. Bake in 425 oven for 18 minutes or until chicken is cooked through.
3. Heat chicken broth and green onions in 1-quart pan and bring to a boil. Stir in couscous. Cover; let stand 5 minutes. Stir in grated parmesan, 2 tbsp bread crumbs, egg, 1 tsp chopped oregano, and 1/8 tsp each salt and pepper. Shape into 8 patties; coat with remaining 2 tbsp bread crumbs.
4. Cook in 2 tsp olive oil in 12-inch nonstick skillet on medium, 4 minutes per side. Serve with chicken.

Chicken with Quinoa and Vegetables

Ingredients:

1 cup rinsed quinoa
2 cups chicken broth
2 tbsp extra-virgin olive oil
2 garlic scrapes, chopped
1 small onion, chopped
2 skinless, boneless chicken breast halves – cut into strips
2 tbsp extra-virgin olive oil
1 zucchini, diced
1 cup broccoli florets
1 tomato, diced
4 oz crumbled feta cheese
8 fresh basil leaves
1 tbsp lime juice

Directions:
1. Bring the quinoa and chicken broth to a boil in a saucepan; reduce heat to a simmer and cover the pan. Simmer until the broth is absorbed, the quinoa is fluffy, and the white line is visible in the grain, about 12 minutes.
2. Heat 2 tbsp of olive oil in a skillet; cook and stir the garlic scrapes and onion until onion is translucent, about 5 minutes. Stir in the chicken breast strips and cook until the chicken is still slightly pink in the middle, about 5 more minutes. Remove the chicken meat and set aside.
3. Pour 2 more tbsp of olive oil in the skillet and cook and stir the zucchini, broccoli florets, and tomato until the veggies are tender, 5 to 8 minutes. Return chicken to skillet and sprinkle with feta cheese, basil leaves, and lime juice. Cook until the chicken is fully cooked and hot, about 10 more minutes. Serve over hot quinoa.

Chicken Marengo

<u>Ingredients:</u>

4 (6 oz each) skinless, boneless chicken breast halves
¼ cup all-purpose flour
½ tsp salt and ¼ tsp black pepper
¼ cup extra-virgin olive oil
3 large portabella mushrooms, stems discarded, and caps thinly sliced
12 medium to large shrimp, deveined and cleaned, tails on
1 small shallot, finely chopped
1 garlic clove, minced
½ tsp dried thyme, crumbled
½ cup dry red wine
1 (14 to 15 oz) can whole tomatoes, drained and chopped
½ cup beef or veal demi-glace* plus ½ cup water (See note below.)

<u>Directions:</u>

1. With oven rack in middle position, preheat oven to 350. Pat chicken dry, then combine flour, salt, and pepper in a large sealable plastic bag and add chicken. Seal bag and shake to coat, then remove chicken, knocking off excess flour. Arrange in 1 layer on a plate.

2. Heat oil in a 12-inch heavy ovenproof skillet over moderately high heat until hot but not smoking. Sauté chicken, smooth sides down, until golden, about 2 minutes. Turn over and sauté 1 minute more. Scatter mushrooms around chicken and transfer skillet to oven, then bake, uncovered, until chicken is cooked through, 5 to 10 minutes.

3. Transfer chicken to a plate. Add shrimp to skillet and sauté one minute on each side (shrimp will continue to cook during next steps).

4. Add shallot, garlic, and thyme to skillet and sauté over medium high heat, stirring, 1 minute. Add wine and boil, stirring and scraping up brown bits, until reduced by half, about 1 minute. Add tomatoes, demi-glace, and ½ cup water and simmer until mushrooms are tender and sauce is reduced by half, about 4 minutes. Return chicken to skillet and simmer to warm. Serve over rice, couscous, or mashed potatoes.

<u>Note:</u>

*If you cannot find demi-glace you can use ½ cup au jus or beef stock mixed with 1 tbsp tomato paste.

Perfect Moist & Tender Chicken Breasts Every Time

<u>Ingredients:</u>

1 to 4 boneless, skinless chicken breasts, of similar size
salt and freshly ground black pepper
1 tbsp olive oil, unsalted butter, or combination of both

<u>Directions:</u>

1. Flatten the chicken breasts. Pound the chicken breasts to an even thickness with a meat tenderizer.
2. Lightly season the chicken with salt and pepper.
3. Heat to medium-high heat a frying pan large enough to fit the chicken in a single layer. When the pan is quite hot, add the olive oil (or butter, if using). Swirl the pan so bottom is lightly covered with the olive oil.
4. Reduce the heat to medium and add the chicken breasts. Cook for 1 minute without moving to help them get a little golden on one side (you are not actually searing or browning them).
5. Flip each chicken breast over.
6. Reduce the heat to low. Cover the pan with a tight-fitting lid. Set a timer for 10 minutes, and walk away. Do not lift the lid; do not peek.
7. After 10 minutes have elapsed, turn off the heat. (If you have an electric stove, remove the pan from the heat.) Reset the timer for 10 additional minutes and leave the chicken breasts in the pan. Again, do not lift the lid; do not peek.
8. After this second 10 minutes is up, uncover and your chicken is done. Make sure there is no pink in the middle of the chicken breasts. If you want to be absolutely sure it is cooked, you can use an instant-read thermometer to check—the chicken should be at least 165°F. Slice and eat.

<u>Notes:</u>

This is a how-to for tender chicken breasts that I can use in any recipe or just to slice for sandwiches. Here are a couple of tips to make the chicken even more perfect: You can dredge the breasts in flour before cooking and season the flour with the spices or fresh herbs of your choice. And if you want to go the extra step to make the chicken even juicier and more flavorful, put the raw chicken in a quick brine before starting. Just 15 minutes in a simple salt/water/sugar brine makes a difference. For brine, mix 1 gallon warm water, ¾ cup kosher salt, and 2/3 cup sugar. However, even without these extra steps, cooking boneless, skinless chicken breasts this way prevents them from becoming tough and dry.

Pesto Chicken Florentine

Ingredients:

2 tbsp olive oil
2 garlic cloves, finely chopped
4 boneless, skinless chicken breast halves, cut into strips
2 cups fresh spinach leaves
1 envelope Alfredo sauce (I skip this and add additional pesto)
2 tbsp pesto sauce
1 (8-oz) package dry penne pasta
1 tbsp Romano cheese, grated (or more to taste)

Directions:
1. Heat oil in a large skillet over medium high heat. Add garlic, sauté for 1 minute; then add chicken and cook for 7 to 8 minutes on each side. When chicken is close to cooked through (no longer pink inside), add spinach and sauté all together for 3 to 4 minutes.
2. Meanwhile, prepare Alfredo sauce (if using) according to package directions. When finished, stir in 2 tbsp pesto; set aside.
3. In a large pot of salted boiling water, cook pasta for 8 to 10 minutes or until al dente. Rinse under cold water and drain.
4. Add chicken/spinach mixture to pasta, then stir in pesto/Alfredo sauce. Mix well, top with cheese and serve.

Notes:
I use about 3 tbsp pesto (recipe p. 250), and no Alfredo sauce packet. I also serve an additional small dish of grated cheese on the side.

Pickle Juice and Buttermilk Brined Fried Chicken

<u>Ingredients:</u>

4 or more chicken thighs or your favorite chicken parts
2 cups dill pickle juice
vegetable oil for frying (I use canola)
1 cup buttermilk
1 cup all-purpose flour
1 tsp salt
dash cayenne (or to taste)
¾ tsp ground black pepper

<u>Directions:</u>

1. Place chicken thighs or other chicken pieces in a resealable plastic bag; cover with pickle juice. Seal and refrigerate for 3 hours.
2. Drain pickle juice from chicken. Cover; refrigerate until ready to fry.
3. Preheat oven to 350.
4. Heat 2 inches oil in a Dutch oven or large frying pan over medium-high heat.
5. Pour buttermilk and flour into 2 separate bowls. Season flour with salt and pepper. Pat the chicken with paper towels to make sure it is dry. Dredge in buttermilk. Then dredge in flour. Return to buttermilk and dredge in both buttermilk and flour a second time. Place chicken on a rack set over a baking sheet.
6. Fill Dutch oven or large frying pan with as many pieces of chicken as possible without crowding. Cook until golden brown, 5 to 7 minutes per side. Place chicken on the baking sheet. Repeat until all pieces are fried. Transfer chicken to the oven.
7. Bake in the preheated oven until no longer pink in the center and the juices run clear, 5 to 8 minutes. You want to make sure chicken is fully cooked, but not overdone. Season with a pinch of salt.

Slow Cooker Turkey Breast

Ingredients:

10-pound turkey breast
2 (1 oz each) pkg dry onion soup mix
¾ cup water
2 tbsp garlic powder
2 tbsp onion powder
1 tbsp dried parsley
1 tbsp seasoning salt
1 tbsp dried basil
1 tbsp dried oregano

Directions:

1. Place turkey breast into a large slow cooker. Whisk soup mix and water in a bowl and pour mixture over the turkey breast, spreading it out to evenly cover the meat.
2. Stir remaining ingredients in a bowl until thoroughly combined; sprinkle over the turkey breast.
3. Cook on low until turkey is very tender, about 8 to 9 hours.

Slow-Cooker Chicken and Potato Curry

Ingredients:

3 baking potatoes, peeled and cut into 1½-inch pieces
2 red onions, cut into wedges
3 tbsp chopped fresh ginger
8 garlic cloves, chopped (about 2 tbsp)
2 tbsp curry powder
1 tsp coriander seeds, crushed
1 tsp kosher salt
½ tsp black pepper
6 skinless chicken legs (3 pounds)
1 (15-oz) can unsweetened coconut milk
chopped cilantro and steamed basmati rice, for serving

Directions:

1. Combine the potatoes and onions in a 6-quart slow cooker. Mix the ginger, garlic, curry powder, coriander, salt, and pepper in a large bowl. Add the chicken and toss to coat.

2. Place the chicken in the slow cooker, pouring over any loose spices and the coconut milk. Cover and cook 6 to 7 hours or on high or for 4 to 5 hours on low until the chicken is tender and cooked through.

3. Garnish the curry with chopped cilantro.

Thanksgiving Turkey (Carving)

Step 1: After the turkey is cooked, let it sit for at least 20 minutes to cool. Don't let it sit for longer than 40 minutes, as carving will add cooling time.

Step 2: While the turkey is cooling, set up your carving station. If you're using a large cutting board, place a rag or towel beneath for stability. Select and sharpen a thin carving knife—knife experts say the thinner the better for slicing. If you don't have a carving knife, you can use a chef's knife.

Step 3: Once the turkey has cooled, place it on the cutting board. Use the sharpened knife to remove the leg and thigh from one side of the bird.

Step 4: Cut all the way through the joint to separate the drumstick from the body.

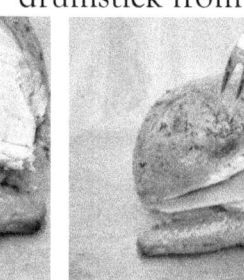

Step 5: On the same side, remove the breast and wing. To do so, cut through the wing joint as you did with the leg. Then, make a slice underneath the breast, as shown. Repeat steps 3-5 on the other side of the turkey.

Step 6: Slice the breast and thigh meat. While the breast meat is still attached to the bird, cut it into slices. Do the same for the thigh meat.

Step 7: Arrange the sliced meat on a platter and serve.

<u>Note</u>: I found these instructions online and need them every year at Thanksgiving, so I included them in this book where I'll always have them.)

Brining a Turkey: If you want a juicier turkey, brine it first. For a 16-24-pound turkey use 2 gallons cold water, 10 ounces Soy Sauce, ½ cup kosher salt, ½ cup sugar, 2 tbsp dried sage, 2 tbsp dried celery seed, and 1 tbsp dried thyme. Remove giblets and neck; rinse turkey inside and out. Mix ingredients and place in large stock pot or 5-gallon container. Add turkey. Cover and refrigerate overnight. Remove from brine, pat dry, and cook per normal instructions.

Two Good Marinades

For Beef (steaks):
Ingredients:

½ cup balsamic vinegar
¼ cup soy sauce
3 tbsp minced garlic
2 tbsp honey
2 tbsp olive oil
2 tsp ground black pepper
1 tsp Worcestershire sauce
1 tsp onion powder
½ tsp salt
½ tsp liquid smoke
pinch cayenne pepper

Directions:
Mix all ingredients. Place steaks in large baking dish and pour marinade over them, turning to make sure all surfaces of meat are covered. Cover dish with plastic and refrigerate overnight. Drain and discard marinade and grill steaks.

For Shrimp:
Ingredients:

2 tsp dried oregano
1 tsp salt
1 tsp black pepper, freshly ground
1 cup olive oil
1 tbsp parsley flakes
1 lemon (juiced)
1 tbsp tomato paste or ketchup
1 clove garlic

Directions:
Whisk all ingredients and pour into large, sealable plastic bag. Add raw, peeled, deveined shrimp. Marinate overnight. Discard marinade and put shrimp on skewer and grill.

Pies

"You can say this for ready-mixes – the next generation isn't going to have any trouble making pies exactly like mother used to make." **Earl Wilson**

"We must have a pie. Stress cannot exist in the presence of a pie."
David Mamet

"A cherry pie is . . . ephemeral. From the moment it emerges from the oven it begins a steep decline: from too hot to edible to cold to stale to moldy, and finally to a post-pie state where only history can tell you that it was once considered food. The pie is a parable of human life." **Nick Harkaway**

"Pies mean Thanksgiving and Christmas and picnics." **Janet Clarkson**

"Never say 'no' to pie. No matter what, wherever you are, diet-wise or whatever, you know what? You can always have a small piece of pie, and I like pie. I don't know anybody who doesn't like pie. If somebody doesn't like pie, I don't trust them. I'll bet you Vladimir Putin doesn't like pie." **Al Roker**

Apple Cider Pie

Ingredients:

prepared crust (See pie crust recipes starting on p. 334.)
2 cups apple cider
1/3 cup sugar
3 tbsp cornstarch
2 tbsp fresh lemon juice
2 tsp vanilla extract
1¼ tsp pumpkin-pie spice
7 Braeburn apples, peeled and quartered (about 3 pounds)
cooking spray
1 large egg, lightly beaten
1 tbsp water
1 tbsp sugar

Directions:
1. Bring cider to a boil in a large, heavy saucepan over high heat. Cook until reduced to ½ cup (about 20 minutes). Cool completely. Preheat oven to 450.
2. Combine cooled cider, 1/3 cup sugar, cornstarch, lemon juice, vanilla, and pie spice in a large bowl. Cut each apple quarter crosswise into ¼-inch-thick slices. Stir apple slices into cider mixture.
3. Make crust for a two-crust pie. Line lightly sprayed 9-inch pie pan with one crust. Fill with apple mixture. Cover with second crust, fold edges under and flute. Cut 6 (1-inch) slits into top of pastry using a sharp knife. Combine egg and 1 tbsp water. Brush top and edges of pie with egg mixture, and sprinkle with 1 tbsp sugar.
4. Place pie on a baking sheet, and bake at 450 for 15 minutes. Reduce oven temperature to 350 (do not remove pie from oven), and bake an additional 45 minutes or until golden. Cool on a wire rack.

Notes:
I often use a streusel topping instead of a top crust. **Streusel Topping**: ½ tsp cinnamon, 1 cup brown sugar, ½ cup oatmeal, 1 cup flour, ½ cup butter. Mix until crumbly. Sprinkle over filled pie when you reduce temperature.

Bumbleberry Pie

Ingredients: (filling enough for two pies)
- 4 cups apples—peeled, cored, and chopped
- 2 cups chopped fresh rhubarb
- 2 cups sliced fresh strawberries
- 2 cups fresh blueberries
- 2 cups fresh raspberries
- 2 tbsp lemon juice
- 2 cups white sugar
- 2/3 cup all-purpose flour
- 2 tbsp tapioca
- 1 egg yolk, beaten
- 2 tbsp water

Directions:
1. Preheat oven to 350. In a large bowl, combine apples, rhubarb, strawberries, blueberries, raspberries, and lemon juice.
2. Mix together 2 cups sugar, 2/3 cup flour, and tapioca; gently toss with fruit mixture. Divide into 2 pastry lined pie pans. Cover with top crusts (or cut-outs if you like less crust); trim and crimp edges. Brush tops with egg wash (1 egg beaten with 2 tbsp water). Cut a few slits in the top to allow steam to vent.
3. Bake in preheated oven for 50 to 60 minutes, or until filling is bubbly in center and top is golden brown.

Caramel Pecan Pie

<u>Ingredients:</u>

1 (9 inch) unbaked pie crust (See pie crusts recipes starting on p. 334.)
36 individually wrapped caramels, unwrapped
¼ cup butter
¼ cup milk
¾ cup white sugar
3 eggs
½ tsp vanilla extract
¼ tsp salt
1 cup pecan halves, lightly toasted

<u>Directions:</u>

1. Preheat oven to 350. In a saucepan over low heat, combine caramels, butter, and milk. Cook, stirring frequently, until smooth. Remove from heat and set aside. (I melt the caramel mixture in microwave, but am careful not to overcook.)
2. In a large bowl, combine sugar, eggs, vanilla, and salt. Gradually mix in the melted caramel mixture. Stir in pecans. Pour filling into unbaked pie crust.
3. Bake in the preheated oven for 45 to 50 minutes, or until pastry is golden brown. Allow to cool until filling is firm.

Dutch Apple Pie

<u>Ingredients:</u>

one 9-inch pie shell (See pie crust recipes starting on p. 334.)
5 cups apples—peeled, cored, sliced (Granny Smith or Yellow Delicious)
2 tbsp all-purpose flour
2/3 cup white sugar
½ tsp ground cinnamon
¼ tsp ground nutmeg
¼ tsp ground allspice
2 tbsp butter
¾ cup all-purpose flour
½ tsp ground cinnamon
½ cup packed brown sugar
¾ cup rolled oats
1 tsp lemon zest
½ cup butter

<u>Directions:</u>

1. Preheat oven to 425. Place 9-inch crust in pan and put in freezer.
2. To Make Apple Filling: Place apples in a large bowl. In a separate small bowl combine 2 tbsp flour, white sugar, ½ tsp cinnamon, nutmeg, and allspice. Mix well, then add to apples. Toss until apples are evenly coated.
3. Remove pie shell from freezer. Place apple mixture in shell and dot with 2 tbsp butter. Lay a sheet of aluminum foil lightly on top of filling, but do not seal. Bake in preheated oven for 10 minutes.
4. While filling is baking, make Streusel Topping: In a medium bowl combine ¾ cup flour, ½ tsp cinnamon, brown sugar, oats, and lemon peel. Mix thoroughly, then cut in ½ cup butter or margarine until mixture is crumbly. Remove pie from oven and sprinkle streusel on top.
5. Reduce heat to 375 degrees. Bake an additional 30 to 35 minutes, until streusel is browned and apples are tender. Cover loosely with aluminum foil to prevent excess browning.

Fresh Strawberry Pie (Version One)

<u>Ingredients:</u>

6 cups fresh whole strawberries, hulled, divided
1 cup sugar
3 tbsp cornstarch
¾ cup water
few drops red food coloring, optional
1 pastry shell (9 inches), baked (or graham cracker shell)
whipping cream
2 tbsp confectioners' sugar
1 tsp vanilla extract

<u>Directions</u>

1. Mash 1 cup strawberries; set aside.
2. In a saucepan, combine sugar and cornstarch; stir in water and mashed berries. Bring to a boil, stirring constantly. Stir in food coloring if desired. Cook and stir 3 minutes more. Cool for 10 minutes.
3. Spread about 1/3 cup glaze over bottom and sides of pie shell. Halve remaining strawberries; arrange in shell. Spoon remaining glaze over berries. Chill for 1-2 hours. Just before serving, garnish with whipped cream. (Using mixer, beat cream on high speed to soft peak stage, add confectioners' sugar and vanilla). Pie is best served the day it's made.

Fresh Strawberry Pie with Whipped Cream

<u>Ingredients:</u>
>1 pint whole, large, very red strawberries, cleaned and cored
>2 tbsp corn starch
>2½ cups cold water
>1 regular pkg strawberry Jell-O gelatin
>1 pie crust, baked and ready to fill or one homemade pie crust

<u>Directions:</u>
1. In a sauce pan, dissolve the cornstarch in the cold water. Slowly bring to a boil. As the mixture becomes thick and clear, stir in the gelatin. Bring back to boil and remove from heat immediately. This creates a glaze for the berries.
2. Place the prepared strawberries in the pie shell with the points up and in a single layer.
3. Pour the glaze over the berries, allowing the tips of the berries to show.
4. Cover with plastic wrap and refrigerate.
5. Serve with dollops of sweetened whipped cream and a garnish of a mint leaf.

<u>Notes:</u>
This recipe came from Jan Kinzel. It's is a simple way to make a truly fresh strawberry pie! No cooked or mushy strawberries.

Key Lime Pie

<u>Ingredients:</u>

1½ cups graham-cracker crumbs
6 tbsp unsalted butter, melted and cooled
3 tbsp sugar
½ cup freshly squeezed key-lime juice
1 tbsp grated key lime zest, plus more for garnish
1 can (14 ounces) can sweetened condensed milk
4 large egg yolks
1½ cups heavy cream, chilled
2 tbsp confectioners' sugar
1 tsp vanilla extract

<u>Directions:</u>

1. Heat oven to 375. Combine graham-cracker crumbs, butter, and 3 tbsp sugar in a medium bowl; mix well. Press into a 9-inch pie plate, and bake until lightly browned, about 12 minutes. Remove from oven, and transfer to a wire rack until completely cooled.
2. Lower oven temperature to 325. In a medium bowl, gently whisk together condensed milk, egg yolks, key lime juice, and zest. Pour into prepared, cooled crust.
3. Return pie to oven, and bake until the center is set but still quivers when the pan is nudged, 15 to 17 minutes. Let cool completely on a wire rack.
4. Shortly before serving, whip heavy cream to soft peak stage. Add confectioners' sugar and vanilla. Spoon over cooled pie, garnish with zest, and serve immediately.

<u>Notes:</u>

I fell in love with key lime pie when visiting our friends, Maureen and Ray Scully. I think they got their pie at Publix, but I found my own recipe. I don't make it often because squeezing tiny key limes is a pain. I've even used the key lime concentrate. No matter how you make it, it's a terrific summer treat.

Lemon Meringue Pie

<u>Ingredients:</u>

1 single pie crust (See pie crust recipes starting on p. 334.)

Filling »»

1 cup sugar
¼ cup cornstarch
1/8 tsp salt
4 large egg yolks
2 cups milk
1/3 cup fresh lemon juice
3 tbsp butter or margarine
1 tsp grated lemon rind
½ tsp vanilla extract

Meringue »»

6 egg whites
½ tsp vanilla extract
6 tbsp sugar

<u>Directions:</u>

1. Fit piecrust into a 9-inch pie plate (about 1 inch deep); fold edges under, and crimp. Prick bottom and sides with a fork. Freeze 10 minutes. Line piecrust with parchment paper; fill with pie weights or dried beans. Bake at 425 for 10 minutes. Remove weights and parchment paper; bake 12 to 15 more minutes or until crust is lightly browned. (Shield edges with foil if they are browning too quickly.) Set aside.

2. Whisk together sugar, cornstarch, and salt in a heavy, non-aluminum, medium saucepan. Whisk together egg yolks, milk, and lemon juice in a bowl; whisk into sugar mixture in pan over medium heat. Bring to a boil, and boil, whisking constantly, one minute. Remove pan from heat; stir in butter, lemon rind, and vanilla extract until smooth. Pour into piecrust. Cover with plastic wrap, placing wrap directly on filling. (Proceed immediately with next step to ensure that the meringue is spread over the pie filling while it is still warm.)

3. **Meringue:** Beat egg whites and vanilla extract at high speed with an electric mixer until foamy. Add sugar, 1 tbsp at a time, and beat 2 to 4 minutes or until stiff peaks form and sugar dissolves. Remove plastic wrap from pie, and spread meringue evenly over warm lemon pie filling, sealing edges. Bake at 325 for 20 to 25 minutes or until golden brown. Cool pie completely on a wire rack. Store leftovers in the refrigerator.

<u>Notes:</u>

My mother, Bonnie Albrecht, made this great lemon pie. She realized her son-in-law loved it so often had one waiting for him when we went to visit.

Mixed Berry Pie

Ingredients:
>pastry for a Double-Crust Pie (See pie crust recipes starting on p. 334.)
>1 cup fresh strawberries, halved
>2 cups fresh raspberries
>1½ cups fresh blueberries
>1 tbsp freshly squeezed lemon juice
>½ cup white sugar (slightly more if you like it sweet)
>¼ cup cornstarch

Directions:
1. Line pie plate with one pie crust and place in the refrigerator. Keep second pie crust in refrigerator to roll and use as top crust.
2. In a large mixing bowl, stir together the sugar and cornstarch. Add the strawberries, raspberries, blueberries, and lemon juice; toss until berries are coated. Allow fruit mixture to stand for about 15 minutes.
3. Preheat the oven to 375. Place a cookie sheet in the oven to preheat. Stir the berry mixture and pour the filling into the pastry-lined pie plate. Place the top crust over the pie and trim the edges, leaving a ½-inch overhang.
4. Crimp the edges of the crust to seal and cut vents in the top to allow steam to escape. To prevent over-browning, cover the edge of the pie with foil.
5. Bake in the preheated oven on the cookie sheet for 25 minutes. Remove the foil. Bake for an additional 20 to 30 minutes, or until the filling is bubbling and the crust is golden. Cool on a wire rack.

Notes:
You can use blackberries in place of raspberries. You can also use frozen berries, but drain slightly.
I often do a lattice top rather than a two crust.

Mud Pie

<u>Ingredients:</u>

1 Oreo crust
1 pint coffee ice cream
1 pint chocolate mocha ice cream
1 cup pecans, chopped and toasted
1 (12 oz) jar hot fudge topping
½ (18 oz) pkg crushed Oreos, divided
1 pint whipping cream
2 tbsp confectioners' sugar
1 tsp vanilla
¾ cup chocolate syrup

<u>Directions:</u>
1. Freeze the crust until firm, about 30 minutes. Place chocolate mocha ice cream into a bowl, and let it stand about 10 minutes to soften. Mix softened ice cream with the toasted chopped pecans. Spread the ice cream/pecans in an even layer over the frozen crust. Cover with plastic wrap, and freeze for 2 hours.
2. Heat the topping in the microwave on low until warm and easy to pour, 30 seconds to 1 minute (do not let the sauce get hot). Pour into a bowl. Set aside 2 tbsp cookie crumbs for garnish; stir remaining cookie crumbs into the fudge topping. Remove the pie from the freezer, and layer the cookie crumbs/fudge topping mixture over the chocolate mocha layer of ice cream. Cover with plastic wrap, and return to freezer for 2 hours.
3. Take coffee ice cream from the freezer, and let stand for about 10 minutes to soften. Layer the ice cream over the layer of cookie crumbs/fudge topping. Cover and return to freezer for 2 more hours. Remove pie, and frost the top of the pie with whipped cream (Whip cream until it stands in soft peaks. Add confectioners' sugar, and vanilla). Sprinkle with reserved cookie crumbs. Freeze for 2 more hours to freeze the whipped topping layer. Cut the pie into serving pieces, and drizzle each with about 1 tbsp of the chocolate syrup.

<u>Notes:</u>
You can vary the flavors of ice cream (i.e. chocolate mint, vanilla, etc.). Take pie from freezer about 15 minutes before slicing or it may be too hard to cut easily.

Pear-Butterscotch Pie

<u>Ingredients:</u>

3 tbsp all-purpose flour
1 tsp cinnamon
½ tsp grated nutmeg
1/8 tsp salt
½ cup packed dark brown sugar
2½ pounds ripe Bartlett or Anjou pears (about 5), peeled,
and each cut into 6 wedges, and cored
1 tbsp fresh lemon juice
1 tsp pure vanilla extract
double crust 9-inch all-butter pastry (see pie crust recipes starting on p. 334.)
1 tbsp unsalted butter, cut into bits
1 large egg beaten with 1 tbsp warm water
1 tbsp granulated sugar

<u>Directions:</u>
1. Put a baking sheet on middle rack of oven and preheat oven to 425.
2. Whisk together flour, cinnamon, nutmeg, and salt, then whisk in brown sugar, breaking up any lumps. Gently toss pears with brown sugar mixture, lemon juice, and vanilla and let stand 5 to 15 minutes to macerate fruit.
3. Roll out bottom crust (keep dough for top crust refrigerated) on a lightly floured surface with a lightly floured rolling pin into a 13-inch round. Fit into a 9-inch pie plate. Reserve scraps.
4. Transfer filling to the dough-lined pie pan. Dot with butter, then cover with rolled out second pastry round. Trim edges, leaving a ½-inch overhang (reserve scraps). Press edges together to seal, then fold under. Lightly brush top crust with some of egg wash, then cut 3 (1-inch-long) vents.
5. Roll out dough scraps about 1/8-inch-thick and cut shapes with cookie cutters. Arrange decoratively on top of pie, pressing gently to help them adhere. Lightly brush cutouts with egg wash and sprinkle top of pie with granulated sugar.
6. Bake pie on hot baking sheet 20 minutes. Reduce to 375 and bake until crust is golden and filling done, 40 to 45 minutes more. Cool to warm or room temperature, 2 to 3 hours. For true decadence, drizzle with caramel sauce. (See index for caramel recipes in this book.)

Pumpkin Praline Pie

<u>Ingredients:</u>
    1 recipe for single butter crust (See pie crust recipes starting on p. 334.)

<u>Filling:</u> »»

    1 (15-ounce) can plain pumpkin puree
    ¾ cup packed (5¼ ounces) dark brown sugar
    2 tsp ground cinnamon
    1 tsp ground ginger
    ½ tsp ground allspice
    pinch of ground cloves
    ½ tsp table salt
    1 cup evaporated milk
    3 large eggs
    2 tsp vanilla extract

For the praline topping: »»

    1 cup (4 ounces) pecans, chopped fine
    ½ cup packed (3½ ounces) dark brown sugar
    pinch of table salt
    2 tsp dark corn syrup
    1 tsp vanilla extract
    2 tsp granulated sugar

<u>Directions for crust:</u>

1. Adjust oven rack to lowest position, place rimmed baking sheet on oven rack, and heat oven to 425.

2. Line pie plate with one unbaked, rolled out crust Trim overhang to ½ inch beyond lip of pie plate. Fold overhang under itself; folded edge should be flush with edge of pie plate. Flute dough or press the tines of a fork against dough to flatten it against rim of pie plate. Refrigerate dough-lined plate until firm, about 15 minutes.

3. Line dough with foil, and fill with metal or ceramic pie weights. Bake for 15 minutes. Remove foil and weights, rotate plate, and bake for five to ten additional minutes, until crust is golden brown and crisp. Remove from oven, and reduce oven temperature to 350.

<u>Directions:</u>

For the filling»»

    (Recipe continued on next page.)

1. Mix pumpkin puree, brown sugar, spices, and salt, and mix until smooth, about one minute. Cook mixture in large saucepan over medium-high heat until sputtering and thickened, about 4 minutes, and remove from heat.

2. Whisk evaporated milk into pumpkin mixture, and then whisk in eggs and vanilla. Pour filling into warm (If the crust has completely cooled, put it back in oven to warm slightly.) pie crust, and bake until filling is puffed and cracked around edges and the center barely jiggles when pie is shaken, about 35 minutes.

Directions:

For the topping »»

1. While pie is baking, toss pecans, brown sugar, and salt in bowl. Add corn syrup and vanilla, using fingers to ensure that ingredients are well blended.

2. Scatter topping evenly over puffed filling and sprinkle with granulated sugar. Bake until pecans are fragrant and topping is bubbling around edges, about 10 minutes. Cool pie completely on wire rack, at least two hours. Pie can be wrapped in plastic and refrigerated for up to two days. Serve pie at room temperature.

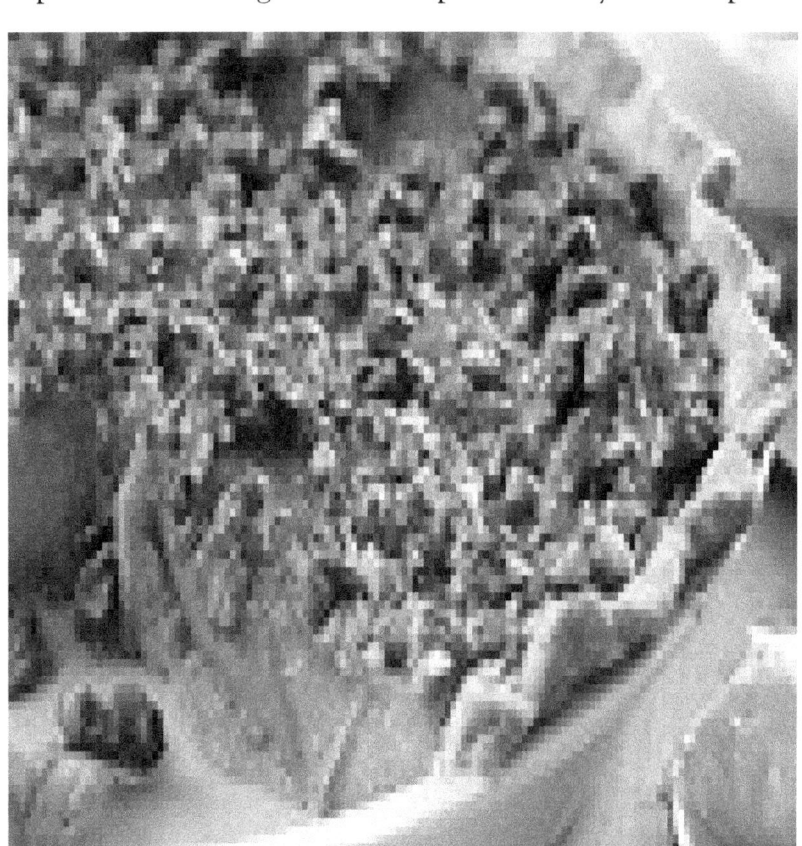

Notes:

It's confession time. I've never tried this recipe, although I have kept it around forever. When I went through my recipes to compile this book, I just couldn't throw it away. My family doesn't like pumpkin pie. But this just looked and sounded too good to discard. I can't eat a whole pie (although I could make a good attempt). Maybe this year, I'll try it for Thanksgiving and see if I have any takers!

Pecan Pie with Brownie Crust and Vanilla Sauce

<u>Ingredients:</u>

Brownie Crust »»

2 large eggs
1 tsp vanilla extract
10 tbsp unsalted butter
1¼ cups granulated sugar
¾ cup unsweetened cocoa powder
¼ tsp salt
½ cup all-purpose flour

Pecan filling »»

1 cup packed light brown sugar
1 cup light corn syrup
4 large eggs
1 tbsp vanilla extract
½ cup unsalted butter, melted
3 tbsp bourbon (optional)
4 cups pecans, chopped and toasted

Vanilla sauce »»

½ cup heavy cream
1 cup milk
½ vanilla bean, split (or 1 tsp vanilla extract)
3 large egg yolks
½ cup granulated sugar

<u>Directions:</u>

Make the brownie crust:

1. Preheat oven to 325. In small bowl, beat the eggs and vanilla, and set aside.
2. Put the butter, sugar, cocoa powder, and salt in a large metal bowl. Set the bowl over a pan of simmering water and stir until the butter is melted and the mixture is warm; remove the bowl from the pan.
3. Whisking constantly, add the egg mixture and continue to whisk until thoroughly incorporated.
4. Beat in the flour, then spread the batter evenly in a 9-inch round cake pan that is 2 inches deep. Bake for 15 minutes, then cool to room temperature.

Make the pecan filling:

(Recipe continued on next page.)

1. In large bowl using an electric mixer, beat the sugar and corn syrup until very smooth, about 3-4 minutes.
2. Add the eggs and vanilla and beat until just combined.
3. Add the butter and the bourbon, if using bourbon, and beat until just combined.
4. Fold in the pecans, then pour the mixture into the baked and cooled brownie crust. Bake for 45 minutes, until firm in the center, then cool to room temperature on wire rack.

Make the vanilla sauce:

1. In small saucepan, combine the cream and milk. Scrape the vanilla bean and add the seeds and bean to the pan. (If using vanilla extract, do not add extract until end of sauce process.)
2. Bring just to a simmer, then remove from the heat and let steep for 30 minutes. Remove the vanilla bean.
3. In medium bowl, whisk the egg yolks and ¼ cup of the sugar until smooth. Stir the remaining ¼ cup sugar into the milk mixture and bring to a bare simmer. Whisk about ½ cup of the milk mixture into the egg mixture, then slowly pour the egg mixture into the saucepan and whisk to combine.
4. Cook over low heat, stirring constantly, until thick enough to coat the back of the spoon; do not boil. (Add vanilla extract at this point if you are using that instead of vanilla bean.) Pour through a fine-mesh sieve set over a bowl, then set the bowl in a larger bowl of ice water and cool to room temperature. Serve slices of the pie drizzled with the sauce.

Pecan Pie without Corn Syrup

<u>Ingredients:</u>

    crust for single crust pie (See pie crust recipes starting on p. 334.)
    3 eggs
    1 cup dark brown sugar
    ¼ cup white sugar
    4 tbsp butter, melted
    ¼ cup milk
    3 tbsp flour
    ¼ tsp salt
    1½ cups chopped pecans (extra whole pecans for top of the pie)

<u>Directions:</u>

1. Preheat oven to 350. Refrigerate a single pie crust. Spray pie pan with cooking spray. Place crust in 9-inch pie pan and prick the crust all over. Bake for 10 minutes or until the edges are just starting to turn golden. Remove from oven.
2. For the filling: While the crust is baking, make the filling. In a large bowl, beat eggs and sugars with a mixer on medium-high speed, until the mixture becomes fluffy and starts to thicken, 5 minutes.
3. Add the melted butter and milk. Continue beating on low speed to combine. Sift the flour and salt into the sugar mixture and beat on low speed until combined and smooth. Pour filling into crust.
4. While making the filling, toast the pecans: spread pecans on baking pan and put in oven to toast after you remove crust from oven. Be careful not to burn the pecans.
5. Assembly: Distribute 1½ cups chopped pecans evenly over the crust. Pour the filling over pecans. Top with pecan halves, if desired.
6. Bake the pie for 30 minutes, tented loosely with aluminum foil. After 30 minutes, remove the aluminum foil and continue to bake the pie for 10-15 min, until it is firm to the center.

<u>Notes:</u>

This sweet, rich, Southern version of pecan pie can be made up to 2-3 days ahead of time and refrigerated, covered, until you are ready to eat it. Remove from refrigerator 1 hour before serving.

Raspberry Pie with Crème de Cassis

Ingredients:
>crust for a 10-inch, two-crust pie (See pie crust recipes starting on p. 334.)
>5 cups raspberries, picked over
>1 cup sugar
>1/3 cup crème de cassis (black currant liqueur)
>5 tbsp cornstarch
>1 tbsp plus 1 tsp fresh lemon juice
>pinch of salt
>2½ tbsp unsalted butter, sliced paper thin

Directions:
1. Preheat the oven to 425. Toss the berries and sugar together in a mixing bowl. Whisk the cassis and cornstarch together in a small bowl until smooth. Stir the crème de cassis mixture, lemon juice, and salt gently into berries.
2. Roll out one half of the pie dough and line a 9-inch pie pan. Leave the edges untrimmed. Spoon in the berries into the pie and dot with butter.
3. Roll out the remaining dough into a 10-inch round and cut into ½-inch strips. Arrange the strips over the berries in a lattice pattern. Trim the overhanging pastry, bring the edge of lower crust over the lattice, and crimp the edge decoratively.
4. Set the pie on the middle rack of the oven and bake 15 minutes. Lower the heat to 350 and bake for another 30-40 minutes, or until the crust is golden brown and the filling is bubbling.

Ryan's Easy Peanut Butter Pie

Ingredients:

8-oz. cream cheese, softened
2 cups confectioners' sugar
¾ cup peanut butter
1 cup milk
16-oz. Cool Whip, softened
2 9-inch graham cracker crusts
chocolate syrup and Reddi-wip for garnish

Directions:
1. Whip cream cheese and gradually add sugar continuing to beat. Continue beating as you add peanut butter and then milk. Blend in the cool whip.
2. Pour into 2 regular graham cracker crusts and freeze.
3. Remove from freezer 10-minutes before serving. Spray each piece with Reddi-whip and drizzle each piece lightly with chocolate syrup.

Notes:
When I started revising this recipe book, my cousin, Linda Dawson Cutler, told me that her grandson Ryan loved her easy peanut butter pie. She searched and searched but couldn't find the recipe. Then, just before I sent this book to the publisher, she was going through some files and there it was. So, I made space for an additional recipe. Thanks Linda.

Pie Crust One (Basic)

<u>Ingredients:</u> (two crust)

2 cups all-purpose flour, divided
1/3 cup ice water
½ tsp salt
½ cup chilled stick margarine or butter, cut into small pieces
½ cup vegetable shortening

<u>Directions:</u>
1. Lightly spoon flour into dry measuring cups; level with a knife. Combine 1/3 cup flour and ice water, stirring with a whisk until well-blended. Combine 1 2/3 cups flour and salt in a bowl; cut in margarine and shortening with a pastry blender or 2 knives until mixture resembles coarse meal.
2. Add ice water mixture; toss with a fork until moist. Divide dough in half. Gently press each half of mixture into a 4-inch circle on heavy-duty plastic wrap or waxed paper, and cover with additional plastic wrap or waxed paper. Roll one half of dough, still covered, into a 12-inch circle, and chill. Roll other half of dough, still covered, into an 11-inch circle; chill for at least one hour before using.

Pie Crust Two (with Vinegar)

<u>Ingredients:</u> (two crust)

3 cups sifted all-purpose flour
1¼ cups shortening
½ tsp salt
1 egg
2 tsp distilled white vinegar
5 tbsp ice water

<u>Directions:</u>
1. In a large bowl, mix flour and salt. With a pastry blender, cut in the shortening until pea-sized.
2. Beat together egg, vinegar and water. Mix liquid with flour mixture, using a fork, until mixture forms a ball (Note: add liquid one tbsp at a time. You probably will not use all of it.)
3. Roll out on lightly floured pastry cloth with cloth covered roller.
Brush the crust with milk and sprinkle with sugar before baking.
<u>Notes:</u> This pie crust was a contest winner, but it's a little harder to roll out.

Pie Crust Three (Butter Crust)

<u>Ingredients:</u> (one crust)

1¼ cups all-purpose flour
¼ tsp salt
½ cup butter, chilled and diced
¼ cup ice water

<u>Directions:</u>
1. In a large bowl, combine flour and salt. Cut in butter until mixture resembles coarse crumbs. Stir in water, a tbsp at a time, until mixture forms a ball. Wrap in plastic and refrigerate for 4 hours or overnight.
2. Roll dough out to fit a 9-inch pie plate. Place crust in pie plate. Press the dough evenly into the bottom and sides of the pie plate.

Pie Crust Four (Lard and Butter)

<u>Ingredients:</u> (two crust)

2½ cups unbleached all-purpose flour
1½ tsp sugar
1 tsp salt
½ cup (1 stick) chilled unsalted butter, cut into ½-inch cubes
½ cup chilled lard cut into ½-inch cubes
5 tbsp (or more) ice water

<u>Directions:</u>
1. Blend flour, sugar, and salt in processor or using pastry blender.
2. Cut in butter and lard; blend until mixture resembles coarse meal.
3. Transfer mixture to medium bowl. Add 5 tbsp ice water and mix with fork until dough begins to clump together, adding more water by tsp if dry. Gather dough together. Divide dough in half; flatten each half into disk. Wrap each disk in plastic and refrigerate at least one hour.

Pie Crust Five (Lard)

<u>Ingredients:</u> (one 10-inch crust)

1½ cups all-purpose flour
pinch of salt
½ cup lard

(Recipe continued on next page.)

3 to 4 tbsp cold water

Directions:
1. In a bowl, combine flour and salt. Cut in lard until mixture resembles coarse crumbs. Sprinkle in water, a tbsp at a time, until pastry holds together. Shape into a ball; chill for 30 minutes.
2. On a lightly floured surface, roll dough to 1/8-inch thickness. Transfer to a 10-inch pie plate. Flute edges; fill and bake.

Pie Crust Six (No Fail with Vinegar and Lard)

Ingredients: (makes four crusts)
4 cups all-purpose flour
1 tsp baking powder
2 tsp salt
1 2/3 cups lard
½ cup water
1 egg, beaten
1 tbsp distilled white vinegar

Directions:
1. In a large bowl, mix together flour, baking powder, and salt. Cut in lard until mixture resembles coarse meal.
2. In a small bowl, mix together water, egg, and vinegar. Pour into lard mixture and stir until dough is thoroughly moistened and forms a ball. Divide into 4 portions and wrap tightly. Use dough within three days or freeze.

Pie Crust Seven (Butter, shortening, and vinegar)

Ingredients: (2 10–inch crusts)
12 tbsp (1½ sticks) very cold, unsalted butter
1/3 cup very cold butter-flavored Crisco
3 cups all-purpose flour
1 tsp kosher salt
1 tbsp sugar
6 to 8 tbsp ice water
1 tbsp white vinegar

Directions:
1. Dice the butter and return it to the refrigerator while you prepare the flour
(Recipe continued next page.)

mixture. Place flour, salt, and sugar in a large bowl and mix.
2. Add butter and shortening. Using a pastry cutter work until coarse and crumbly.
3. Add vinegar to water and sprinkle about 2/3 over the crumbly flour mixture. Using a fork gather the mixture into a ball, add remaining water/vinegar as needed.
4. Form into 2 balls and flatten into discs. Refrigerate at least an hour before rolling out on a floured pastry board.

Notes:

I've probably tried every pie crust recipe out there. Which is my favorite? I can unequivocally say that twenty-five years ago I made pies that were much better than those I make today, and I made them with lard. They never failed. I was often asked for my recipe. I hated to admit I used lard (but let's be real, since when is a cup of butter healthy?). I got strange looks that said, "Oh, really?" Then, for whatever reason, the brand of lard I used was no longer available. My pie crusts were never as good. I often make Pie Crust Three with butter because I think it's the best tasting crust. I think a butter crust is a little harder to work with and often use a mix of shortening and butter (recipe Seven).

Great Meringue

Ingredients:

1 cup egg whites (about 6 whites)
2 cups granulated sugar
1 tsp vanilla extract

Directions: (enough for two pies)

1. Put all three ingredients into a double boiler and cook to 120 degrees. Beat until stiff. Pile high on pies. Can be put directly onto hot pies.
2. Place pies in 400-degree oven for 3-5 minutes, watching carefully. Meringue should be browned.

Notes:

I got this recipe at Zender's Restaurant in Frankenmuth when my mom, Aunt Edie, Cousin Linda, and I attended an Apple Bake Off Contest.

Sandwiches and Soups

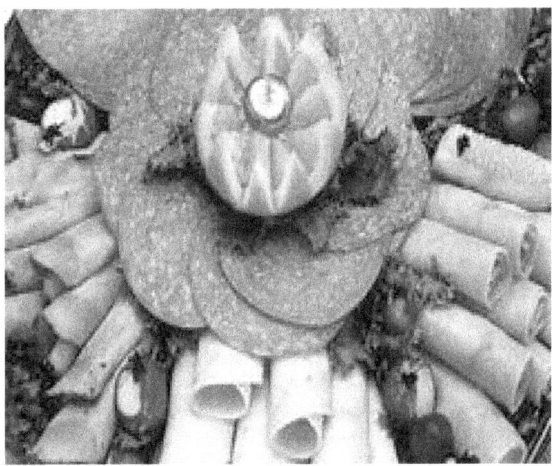 

"Soup is just a way of screwing you out of a meal." **Jay Leno**

"As the days grow short, some faces grow long. But not mine. Every autumn, when the wind turns cold and darkness comes early, I am suddenly happy. It's time to start making soup again." **Leslie Newman**

"A hot dog at the game beats roast beef at the Ritz." **Humphrey Bogart**

"To feel safe and warm on a cold wet night, all you need is soup." **Laurie Colwin**

"A first-rate soup is more creative than a second-rate painting." **Abraham Maslow**

"It's never about the screwup—it's always about the recovery. That's the thing about it . . . if it comes out a little rare you call it carpaccio. It comes out a little overcooked, you shred it up and put in on a sandwich." **Tyler Florence**

~~~Sandwiches~~~

Black Bean Burgers

<u>Ingredients:</u>

1 can (15 ounces) black beans, rinsed and drained
1 packet (1.25 ounces) taco seasoning mix
kosher salt and black pepper to taste
½ cup frozen corn, do not thaw
1 packet instant original oatmeal
1 egg, beaten
3 tbsp olive oil
4 multi-grain wheat buns, toasted
4 tsp mayonnaise
shredded lettuce
prepared salsa

<u>Directions:</u>
1. Mash beans in large bowl or plastic bag, leaving a few chunks. Stir in taco seasoning, salt, and pepper as desired. Stir in corn, oats, and egg. Refrigerate mixture 10 minutes to hydrate the oats.
2. Heat oil in large skillet over medium heat. When oil begins to swirl, scoop one-fourth of the bean mixture and drop onto pan, slightly smoothing it into a circle.
(Recipe continued on next page.)

Cook on one side until golden and a bit crisp, about 8 minutes; flip and cook on the other side 8 minutes more.

3. Spread bottom of each bun with thin layer of mayonnaise. Top with lettuce, black bean patties, salsa, and bun top.

Notes:

I got this recipe when we had sold our house and were waiting for the new house to be built. We stayed at the Extended Stay, and they offered this recipe because it was simple and could be made stovetop. It seemed pretty healthy because I could skip the mayo and use more salsa. I actually like this burger.

Chicken Curry Tea Sandwiches

<u>Ingredients:</u>

2 cups cubed, cooked chicken
1 unpeeled red apple, chopped
¾ cup dried cranberries
½ cup thinly sliced celery
¼ cup chopped pecans
2 tbsp thinly sliced green onions
¾ cup mayonnaise
2 tsp lime juice
½ tsp curry powder
12 slices bread
12 lettuce leaves

<u>Directions:</u>
1. Combine chicken, apple, cranberries, celery, pecans, and green onions in a bowl.
2. Mix mayonnaise, lime juice, and curry powder in a small bowl.
3. Fold mayonnaise mixture into chicken mixture; stir to coat. Cover and refrigerate until ready to serve.
4. Cut each bread slice with a 3-inch heart-shaped cookie cutter or cut crusts off the bread and slice diagonally. Top with a lettuce leaf and chicken salad, then second piece of bread.

<u>Notes:</u>
A recipe from my Grandma-Granddaughter tea parties. It would also be nice for a fancy luncheon.

Cucumber Tea Sandwiches

Ingredients:

1 cucumber, peeled and thinly sliced
1 (8 oz) pkg cream cheese, softened
¼ cup mayonnaise
¼ tsp garlic powder
¼ tsp onion salt
1 dash Worcestershire sauce
1 (1 pound) loaf high-quality sliced bread, crusts removed
1 pinch lemon pepper (optional)

Directions:

1. Place cucumber slices between 2 paper towels set in a colander. Allow liquid to drain, about 10 minutes.
2. Mix cream cheese, mayonnaise, garlic powder, onion salt, and Worcestershire sauce in a bowl until smooth.
3. Spread cream cheese mixture evenly on one side of each bread slice.
4. Divide cucumber slices over half of the bread slices; sprinkle lemon pepper on cucumber.
5. Stack the other half of the bread slices with spread sides down over the cucumber slices to make sandwiches.

Notes:

I made these for "high tea" with my granddaughters, Lauren and Kaelin. Now, the second wave of grandchildren (Noah and Ezra) have found that they love these sandwiches which I make for our Valentine's Day Tea. However, I replace the garlic and onion salt with fresh dill, and I cut the sandwiches diagonally with a very sharp knife. Knife has to be sharp to cut through cucumber without messing up the sandwich.

Egg Dipped Ultimate Grilled Cheese Sandwich

<u>Ingredients:</u>

2 tbsp butter
½ cup chopped fresh mushrooms
¼ cup chopped onion
8 slices crisp fried bacon, patted dry
pinch of black pepper
8 slices bread
4 slices Swiss or cheddar cheese, sliced
4 slices mozzarella cheese, sliced
extra butter, for frying

2 eggs
3 tbsp milk
½ tsp salt

<u>Directions:</u>

1. To prepare the sandwiches, melt the butter over medium heat in a medium-size frying pan. Add the mushrooms, onion, and pepper and cook until the vegetables are tender, about 5 minutes. Remove vegetables from pan, drain well and pat dry.
2. For each sandwich, layer a slice of bread, a slice of Swiss or cheddar cheese, some of the mushroom-onion mixture, a slice of mozzarella cheese and another slice of bread.
3. To prepare the egg coating, whisk the eggs, milk, and salt together in a shallow bowl. Dip the sandwiches in the egg mixture to coat on both sides.
4. Wipe out the frying pan; melt a little more butter in it and swirl to cover the bottom. Add two sandwiches and brown on one side over medium heat, 3 to 5 minutes. Add a little more butter and turn the sandwiches over to brown the second side. Keep warm while you cook the remaining two sandwiches in the same way.

<u>Notes:</u>

I found dipping the entire sandwich in the egg coating was cumbersome and the sandwich sometimes fell apart. So, instead I make the egg dip as directed. I then brush one side of a slice of bread with mixture, lay that slice, egg-brushed side down, on melted hot butter in pan, build sandwich on unbrushed side of that slice, add second slice of bread and brush the outside of that slice.

Fat Doug Burger

<u>Ingredients:</u>

½ head Napa cabbage, shredded
½ clove garlic (minced)
½ small red onion
½ fresh jalapeno (minced)
3 tbsp champagne vinegar
1 tbsp sugar
1 tbsp Dijon mustard
2 tbsp yellow mustard
¼ cup mayonnaise
1½ tsp salt
1 tbsp Worcestershire Sauce
½ pound ground sirloin
½ pound ground brisket
½ pound ground boneless short rib
salt and freshly ground pepper
½ pound pastrami (thinly sliced)
4 slices Swiss cheese (medium thick)
1½ tbsp unsalted butter (melted)
4 brioche or egg buns (split)

<u>Directions:</u>

1. Prepare the slaw: In a medium bowl, mix together the cabbage, garlic, onion, jalapeno, vinegar, mustard, mayonnaise, sugar, salt, and Worcestershire sauce. Cover and refrigerate one hour.
2. Make the burgers: Build a charcoal fire or heat a gas grill. On a work surface, combine the meats and form the burgers into 4 equal-size patties. Season liberally with salt and pepper.
3. Grill the burgers over high heat until medium rare, 3 to 5 minutes per side.
4. Meanwhile, heat a large sauté pan over medium heat. Place 4 heaping piles of pastrami in the pan. After two minutes, top each pile with a slice of Swiss cheese. Remove them when the cheese is melted; set aside.

(Recipe continued on next page.)

5. Put butter into the pan. Place the buns in the pan, cut-side down, and toast, about two minutes.

6. Place a heaping tablespoon of the slaw on the bottom half of each bun. Top with a burger and a mound of pastrami and cheese. Cover each with the top half of the bun and serve immediately.

Notes:

I've had trouble getting ground short rib and used a combination of extra lean hamburger and ground brisket. The key here is simply having a good slaw (feel free to substitute your own), pastrami, and Swiss.

Grandma Bertha's Sloppy Joes

Ingredients:

1½ pounds ground beef
2 stalks celery
1 chopped onion
1 small bottle ketchup (1¼ cups)
1/3 cup water
3 tbsp Worcestershire sauce
2 tbsp vinegar
2 tbsp brown sugar
1 tbsp prepared mustard
salt and pepper to taste

Directions:
1. Finely chop celery and onion and place in large skillet. Add ground beef and brown.
2. Add remaining ingredients and simmer for fifteen minutes. Serve on hamburger buns.

Notes:
I got this recipe from my cousin, Linda Dawson Cutler. She tells the story that every November when she was a child, our grandpa (Ray Dawson), our Uncle Carlton, and her father plus any other male relatives they could induce to join them, loaded up their cars and headed to the Upper Peninsula for a week of deer hunting. Linda and her mom (my Aunt Edie) spent the week with Grandma Bertha Dawson. They always slept in the spare bedroom, and Linda remembers the bed was made with flannel sheets. And Grandma always had a jar of these sloppy joes in the refrigerator.

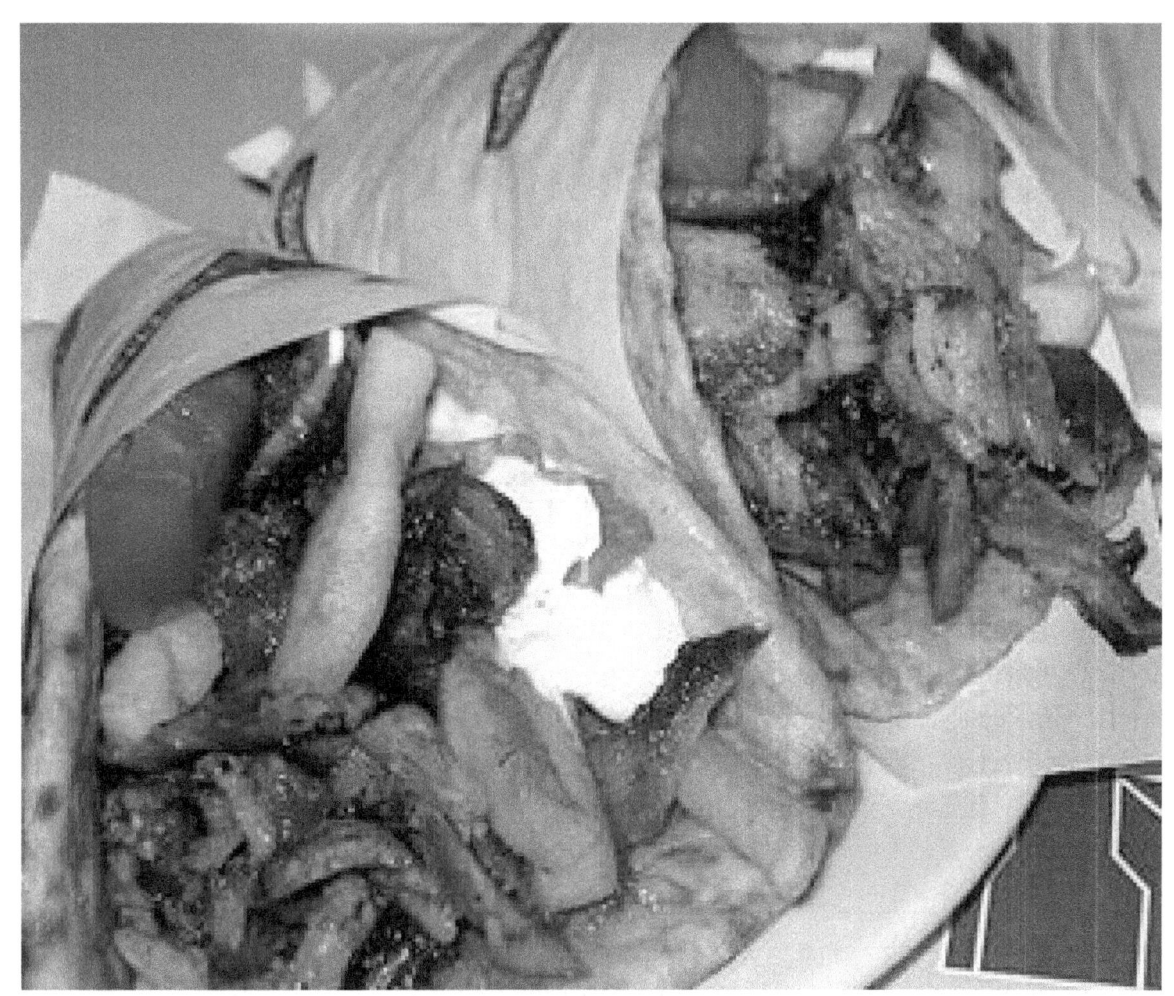

Greek Pork Gyros Souvlaki

<u>Ingredients:</u>

2 pounds pork loin roast
1 tsp dried oregano
1 tsp Greek adobo seasoning
¼ cup water
¼ cup extra virgin olive oil
2 tbsp lemon juice
2 tbsp vinegar
1 tbsp soy sauce
2 garlic cloves
(Recipe continued on next page.)

½ medium onion
1 tbsp honey
salt
Greek pita bread
lettuce, sliced onion, chopped tomato for serving
sauce: below

Directions:
1. Cut pork loin into strips about 1½-inch in diameter.
2. Mix the dried herbs, water, olive oil, lemon juice, soy sauce, vinegar, and honey in a bowl deep enough to hold the pork roast strips.
3. Coat pork roast strips with the marinade.
4. Slice the garlic and onion and spread over top of meat.
5. Cover and refrigerate for at least two hours, turning and coating several times.
6. Place contents of bowl (including marinade) in slow cooker and cook on medium 4 to 4.5 hours, basting roast often with its own juices. Allow to cool to touch. Slice or "pull" the meat.
7. Before serving, dry fry (no oil) the meat in a non-stick skillet. This will produce crispy golden-brown bits nearly identical to that from a rotisserie.

Ingredients for the Tzatziki sauce:
1 cucumber
2 cloves of garlic
¼ cup extra virgin olive oil
pint low fat, plain Greek yogurt
1-2 tbsp of red wine vinegar
salt and freshly ground pepper to taste

Directions for sauce and assembly:
1. Mix all ingredients.
2. Cut top 1/3 off pita bread and stuff with cooked meat mixture.
3. Add Tzatziki sauce and onion, tomato, and lettuce as desired.

Lum's Beer Steamed Hot Dogs with Chili Sauce

<u>Ingredients:</u> Chili Sauce »»

1 pound ground beef (85%)
1 large onion (finely chopped)
2 tbsp chili powder
½ tsp salt and ¼ tsp freshly ground black pepper
¼ tsp ground allspice
¼ tsp ground mustard
½ tsp garlic powder
1/8 tsp ground cumin
1/8 tsp ground cinnamon
1/8 tsp ground cayenne pepper
¼ cup Heinz Ketchup
2 cups beef broth

8 hot dogs, preferably Koegels and 8 hot dog buns
1 tbsp neutral oil, like canola
½ bottle of Bud beer

<u>Directions:</u>
1. Chili Sauce: In a medium saucepan, brown the ground beef; drain well. To the ground beef add remaining chili ingredients (save out a small amount of finely chopped onion for topping) and simmer for two hours.
2. Hot dogs: pour oil in pan and heat to medium-high. Sear hot dogs one minute. Add beer (Lum's used Bud, but you can use your favorite) and steam for ten minutes. Steam buns or put in microwave for thirty seconds.
3. Assemble: Put a hot dog in each bun, add 2 tbsp chili and condiments of choice (shredded cheddar, chopped onions, and mustard) to taste.

<u>Notes:</u>
If you watched the *Irishman* on Netflix, you saw De Niro's character, Frank Sheeran, stop at the bygone Lum's for beer steamed hotdogs. I researched online and created this recipe. Lum's menu offered many toppings including sauerkraut.
Chili Sauce would always be my first choice. After a hearty scoop of sauce, I'd pile on the cheddar, onions, and mustard.

Marilyn's Favorite Sloppy Joes

Ingredients:

2 pounds lean ground beef
1 tbsp mustard
3½ tbsp brown sugar
1 1/3 cups catsup
1 tbsp molasses
½ tsp garlic powder

Directions:
1. Brown ground beef, breaking up as you cook so it's in small pieces. Drain.
2. Add remaining ingredients and heat through. Serve on hamburger buns.

Notes:

This is the recipe from the Ottawa Towers Cafeteria where we often ate lunch when I worked for the Health Professionals Division of the Attorney General. Marilyn Parr was my secretary, and she asked for and was given this recipe.

Pulled Pork Biscuit Sliders

Ingredients:
Biscuits »»

2 cups all-purpose flour
1 tbsp sugar
1 tbsp baking powder
1 tsp salt
½ cup butter, chilled and cut into small chunks
¾ cup cold milk

Filling »»

2 cups BBQ pulled pork (recipe under Pulled Pork in this book) warmed
10 dill pickle chips
3 slices sharp cheddar cheese, cut into quarters
Dijon mustard (can also use spicy brown mustard)

Directions:
1. Preheat oven to 450. In a medium bowl mix together the flour, sugar, baking powder, and salt. Add in butter and cut with a pastry blender until you have coarse crumbs. Stir in the milk until the dough starts to leave the sides of the bowl.
2. Place dough on a work surface and knead lightly 10 times. This will also help to finish mixing your dough together. Roll dough to ½-inch thick and use a 2½-inch biscuit cutter. Place on ungreased baking sheet and bake for 10-15 minutes or until golden brown. Cool slightly.
3. Cut biscuits in half and spread a small amount of mustard on each half. Put a small amount of pork on the bottom half and top with a square of cheese, pickle and place top back on. Repeat with other biscuits. Makes 10 sliders.

Putting on the Ritz Egg Salad Tea Sandwiches

Ingredients:

8 hard-cooked eggs
½ cup mayonnaise
salt and pepper to taste
1 tbsp finely-chopped fresh dill weed
6 tbsp unsalted butter, room temperature
20 slices best-quality white bread

Directions:

1. Peel eggs and place into a medium bowl. Slice eggs and then coarsely mash them with the back of a fork. Add mayonnaise, salt, pepper, and dill; stir until well blended.
2. Spread butter onto one side of each slice of bread. Spread the buttered side of 10 slices of bread with 2 tbsp egg mixture. Top with remaining slices of bread, buttered side down.
3. Carefully cut the crusts from sandwich with a long, sharp, serrated knife. Cut in half diagonally, then cut in half again. 40 sandwich quarters.

Note:

Another recipe from my tea parties with granddaughters, Lauren and Kaelin.

Turkey Burgers

Ingredients:

2 pounds ground turkey
¾ tsp salt
½ tsp cracked black pepper
4 tsp Worcestershire sauce
1 tsp garlic powder
1 tsp dried thyme
½ tsp dried rosemary
4 tsp Dijon mustard
⅔ cup ricotta cheese

Directions:
1. Mix all ingredients together with hands. Form into patties of desired size and thickness. If you keep them fairly thick, they will be moister.
2. Place into lightly greased, nonstick skillet on medium high. Cook without moving until bottom side is dark brown and crusted, approximately 4 to 5 minutes. Turn over, then reduce heat to medium and cook 8-10 minutes longer or until center is no longer pink and juices run clear.
3. Serve on ciabatta rolls with mayo, more Dijon, a slice of pepper jack cheese, lettuce, tomato, and avocado.

Notes:
I'm never going to convince my husband this is beef, but the ricotta does make a moister burger. I also add ¼ cup of cilantro, and a tbsp of chili powder. With all of the condiments, this is pretty decent.

Smoked Salmon Sandwich on Pumpernickel with Capers and Avocado

<u>Ingredients:</u>

5 tbsp unsalted butter, softened
1 tbsp fresh lemon juice
1 tbsp drained, bottled capers
8 slices of pumpernickel bread
½ pound thinly sliced smoked salmon
1 small red onion, sliced thin
1 avocado, pitted, peeled, cut into 12 wedges, and sprinkled with the juice of ½ lemon
1 cup alfalfa sprouts

<u>Directions:</u>

1. In a small bowl cream together the butter, lemon juice, capers. Salt and pepper to taste. Spread the lemon caper butter on one side of each slice of bread. Layer half the bread slices with the salmon, the onion, the avocado, and the sprouts and top the sandwiches with the remaining bread slices, pressing them firmly.

<u>Note:</u>
I often add thinly sliced cucumber because my grandson, Noah, loves sliced cucumbers.

Upscale Philly Cheese Sandwiches

<u>Ingredients:</u>

2 tbsp all-purpose flour
½ of a 17.3-oz pkg Pepperidge Farm Puff Pastry Sheets (1 sheet), thawed
1 tbsp vegetable oil

1 medium onion, cut in half and sliced (about 1 cup)
6 oz frozen beef sandwich steaks (4 portions), cut into thick strips
4 slices processed American cheese food product
1 egg, beaten

<u>Directions:</u>

1. Heat the oven to 400.
2. Sprinkle flour on the work surface. Unfold the pastry sheet on the work surface. Roll the pastry sheet into a 10-inch square. Cut into 4 (5-inch) squares.
3. Heat the oil in a 10-inch skillet over medium heat. Add the onion and cook until tender, stirring occasionally. Remove the onion from the skillet.
4. Increase the heat to medium-high. Add the sandwich steaks to the skillet and cook for 3 minutes or until cooked through, stirring occasionally.
5. Spoon ¼ of the onion and ¼ of the sandwich steaks on the bottom third of **each** pastry square. Top each with 1 slice cheese. Fold **2** opposite sides over the filling. Roll up like a jelly roll. Brush the pastries with the egg. Place the pastries onto a baking sheet.
6. Bake for 20 minutes or until the pastries are golden brown. Let the pastries cool on the baking sheet on a wire rack for 10 minutes. Cut the pastries in half diagonally to serve.

~~~Soups~~~

Authentic Chicken and Andouille Sausage Gumbo

<u>Ingredients:</u>

1½ gallons water
1 (4 pounds) chicken, cut up
5 bay leaves
5 parsley sprigs
3 whole garlic cloves
1 pound andouille or smoked sausage, diced
2 medium onions, chopped
1 large green bell pepper, chopped
1 large celery rib, chopped
3 tbsp minced garlic
4 chicken bouillon cubes
1¼ cups vegetable oil
1½ cups all-purpose flour
1 tbsp salt
1 tsp ground red pepper
1 tsp ground black pepper
1 bunch green onions, chopped
½ cup chopped fresh parsley
½ tsp filé powder
hot cooked rice

(Recipe continued on next page.)

Directions:
1. Bring first 5 ingredients to a boil in a large stockpot; cover, reduce heat, and simmer 1 hour.
2. Remove chicken, reserving broth. Skin, debone, and coarsely chop chicken; set aside. Pour broth through a wire-mesh strainer into a large bowl, discarding solids.
3. Measure 1-gallon broth, and return to stockpot. Add sausage and next 5 ingredients; simmer, stirring occasionally, one hour. Heat oil in a heavy skillet over medium heat; gradually whisk in flour, and cook, whisking constantly, until flour is a dark caramel color (about 20 minutes).
4. Stir into sausage mixture and simmer, stirring occasionally, one hour. Stir in chicken, salt, and red and black pepper; simmer, stirring occasionally, 45 minutes. Skim off fat.
5. Stir in green onions and parsley; simmer, stirring occasionally, 10 minutes. Remove from heat, and stir in filé powder. Serve over hot cooked rice with hot sauce, if desired.

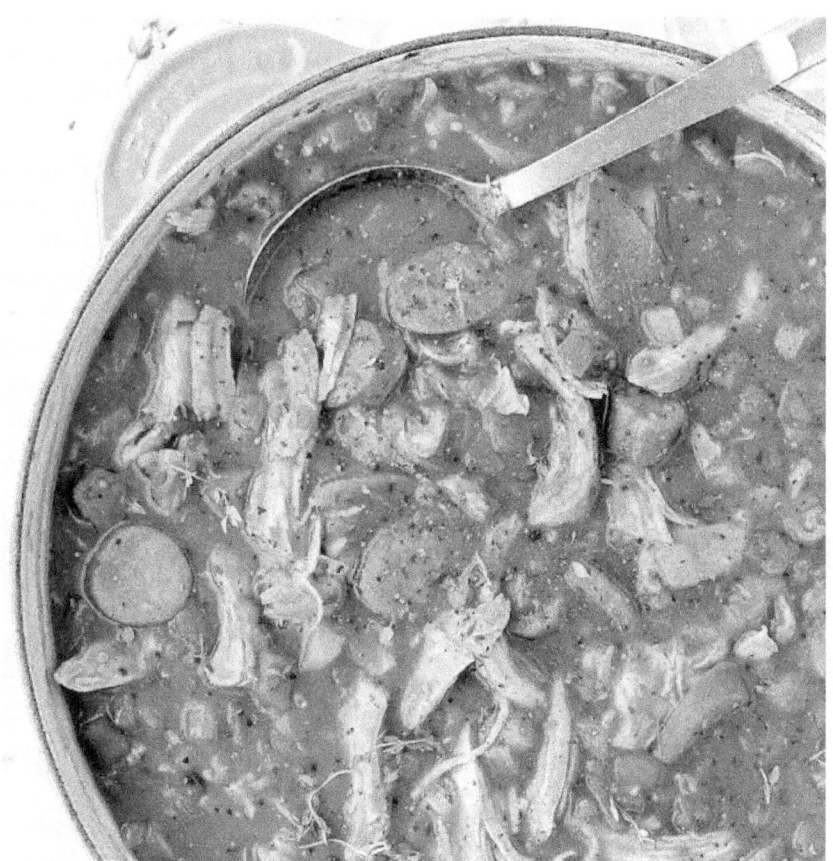

Note:
This recipe suggestion came from our neighbor, Heidi Landry. She served gumbo at her Mardi Gras celebration.

Barley Mushroom Soup

<u>Ingredients:</u>

3 or 4 carrots, peeled
3 or 4 celery stocks
1 large onion
a few sprigs parsley and fresh dill
10-12 white mushrooms, sliced
¼-½ cup of quick-cook barley
48 oz low-sodium chicken broth
olive oil
salt and pepper
Creole spice if desired
heavy cream to taste

<u>Directions:</u>

1. In a food processor put chunks of all vegetables other than the mushrooms. Process until chopped fine.
2. Heat olive oil in soup pot and lightly sauté all vegetables, including mushrooms.
3. Add barley and chicken broth. Bring to a boil. Turn down heat to low and simmer for 45-60 minutes. Once ready, you may add heavy cream to taste.

<u>Notes:</u>
This recipe comes from my dear friend, and my daughter's mother-in-law, Shlomit Elitzur. We have enjoyed this soup at her home many times and were grateful she shared the recipe. Shlomit uses Trader Joe's 10 Minute Barley and Swanson's broth.

Bean Soup with Smoked Turkey

Ingredients:

1 pound dry Great Northern beans
8 cups water (see notes below)
½ tsp salt
2 smoked turkey legs (meat and bone)
1 cup chopped carrots
1 stalk celery, chopped
2 potatoes, peeled and in small chunks
1 cup chopped onion
1 tsp minced garlic
1 tsp mustard powder
2 bay leaves
½ tsp freshly ground pepper

Directions:
1. Rinse beans, sorting out and discarding any broken or discolored ones. In a large pot over high heat, bring the water to a boil. Add the salt and the beans and remove from heat. Let beans sit in the hot water for at least 60 minutes.
2. After an hour of soaking, return the pot to high heat and place the turkey legs, carrots, celery, potatoes, onion, garlic, mustard, and bay leaves in the pot. Stir well, bring to a boil, reduce heat to low and simmer for 60 more minutes.
3. Remove turkey legs, and remove meat. Discard bones and stir meat back into the soup pot and simmer for 30 more minutes. Remove bay leaves. Season with pepper to taste.

Notes:
Instead of 8 cups of water, I use one large box of chicken or beef stock and four cups water. I get the smoked turkey legs at the meat counter of Safeway. They usually yield about two cups of meat pieces. Also, I let the beans sit overnight in cold water and then start with step 2.

Butternut Squash, Corn, Potato, and Pea Soup

<u>Ingredients:</u>

1 tbsp olive oil
1 clove garlic, minced
1 onion, chopped
1 butternut squash, peeled and cubed
1 cup corn
1 cup frozen peas
2 large potatoes, peeled and cut into small pieces
3 cups vegetable stock
1 tsp dried basil
½ tsp ground black pepper
½ cup plain yogurt
½ tsp ground nutmeg

<u>Directions:</u>

1. Heat the olive oil in a Dutch oven over medium-high heat. Cook and stir the garlic and onion in the oil until soft and translucent. Add the butternut squash, potatoes, and corn and cook for 3 more minutes. Pour the stock into the Dutch oven and bring to a boil; season with basil and black pepper.
2. Reduce the heat to medium-low and simmer uncovered until the squash and potatoes are tender, about 15 minutes. Remove the Dutch oven from the heat and using a hand blender, or working in batches with a counter top blender, process the soup until smooth. Stir in the yogurt and nutmeg.

Butternut Squash with Apple Cider Soup

<u>Ingredients:</u>

2 tbsp butter
1 onion, diced
1 butternut squash—peeled, seeded, and cut into large chunks
2 white potatoes, peeled and chopped
1 apple, peeled and chopped
1 large carrot, peeled and diced
2 stalks celery, chopped
2 (14 oz) cans chicken broth
½-gallon apple cider
¾ cup half-and-half cream
½ tsp ground cinnamon
¼ tsp ground cloves
½ cup sour cream, or as needed
1 pinch ground nutmeg, or to taste

<u>Directions:</u>
1. Heat butter in a large pot over medium heat; cook and stir onion in the melted butter until translucent, 5 to 10 minutes. Add butternut squash, potatoes, apple, carrot, and celery to onion; pour in chicken broth and enough apple cider to cover vegetables. Bring mixture to a boil and cover pot. Reduce heat and simmer, adding more apple cider as needed, until vegetables are tender, 35 to 40 minutes.
2. Blend vegetable mixture with an immersion blender until smooth; stir in cream, cinnamon, and cloves. Simmer until heated through, 5 to 10 minutes. Spoon soup into serving bowls; top each with about 1 tbsp sour cream and a pinch of nutmeg.

Chicken Chili with Black Beans

Ingredients:
>3 whole boneless skinless chicken breasts (1¾ pounds), cubed
>2 medium sweet red peppers, chopped
>1 large onion, chopped
>3 tbsp olive oil
>1 can (4 oz) chopped green chilies
>4 garlic cloves, minced
>2 tbsp chili powder
>2 tsp ground cumin
>1 tsp ground coriander
>2 cans (15 oz each) black beans, rinsed and drained
>1 can (28 oz) Italian stewed tomatoes, cut up
>1 cup chicken broth or beer

Directions:
1. In a Dutch oven, sauté the chicken, red peppers, and onion in oil for five minutes or until chicken is no longer pink. Add the green chilies, garlic, chili powder, cumin, and coriander; cook one minute longer.
2. Stir in the beans, tomatoes and broth or beer; bring to a boil. Reduce heat and simmer, uncovered, for 15 minutes, stirring often. Yield: 10 servings (3 quarts.)

Notes:
I often add a can of corn to the soup. It is good with onions and shredded cheddar on top.

Chili with Pulled Pork and Beef

<u>Ingredients:</u>

4 pounds boneless beef chuck roast, patted dry
8 country-style pork ribs, patted dry
½ cup vegetable oil or other flavorless oil
salt and freshly ground black pepper
1 tbsp ground cumin
1 cup mild chili powder
4 tsp dried oregano
4 tsp ground cumin
4 large onions, diced
2 (28 oz each) cans + 1 (16 oz) can crushed tomatoes
1 small bag frozen corn
12 garlic cloves, minced
2 oz bittersweet chocolate, coarsely chopped
2 (15.5 oz each) cans kidney beans, rinsed (optional)
2 (15.5 oz each) cans black beans, rinsed (optional)

<u>Directions:</u>

1. Adjust oven rack to middle position; heat oven to 450. Set a large, heavy-duty roasting pan over 2 burners on medium heat.
2. Pour 2 tbsp oil into a medium bowl. Add as much of meat as fits comfortably. Generously sprinkle with salt, pepper, and 1 tbsp cumin. Increase heat under roasting pan to medium-high. Cook until a solid brown crust forms on one side, 4 to 5 minutes. Turn over; cook until a crust again forms, 4 to 5 minutes.
3. Transfer meat to a soup pot. Brown remaining meat; add to soup pot.
4. Set roasting pan aside. Add 2½ cups water to the soup pot and cover with heavy-duty foil, pressing down so foil is concave and touches the meat. Seal foil around the top of the pot so it is airtight; place lid on pot. Heat until you hear pan juices bubble. Set pot in oven. Cook, without checking, 90 minutes (meat should be very tender).
5. Carefully remove from oven and let cool. Shred pork and beef into bite-size pieces, discarding pork bones. Measure meat juices, then add enough water to equal 12 cups.
6. Meanwhile, in a medium skillet over low heat, slow-toast chili powder, oregano, and remaining 4 tsp cumin, stirring constantly, until spices are fragrant and darker

(Recipe continued on next page.)

in color; be careful not to burn.

7. Set roasting pan over two burners on medium-high heat; add remaining ¼ cup oil. Add onions; sauté until soft, 7 to 8 minutes. Add spices, tomatoes, frozen corn, meat and juices.

8. Simmer until flavors are unified, 1 to 1½ hours. Add garlic, chocolate and optional beans; simmer 5 minutes. Serve with onions, cheddar cheese, Fritos (in place of crackers), and sour cream.

<u>Notes:</u>

I sent a huge pot of this chili on a ski trip. I can guarantee that no one in the male-only group left the table hungry. When I typed up recipes for this book, I had a hard time deciding if I should include this recipe in the section on One Dish Meals, or here under soups.

Our family loves this or any chili over Fritos because they don't get as soggy as crackers. And sometimes, instead of crackers or Fritos, I serve cornbread with my chili.

Cincinnati Skyline Chili

<u>Ingredients:</u>

2 pounds lean ground beef
2 cups onion, chopped
4 cups beef stock
2 (8 oz) cans tomato sauce
1 clove garlic, crushed
1 tbsp Worcestershire sauce
1 tsp ground cinnamon
dash of nutmeg
1 tsp apple cider vinegar
2½ tbsp unsweetened cocoa powder or ½ oz square of chocolate
1 pinch cayenne pepper
1 tsp ground cumin
salt and pepper to taste
optional: 1 pound uncooked spaghetti
toppings: finely shredded cheddar cheese, kidney beans, and chopped onion

<u>Directions:</u>

1. Cut beef into very small pieces. Place beef, onion, and beef stock in 4-quart pot. Simmer for 30 minutes. Stir often.
2. Add tomato sauce, garlic, Worcestershire sauce, cinnamon, vinegar, cocoa powder, cayenne pepper, salt, and pepper. Simmer, uncovered, over low heat for 3-4 hours. Refrigerate overnight and then reheat and eat plain or over spaghetti with your choice of toppings.

<u>Notes:</u>

I lived for several years in Cincinnati. It is where my children were born and where I attended both graduate and law school. Skyline Chili is a local institution. I got mine in Clifton, just a short distance from the University of Cincinnati. It was served plain (1 way), over spaghetti (2 way), over spaghetti with cheese (3 way), over spaghetti, with cheese and onion (4 way), or over spaghetti with cheese, onion, and beans (5 way). The recipe came from a Greek immigrant and there is NO chili powder in it.

A fellow law school student and close friend, Mike Dudley, and I always said we were going to move to Lansing (we both did) and open our version of Skyline Chili (we never did).

Cioppino (Fish Stew)

Ingredients:

¾ cup butter
2 large onions, chopped
2 cloves garlic, minced
1 bunch fresh parsley, chopped
2 (14.5 oz each) cans crushed tomatoes
2 (14.5 oz each) cans chicken broth
2 bay leaves
1 tbsp dried basil
½ tsp dried thyme
½ tsp dried oregano
1½ cups dry white wine
1½ pounds large shrimp, peeled and deveined
1½ pounds bay scallops
18 small clams
18 mussels, cleaned and debearded
2 pounds shell-on king crab legs
1½ pounds cod filets (or snapper or whitefish), cubed

Directions:

1. Over medium-low heat melt butter in a very large stockpot, add onions, garlic, and parsley. Cook slowly, stirring occasionally until onions are soft.
2. Add tomatoes, chicken broth, bay leaves, basil, thyme, oregano, water, and wine. Mix well. Cover and simmer 30 minutes.
3. The above stew base can be made a day ahead, and the flavors mingle well. Reheat and proceed with step 4 below.
4. Stir in the fish in this order: first, clams for about 5 minutes until they open. Remove any clams that don't open. Then add crab legs which have been chopped into several large pieces (use large, heavy knife) and cook one additional minute. Next stir in the mussels, shrimp, squid, scallops. Cook about three minutes, until mussels open. Finally, lay the chunks of cod on top and continue cooking until cod is done. Serve immediately with warm, crusty bread.

Clam Chowder

Ingredients:

3 (8 oz each) bottles clam juice
1 pound russet potatoes, peeled, cut into ½-inch pieces
2 tbsp (¼ stick) butter
3 slices bacon, finely chopped
2 cups chopped onions
1¼ cups chopped celery with leaves (about 2 large stalks)
2 garlic cloves, chopped
1 bay leaf
¼ cup all-purpose flour
6 (6½ oz each) cans chopped clams, drained, juices reserved
1¼ cups half and half
1 tsp hot pepper sauce

Directions:

1. Bring bottled clam juice and potatoes to boil in heavy large saucepan over high heat. Reduce heat to medium-low; cover and simmer until potatoes are tender, about 10 minutes. Remove from heat.
2. Melt butter in heavy large pot over medium heat. Add bacon and cook until bacon begins to brown, about 8 minutes. Add onions, celery, garlic, and bay leaf and sauté until vegetables soften, about 6 minutes.
3. Stir in flour and cook 2 minutes (do not allow flour to brown). Gradually whisk in reserved juices from cans of clams. Add potato mixture, clams, half and half and hot pepper sauce. Simmer chowder 5 minutes to blend flavors, stirring frequently.
4. Season to taste with salt and pepper. Can be prepared 1 day ahead. Refrigerate uncovered until cold, then cover and keep refrigerated. Bring to simmer before serving.)

Notes:

I cannot bring myself to put clam chowder (think fishy smell) in the refrigerator uncovered. I wait until it is lukewarm, then cover and refrigerate. Also, I have an aversion to any bacon that isn't fully cooked and crisp, so I make sure my bacon is done and not just "beginning to brown."

Crab and Corn Chowder

<u>Ingredients:</u>

4 oz thick-sliced smoked bacon, cubed
4 tbsp unsalted butter
1 cup corn
2 yellow onions, diced
1 chili, diced
2 celery stalks, diced
2 cloves garlic, finely chopped
1 tsp Old Bay seasoning
½ tsp chipotle chile powder
1 jalapeño, cut in half, seeds removed
½ tsp freshly ground white pepper
4 sprigs fresh thyme, stemmed, leaves chopped
1 fresh bay leaf
1-quart crab (seafood) stock
2 pounds potatoes, diced
1½ cups heavy cream
2 oz cream cheese
1 pound fresh Dungeness crabmeat
cilantro pesto (1 bunch chopped cilantro pureed with ½ cup olive oil)

<u>Directions:</u>

1. In a 4 to 6-quart pot set over low heat, cook the bacon until it renders its fat, then increase the heat to medium to make the bacon crisp. Remove the bacon from the pan and set aside. Leave about half the bacon fat in the pan.

2. Add butter and sauté the corn for 4 to 6 minutes. Transfer corn to a heatproof bowl and set aside. Add the onions and sauté until translucent, 4 to 6 minutes, being careful not to let them brown. Add the pasilla pepper and sauté for 4 minutes more. Transfer the mixture to the bowl with the corn. Add celery, sauté 2 to 3 minutes, then add the garlic and continue to sauté for 2 minutes more, being careful not to let the garlic burn.

3. Return sautéed vegetables and bacon to the pan. Add Old Bay seasoning, ground chipotle, jalapeño, pepper, thyme and bay leaf. Add just enough crab stock to barely cover the vegetables. Add the diced potatoes, increase the heat to high

(Recipe continued on next page.)

and boil the potatoes vigorously for about 4 minutes. The goal is to soften the outside of the potato to help thicken the chowder, while keeping the potato al dente.

4. Add the cream and cream cheese. Cook and stir for 2 minutes, then remove from heat. If you need to thicken the chowder, smash a few of the potato pieces against the side of the pot. Gently fold in the crabmeat and simmer just until warmed through. Season to taste with salt and pepper. Remove the jalapeño pepper before serving.

5. To serve, ladle chowder into bowls and garnish with cilantro pesto or bacon bits.

Note:

If you can't get pasilla chili, you can substitute ancho chili, mulato chili, or another chili.

Cream Soup with Mushrooms

Ingredients:

3 tbsp olive oil
¼ medium onion, minced
1 clove garlic, minced
1 pound mushrooms, sliced
½ cup all-purpose flour
4½ cups milk (non-fat works but is less creamy)
1 bay leaf
1 tsp salt
1/8 tsp ground black pepper
½ tsp dry basil
2 tbsp fresh parsley, chopped
½ cup white wine
1 cup half and half

Directions:

1. In a bowl, combine flour and ½ cup milk. Mix well and set aside.
2. In a soup pot, add olive oil, onion, and garlic. Sauté over medium heat. Add mushrooms and sauté until golden brown.
3. Add 4 cups milk, bay leaf, basil, parsley, salt, and pepper. Bring to a gentle boil, stirring constantly. Reduce heat and simmer for 5 to 10 minutes.
4. Slowly add flour and milk thickening mixture, stirring constantly. Continue simmering and stirring until soup thickens, an additional 10 to 20 minutes, adding salt and pepper to taste.
5. Add white wine and half and half. Bring back to a boil and serve.\

Notes:

This recipe came from one of my writer friends, Neva Hodges, who prepared it for us at a luncheon she served at her house. We all loved it.

Curried Butternut Squash and Apple Bisque

<u>Ingredients:</u>

2 butternut squash, halved lengthwise and seeded
olive oil
2 sweet onions (such as Vidalia), diced
6 cloves garlic, minced
2 quarts vegetable stock
1 (8.4 oz) pkg medium-hot curry sauce (See recipe below)
2 Granny Smith apples, cored and diced
1 cup peeled and chopped potatoes
1/3 cup dry sherry
1½ cups half and half
¼ cup toasted pine nuts or ¾ cup blue cheese for garnish
16 fresh cilantro leaves, or to taste

<u>Directions:</u>

1. Preheat oven to 350. Place squash onto a baking sheet cut-side down. Bake squash in preheated oven until the skin loosens from the flesh, about 40 minutes. Set aside.
2. Heat olive oil in a 5-quart stockpot over medium-high heat. Cook and stir onion and garlic in hot oil until the onion is translucent, 5 to 7 minutes. Add vegetable stock, curry sauce, apples and potatoes to the stockpot; bring to a simmer, stirring frequently. Reduce heat to medium-low.
3. Cut squash into 1-inch cubes; add to the stockpot. Bring the mixture again to a simmer, place a cover on the pot, and cook, stirring once every 15 minutes, until the squash is tender and breaks apart easily when stirred, about 2 hours.
4. Remove pot from heat and blend soup with an immersion blender until completely pureed. Pour half and half and sherry into the soup; continue blending until creamy. Top each serving with toasted pine nuts or blue cheese and a couple of leaves of cilantro.

Curry Sauce

<u>Ingredients:</u>

2 tbsp peanut oil
(Recipe continued on next page.)

1 tbsp margarine or butter
1 large onion, chopped
1 tbsp minced fresh ginger root
2 tbsp minced garlic
1 tsp ground cinnamon
1 tsp ground black pepper
2 tbsp ground coriander
2 tbsp ground cumin
¼ tsp ground turmeric
1 tsp cayenne pepper
2 tomatoes
2 serrano chile peppers, seeded
½ cup fresh cilantro
½ cup yogurt, whisked until smooth
3 cups water

Directions:
1. Heat oil and margarine in a small skillet or wok over medium high heat. Add onion and sauté until very brown, 10 to 15 minutes. (Note: This is an important step; if onion is not cooked well, sauce will taste funny.)
2. Add ginger and garlic to onion and sauté for an additional 2 minutes. Process onion/ginger/garlic mixture in food processor until smooth. Do not rinse food processor.
3. Place onion mixture in a large saucepan. Stir in the cinnamon, black pepper, coriander, cumin, turmeric, and cayenne pepper and cook over low heat until mixture is thick and has the consistency of a paste.
4. Puree tomatoes, chile peppers, and cilantro in food processor until smooth. Add to onion mixture and stir well over low heat, cooking off moisture from tomatoes and cilantro. Add yogurt a little bit at a time, stirring constantly to avoid curdling. Blend the whole mixture in food processor to puree it (for a very smooth sauce).
5. Return to saucepan, add water and increase heat to high; bring sauce to a rolling boil. Cover saucepan and boil for 3 to 5 minutes. Reduce heat and simmer until desired consistency is reached.
6. Use in previous recipe or serve with cooked meat simmered in sauce for 10 minutes and serve over rice.

Finch Bay Tomato Soup

Ingredients:

¼ cup plus 2 tbsp olive oil
3 pounds ripe tomatoes, peeled and diced
salt and pepper to taste
1 tbsp sugar
2 cups chopped onion
6 garlic cloves, minced
3 oz tomato paste
2 tbsp unsalted butter
¼ tsp crushed red pepper flakes
4 cups chopped basil leaves, packed
1 quart vegetable or chicken stock

Directions:

1. Preheat the oven to 400. Toss together the tomatoes, ¼ cup olive oil, salt, pepper, and sugar. Spread the tomatoes in a single layer on a baking sheet and roast for 45 minutes.
2. In a large stockpot over medium heat, sauté the onions and garlic with the remaining 2 tbsp of olive oil, the butter, and red pepper flakes for 10 minutes, until the onions start to brown. Add the tomato paste, basil, thyme, and vegetable or chicken stock. Add the oven-roasted tomatoes, including the liquid on the baking sheet. Bring to a boil and simmer uncovered for 40 minutes. In batches, puree in blender. Serve with buttery garlic bread.

Notes:

I got this recipe from a chef at Finch Bay Resort in the Galapagos. He served it for dinner. I was impressed and boldly asked our server if he could possibly get the recipe. The server talked to the chef who attempted to put it in English and typed out a copy for me. I brought it home, tried to convert grams to U.S. system of measurement and checked a couple of internet recipes to make sure I wasn't too far off. I came up with this.

French Onion Soup

<u>Ingredients:</u>

5 tbsp olive oil, divided
1 tbsp butter
8 cups thinly sliced onions (about 3 pounds)
3 garlic cloves, minced
½ cup port wine
2 cartons (32 oz each) beef broth
½ tsp pepper
¼ tsp salt
24 slices French bread baguette (½ inch thick)
2 large garlic cloves, peeled and halved
1¼ cups shredded Gruyere or Swiss cheese

<u>Directions:</u>
1. In a Dutch oven or large soup pot, heat 2 tbsp oil and butter over medium heat. Add onions; cook and stir for 10-13 minutes or until softened. Reduce heat to medium-low; cook for 30-40 minutes or until deep golden brown, stirring occasionally. Add minced garlic; cook 2 minutes longer.
2. Stir in wine. Bring to a boil; cook until liquid is reduced by half. Add the broth, pepper, and salt; return to a boil. Reduce heat; simmer for 1 hour, stirring occasionally.
3. Meanwhile, place baguette slices on a baking sheet; brush both sides with remaining oil. Bake at 400 for 3-5 minutes on each side or until toasted. Rub toasts with halved garlic.
4. To serve, place twelve 8-oz broiler-safe bowls or ramekins on baking sheets. Place two toasts in each. Ladle with soup; top with cheese. Broil 4 inches from heat until cheese is melted.

<u>Notes:</u>
This was one of my mom's favorites, and I almost always fixed it when she visited. It doesn't hurt that Bob and I love it too.

Gazpacho

<u>Ingredients:</u>

2 cups extra-virgin olive oil, more for drizzling (see note)
¼ cup sherry vinegar, more as needed
1 tsp Tabasco or other hot pepper sauce
½ medium red onion, peeled and cut into large chunks
½ medium cucumber, trimmed and cut into large chunks
leaves from 6 large sprigs flat-leaf parsley
10 to 12 large fresh basil leaves
1 large clove garlic
kosher salt
4 medium Roma tomatoes, cored and cut into large chunks
3 medium heirloom tomatoes, cored and cut into large chunks

<u>Directions:</u>

1. Put the oil, vinegar, and Tabasco in a blender and blend briefly. Add the onion, cucumber, parsley, basil, garlic, and 1 tbsp salt and blend until smooth.
2. Add the tomatoes a few at a time, blending as you go. When the blender is about three-fourths full, pour out half of the liquid into a medium bowl. Continue to puree and add the tomatoes a few at a time until all the tomatoes are incorporated and the mixture is smooth. Pour the blender contents into the bowl and stir to blend. If you want a super-smooth texture, pass the soup through a fine-mesh strainer.
3. Chill for at least 2 hours before serving. Whisk to blend, then taste and add more salt or vinegar as needed. Garnish each serving with a drizzle of extra-virgin olive oil.

<u>Notes:</u>

This may seem like a lot of olive oil, but any less and it doesn't work. Besides, olive oil is pretty healthy. ☺.

Hearty Chicken Soup with Noodles and Vegetables

Ingredients:

1 (3 pounds) whole chicken
1 onion, cut into thick slices
5 stalks celery, thickly sliced
1 tbsp salt
1 tsp packed fresh basil leaves
1 tsp coarse ground black pepper
5 carrots, sliced
1 yellow squash, thinly sliced
1 zucchini, thinly sliced
1 pound fresh mushrooms, sliced
1 red bell pepper, sliced
2 tbsp chicken soup base
2 cups uncooked wide egg noodles

Directions:

1. Place chicken, onion, celery, salt, basil, and pepper in a 10-quart stock pot. Fill stock pot with water until ingredients are fully covered and bring to a boil. Let simmer for 1½ hours or until chicken is tender.
2. Remove chicken from pot with slotted spoon and set aside.
Add carrots, squash, zucchini, mushrooms, red pepper, tortellini, chicken soup base and uncooked noodles to stock pot and increase temperature to medium heat.
3. While noodles and vegetables are cooking, tear chicken apart from bones. Cut up into pieces and add back into soup in stock pot. Be sure to add additional water if ingredients are not fully covered. Bring to a boil, then reduce to a simmer for about 10 minutes or just until noodles are cooked.

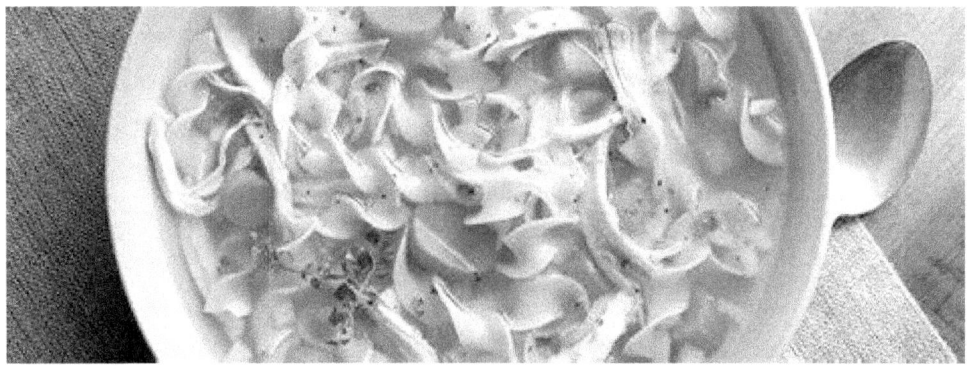

Minestrone Soup

<u>Ingredients:</u>

6 oz pancetta
3 tbsp olive oil
3 cloves garlic, chopped
2 onions, chopped
2 cups chopped celery
5 carrots, chopped
2 tbsp tomato paste
4 cups chicken broth
2 cups tomato sauce
2 cups diced tomatoes
3 potatoes, peeled and in small chunks
1 tbsp chopped fresh oregano
2 tbsp chopped fresh basil
1 tbsp fresh rosemary
2 cups baby spinach, rinsed
salt and pepper to taste
½ cup red wine (optional)
1 can each kidney, cannellini, and green beans, drained
½ cup seashell or Rotella pasta, cooked according to pkg directions
4 tbsp freshly grated parmesan cheese and more for topping

<u>Directions:</u>
1. Over medium heat in a large stock pot, heat olive oil. Sauté garlic 2 to 3 minutes. Add onion and sauté 4 to 5 minutes. Add pancetta, celery, and carrots, sauté 1 to 2 minutes. Add tomato paste, stir.
2. Add chicken broth, spinach, tomato sauce, diced tomatoes, bring to boil, stirring frequently. Add oregano, basil, rosemary, salt, and pepper. If desired, add red wine at this point. Reduce heat to low and simmer for one hour. Add kidney beans, cannellini beans, green beans, pasta, and 4 tbsp parmesan. Serve with more grated parmesan.

<u>Notes:</u>
For thicker soup, put about ¼ of soup in blender and blend, then add back to pot. This recipe makes a lot of soup, but it freezes well.

Potato Soup Chowder

<u>Ingredients:</u>

3½ cups peeled and diced potatoes
1/3 cup diced celery
1/3 cup finely chopped onion
¾ cup diced cooked ham
3¼ cup low sodium chicken broth
6 tbsp butter
6 tbsp all-purpose flour
2 cups milk
salt and pepper to taste

<u>Directions:</u>

1. Combine the potatoes, celery, onion, ham, corn, and chicken broth in a stockpot. Bring to a boil, then cook over medium heat until potatoes are tender, about 10 to 15 minutes. Add corn and continue boiling an additional 2 minutes.
2. In a separate saucepan, melt butter over medium-low heat. Whisk in flour with a fork, and cook, stirring constantly until thick, about 1 minute. Slowly stir in milk so as not to allow lumps to form until all of the milk has been added. Continue stirring over medium-low heat until thick, 4 to 5 minutes.
3. Stir the milk mixture into the stockpot, and cook soup until heated through. Serve immediately.

<u>Notes:</u>

I often use the meat from a smoked turkey leg in place of the ham. Be careful how much salt you add since the turkey leg and broth both have salt. When I feel like throwing cholesterol caution to the wind, I add a cup of sharp cheddar cheese to the milk/flour mixture after step 2 and stir until melted and smooth. Garnish with chopped chives.

Slow Cooker Bean and Vegetable Soup

<u>Ingredients:</u>

2 **pounds** smoked turkey leg (or you can use ham)
1 **pound** dried navy beans, sorted, rinsed
4 medium stalks celery, sliced (1 cup)
1 large onion, chopped (½ cup)
4 medium carrots, sliced (2 cups)
2 large potatoes, peeled and cut into chunks (2 cups)
6 cups low sodium chicken broth
½ **tsp** dried thyme leaves
½ **tsp** liquid smoke
several dashes of hot sauce
½ **cup** chopped fresh parsley

<u>Directions:</u>
1. Soak beans overnight, or in large pot cover beans with water, bring to boil, and cook on low for an hour.
2. In 3½ to 4-quart slow cooker (large slow cooker), mix all ingredients except parsley.
3. Cover; cook on low heat setting 10 to 12 hours or medium 4-5 hours, until beans and meat are tender.
4. Remove turkey legs and strip off meat. Discard bones. Stir meat back into beans. Stir in parsley before serving.

<u>Notes:</u>
Especially good served with cornbread. Also, this can be an overnight recipe if you want to start it late at night before you go to bed and have it for lunch the next day.

Smoked Salmon Chowder

<u>Ingredients:</u>

2 tbsp butter
1 tbsp olive oil
1 cup chopped onion
2 cloves garlic, chopped
½ cup chopped celery
½ cup all-purpose flour
6 cups chicken broth or vegetable broth
1 pound potatoes, peeled and cubed
1 tsp dried dill weed
1 tsp dried tarragon
1 tsp dried thyme
½ tsp paprika
8 oz smoked salmon, cut into ½-inch pieces
¼ cup white wine
1 tbsp fresh lemon juice
¼ tsp hot sauce
1 tsp salt and 1 tsp fresh-ground black pepper
1 cup half and half

<u>Directions:</u>

1. In a large stockpot over medium-high heat, combine the butter, olive oil, onion, garlic, and celery. Cook 8 to 10 minutes, or until the onions are transparent. Sprinkle flour over the mixture and stir well to make a dry roux. Gradually add the chicken broth and stir until slightly thickened. Stir in the potatoes, dill, tarragon, thyme, and paprika. Reduce heat to medium, cover, and simmer for 15 minutes.
2. Stir in the salmon, wine, lemon juice, hot sauce, salt, and pepper. Simmer over low heat, uncovered for 10 minutes. Mix in the half-and-half and continue to simmer for 30 minutes, stirring occasionally. Do not let the chowder boil after adding the half-and-half. Serve hot.

<u>Notes:</u>

My friend, Susan Jurkiewicz suggested this for a dinner party I was hosting. It was appreciated.

Smoked Turkey Leg and Split Pea Soup

<u>Ingredients:</u>

1 tbsp olive oil
1 yellow onion, diced
2 cloves garlic, chopped
6 cups low-sodium beef broth
2 pounds dried split peas
1 carrot, peeled and diced
2 small potatoes, peeled and diced
2 tbsp soy sauce
1 tbsp dried basil
1 tbsp dried parsley
2 tsp crushed red pepper flakes
1 tsp ground sage
2 bay leaves
2½ pounds smoked turkey legs (you can use ham)
coarse salt and pepper to taste
2½ tbsp sour cream, for garnish

<u>Directions:</u>

1. Heat the oil in a large pot over medium-high heat. Cook the onion in the hot oil until translucent, about 5 minutes; stir in the garlic and cook another 30 seconds. Pour in the beef broth; add split peas, carrot, potatoes, soy sauce, basil, black pepper, parsley, red pepper flakes, sage, kosher salt, and bay leaves.
2. Place the smoked turkey legs into the pot and pour in enough water to cover the peas by about 1 inch. Push the meaty ends of the turkey legs down into the liquid. Bring to a boil, cover, reduce heat to medium-low. Simmer until the peas have softened, about 45 minutes.
3. Remove the turkey legs from the soup and set aside to cool. When cool enough to handle, strip the meat from the bones and tendons, finely chop the turkey meat, and set aside.
4. Put 1/3 of the soup mixture into a blender and puree. Add pureed soup to soup pot to thicken. Add turkey meat. Serve bowls of soup topped with dollop of sour cream.

Three Alarm Vegetarian Chili

<u>Ingredients:</u>

2 tbsp corn oil
1½ cups chopped onions
3 cloves garlic, minced
2 tbsp chili powder
¼ tsp crushed red pepper
½ tsp ground cumin
1 cup diced carrots
1 green pepper, chopped
2 cans (14½ to 16 oz each) tomatoes in juice, undrained
1 can (16 oz) chick peas, drained
1 can kidney beans
1 pkg (10 oz) frozen corn, thawed

<u>Directions:</u>
1. In a 5-quart saucepot, heat corn oil over medium heat. Add onions, garlic, chili powder, red pepper, and cumin. Sauté 5 minutes or until tender.
2. Add carrots and green pepper; sauté 2 minutes. Add tomatoes with juice, crushing tomatoes with spoon.
3. Stir in chick peas, kidney beans, and corn. Bring to a boil. Reduce heat, cover and simmer 30 to 35 minutes. Serve with hot sauce in case anyone wants it even hotter.

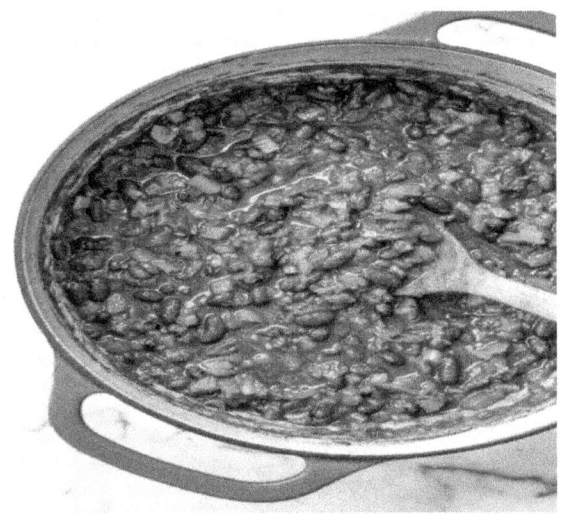

<u>Notes:</u>
This is a spicy vegetarian and gluten free dish. I serve with shredded cheddar, sour cream, and chopped onions. Neither Bob nor I are vegetarian nor do we eat with concern for gluten-free, but every now and then we have friends for dinner who avoid either meat or gluten, so I keep a couple of recipes I can pull out for such occasions.

Veggie Soup

<u>Ingredients:</u>

4 cups cubed red potatoes (do not peel)
1½ cups coarsely chopped carrots
1 cup coarsely chopped celery
½ cup green beans
1 green, red, or yellow bell pepper, coarsely chopped
1 cup frozen sweet peas
1 large onion, peeled and coarsely chopped
1 (10 oz) bag spinach
2 cups of tomato juice or V8
2 cups water
½ stick of butter
1½ tsp salt
1 tsp black pepper
1½ tsp dried sage
1 tbsp dried basil
¼ cup chopped fresh parsley

<u>Directions:</u>
1. Place vegetables in a Dutch oven. Add tomato juice and water; bring to a boil. Add butter, salt, pepper, and herbs.
2. Simmer until vegetables are tender, about 30 minutes.

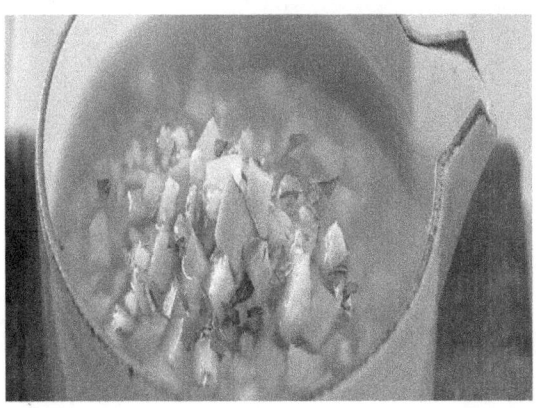

<u>Notes:</u>
This is my go-to recipe when I've eaten way too much of everything else in this book. I'll avoid using the "D" word and simply say it's my healthy-get-back-on-track recipe. I decrease the amount of potatoes and add a half of a head of chopped cabbage and a can of diced tomatoes. I substitute 2 tbsp olive oil for the half stick of butter and add a few dashes of hot sauce. It is a fairly bland soup so I often add garlic, a couple of bay leaves, and some combination of other spices including: marjoram, cumin, paprika, chili powder, and thyme. I also squeeze a half lemon into the soup and remove the bay leaves when the soup has finished simmering.

Salads and Side Dishes
(Veggies, Potatoes, and Rice)

"Life Expectancy would grow by leaps and bounds if vegetables smelled like bacon." **Doug Larsen**

"What I say is that, if a man likes potatoes, he must be a pretty decent sort of fellow." **A.A. Milne**

"Friends are the bacon bits in the salad of life."

Chocolate comes from cocoa which is a tree. That makes it a plant. Chocolate is salad.

~~~Salads~~~

April's Asian Salad

Ingredients:

1 cup cut-up lettuce
2 green onions, cut in thin slices
2 slices cooked, crisp bacon, in pieces
1 small can mandarin oranges, drained
2 chicken breasts, cooked and cubed
1 cup Chinese chow Mein noodles
sweet and sour dressing

Directions:
1. Cook bacon and chicken. Crumble the bacon and cut chicken into small cubes.
2. Mix all ingredients and then add dressing to taste.

Notes:
This recipe came from my second cousin, April Cutler. (See next page for Sweet and Sour Dressing for this salad.)

April's Sweet and Sour Dressing

<u>Ingredients:</u>

1 cup vegetable oil
2/3 cup white sugar
1/3 cup distilled white vinegar
¼ small onion, finely diced
1 tsp salt
¾ tsp dry mustard
½ tsp celery seed

<u>Directions:</u>
Mix or shake all ingredients in a blender or salad dressing shaker.

~ ~ ~

Bacon Potato Salad

<u>Ingredients:</u>

4 tsp red-wine vinegar
4 slices bacon
1½ pounds new potatoes, thinly sliced
6 oz wax beans, trimmed and halved
6 oz green beans, trimmed and halved
3 tbsp capers, rinsed and drained
1 tsp extra-virgin olive oil
2 scallions, thinly sliced

<u>Directions:</u>
1. Preheat oven to 450 with racks in upper and lower thirds. Divide bacon between two rimmed baking sheets; cook until browned, 8 minutes. Drain bacon on paper towels, reserving sheets. Crumble bacon into bite-size pieces.
2. Add potatoes to sheets, season with pepper, and toss to coat with bacon drippings. Cook until potatoes are brown on bottoms, 15 minutes, rotating sheets halfway through. Remove sheets from oven and flip potatoes with metal spatula.
3. In a bowl, combine beans, capers, and oil; divide between sheets with potatoes. Cook until potatoes and beans are tender, about 15 minutes, rotating sheets halfway through. Transfer potato mixture to a large bowl; toss with bacon, scallions, and vinegar, and serve.

Bread Salad (Panzanella)

Ingredients:

1 clove garlic
1 (1 pound) loaf Italian bread
1 cup chopped tomatoes
1 cup cucumber—peeled, seeded and chopped
1 cup chopped red onion
1 cup mozzarella balls
1 clove garlic, minced
2 cups chopped fresh basil
1/8 cup chopped fresh thyme
¼ cup olive oil
2 tbsp balsamic or red wine vinegar

Directions:
1. Rub a peeled clove of garlic around a salad bowl.
2. Cut bread into small chunks. Heat olive oil in large pan and toast bread cubes until browned. Do not add bread to salad until you are ready to serve.
3. In the prepared salad bowl, combine tomatoes, cucumbers, red onions, mozzarella, garlic, basil, and thyme. Add bread just before serving. Add enough olive oil and vinegar to lightly coat, toss and serve.

Broccoli, Raisin, Bacon, and Almond Salad

<u>Ingredients:</u>

6 cups small broccoli florets
½ cup chopped celery
½ cup raisins
10 slices cooked crisp, crumbled bacon
3 sliced green onions
2/3 cup mayonnaise
¼ cup honey
fresh lemon juice
1 (3.75 oz) package honey roasted sliced almonds

<u>Directions:</u>

1. In a medium bowl, combine first 5 ingredients.
2. In a small bowl, stir together mayonnaise, honey, and lemon juice. Pour over broccoli mixture, tossing gently to coat. Stir in almonds just before serving.

Caprese Salad

Ingredients:

4 cups cooked orzo
8 cups baby arugula
2 large ripe avocados, sliced
2 cups tomato wedges or grape tomatoes cut in half
8 oz fresh mozzarella cheese, torn
16 tbsp fresh basil
¼ tsp freshly ground pepper
16 strips of bacon, cooked crisp and crumbled

Dressing:

¾ cup olive oil
1 tbsp balsamic vinegar
2 tsp Dijon mustard
1 tsp kosher salt

Directions:

Arrange Orzo and arugula in bottom of salad bowl. Top with avocados, tomato, mozzarella, and basil. Sprinkle with pepper and crumbled bacon. Drizzle with dressing.

Notes:
This recipe was served by our neighbor, Gail Leyba Ng. We all loved it, and she shared the recipe.

Caprese Cookie Sheet Salad with Pasta and Roasted Tomato

Ingredients:

2 (10 oz) containers cherry tomatoes, halved
2 tbsp olive oil
2 tsp freshly ground black pepper
1 tsp kosher salt
6 garlic cloves, minced
16 oz whole-grain fusilli pasta, cooked according to package directions until al dente, then drained.
8 oz fresh mozzarella, cut into ½ inch pieces
½ cup fresh basil, roughly chopped
¼ cup freshly grated parmesan cheese (or more to taste)

Directions:

1. Preheat oven to 375. On a rimmed sheet pan, combine tomatoes, olive oil, pepper, salt, and garlic. Toss to coat. Spread in an even layer. Bake 20-25 minutes or until tomatoes are soft and fragrant.
2. Add cooked pasta, mozzarella, and basil to the pan. Toss to combine. Adjust salt and pepper. Drizzle with additional oil. Serve with ¼ cup (or more) grated parmesan.

Chopped Chicken Salad

<u>Ingredients:</u>
Salad »»

>2 large bunches romaine, chopped
>1 head radicchio, chopped
>3 heads Belgian endive, chopped
>1 pound roasted chicken, chopped
>1 pound blue cheese, crumbled
>6 oz bacon, cooked, drained, and crumbled
>2 large apples, peeled and chopped
>½ bunch of parsley, chopped
>½ lemon, juiced

Mustard Vinaigrette »»

>2 tbsp shallots, diced
>¼ cup sherry vinegar
>1 tsp Dijon mustard
>½ tbsp whole grain mustard
>¾ cup extra virgin olive oil
>½ tsp honey
>salt and pepper to taste

<u>Directions:</u>
1. For vinaigrette: Soak the shallots in the vinegar for 5 minutes. Whisk in the mustards, and then the olive oil and honey. Season with salt and pepper.
2. For salad: Place all the ingredients (except the lemon juice) in a large salad bowl. Toss with the vinaigrette and lemon juice. Add salt and pepper to taste.

Corn Salad

<u>Ingredients:</u>
Salad »»

> 12 ears of fresh corn on the cob
> 2 cups tomatoes, seeded and coarsely chopped
> 2 cups cucumbers, chopped
> 1 cup red pepper, chopped
> 1 cup red onion, chopped

Red Wine Vinaigrette »»

> ½ cup red wine vinegar
> ¾ cup extra virgin olive oil
> 2/3 cup fresh shallots, chopped very fine
> ¼ to ½ tsp sugar, if desired
> 2 tbsp fresh basil, chopped
> ¼ cup flat leaf parsley, chopped
> ¼ tsp cayenne
> coarse salt and freshly ground black pepper to taste

<u>Directions:</u>
1. Remove husks and silk from corn. Rub ears with olive oil and sprinkle with salt and pepper. Wrap ears in aluminum foil and bake at 400 for 20 minutes. Corn should be soft and steaming. When cool enough to handle, cut corn from cobs and place in large bowl.
2. Add tomatoes, cucumbers, red pepper, onion.
3. Prepare vinaigrette by mixing remaining ingredients and then pour over salad and stir to coat corn mixture completely.

<u>Notes:</u>
My daughter, Courtney Phillips, brought this to an open house celebrating Bob's 70th birthday. It was a hit. Best chilled before serving.

Curry Chicken and Fruit Salad

Ingredients:

4 skinless, boneless chicken breast halves - cooked and diced
1 stalk celery, chopped
1 small apple, peeled, cored, and chopped
4 green onions, chopped
⅓ cup golden raisins
⅓ cup seedless green grapes, halved
½ cup chopped toasted pecans
⅛ tsp ground black pepper
½ tsp curry powder
¾ cup mayonnaise

Directions:
1. In a large salad bowl combine all ingredients. Good served as a separate side salad or on a croissant as a sandwich.

~ ~ ~

Creamy Coleslaw

Ingredients:

1 (16 oz) bag coleslaw mix
2 tbsp finely diced onion
2/3 cup Miracle Whip
3 tbsp canola oil
½ cup white sugar
1 tbsp white vinegar
¼ tsp salt
½ tsp poppy seeds

Directions:
1. Combine the coleslaw mix and onion in a large bowl.
2. Whisk together the salad dressing, canola oil, sugar, vinegar, salt, and poppy seeds in a medium bowl; blend thoroughly. Pour dressing mixture over coleslaw mix and toss to coat.
3. Chill at least 2 hours before serving.

Note:
It's the poppy seeds that set this apart from other coleslaw. It's our favorite.

Easy and Versatile Fruit Salad

Ingredients:

    2 cups green grapes
    2 cups sliced strawberries
    2 cups sliced peaches
    2 cups orange segments
    1 cup peeled sliced kiwi
    ½ cup orange juice
    ½ cup Triple Sec
    2 tbsp white sugar
    1 cup toasted walnuts
    1 cup dates, cut in half

Directions:
1. Mix grapes, strawberries, peaches, orange segments, and kiwi in a large bowl.
2. Whisk orange juice, Triple Sec, and sugar together in small bowl until sugar dissolves; gently stir into fruit until evenly coated. Cover bowl with plastic wrap and refrigerate up to 8 hours.
3. Before serving add walnuts and dates and stir.

Notes:
This recipe works for so many occasions: brunch, light dessert, picnic, side dish. Variations are limited only by your imagination. Cut up apples work well. Amounts don't need to be precise, so weight it in favor of your favorite fruit.

Endive, Orange, and Roquefort Salad With Vinaigrette

Ingredients:

Orange Vinaigrette »»

½ tsp grated orange zest
¼ cup orange juice
¼ cup olive oil
1 tsp white wine vinegar

Salad »»

2 heads Belgian Endive
½ cup toasted walnut halves
4 oz Roquefort or Blue Cheese
1 sweet red apple, cored, unpeeled, and medium diced
4 oz baby arugula
1 orange

Directions:
1. Cut endives in half lengthwise, wash, and remove the hard inner triangle. Let leaves separate and cut them in half.
2. Place endive in large bowl and drizzle with vinaigrette.
3. Add walnuts, Roquefort, apple, and arugula and toss.
4. Zest the orange into the salad with a strip zester.
5. Separate orange sections, remove membranes, and toss them on the salad.
6. Sprinkle with salt and serve.

Fig and Blue Cheese Salad

Ingredients:

¼ cup extra-virgin olive oil
2 tbsp apple cider vinegar
½ tbsp whole-grain mustard
sea salt
pepper
6 slices of bacon
1½ tbsp salted butter
1 crisp Fuji apple, halved, cored, and thinly sliced
1/3 cup toasted hazelnuts, chopped
2 cups mesclun greens
3 oz Roquefort cheese, crumbled
½ pound small, seedless dark grapes, halved
4 fresh figs, cut into wedges

Directions:
1. In a small bowl, whisk the olive oil with the apple cider vinegar and whole-grain mustard. Season with salt and pepper.
2. In a large nonstick skillet, cook the bacon slices over moderate heat, turning, until golden and crisp, about 5 minutes. Transfer to a paper towel–lined plate to drain. Break the bacon into pieces.
3. In the same skillet, melt the butter. Add the apple and cook over moderate heat until lightly golden, 3 to 4 minutes. Stir in the hazelnuts and cook until deep golden, 1 to 2 minutes. Let cool slightly.
4. Arrange the greens on a platter. Top with the apple, hazelnuts, cheese, grapes, figs, and bacon. Drizzle with the vinaigrette and serve.

Freezer Cole Slaw

<u>Ingredients:</u>

1 medium head cabbage, shredded
1 green bell pepper, finely chopped
1 small onion, finely chopped
1 carrot, shredded
2 cups boiling water
2 tsp salt
1½ cups white sugar
1 cup water
1 cup cider vinegar
2 tsp celery seed
1 tsp mustard seed

<u>Directions:</u>

1. Combine cabbage, green bell pepper, onion, and carrots in a large bowl. Mix boiling water and salt together in a bowl and pour over cabbage mixture. Set aside for salt to draw out extra water from vegetables, about 1 hour. Drain well.
2. Mix sugar, 1 cup water, cider vinegar, celery seed, and mustard seed in a saucepan; bring to a boil. Cook and stir until sugar is dissolved, about 1 minute. Remove saucepan from heat and cool completely.
3. Pour cooled sugar-vinegar mixture over drained cabbage mixture in a large bowl and toss until slaw is well mixed. Spoon slaw into resealable plastic bags and freeze.

<u>Notes:</u>

I originally got this recipe from my cousin, Judy Albrecht. I made a few changes, but like she told me when she gave me the directions, this is nice to have in the freezer for when company comes. Or in my case, when I've been in San Francisco playing with my grandsons and get home too late to cook. It thaws quickly.

Fresh Zucchini and Corn Salad

Ingredients:

¼ cup butter
½ small white onion, finely diced
3 small zucchinis, diced
3 ears corn, husks and silk removed
sea salt to taste
freshly ground black pepper to taste

Directions:

1. Heat butter in a skillet over medium heat, stirring occasionally, until lightly browned, 1 to 2 minutes. Cook and stir onion in the melted butter until translucent, about 5 minutes. Cut kernels from the ears of corn. Add zucchini and corn; cook and stir until zucchini is tender, about 8 minutes. Season with sea salt and pepper.
2. This can be served as a side dish, or as a salad with a light lemon/oil dressing.

~ ~ ~

German Potato Salad

Ingredients:

½ pound bacon, cooked, drained, and crumbled
¾ cup chopped onion
2 tbsp all-purpose flour
1 tsp celery seed
1 tsp salt
1/8 tsp pepper
1 cup water
4 tbsp beer
2/3 cup cider vinegar
¼ cup sugar
6 cups peeled, sliced, and cooked potatoes

Directions:

1. In a large skillet, fry bacon until crisp; remove, and set aside. Drain all but 4-5 tbsp of drippings. In remaining drippings, cook onion until tender. Stir in the flour, celery seed, salt, and pepper until blended. Add water, beer, and vinegar; cook and stir for 1 minute or until slightly thickened. I sometimes use the whole pound of bacon. (Recipes and notes continued on next page.)

2. Stir in sugar until dissolved. Crumble bacon; gently stir in bacon and potatoes. Heat through, stirring lightly to coat potatoes. Serve hot.

Notes:
I can't be German without a good family recipe for German Potato Salad. I think I got this one from my Grandma Emma Albrecht, but I can't say for sure. I'll give her the credit anyway. Now if I could just make her amazing homemade bread.

~ ~ ~

Guest-Worthy Caesar Salad

Ingredients:

1 egg yolk
3 tbsp fresh lemon juice
1 tbsp minced garlic
½ tsp Worcestershire sauce
¼ tsp red pepper flakes
1 tbsp Dijon mustard
2 anchovy fillets, mashed
scant 1 cup vegetable oil
1/3 cup extra-virgin olive oil
salt and freshly ground black pepper
1 large head romaine lettuce, cleaned and cut into 1 to 2-inch pieces
freshly grated parmesan
2 cups croutons

Directions:
1. In a medium bowl, whisk together the egg yolk, lemon juice, garlic, Worcestershire, pepper flakes, mustard, and anchovies.
(Recipe continued on next page.)

2. Slowly whisk in the oils to emulsify. Season, to taste, with salt and pepper. Place the lettuce in a large bowl. Sprinkle with parmesan and black pepper. Drizzle with desired amount of dressing and toss well. Sprinkle top with croutons.

~ ~ ~

Grilled Potatoes with Chevre and Cilantro Vinaigrette

<u>Ingredients:</u>
Salad »»

2 pounds medium red-skinned potatoes
olive oil for brushing
2 clove garlic, crushed
2 oz goat cheese, crumbled

Cilantro Vinaigrette »»

1 large clove garlic
½ cup fresh cilantro
¼ cup fresh basil
1 tsp toasted cumin seeds, or ½ tsp ground cumin
1 tsp toasted fennel seeds
½ tsp crushed red pepper flakes
¼ tsp sea salt and freshly ground black pepper to taste
2 tbsp apple cider vinegar, or white wine vinegar
¼ cup extra-virgin olive oil

<u>Directions:</u>
1. Place all vinaigrette ingredients in a blender and puree. Adjust by seasoning with more salt and pepper, if desired.
2. In a large pot of salted water, gently simmer potatoes until just turning soft, about 10 to 15 minutes. Drain, rinse with cool water, drain again, and slice into ½-inch slices.
3. Put olive oil, garlic, sea salt, and freshly ground black pepper into a large plastic sealable bag. Add sliced potatoes and gently shake until potatoes are covered.
4. Spray grate and preheat grill. Grill potatoes until browned, 20-25 minutes. Transfer to serving platter, top with goat cheese, and ladle dressing over all.

<u>Note:</u>
I used this recipe before we had a grill, and I oven roasted the potatoes at 400 degrees until browned (I skipped boiling them first).

Mandarin Chicken Salad

Ingredients:
>3 cups cooked, diced, cubed, and cooled chicken (preferably baked)
>1 cup diced celery
>2 tbsp lemon juice
>1 tbsp minced onion
>½ tsp salt
>⅓ cup mayonnaise
>1 cup green seedless grapes
>1 (11 oz) can mandarin oranges, drained
>1 (2 oz) package slivered almonds, toasted
>1½ cups elbow macaroni, cooked per pkg directions, or 1 head leaf lettuce
>additional mandarin orange section (optional)
>clusters green grapes (optional)

Directions:
1. Sprinkle chicken with olive oil. Combine chicken, celery, lemon juice, onion, and salt; stir well. Cover and chill.
2. Add mayonnaise, grapes, oranges, and almonds to chicken mixture; toss well. Mix into cooked, drained, and cooled elbow macaroni or serve on lettuce. Garnish with additional orange slices and grapes if desired.

Notes:
I originally got this recipe from my cousin, Jean Ann Albrecht Wendt, but the above is how I've modified it a bit since then. I sometimes use apple instead of oranges and sliced instead of slivered almonds.

New Potato, Avocado, and Egg Salad

Ingredients:

1½ pounds tiny red potatoes, quartered
¾ cup mayonnaise
2 tbsp cider vinegar
2 tbsp chopped fresh dill weed or 2 tsp dried dill weed
1 tbsp yellow mustard
1 medium red or orange sweet pepper, chopped (about 1 cup)
½ cup chopped celery
1 small red onion, chopped
½ cup chopped dill pickles
1 firm ripe avocado, halved, pitted, peeled, and sliced
4 hard cooked eggs, peeled and sliced
iceberg lettuce

Directions:
1. Place potatoes in a large saucepan; cover with water. Bring to boil; reduce heat. Cook, covered, for 8 to 10 minutes or until just tender. Drain and run cold water over potatoes to cool. Drain and set aside.
2. Meanwhile, stir together the mayonnaise, vinegar, dill weed, and mustard in a large bowl.
3. Stir in the sweet pepper, celery, onion, and pickles. Gently stir in the potatoes, avocado, and eggs until just combined. Season to taste with salt and pepper. Serve over lettuce.

Pear, Gorgonzola, and Candied Walnut Salad

<u>Ingredients:</u>

1 tbsp unsalted butter
2 tsp brown sugar
½ cup walnut pieces
1 medium ripe pear, cored
handful of dried cranberries
½ cup crumbled Gorgonzola cheese
4 cups packed frisee lettuce (I use Romaine)
2 tbsp olive oil
2 tbsp balsamic vinegar
salt and pepper (to taste)

1. In a medium skillet, melt butter and whisk in brown sugar over medium low heat. Add walnuts and let cook. Stir often, until sugar has caramelized on the walnuts, about 3 to 4 minutes. Remove from skillet and set aside.
2. Slice pear into 1/8 to ¼ inch thick slices.
3. Whisk together olive oil, balsamic vinegar, salt, and pepper. Toss dressing with lettuce.
4. To assemble salad: place lettuce in a bowl and top with walnuts, pears, and Gorgonzola cheese. Drizzle with dressing.

<u>Notes:</u>
I usually use two pears instead of one. I often add cooked and crumbled bacon to this salad, and I sometimes substitute chopped granny smith apple in place of the pear.
You can mix it up more and add grilled zucchini slices. When I do that, I use toasted, but not candied walnuts.

Potato Salad with Mayonnaise Dressing

Ingredients:

6 medium potatoes
1 small onion, finely chopped
1 cup celery, chopped
1 tsp salt
6 hard-cooked eggs, peeled, diced
1 tbsp sweet pickle relish
1 tbsp capers
2 eggs, beaten
½ cup white sugar
1 tsp cornstarch
salt to taste
½ cup vinegar
1 (5 ounce) can evaporated milk
1 tsp prepared yellow mustard
¼ cup butter
1 cup mayonnaise
sliced radishes/green peppers as garnish (Optional)

Directions:
1. Place the potatoes into a large pot, and fill with enough water to cover. Bring to a boil, and cook for about 20 minutes, or until easily pierced with a fork. Drain. Cool, peel, and dice. Transfer to a large bowl, and toss with the onion, celery, 1 tsp of salt, hard-cooked eggs, and sweet relish.
2. While the potatoes are cooking, whisk together remaining 2 eggs (raw), sugar, cornstarch, and salt in a saucepan. Stir in the vinegar, milk, and mustard. Cook over medium heat, stirring frequently, until thickened, about 10 minutes. Remove from heat, and stir in the butter. Refrigerate until cool, then stir in the mayonnaise.
3. Stir the dressing into the bowl of potato salad until evenly coated. Chill several hours or overnight before serving for best flavor.

Notes:
For me, baked beans and potato salad make it a picnic. If you are going to make a potato salad with a mayonnaise dressing, I think this one is the best.

Salad Niçoise

<u>Ingredients:</u>

1 large shallot, minced
1 tbsp capers
2 tbsp Dijon mustard
2 tbsp white-wine vinegar
1 tsp coarse salt and ¼ tsp freshly ground pepper
6 tbsp extra-virgin olive oil
½ pound green beans
1 pound small red potatoes
2 large eggs
1 small head Romaine lettuce, cut into bite-size pieces
1 stalk celery, cut into ¼-inch slices
2 tomatoes, cut into wedges
4 radishes, thinly sliced
2 (6 oz each) cans water-packed solid albacore white tuna, drained
3 oz Niçoise or other olives (about 24)
8 anchovies (optional)

<u>Directions:</u>
1. Vinaigrette: Whisk together shallot, capers, Dijon, vinegar, salt, and pepper. Slowly whisk in oil; set dressing aside.
2. Fill large bowl with ice water; set aside. Bring a pan of water to a boil. Add beans. Cook beans about 1½ minutes. Drain; plunge into ice water, drain again, cut into 1½-inch pieces. Set aside.
3. Refill saucepan with cold water, add potatoes. Bring to a boil, reduce to a simmer; cook until potatoes are tender, about 15 minutes. Drain potatoes; cool slightly. When cooled, cut potatoes into 1-inch pieces. Place in a bowl; toss with ¼ cup of the vinaigrette; set aside.
4. Place eggs in a small saucepan of cold water. Bring to a boil; cover. Remove from heat. Set aside for 11 minutes. Rinse in cold water; peel; cut into wedges; set aside.
5. To assemble: Arrange lettuce on individual plates. Arrange green beans, potato salad, sliced eggs, celery, tomatoes, radishes, tuna (I prefer to use fresh poached Ahi tuna), olives, and anchovies. Drizzle remaining dressing, and serve.

<u>Notes:</u>
When my grandson Ezra was four, Salad Niçoise was his choice for a family night dinner. His mom started family night dinners for the extended family. We got together every Sunday night and alternated houses. Ezra wanted to help me make the salad, but had to stand on a stool to reach the counter. It is my first distinct memory of cooking with him.

Shrimp Cole Slaw

<u>Ingredients:</u>

1 large head of cabbage, shredded
¼ cup bell pepper, chopped fine
½ cup onion, chopped fine
½ cup celery, chopped fine
½ cup Italian dressing
2 tsp garlic salt
1 tsp garlic powder
1 tsp onion salt
½ cup mayonnaise
1 pound small pre-cooked shrimp

<u>Directions:</u>
1. In large mixing bowl, combine first four ingredients.
2. Mix dressing, garlic salt, garlic powder, onion salt, and mayonnaise in small bowl, then pour over ingredients in first bowl. Mix well.
3. Add shrimp.
4. Chill until served.

Shrimp Pasta Salad

<u>Ingredients:</u>

1 (16 oz) pkg uncooked penne pasta
¼ pound bacon
1 pound cooked shrimp, peeled and deveined
2 avocados, peeled, pitted, and diced
1 cup shredded Cheddar cheese
1 cup mayonnaise
¼ cup lemon juice
2 tomatoes, diced and seeded
1 tsp crushed red pepper
4 cups shredded lettuce

<u>Directions:</u>

1. Bring a large pot of lightly salted water to a boil. Place pasta in the pot, cook for 8 to 10 minutes, until al dente, and drain. Rinse under cold running water to cool.

2. Place bacon in a skillet over medium high heat, and cook until evenly brown. Drain and crumble.

3. In a large bowl, gently toss together the pasta, bacon, shrimp, avocados, cheddar cheese, mayonnaise, lemon juice, tomatoes, and red pepper. Serve over shredded lettuce.

Smoked Salmon Potato Salad with Dill

<u>Ingredients:</u>
Salad »»

    2 pounds red skinned potatoes, washed
    1 tsp salt
    1 medium red onion, sliced
    4 slices smoked salmon (about 5 oz), cut into strips
    1 tbsp capers (optional)

Dressing »»

    ¼ cup half and half
    ½ cup plain Greek style yogurt
    1 tsp Dijon mustard
    1 tbsp lemon juice
    1 tbsp fresh dill, chopped

<u>Directions:</u>

1. Cut potatoes into 1-inch pieces and rinse them. Place potatoes in a large pan, cover with water, add salt and cook on high heat. Bring the water to a boil and cook 10 minutes or until tender. Drain the potatoes in a colander and let cool completely.
2. Make the dressing while potatoes are cooling: in a small bowl, combine half and half, yogurt, mustard, lemon juice, and fresh dill. Mix well and keep in the refrigerator.
3. In a salad bowl, mix potatoes, onion, capers, and smoked salmon together.
4. When ready to eat, pour dressing on the salad, and mix well to coat. Best served chilled.

<u>Note:</u>
This salad can be made ahead, but add the dressing just before serving.

Sweet Potato Cakes with Kale Bean Salad

Ingredients:

3 sweet potatoes, peeled and shredded
2 green onions, thinly sliced
¼ tsp salt
¼ tsp pepper
¼ cup light or regular mayonnaise
2 tbsp lime juice
1 tbsp soy sauce
5 oz baby kale
2 (14 oz each) cans black beans, rinsed and drained
2 cups shelled frozen edamame

Directions:
1. Preheat oven to 450. Spray cookie sheet with cooking spray.
2. In large bowl, toss sweet potatoes, green onions, and salt and pepper. With ¼ measuring cup, scoop packed sweet potatoes onto pan to form 12 mounds, 2 inches apart. Flatten slightly. Spray tops with cooking spray. Bake 25 minutes or until browned at edges.
3. Dressing: In large bowl, whisk mayonnaise, lime juice, and soy sauce.
4. When cakes are cooked, add baby kale, black beans, and edamame to dressing. Toss until coated. Serve cakes over salad.

Tangy Two Potato Salad

<u>Ingredients:</u>

1½ pounds red potatoes
1 pound sweet potatoes
¼ cup champagne vinegar
¼ cup grainy Dijon mustard
1 medium shallot
3 tbsp fresh lemon juice
3 tbsp olive oil
8 oz fresh green beans, ends cut off
6 radishes
¼ cup finely chopped parsley

<u>Directions:</u>

1. In large saucepot, combine potatoes, 1 tbsp salt, and enough water to cover potatoes by 1 inch. Cover; bring to a boil and then reduce heat; simmer, partially covered, 5 minutes.

2. Meanwhile, in large bowl, whisk vinegar, mustard, shallot, lemon juice, oil, 1 tsp salt, and ½ tsp pepper until combined; set aside.

3. Add beans to potatoes. Cook 6 minutes or until vegetables are tender. Drain well; gently toss with vinaigrette until coated. Cool 15 minutes; fold in radishes and parsley.

~ ~ ~

Thai Cucumber and Tomato Salad with Lime/Peanut Dressing

<u>Ingredients:</u>

1 large cucumber
2 tomatoes, seeded and cut into wedges
¼ red onion, thinly sliced
¼ cup rice vinegar
2 tbsp lime juice
1 tsp white sugar, or to taste
3 tbsp chopped fresh cilantro
3 tbsp chopped peanuts, optional

<u>Directions:</u>

1. Peel the cucumber in strips lengthwise with a vegetable peeler, alternating skinned strips with peel for a decorative effect. Slice the cucumber in half

(Recipe continued on next page.)

lengthwise, and then thinly slice. Place the cucumber in a salad bowl with the tomato and red onion, and mix together.

2. Pour the rice vinegar and lime juice into a separate bowl, and stir in the sugar until dissolved. Pour the dressing over the salad; mix, cover, and refrigerate until chilled, at least 30 minutes. Just before serving, stir in the cilantro and sprinkle with chopped peanuts.

~ ~ ~

Salad Dressings:

1. **Basic oil/vinegar/lemon juice dressing:** Mix juice from ½ freshly squeezed *lemon*, ¼ cup high quality *olive oil*, 1 tbsp *red wine vinegar*, 1 tsp *Dijon mustard*, 2 tbsp *fresh parsley*, *salt* and *pepper* to taste. (Add ¼ cup *honey* for honey mustard.)

2. **Creamy Blue Cheese Dressing:** In small bowl, mash 2½ tbsp *blue cheese*. Add 3 tbsp *buttermilk*, 3 tbsp *sour cream*, 2 tbsp *mayonnaise*, 2 tsp *white wine vinegar*, ¼ tsp *sugar*, 1/8 tsp *garlic powder*, and *salt* and *pepper* to taste. Mix well.

3. **Creamy Brie Dressing:** Blend 8 oz *brie cheese*, rind removed; ¼ cup each *milk* and fresh *lemon juice*; 3 tbsp extra virgin olive oil; 1 *clove garlic*; 1 tsp *honey*; and ¼ tsp each *salt* and *pepper* until smooth.

4. **Green Goddess Dressing:** Blend ½ cup each *sour cream*, packed fresh *tarragon*, and packed fresh *parsley*; 1/3 cup *mayonnaise*; 3 tbsp fresh *lemon juice*; 5 *anchovy filets*; 2 tbsp snipped fresh *chives*; 1 tbsp *cider vinegar*; ¼ tsp *salt* until smooth.

5. **Julia Child's Lemon-Oil Dressing:** 1 tbsp fresh *lemon zest*, ¼ tsp *salt*, plus more to taste, ½ tbsp *Dijon mustard*, 2 tbsp freshly squeezed *lemon juice*, ½ cup fine fresh *oil*, and freshly ground *pepper* to taste. Put all ingredients in small jar and shake.

6. **Raspberry Vinaigrette:** ½ cup unsweetened frozen *raspberries*, thawed, ¼ cup extra virgin *olive oil*, 2 tbsp fresh *lemon juice*, 1 tbsp *honey*, *coarse sea salt*, and freshly ground *black pepper* to taste. Put all ingredients in small jar and shake.

7. **Tomato-Miso Dressing:** In 10-inch skillet cook ¼ cup *canola oil*; 1 small *shallot*, sliced, 1 *jalapeno chili*, sliced; and 1 *clove garlic*, chopped. Use medium heat and cook 3 to 4 minutes or until mixture is slightly browned. Stir constantly. Add 8 oz *tomatoes*, chopped. Cook 5 minutes, stirring. Cool. Blend with 3 tbsp *miso*, 3 tbsp *rice vinegar*, and 1 tbsp *water*.

 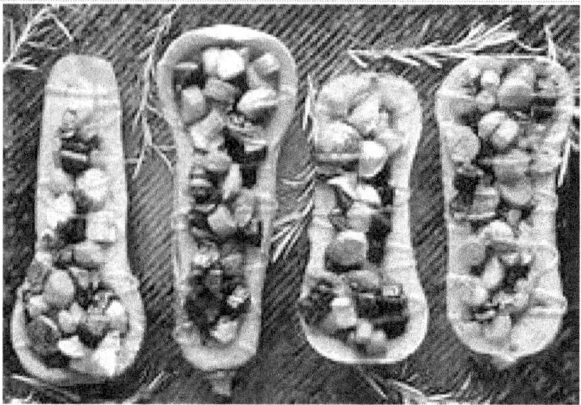

~~~Side Dishes~~~

Asparagus Made Foolproof

<u>Ingredients:</u>

2 to 4 bunches of asparagus, any thickness you prefer
1 tbsp kosher salt
boiling water

<u>Directions:</u>

1. Place trimmed and cleaned asparagus spears in a glass dish that has a lid, such as Corning ware. Sprinkle spears with salt. Pour boiling water over the spears to cover and immediately cover with the lid. Let the asparagus sit in the boiling water until the water is no longer hot. The asparagus will be perfectly cooked with the right amount of crunch. If you want it less crunchy, or it is thick asparagus spears, drain the water, and give it another bath of boiling water.
2. Drain the water. Serve hot or cold.

<u>Toppings:</u>

If served warm, top with melted butter and lemon, or freshly grated parmesan cheese. If served cold, mix 1 cup mayo and 1 tbsp cream and stir. Add three minced garlic cloves, stir, and pour over asparagus.

<u>Notes:</u>

I have included this *recipe* because I never could get asparagus cooked right. My friend, Jan Kinzel, shared this method.

Asparagus with Lemon Zest, Goat Cheese, and Roasted Almonds

Ingredients:

2/3 cup coarsely chopped almonds
1 tbsp olive oil
1 tsp coarse salt
2 pounds fresh asparagus, trimmed
1 tbsp olive oil
½ cup vegetable broth
6 ounces soft goat cheese, crumbled
1 tbsp lemon juice
1 tsp grated lemon zest
I tbsp finely shredded fresh basil leaves

Directions:

1. Set the oven to 350. In small bowl chop almonds and mix with 1 tbsp of olive oil and 1 tsp salt. Place on roasting pan and roast the chopped almonds for 12 to 14 minutes. Don't let almonds overcook. Remove from oven and set aside.
2. Spray roasting pan with cooking spray. Stir the asparagus and 1 tbsp oil in the pan. Season the asparagus with salt and pepper as desired. Add the broth.
3. Roast the asparagus for 20 minutes or until tender, stirring once during cooking. Top with the cheese, lemon juice, lemon zest, and roasted almonds.

Notes:

You can divide recipe in half if you don't need 2 pounds. Also, you can use a lemon-honey mustard dressing rather than just sprinkling with lemon juice. Honey mustard dressing: 1 large egg, hard-boiled, white discarded, and yolk chopped, juice from 1 lemon, 1 tbsp Dijon mustard, 2 tbsp honey, salt, pepper, ½ cup olive oil. Whisk all ingredients. Pour on asparagus after topping with cheese and almonds.

Asparagus with Pistachio Pesto

Ingredients:

1 bunch asparagus, ends snapped off
2 tbsp olive oil
pinch salt and freshly ground black pepper
½ cup shelled pistachios
½ cup basil leaves
½ cup parsley
1 clove garlic
½ lemon, juiced
1/3 cup olive oil

Directions:

1. Preheat the oven to 500. Put a rimmed cookie sheet into the oven to preheat for at least 5 minutes. It needs to be very hot.
2. Toss the asparagus in the olive oil, salt, and pepper. Quickly (and carefully) take the hot pan from the oven and lay the oiled asparagus onto it. Spread the spears out evenly in a single layer and return pan to the oven for 4-5 minutes.
3. While the asparagus is in the oven, make pesto: put remaining ingredients into your food processor or blender and pulse until coarsely chopped and mixed well.
4. Remove asparagus from the oven and top with the pesto. Serve hot or at room temperature.

Brown Rice with Peppers and Onion

<u>Ingredients:</u>

2 cups low sodium chicken broth
1 cup long grain brown rice
1 tbsp olive oil
1 small sweet onion, finely chopped
3 cloves garlic, minced
1 small green bell pepper, chopped
1 small red bell pepper, chopped
1 tsp dried basil
1 tsp dried oregano
½ tsp ground black pepper
pinch of salt
splash dry white wine
1 tbsp grated parmesan cheese (optional)

<u>Directions:</u>

1. Bring water and rice to a boil in a saucepan. Reduce heat to medium-low, cover, and simmer until the rice is tender and liquid has been absorbed, 20 to 25 minutes.
2. Heat oil in a large skillet over medium-high heat. Cook and stir onion in the hot oil until tender, about 3 minutes. Add garlic and continue to cook and stir until onion is translucent, 2 to 3 minutes more. Stir green bell pepper and red bell pepper into onion mixture; cook until tender, about 5 minutes. Season with basil, oregano, black pepper, and salt.
3. Pour wine into vegetable mixture and reduce heat to medium low. Simmer until liquid is reduced, about 5 minutes. Stir rice into vegetables. Top with parmesan cheese before serving.

Boston Baked Beans

Ingredients:

2 cups navy beans
½ pound bacon, chopped into 1-inch pieces, half cooked, and drained
1 onion, finely diced
3 tbsp molasses
2 tsp salt and ¼ tsp ground black pepper
¼ tsp dry mustard
½ cup ketchup
1 tbsp Worcestershire sauce
¼ cup brown sugar

Directions:

1. Pick over beans for stones, wash and drain. Soak overnight in cold water. Simmer the beans in the same water until tender, 1 to 2 hours. Drain and reserve the liquid.
2. Preheat oven to 325. Put beans in a 2-quart bean pot or casserole dish in portions, layering them with bacon and onion.
3. In a saucepan, combine molasses, salt, pepper, dry mustard, ketchup, Worcestershire sauce, and brown sugar. Bring the mixture to a boil and pour over beans. Pour in just enough of the reserved bean water to cover the beans.
4. Cover the dish with a lid or aluminum foil. Bake for 3 to 4 hours in the preheated oven, until beans are tender. Remove the lid about halfway through cooking, and add more liquid, if necessary, to prevent beans from getting too dry.

Notes:

When I was growing up, it wasn't a picnic without baked beans. I often modify this and use a slow cooker. I soak the beans overnight as directed. I use 1 pound of bacon, and 1½ times the remaining ingredients and put everything into the slow cooker and cook for 6 to 8 hours on low, adding liquid if beans get dry. During the last hour, I add one can each of kidney and black beans.

Butternut Squash and Mascarpone Bake

Ingredients:
  1½ pounds butternut squash, peeled, seeded, and cut in 1-inch cubes (3 cups)
  2 tbsp olive oil
  8 oz dried extra-wide noodles
  4 tbsp butter
  6 shallots, chopped
  1 tbsp lemon juice
  1 8-oz carton mascarpone cheese
  ¾ cup grated parmesan cheese
  ½ cup fresh Italian (flat-leaf) parsley, snipped
  1 cup Panko bread crumbs or soft bread crumbs

Directions:
1. Preheat oven to 425. In bowl, toss squash in oil; place in oiled 15x10-inch baking pan. Roast, uncovered, 30 minutes, until lightly browned and tender, stirring twice.
2. Meanwhile, in large pot or Dutch oven, cook noodles according to package directions. Drain; set aside. In same pot, melt 2 tbsp of the butter. Add shallots; cook and stir over medium heat for 3 to 5 minutes, until shallots are tender and butter just begins to brown. Stir in lemon juice.
3. Add noodles and squash to shallot mixture. Stir in mascarpone, ½ cup of the parmesan, ¼ cup parsley, and ¼ tsp each salt and black pepper. Transfer to a greased 2-quart oval gratin dish or baking dish.
4. In small saucepan melt remaining 2 tbsp butter; stir in bread crumbs, remaining parmesan, and parsley. Sprinkle on noodle mixture. Bake, uncovered, 10 minutes, until crumbs are golden. Serves 8.

Corn Bread with Cream Style Corn

<u>Ingredients:</u>

3 boxes Jiffy corn muffin mix
2 sticks of butter, softened
16 oz sour cream
1 (16 oz) can creamed style corn
1 (16 oz) can whole kernel corn, drained
4 eggs

<u>Directions:</u>

1. Preheat oven to 350.
2. Mix all ingredients together and pour into an 11x15-inch butter greased pan, and bake for 45 minutes until well-browned.

<u>Notes:</u>

This recipe came from Linda Dawson Cutler, who said that although she doesn't like corn bread, she thinks this is delicious. If you don't have an 11x15 pan, this can be made in two 9 x 9-inch pans.

Corn Mushroom Bake

<u>Ingredients:</u>

6 tbsp butter, divided
¼ cup finely chopped green or red pepper
¼ cup minced onion
8 oz mushrooms, washed and chopped
½ cup all-purpose flour
2 cans (14¾ oz each) cream-style corn
1 tsp salt
¼ tsp pepper
2 pkg (3 oz each) cream cheese, cubed
2 cans (15¼ oz each) whole kernel corn, drained
1 cup shredded Swiss cheese
2 cups soft bread crumbs

<u>Directions:</u>

1. In a large saucepan, sauté pepper, mushrooms, and onion in 3 tbsp butter until tender. Stir in flour, cream corn, salt, and pepper until blended. Add cream cheese; stir until melted. Stir in the whole kernel corn, mushrooms, and Swiss cheese.
2. Transfer to a greased 3-quart baking dish. Melt remaining butter; toss with bread crumbs. Sprinkle over the corn mixture.
3. Bake, uncovered, at 400 degrees for 20-25 minutes or until heated through.

<u>Notes:</u>
I make no representation that this is a healthy side dish. It is comfort food pure and simple. I make it rarely, but I try to enjoy it guilt-free on those occasions when I do.

Cornbread Stuffing

Ingredients:

1 pound ground sausage
2 cups chopped celery
2 large onions, chopped
5 cups crumbled cornbread (see note below)
5 cups seasoned bread crumbs
2¼ cups chicken broth
¾ cup butter, melted
1½ tsp poultry seasoning
1 tsp sage
1 tsp dried thyme
salt and pepper to taste

Directions:
1. Preheat oven to 325. Place sausage, celery, and onions in a large, deep skillet. Cook over medium high heat until evenly brown. Drain, crumble, and set aside.
2. In a large bowl combine sausage mixture with cornbread, bread crumbs, chicken broth, butter, poultry seasoning, sage, and thyme.
3. Mix well and transfer to a buttered 9x12-inch baking dish. Bake, covered, for 45 minutes, or until well set and cooked through.

Notes:
For this recipe, I've bought cornbread, made it with Jiffy Mix, or made it from scratch. All work well. Of course, if I had to choose, I'd take the version with homemade cornbread to which I generally add a can of cream style corn.

Cranberry Sauce with Dried Cherries

<u>Ingredients:</u>
>1 pound fresh or thawed frozen unsweetened cranberries (4 cups)
>1½ cups dried sour cherries (9 oz)
>1½ cups sugar
>½ cup pure cranberry juice
>juice from ½ navel orange (¼ cup)
>kosher salt

<u>Directions:</u>
1. In a medium saucepan, combine all of the ingredients except the salt and bring to a simmer. Cook over moderate heat, stirring occasionally, until the cranberries burst, and the sauce is about the consistency of jam, approximately 15 minutes.
2. Scrape the cranberry sauce into a heatproof bowl and let cool completely. Season with salt and refrigerate until chilled. Serve the sauce cold or at room temperature; stir in small amount of water if the sauce is too thick.

<u>Note:</u>
This sauce can be made several days ahead, put in a pretty holiday bowl and covered with plastic wrap until you are ready to serve it.

~ ~ ~

Cranberry Sauce with Pineapple and Walnuts

<u>Ingredients:</u>
>15 oz can whole cranberry sauce
>15 oz can crushed pineapple
>3 oz raspberry or cherry Jell-O dissolved in 1 cup boiling water
>1 cup coarsely chopped walnuts

<u>Directions:</u>
1. Dissolve Jell-O in boiling water. Add remaining ingredients. Pour in a 13x9-inch pan and refrigerate. Before serving, stir and put in bowl.

<u>Notes:</u>
This recipe came from my friend, Susan Jurkiewicz, and for many years was a Thanksgiving staple. In recent years, I've mixed it up a bit and tried other cranberry dishes, but this remains a favorite.

Creamy Slow Cooker Mashed Potatoes

<u>Ingredients:</u>

    5 pounds russet or Yukon gold potatoes (peeled and quartered)
    1 (8-oz) pkg cream cheese (softened)
    1 cup sour cream
    1 tsp onion powder
    1½ tsp salt
    ¼ tsp garlic powder
    ¼ tsp white pepper
    1 egg (beaten)
    1/3 cup butter

<u>Directions:</u>

1. Cook the potatoes in large pot of boiling salted water until they are tender, about 20 to 30 minutes.
2. Drain the potatoes in a colander, return the potatoes to the dry pot. Shake over low heat for about 1 minute. This helps make the potatoes fluffy and removes excess moisture.
3. Mash the potatoes until there are no lumps. Beat in the cream cheese, sour cream, onion powder, salt, pepper, and egg.
4. Place the mashed potatoes in a greased 5-quart crockpot insert. Melt the butter and drizzle over the potatoes. Cool for 20 minutes, then cover and refrigerate up to three days.
5. Take the potatoes out of the refrigerator about 3½ hours before serving time. Stir the potato mixture well. Cover and cook on low heat for 3 to 4 hours, stirring once or twice.
6. Add more melted butter or milk if you desire a softer consistency. The potatoes can be kept warm in the slow cooker an additional 30 minutes on low. If you want them to stay warm on a buffet, turn crockpot to warm for up to two more hours.

<u>Notes:</u>

Under most circumstances, making mashed potatoes this way is just an extra bother. However, when I'm having a dinner party and want mashed potatoes, I find that draining and mashing potatoes at the last minute, when there are a hundred other little details that demand attention, can be difficult. This method allows me to take care of the time consuming or messy part of mashed potatoes ahead of time. Besides, these are quite delicious.

Everyday Recipe for Perfect Mashed Potatoes

<u>Ingredients:</u>

    4 pounds potatoes cut into smallish pieces
    2 tsp salt
    1 stick butter
    1 cup milk

<u>Directions:</u>

1. Place potatoes in a pot. Cover with cold water, add two tsp salt. Bring to a boil and then simmer until tender.
2. Drain potatoes in a colander. Return to pot and with burner on low, let heat dry any remaining water. These two steps (draining and returning to the pot) make all of the difference.
3. Beat on med-high until pretty much lump free.
4. Add one stick of butter and 1 cup milk (more or less to obtain your desired consistency.

~ ~ ~

Gingered Applesauce

<u>Ingredients:</u>

    5 medium apples, (Granny Smith or other tart apple)
    1 (1-inch) piece of ginger, peeled and sliced into 1/8-inch pieces
    ½ cup water
    1 tsp lemon juice
    2 tbsp brown sugar (heaping tbsp)
    ¾ tsp cinnamon, ground
    ¼ tsp ginger, ground

<u>Directions:</u>

1. Peel and core apples and chop into 1-inch pieces. Into a medium saucepan over medium heat, place apples, pieces of ginger, water, and lemon juice. Cover and simmer for 15-20 minutes, stirring occasionally. Check to make sure mixture doesn't boil dry.
2. When apples are soft, drain, and mash until reaching your preferred chunky consistency. Remove pieces of ginger. Stir in brown sugar, cinnamon, and ground ginger until thoroughly incorporated.

Grilled Chile-Lime Corn on the Cob

Ingredients:

4 ears corn, in husk
3 tbsp unsalted butter, at room temperature
1 tsp lime zest
1 tbsp lime juice
1 tsp chili powder
¼ tsp granulated garlic
1 tsp salt
½ tsp freshly ground black pepper

Directions:
1. In a small bowl, combine butter, lime zest and juice, chili powder, garlic, and salt and pepper. Set aside.
2. Carefully peel back husk from the ears of corn, without detaching from the bottom, remove silk, fold the husk back around the ears and soak in water for 30 to 45 minutes. Make sure to weigh down the ears so that they are fully submerged.
3. Preheat a grill to medium, indirect heat. Remove ears from water, drain, open husk, dry ears with paper towel, and spread butter mixture evenly on corn. Fold husk back over corn and grill, turning often, for 35 minutes (change heat to medium-high for the last ten minutes.) Serve immediately.

Hasselback Potatoes

<u>Ingredients:</u>

3 pounds baking potatoes
1 tsp salt
2-3 tbsp melted butter
2-3 tbsp of olive oil
2-3 tbsp chopped fresh herbs (parsley, chives, thyme, sage, etc.)
or 2 -3 tsp dried herbs
4 tbsp grated cheddar cheese
1½ tbsp parmesan cheese
3 tbsp fine bread crumbs (or panko)

<u>Directions:</u>
1. Preheat the oven to 425.
2. Peel the potatoes, and place in bowl of cold water to prevent browning.
3. One by one, place potatoes on a large wooden or metal spoon. Using a sharp knife, make slices across the potato the short way about 1/8 to ¼ inch apart, making sure to cut down to the lip of the spoon, not all the way through the potato. The slices should stay connected at the bottom, and the spoon helps keep the depth even. Return the potato to the bowl of water, and proceed with the remaining potatoes.
4. When all of the potatoes are cut, place them cut side up in a shallow baking dish.

(Recipe continued on next page.)

5. Mix olive oil and butter. Drizzle potatoes with half of the butter-olive oil mixture, then sprinkle and season with herbs and salt and pepper.

6. Bake for 45 minutes to an hour (until potatoes are nearly done) in the preheated oven. Remove from the oven, and drizzle with the remaining butter/olive oil. Sprinkle cheeses and bread crumbs onto the tops of the potatoes, and season with a little more salt and pepper. Return to the oven, and bake for an additional 20 minutes, or until nicely browned.

<u>Notes:</u>

It is easy to vary the quantity to meet your needs. I sometimes use small red potatoes (adjusting the time so they don't get mushy), other times larger baking potatoes. I usually plan four or five small new potatoes per person. You can also serve with herbed sour cream (Sour cream with a bit of garlic powder, salt, pepper, and fresh parsley).

~ ~ ~

Grand Marnier Cranberry Sauce

<u>Ingredients:</u>

1 (12-oz) pkg fresh cranberries
1¼ cups sugar
2 tbsp frozen orange juice concentrate, thawed
2 tbsp Grand Marnier or another orange-flavored liqueur

<u>Directions:</u>

1. Preheat oven to 325. Place cranberries in 8x8x2-inch glass baking dish. Sprinkle sugar, then orange juice over cranberries. Cover tightly with foil.

2. Bake until juices form and cranberries are very soft, about 1 hour.

3. Uncover; mix in liqueur. Cover and refrigerate until very cold, about 4 hours. Can be prepared 3 days ahead. Keep chilled.

<u>Notes:</u>

I got this from *Bon Appétit Magazine* while I was waiting . . . and waiting . . . and waiting . . . in my ophthalmologist's office. I fixed it to serve with turkey for Christmas that year and thought it was much superior to canned cranberry sauce.

Jacques Pepin's Pumpkin Gratin

Ingredients:

1 can (15.5 oz) pure pumpkin puree (**not** pumpkin pie filling)
3 large eggs
1 cup heavy cream
¾ cup grated Swiss cheese
¾ tsp salt
½ tsp freshly ground black pepper
1 tsp unsalted butter
1 tbsp grated parmesan cheese

Directions:

1. Preheat the oven to 350. Spoon the pumpkin puree into a food processor and add the eggs, cream, Swiss cheese, salt, and pepper. Process for 10 to 15 seconds to combine.
2. Coat a 6-cup gratin dish with the butter. Fill the dish with the pumpkin mixture. Sprinkle the parmesan cheese on top and bake for 35 to 45 minutes, until set and lightly browned on top. Serve hot as a side dish.

Notes:

This recipe came from Lani Longshore, a member of my writers' group. It is vegetarian and gluten free.

Roasted Asparagus and Mushrooms

<u>Ingredients:</u>

1 bunch fresh asparagus, trimmed
½ pound fresh Baby Bella mushrooms, quartered
1 tbsp balsamic vinegar
2 tbsp olive oil
kosher salt to taste
freshly ground black pepper to taste

<u>Directions:</u>

1. Preheat oven to 400. Lightly spray a cookie sheet with cooking spray.
2. Place the asparagus and mushrooms in a bowl. Drizzle with the olive oil and balsamic, salt, and pepper; toss well. Lay the asparagus and mushrooms out on the prepared pan in an even layer. Roast in the preheated oven until the asparagus is crisp-tender, about 15 minutes.

<u>Notes:</u>

Cooking time will vary depending upon thickness of asparagus. So, while I love roasted asparagus, you have to be careful. Thin asparagus may burn, thick may take a couple additional minutes.

Roasted Mushrooms in Polenta with Goat Cheese, Caramelized Shallots and Sun-dried Tomatoes

Ingredients:

6 large Portobello mushrooms (about 1½ pounds, stems discarded)
3 tbsp good olive oil
1 tbsp balsamic vinegar
kosher salt and black pepper to taste
2½ cups chicken stock
2 cups half and half
¾ cup fine cornmeal
8 oz can diced marinated artichoke hearts in their own oil
1 heaping tbsp sun-dried tomatoes, snipped into small pieces
¼ cup Italian mascarpone cheese
4 oz Gorgonzola picante, crumbled

Directions:

1. Preheat oven to 400. Wash mushroom caps gently, then arrange them, underside up, on a sheet pan. Drizzle with olive oil and balsamic vinegar, then sprinkle with salt and pepper. Bake for 20 minutes, until tender. Set aside. Lower the oven temperature to 375.

2. While mushrooms are baking, make polenta. Pour the stock and half and half into a large saucepan and bring to a boil. Lower the heat and while whisking constantly, slowly sprinkle the cornmeal into the boiling liquid. Simmer for 6 to 8 minutes, stirring almost constantly with a wooden spoon, until polenta is thick and smooth. Turn off the heat, stir in the mascarpone, artichokes, sun-dried tomatoes, 1 tsp salt, and ½ tsp pepper. Pour into an 8x11x2-inch baking dish.

3. Arrange the mushrooms, underside up, in one layer over the polenta. Sprinkle on the gorgonzola and bake for 25-30 minutes, until the polenta is bubbly and the cheese is melted. Sprinkle with additional salt and pepper to taste. Serve warm.

Note:

This wonderful recipe came from Jan Kinzel and was served at a brunch she hosted for Bob and me when we were moving from our Trevi condominium to our house in West Dublin.

Roasted New Potatoes

Ingredients:

3 pounds new potatoes, quartered
4 tbsp olive oil
4 tsp minced garlic
¾ tsp salt
¾ tsp dried rosemary, crushed
¾ tsp dried thyme
¼ tsp pepper
Pam cooking spray

Directions:

1. In a large resealable plastic bag, combine all ingredients; shake to coat. Place potatoes, cut side down onto a rimmed baking sheet sprayed with Pam.
2. Bake, uncovered, at 450 for 35 minutes or until potatoes are tender. Stir once during baking.

Note:

I have yet to meet a potato I didn't love.

Roasted Vegetable Medley

<u>Ingredients:</u>

2 tbsp olive oil, divided
1 large yam, peeled and cut into 1-inch pieces
1 large parsnip, peeled and cut into 1-inch pieces
1 cup baby carrots
1 zucchini, cut into 1-inch slices
1 bunch fresh asparagus, trimmed and cut into 1-inch pieces
½ cup roasted red peppers, cut into 1-inch pieces
2 cloves garlic, minced
¼ cup chopped fresh basil
½ tsp kosher salt and ½ tsp ground black pepper

<u>Directions:</u>
1. Preheat oven to 425. Grease 2 baking sheets with 1 tbsp olive oil.
2. Place the yams, parsnips, and carrots onto the baking sheets. I line sheets with non-stick aluminum foil to make clean-up easier. Bake in the preheated oven for 30 minutes, then add the zucchini and asparagus, and drizzle with the remaining 1 tbsp of olive oil.
3. Continue baking until all of the vegetables are tender, about 30 minutes more. Once tender, remove from the oven, and let cool for 30 minutes on the baking sheet.
4. Toss the roasted peppers together with the garlic, basil, salt, and pepper in a large bowl until combined. Add the roasted vegetables, and toss to mix. Serve at room temperature or cold.

<u>Notes:</u>
The first time I made this, I felt the asparagus was overcooked. So, the second time I extended the cooking time for the original veggies, added the zucchini after 30 minutes, but the asparagus after 45 minutes. I preferred this warm as a side dish. Substitute any favorite veggie you like (mushrooms, white potato, broccoli), but add at appropriate time to avoid burning.

Scalloped Potatoes

<u>Ingredients:</u>

1½ cups heavy cream
3 bay leaves
2 sprigs fresh thyme, plus more to garnish
2 garlic cloves, chopped
½ tsp freshly grated nutmeg
salt and freshly ground black pepper
unsalted butter
2 pounds russet potatoes, peeled and cut into 1/8-inch-thick slices
½ cup grated parmesan, plus more for broiling

<u>Directions:</u>

1. Preheat the oven to 400. In a saucepan, heat the cream with the bay leaves, thyme, garlic, nutmeg, and salt and pepper to taste. While the cream is heating, butter a casserole dish.

2. Use a slotted spoon to remove the bay leaves and thyme from the heated cream. Pour the cream into a large bowl with the potato slices. Mix gently to coat the potatoes. Dust the parmesan over the potatoes. Mix to gently incorporate. Spoon a little bit of the cream into the bottom of the casserole dish. Then spoon the potatoes in. Level out the potatoes for uniform cooking time. Pour the remaining cream at the bottom of the bowl over the casserole. Top with parmesan and fresh thyme leaves.

3. Cover the dish with foil, but pull back one corner for the steam to escape. Bake for 40 minutes or until potatoes are done.

<u>Notes:</u>
I keep this around as a good basic recipe. I double or triple as needed. I sometimes pour the potatoes into a slow cooker so I don't have to be bothered watching them and can get on to fixing the remainder of the dinner. I like to sauté onion and add to the potatoes. I often add shredded cheddar cheese (or other cheese) or ham to the saucepan when I'm heating the cream.

Simple Bread Stuffing

<u>Ingredients:</u>

¾ cup (1½ sticks) unsalted butter plus more for baking dish
1 pound good-quality day-old white bread, torn into 1-inch pieces (about 10 cups)
2½ chopped yellow onions
1½ cups ¼-inch slices celery
½ cup chopped flat-leaf parsley
2 tbsp chopped fresh sage
1 tbsp chopped fresh rosemary
1 tbsp chopped fresh thyme
2 tsp kosher salt
1 tsp freshly ground black pepper
2½ cups low-sodium chicken broth, divided
2 large eggs

<u>Directions:</u>

1. Preheat oven to 250. Butter a 13x9x2-inch baking dish and set aside. Scatter bread in a single layer on a rimmed baking sheet. Bake, stirring occasionally, until dried out, about 1 hour. Let cool; transfer to a very large bowl.

2. Meanwhile, melt ¾ cup butter in a large skillet over medium-high heat; add onions and celery. Stir often until just beginning to brown, about 10 minutes. Add to bowl with bread; stir in herbs, salt, and pepper. Drizzle in 1¼ cups broth and toss gently. Let cool.

3. Whisk 1¼ cups broth and eggs in a small bowl. Add to bread mixture; fold gently until thoroughly combined. Transfer to prepared dish, cover with foil.

4. Bake in an oven preheated to 350 until an instant-read thermometer inserted into the center of stuffing registers 160, about 40 minutes. Continue to bake stuffing, uncovered, until set and top is browned and crisp, 40-45 minutes longer.

<u>Notes:</u>

This is the basic recipe my mother, Bonnie Albrecht, served with Thanksgiving dinner. It's pretty simple, and sometimes simple is best. Since stuffing (aka dressing in our home) was such a family favorite we always doubled the recipe. If you expect a hectic holiday, you can make this stuffing the day ahead through step 3. Cover and refrigerate. Remove from refrigerator and let sit for one hour to bring to room temperature before baking and then bake according to step 4.

Twice Baked Potatoes

Ingredients:

6 large baking potatoes
1 (16 oz) container sour cream
½ cup shredded Cheddar cheese
1 stick butter
½ pound bacon, cooked, drained, and crumbled
1 small bunch scallions, chopped fine
salt and pepper to taste
3 slices American cheese

Directions:
1. Preheat oven to 350. Bake potatoes for 1 hour or until soft.
2. While potatoes are baking, cook bacon. When crisp, remove, drain, and crumble. Set aside. Cook scallions (or finely sliced green onions) in bacon grease until translucent. Remove with slotted spoon and set aside.
3. Remove baked potatoes from oven and when cool enough to handle, cut in half and scoop out insides leaving about ¼ inch of potato pulp with the skin. Put scooped pulp into a mixing bowl. Add butter, sour cream, cheese, all but a tbsp of bacon crumbles, and scallions. Mix together well. Add salt and pepper to taste.
4. Fill the skins with the mix. Top with bacon crumbles and ½ slice American cheese. Bake for 20 to 25 minutes just until heated through.

Notes:
 I always peel and boil a couple of additional potatoes and mash and add to the mix to give me more quantity for the filling. I also prefer other cheeses to American, so often use shredded cheddar as a topping.

White House Traditional Bread Stuffing

Ingredients:

1 loaf (16 oz) sourdough or other crusty-type bread
3 tbsp olive oil
2 large onion, chopped
2 ribs celery, chopped
1 large carrot, chopped, (I grate the carrot)
4 oz mushrooms, sliced (optional)
2½ cups chicken broth
2 tsp chopped fresh rosemary or ½ tsp dried rosemary
2 tsp chopped fresh thyme or ½ tsp dried thyme
½ tsp salt and ½ tsp freshly ground black pepper

Directions:

1. Cut bread into ¼ inch cubes. Turn into two 15x10x1-inch jelly-roll pans. Heat in 350-degree oven 30 minutes or until dry, tossing occasionally. (Alternatively, you may cover fresh-cut bread cubes with parchment paper and let dry at room temperature 1 to 2 days instead of drying in the oven.)
2. Heat olive oil in a large skillet over medium heat. Add vegetables and sauté 3 to 5 minutes or until slightly tender. If you are adding mushrooms, add them at this point and sauté an additional minute.
3. Place bread cubes in large bowl. Add chicken broth. Toss to moisten. Add vegetables, rosemary, thyme, salt and pepper.
4. Spoon into 2½ to 3-quart shallow baking dish. Cover with aluminum foil. Bake in 350-degree oven 35 minutes or until heated through. Uncover and bake an additional 10 minutes. Makes 10 cups. For a moister stuffing, add more chicken broth as desired to bread cubes.

Notes:

It's not Thanksgiving without stuffing. This is similar to my mother's recipe, but she didn't put in the carrots or mushrooms, and she used stale white bread, not sourdough. I triple the recipe because my family loves stuffing, and we want plenty of leftovers. To make a moister stuffing, I also add ½ cup melted butter, 1 cup if doubling the recipe, 1½ cups if tripling the recipe.

White House Sweet Potatoes and Greens

<u>Ingredients:</u>

2 or 3 large sweet potatoes
¼ tbsp olive oil or vegetable oil
½ tsp cinnamon
¼ tsp ground cloves
salt and pepper to taste
2 bunches of greens (chard, kale, or collards)
2 cloves of garlic
1 tsp honey
juice from half a lemon

<u>Directions:</u>

1. Peel and cut the sweet potatoes into bite-size pieces. Heat half the oil in pan over medium heat and add potatoes. Cook, stirring occasionally, until just brown on all sides and soft (about 12 to 15 minutes, depending on size). When cooked, add spices and salt and pepper to taste. Set aside.

2. While the potatoes are cooking, wash the greens (do not dry), remove stems and cut leaves into small pieces. Heat remaining oil over medium heat, add the garlic and cook for a minute before adding greens. Stir often and cook until tender. Season with salt and pepper to taste.

3. Combine potatoes, honey, and lemon juice with the greens, stir and serve.

<u>Notes:</u>

I figured if it was good enough for President Obama, it was good enough to try on my family. I was an adult before I developed a taste for sweet potatoes, and greens still aren't on my 'favorites' list, but this isn't half bad.

Zucchini Boats (Stuffed)

Ingredients:

4 small zucchinis (about 6 inches in length)
6 oz fresh spinach, coarsely chopped
2-3 tbsp diced red onion (or scallions or sweet onion)
1-2 tbsp jalapeno peppers, finely diced (can substitute sweet peppers)
½ cup diced fresh, seeded tomato
8 slices center cut bacon, cooked (optional)
8 slices sharp cheddar cheese

Directions:
1. Preheat oven to 400.
2. Wash, trim zucchini, cut in half lengthwise, and cut out centers for stuffing. Dice zucchini centers.
3. Mix chopped zucchini centers, spinach, onion, peppers, tomato, and salt and pepper to taste.
4. Stuff/overstuff zucchini. Top with bacon and cheese, cut to fit (may use toothpicks to hold cheese in place).
5. Bake in 400-degree oven until cheese is nicely browned, about 10-15 minutes.

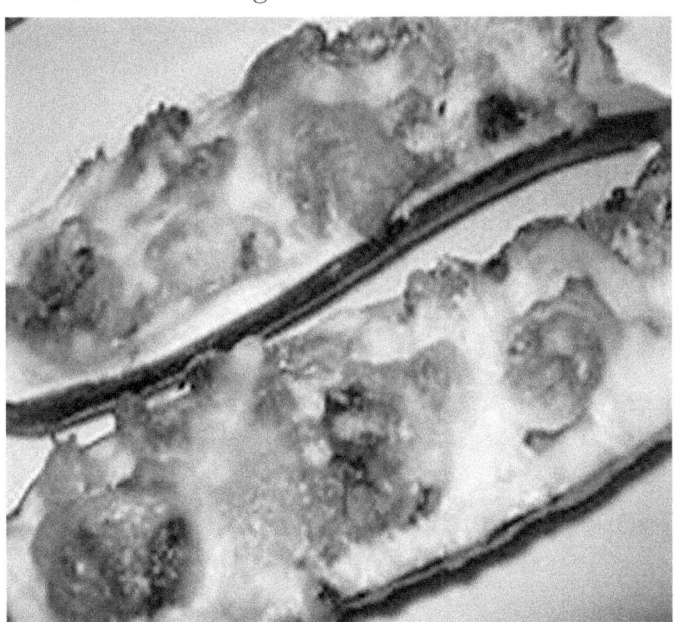

Notes:
This recipe came from my friend, Diane Herron. She says it can be prepared up to a day in advance, covered and refrigerated until needed. Bring to room temperature before baking. She also notes that this recipe is very flexible. You can substitute baby kale for spinach, use a different cheese, add corn, cooked rice, or grains. Even the oven temperature is flexible so if you want to bake something else at the same time you can bake this any temperature between 375 to 425, and adjust cooking time. Diane likes vegetables so makes this as an entree with 3 halves for each person, served with a side salad, rice, grain, or bread. Makes 8 zucchini boats (more if cut small and used as appetizer).

Zucchini Sticks, Oven Roasted with Parmesan

Ingredients:

4 zucchinis, quartered lengthwise
½ grated parmesan
½ tsp dried thyme
½ tsp dried oregano
½ tsp dried basil
¼ tsp garlic powder
kosher salt and freshly ground pepper
2 tbsp olive oil
2 tbsp finely chopped fresh parsley leaves

Directions:
1. Preheat oven to 350. Coat a cooking rack with nonstick spray and place on a rimmed baking sheet. Set aside.
2. In a small bowl, combine parmesan, thyme, oregano, basil, and garlic powder. Salt and pepper to taste.
3. Place zucchini onto prepared baking sheet. Drizzle with olive oil and sprinkle with parmesan mixture. Place in oven and bake until tender, about 15 minutes. Then broil for 2 to 3 minutes or until crisp and golden brown.
4. Garnish with parsley and serve immediately.

Miscellaneous
A few things that didn't seem to go anywhere else...

~ ~ ~

Candied Flower Garnish

Ingredients:

2 tsp meringue powder
2 tbsp water
40 to 50 edible blossoms
1-1¼ cups superfine sugar

Directions:
In a small bowl, dissolve meringue powder in water. Lightly brush over all sides of flowers to coat completely. Sprinkle with sugar. Allow to dry on a waxed paper-lined baking sheet for 1 to 2 days. Use as a garnish for dessert.

Notes:
Edible flowers include: rose petals, carnations, fuchsia, impatiens, marigold, lilacs, violas, and dianthus. Make sure flowers haven't been treated with pesticides or wash very carefully.

~ ~ ~

How to Make Perfect Boiled Eggs

Ingredients:

6 eggs

Directions:
1. Place eggs into a saucepan and pour in cold water to cover; place over high heat. When the water just starts to simmer, turn off heat, cover pan with a lid, and let stand for 17 minutes. Don't peek. (Instructions continued on next page.)

2. Pour out the hot water and pour cold water over eggs. Drain and refill with cold water; let stand until eggs are cool, about 20 minutes. Peel eggs under running water.

~ ~ ~

How to Make Perfect Turkey Gravy

<u>Ingredients:</u>

5 cups turkey stock with pan drippings
1 (10.75 ounce) can condensed cream of chicken soup
1 tsp poultry seasoning
½ tsp black pepper
1 tsp seasoned salt
¼ tsp garlic powder
1 cup milk
1/3 cup all-purpose flour

<u>Directions:</u>
1. Bring the turkey stock to a boil in a large saucepan. Stir in soup, and season with poultry seasoning, pepper, seasoned salt, and garlic powder. Reduce heat to low, and let simmer.
2. Warm the milk in the microwave, and whisk in the flour with a fork until there are no lumps. Return the gravy to a boil, and gradually stir in the milk mixture. Continue to cook, stirring constantly, for 1 minute, or until thickened.

~ ~ ~

Tips for Making Cake Mix Cakes Taste Closer to Homemade

1. Add two additional egg yolks to the eggs called for by the recipe.
2. Substitute milk or buttermilk for the water. Because buttermilk is thicker, add a couple of extra tbsp to the amount of water called for.
3. Butter gives more flavor. Replace oil called for with butter.
4. Other extras (depending on mix flavor) a bit of lemon or lime juice, chocolate chips or dried fruit.

~ ~ ~

Wonderful Imposters

Recipes you may have wished you had from commercial eateries; these replications are pretty darned close.

(Recipes start on the next page.)

1. **Arthur Treacher's Fish and Chip Batter**: Mix together until smooth equal parts of boxed pancake mix and club soda. Dip moistened and lightly floured fish filets into batter, using tip of sharp knife, not tongs. Fry in 385-degree oil until crispy brown on each side.

2. **Colonel Sanders Cole Slaw:** Marinate 3 cups shredded cabbage, ½ cup shredded carrot, 2 tbsp sugar, 4 tbsp milk in refrigerator overnight. Drain well. Mix cabbage/carrot mixture with ½ cup mayonnaise, ¼ cup buttermilk or sour cream, dash Tabasco, 1 tbsp dry minced onion, ¼ tsp celery seed. Refrigerate 1 hour before serving.

3. **Long John Silver's Fish Batter**: With wire whisk in medium bowl, combine 2/3 cup beer or club soda, 1/3 cup lemon juice, 1 egg, ½ cup Bisquick, and ½ cup self-rising flour. When smooth, let stand 10 minutes. Moisten and lightly flour 1½ to 2 pounds fish filets. Let dry a few minutes. Dip to coat with batter. Do not use tongs but rather the tip of a sharp knife to spear filets. Drop batter coated filets into 385-degree oil, a few at a time, frying on each side until golden brown and crispy.

4. **Kentucky Fried Chicken:** Combine 3 cups self-rising flour, 1 tbsp paprika, 2 envelopes tomato Cup of Soup powder, 2 pkgs Good Seasons Italian Dressing Mix powder, 1 tsp seasoning salt. Rinse a 9-piece, 3-pound cut-up fryer in water; drain, and pat dry. Place flour mixture in plastic food bag. Coat 1 piece of chicken at a time in flour mixture. Make a single layer, skin-side-up in a greased baking pan. Drizzle each piece with melted butter (about 2 tbsp per piece). Do not turn pieces. Bake uncovered at 350 for one hour or until golden brown, basting 3 or 4 times with more butter. For extra crispy, dust pieces in a bit more flour mixture and drizzle with more butter to build up coating during baking.

5. **McDonald's Big Mac Sauce**: Combine 1 cup Miracle Whip salad dressing, 1/3 cup bottled creamy French dressing, ¼ cup sweet pickle relish, 1 tbsp sugar, ¼ tsp black pepper, 1 tsp dry minced onion. Stir well and keep refrigerated, tightly covered up to two weeks.

6. **Sanders Hot Fudge Sauce**: In the top of a double boiler over simmering water, combine 14 oz can Eagle Brand Sweetened Condensed Milk, 14 oz light Karo syrup, ½ pound butter (2 sticks), and 12 oz Nestles Milk Chocolate morsels. Stir until smooth and then continue simmering over double boiler without stirring for 30 additional minutes. Put through blender in small amounts using high speed. Makes 1 quart. To heat for serving, rewarm over hot water or in a microwave.

7. **White Castle Sliders**: Soak ¼ cup dry minced onions in ¼ cup hot water until soft. Meanwhile mix 2 pounds ground round, 3 oz jar of strained beef baby food, and 2/3 cup clear beef broth. Keep patties uniform by using a ¼ cup scoop for each patty and flatten to ¼ inch thick. Fry on griddle using 1 tbsp of oil for each patty and put 1 tsp of onion under each patty as you turn to fry second side. Make 3 or 4 holes in each patty while frying. Cut hot dog buns in half and cut off rounded ends to make buns.

Note:
I admit that the idea of adding a jar of baby food to the White Castle Sliders seemed disgusting, but it's the price you pay for nostalgia.

~ ~ ~

Substitutions

I doubt there is a cook among us who hasn't, at one time or another, started a recipe only to find they were missing an ingredient. Here is a helpful list of substitutions for those occasions.

Butter
For cooking, any oil will do. For baking, use an equivalent amount of:
regular (not light) margarine
Lard
Coconut oil (solid)
If you've only got half the amount of butter you need for a baked good recipe, applesauce can work for the rest.

Eggs
For each egg in a baking recipe, swap in:
1/3 cup applesauce
½ pureed banana (¼ cup)
1 tbsp ground flax seeds or chia seeds + 3 tbsp water
¼ cup blended silken tofu

3 tbsp vegetable oil + 1 tbsp water
2 to 3 tbsp mayonnaise (for cakes)

Sour Cream
Replace each cup with:
Plain Greek yogurt, an equivalent amount
¾ cup cream cheese + 3 tablespoons milk
1/3 cup melted unsalted butter + ¾ cup milk + 1 tsp lemon juice (for baking)

Dairy Products
1 cup milk = ½ cup evaporated milk + ½ cup water
1 cup half & half = 1 cup whole milk + 1 tbsp melted unsalted butter OR 1 cup evaporated milk

(Substitutions continued on next page.)

1 cup heavy whipping cream = 2/3 C whole milk + 1/3 C melted unsalted butter
1 C buttermilk = 1 C milk + 1 tsp lemon juice or vinegar

Garlic
For each clove, use:
1/8 tsp garlic powder
½ tsp garlic salt (omit ½ tsp salt from the recipe)
½ tsp jarred minced garlic
½ to 1 tsp minced shallots

Onions
For each medium onion, use:
1½ to 2 tsp onion powder
1 cup chopped shallots
1¼ cups chopped leeks, green onions or scallions (white and light green parts only)
1 cup frozen chopped onions

Lemon
For each tbsp of juice, use 1 ½ tsp white wine vinegar, sherry vinegar, or champagne vinegar
For each tsp of zest, use ½ tsp lemon extract

Fresh Herbs
For each tbsp of chopped fresh herbs, use:
1 tsp dried
¼ to ½ tsp ground or powdered

Breadcrumbs
For each cup, use:
3 to 4 slices oven-dried bread, crushed in a food processor
1¼ cups croutons or stuffing cubes, crushed
¾ cup cracker crumbs
1 cup crushed tortilla or potato chips
1 cup crushed pretzels
1 cup crushed cornflakes

Flour
1 cup all-purpose flour = 1 cup + 3 tablespoons cake flour OR 1 cup self-rising flour (omit baking powder + salt from recipe) OR 1½ cups dry breadcrumbs
1 cup of cake flour = 1 cup pastry flour OR 1 cup minus 3 tbsp all-purpose flour + 3 tbsp cornstarch
1 cup pastry flour = 2/3 cup all-purpose flour + 1/3 cup cake flour
1 cup self-rising flour = 1 cup all-purpose flour + 1½ tsp baking powder + ½ tsp salt

Sugar
1 cup granulated sugar = 1¾ cups unsifted confectioners' sugar OR 1 cup packed light or dark brown sugar OR 1 cup minus 2 tbsp honey, agave nectar, or brown rice syrup + ¼ tsp baking soda (reduce liquid in recipe by 3 tbsp and lower oven temperature by 25°)
1 cup dark brown sugar = 1 packed cup light brown sugar + 1 tbsp molasses OR 1 cup granulated sugar + 2 to 3 tbsp molasses
1 cup light brown sugar = 1 cup granulated sugar + 1 to 2 tbsp molasses OR ½ cup dark brown sugar + ½ cup granulated sugar
1 cup confectioners' sugar = 1 cup granulated sugar + 1 tbsp cornstarch, processed in a food processor

Cocoa Powder
For every 3 tbsp, use:
1 oz unsweetened chocolate (decrease fat in recipe by 1 tbsp)
2 oz semisweet chocolate (decrease fat in recipe by 1 tbsp and sugar in recipe by 3 tbsp)

Table Salt
For each tsp, use:
1½ tsp Morton kosher salt
2 tsp Diamond Crystal kosher salt
2 tsp soy sauce

Rice
For each 1 cup of uncooked white or brown rice, use the following amount of the uncooked substitute:
2 cups orzo pasta
1¼ cups couscous
¾ cup barley
1 cup quinoa
1 cup bulgur
1 1/3 cups wheatberries
1½ cups kasha

Tomatoes
For each pound of fresh tomatoes, use:
1½ cups canned whole tomatoes
6 to 8 sun-dried tomato halves, reconstituted in hot water

(Substitutions continued on next page.)

3 tbsp tomato paste (you may need to add liquid)

Broth

1 cup of broth = 1 bouillon cube + 1 cup boiling water OR 1 tsp bouillon granules + 1 cup boiling water

To replace chicken or vegetable broth, use an equivalent amount of dry white wine, vermouth or water (in small amounts).

To replace beef broth, use an equivalent amount of vegetable broth, red wine or beer.

Wine

For each cup of red, use:

¾ cup red grape juice + 2 tbsp red wine vinegar or lemon juice + 2 tbsp of water (for marinades)

1 cup beef broth (for sauces and stews)

1 cup beer (for stews)

For each cup of white, use:

¾ cup white grape juice, apple juice, or apple cider + ¼ cup white wine vinegar or lemon juice (for marinades)

1 cup sherry, vermouth, sake, mirin, or chicken or vegetable broth (for sauces and stews)

Note:

A word of caution about substitutions: They work better in some recipes than others, so consider the likelihood a substitution will suffice in light of the complexity of the recipe and the other ingredients. If baking a cake and the recipe calls for 1 cup milk, you can probably get away with ½ cup evaporated milk plus ½ cup of water. But if you need whipped cream to top a dessert, you aren't going to be able to turn milk with butter into whipped cream!

INDEX

A List of Contributors

Andrea Beach 15
April Cutler 385
Barb Albrecht 18, 31, 35, 76
Bertha Dawson 161, 169, 180, 346
Bonnie Albrecht 43, 53, 72, 113, 323, 433
Carol Kammer 166
Cora Wiltsie 157, 169
Courtney Phillips 392
Diane Herron 437
Dorothy Albrecht 80
Edith Dawson 70, 97, 100, 101, 116, 154, 172, 179, 185, 200, 204
Emma Albrecht 399
Fred Kosanke 231
Gail Ng 22, 25, 389
George Cramer 61
Heidi Landry 10, 357
Jan and Chris Kinzel 38
Jan Kinzel 140, 235, 321, 412, 429
Jean Ann Albrecht Wendt 74, 94, 152
Jes Phillips 7, 131, 135
Judy Albrecht 26, 31, 89, 115, 397
Julie Rosas 251
Kaelin Royce 197
Lani Longshore 427
Linda Danko 14
Linda Dawson Cutler . 19, 56, 58, 69, 75, 153, 169, 200, 206, 216, 346, 418
Linh Nguyen 28
Margie Lampel 214
Marilyn Albrecht Tackaberry 84, 222
Marilyn Parr 350
Marilyn Royce 246
Maureen and Ray Scully 322, 422
Merry Rosenberg 193
Minna Dubin 57
Neva Hodges 370
Rick Albrecht 176
Rose Houk 226
Sharron Dawson Beckwith 157, 160, 163, 169, 177
Shlomit Elitzur 19, 147, 266, 358
Susan Jurkiewicz 12, 380, 421

Appetizers, Dips, and Snacks

Artichoke and Crab Dip 4
Asparagus Roll-Ups 5
Bacon Horseradish Dip 16
Banh Mi Bruschetta 6
Bay Scallops and Shrimp Ceviche 7
Best Chicken Appetizer Ever 8
Cucumber Dill Dip 16
Filet Mignon Towers 9
French Onion Dip 17
Ginger Lime Fruit Dip 17
Grilled Marinated Shrimp 10
Guacamole Dip 17
Healthy Chimichurri Shrimp Appetizer 11
Hot Artichoke Dip 16
Hot Cheddar Bean Dip 16
Hot Crab Dip 16
Individual Spicy Greek Layered Cups 12
Mushroom and Ricotta Bruschetta 15
Mushroom Croustades 13
Nine Mayonnaise Based Dips 16
Nuts and Bolts 18
Salmon Log 19
Salmon Spread with Herbed Crostini 20
Shrimp Louis Dip 17
Shrimp Salsa 21
Spicy Nuts 22
Spicy Shrimp 23
Spinach and Ham Dip 24
Stuffed Portobello Mushrooms Caps 25
Taco Dip 26

Thai Fried Wonton Wrapped Shrimp 27
Tuna Pâté.. 29
Twice Baked New Potato Skins.................. 30
Vegetable Pizza.. 31

Beverages

Almond Joy 33
Chalet View Lodge Cognac and Champagne
.... 33
Cranberry Margaritas 34
Dirty Snowman 34
Green Magic Punch Or Orange Monster
Punch 35
Green Tea Sangria 36
Honey Deuce Delight 36
Hot Apple Pie Cocktail 36
Julie's Easy Margaritas for a Crowd........... 37
Long Bay Iced Tea 37
Moscato Moscow Mule 38
Moscato Strawberry Lemonade 38
Nino Anejo 35
Party Rum Punch 39
Peach Ginger Bellini.................................. 39
Perfect Pear Punch 40
Pina Colada Slush...................................... 40
Raspberry and Citrus Martini 41
Red Velvet Punch...................................... 42
Sage honey syrup~.................................... 44
Slush 43
Slushie Gin and Tonic................................ 43
Sparkling Sage Grapefruit Cocktail 44

Breads, Rolls, Muffins, and Waffles

Almond-Cherry Filled Braids..................... 46
Bacon Ranch Bread Bites.......................... 47
Banana Blueberry Muffins........................ 48
Banana Bread 49
Banana Bread (No-fat version) 50
Banana Bread (with yogurt and toasted
walnut) 51
Banana Nut Waffles 52
Blueberry Muffins 53
Bran Muffins...54
Cheddar-Corn Bread Rolls........................55
Clotted Cream 78
Coffee Cake with Apple Pie Filling.............56
Corn Fritters with Roasted Peppers,..........57
Dad's Favorite Crumb Coffee Cake 58
French Toast (Baked and Stuffed 59
French Toast Italiano................................60
George Cramer's Holiday Buttermilk Waffles
....61
Healthy Blueberry Bran Muffins 62
Honey Gingerbread 63
Kaiser Rolls from Frozen Bread Dough......64
Oat-Zucchini Bread...................................65
Peachy Bran Muffins.................................66
Pear, Ginger, and Walnut Muffins 67
Pecan Caramel Rolls.................................68
Pecan Rolls 69
Pistachio Coffee Cake...............................70
Poppy Seed Muffins 71
Pull Apart Bacon Cheese Wreath...............72
Pumpkin Oatmeal Muffins 73
Raisin Nut Bread.......................................74
Raspberry Royale Muffins 75
Raw Apple Bread......................................76
Red Lobster Cheddar Biscuits 77
Scones with Clotted Cream......................78
Sour Cream Coffee Cake 80
Strawberry Waffle Topping.......................61
Toasted Garlic Bread 81
Waffle S'mores...82
Whole-Grain Berry Pancakes 83
Zucchini-Chocolate Chip Muffins 84

Cakes and Frostings

Apple Pie Cake with Rum Butter Sauce 86
Apple Sheet Cake 87

Best Ever Banana Cake with Cream Cheese Frosting 88
Banana Dump Cake 89
Bavarian Cream Filling 92
Best White Cake Recipe 90
Boston Cream Pie 92
Brownie Cupcakes 94
Caramel Sauce 126
Caramel Whipped Cream 126
Carrot Cake with Cream Cheese Frosting .. 95
Carrot Cake with Orange Glaze 96
Chocolate Frosting 93
Chocolate Ice Box Cake 98
Cream Cheese Frosting: 105
Flourless Chocolate Cake 99
Fresh Apple Cake 100
Fresh Orange Cake 101
Frozen Chocolate Cake 102
Ghirardelli Individual Chocolate Lava Cakes 103
Hawaiian Carrot Cake 104
Hummingbird Cake 105
Ice Cream Cake (Baskin Robbins Style) 106
Italian Cream Cake 108
Macadamia Fudge Torte 109
Maple-Walnut Topping 128
Marshmallow Frosting 128
Milky Way Cake 111
Mini-Bundt Cakes 112
Mom's Florida Cake 113
Pastry Cream Filling 92
Pumpkin Roll 114
Rhubarb-Upside Down Cake 115
Self-Filled Cup Cakes 116
Strawberry Shortcake with Basil Whipped Cream 117
Texas Sheet Cake (Oatmeal Version) 122
Texas Sheet Cake (Original Chocolate) 119
Texas Sheet Cake (Peanut Butter Version) 120
Texas Sheet Cake (Pumpkin Version) 122
Texas Sheet Cake (White Version) 121
Vanilla buttercream frosting 90
Vanilla Buttercream Frosting 91
Waldorf Astoria Red Cake 124
Walnut Cake with Caramel Whipped Cream 125
Whipped Chocolate Frosting 129

Casseroles, Stews, and One Dish Meals

Chicago-Style Deep Dish Pizza 132
Chicken Pot Pie 133
Creamy Fettuccine with Bacon 134
Ezra's and Noah's Tortilla Casserole 135
Goulash 136
Hearty Beef Pot Pie with Cornmeal Cheese Crust 137
Hearty Beef Stew 138
Lobster Mac and Cheese 139
Macaroni and Cheese 141
Mississippi Pepperoncini Pot Roast 277
Puttanesca Penne Pasta 142
Quick Red Wine Chicken Stew 143
Spicy Chicken Stew 144
Tuna Casserole 145

Cookies, Brownies, and Candy

Almond Cookies 147
Best Ever Oatmeal Cookie 148
Brickle Bars 149
Brownie cupcakes with peanut butter cup 150
Brownie Dress Ups 150
Butterfinger Brownies 151
Calico Meringues 152
Caramel Apples 188
Caramel Corn 189
Caramel Dip 190
Caramel-coconut pecan brownies 150
Caramels to Die For 191
Chewy Chocolate Cookies 153

Chocolate Bon Bon Pops 192
Chocolate Brownie Cups......................... 154
Chocolate Nut Toffee Bars...................... 158
Chocolate Oatmeal Sandwich Cookies 159
Chocolate Peanut Butter Pile Ups 160
Chocolate Volcano Cookies 155
Chocolate Whoopie Pie Cookies.............. 156
Chocolet Cookies 157
Church Windows 161
Clipper Chocolate Chip Cookies............... 162
Coffee brownies with mocha icing 151
Cream de menthe brownies 150
Creamy Double Decker Fudge 193
Crispy Snack Cookies 163
Death by Chocolate Cookie 164
Decadent Candy Bar Cookies................... 165
Delicious Chocolate Dollops 166
Double Tree Chocolate Chip Cookies 167
English Toffee 193
Gingersnap macadamia nut brownies..... 150
Great Harvest Bread Company Chocolate Chip Cookies 168
Hermits 169
Hot Fudge Sauce 194
Lemon Bars with Shortbread Crust 170
Lemon Shortbread Triangles 171
M&M brownies... 150
Meringue Topped Chocolate Coconut Nut Bars 172
Mrs. Field's Chocolate Chip Oatmeal Cookies 173
Paint for Sugar Cookies............................ 181
Peanut Butter Fudge 194
Peanut Butter Temptations..................... 174
Pecan Toffee Bars with Browned Butter Icing 175
Praline Crunch Party Mix...........................195
Raspberry-almond Viennese brownies ... 150
Rick's Spicy Molasses Cookies 176
Roasted Hazelnut Shortbread Cookies.... 183
Rocky road brownies 151
Sand Art Brownies 177
Saucepan Candied Fruit Bars 178
Shortbread Cookies..................................179
Skillet Cookies 180
Spicy Gingerbread Men...........................182
Sugar Cookies..181
Thumbprint Cookies................................184
Top of the Stove Oatmeal Peanut Butter Clusters...185
Triple chocolate brownies.......................150
Triple Treat Shortbread, Caramel, and Chocolate Cookies..............................186
Walnut Crescent Cookies 187

Desserts

Almond Stuffed Chocolate Dipped Strawberries...197
Apple Crisp 198
Apple Turnovers.......................................199
Assorted Tiny Tarts 201
Caramel Cups 204
Cherry-Rhubarb Crunch 205
Cream Puffs in a Pan 206
Elegant Pear Dessert...............................207
Fudgy Ice Cream Sandwiches...................208
Gingerbread with Lemon Curd................209
Gooey Chocolate Caramel Fantasy 211
Hot Fudge Ice Cream Puffs......................212
Individual Bittersweet Chocolate Cheesecakes...213
Mountain Dew Apple Dumplings.............214
Poached Pear in Puff Pastry 215
Pretzel Salad..216
Raisin Pudding Cake with Caramel Sauce 217
Raspberry Mocha Torte 218
Rice Pudding..219

Eggs, Cheese, and Brunch

Baked Eggs on Puff Pastry.......................221
Baked Oatmeal..222
Breakfast Casserole.................................223

Breakfast Strudel 224
Cheesy Hash Brown Potato Casserole 226
Crustless Spinach and Mushroom Quiche 227
Essence Spice 234
Festive French Toast 229
Italian Brunch Torte 230
Joe's Special
   A San Francisco Tradition.................... 231
Make-Ahead Eggs Benedict 232
Make-Ahead Savory Breakfast Bread
   Pudding 233
Mini Breakfast Quiches with Potato Crust
.... 235
Spicy Southwest Bacon-Sausage Bake 236
Turkey Breakfast Pizza 237

Italian, Mexican, Asian, and Other Ethnic Dishes

Afghani Bolani (Potato and Green Onion
   Stuffed Flatbread) 239
Asian Pork and Noodles 241
Authentic Fettuccine 131
Crabmeat Quesadillas 242
Gnocchi with Wild Mushrooms and Basil
   Cream 243
Grilled Asian Flank Steak 244
Hungarian Chicken Paprikash with
   Dumplings 245
Indian Chicken Stew 247
Lasagna with Four Cheese and Meat Sauce
.... 248
Pesto 250
Pesto Cream Tortellini 250
Pesto Egg Salad 250
Pesto Potato Salad 250
Pesto Quesadilla Sauce 250
Pesto-Tomato Soup 250
Quesadillas with Brie, Avocado, Eggs, & Fruit
   Salsa 251
Sali Par Edu 252
Salsa Verde Enchiladas with Chicken and
   Kale 253
Slow Cooker Layered Huevos Rancheros 254
Soft Tacos with Seafood and Vegetables 255
Spaghetti Sauce 257
Sweet and Sour Chicken 258
Sweet and Sour Chicken (Stir-Fry) 259
Taco Dip (Seven Layer) 260
Taco Seasoning 260
Thai Green Curry with Chicken and
   Asparagus 261
Veggie Lo Mein 263
Vietnamese Chicken Noodle Soup 264

Main Dishes, Beef

Beef Bourguignon 266
Beef Stroganoff 267
Best Ever Pot Roast 268
Lobster-Stuffed Beef Tenderloin 269
Meat Loaf Three (Italian) 276
Meat Loaf Two 275
Meatball Dress-Ups 272
Meatballs 272
Meatballs in BBQ Sauce 273
Meatballs in Pesto 273
Meatballs in Pesto Cream 273
Meatballs in Pineapple Sauce 272
Meatballs with Beef/Veal/Pork 271
Meatloaf One 274
St. Louis BBQ Ribs 278
Stuffed Flank Steak 279
Swiss Steak in Wine Sauce 280
Teriyaki Beef Tenderloin 281

Main Dishes, Fish

Almond Crusted Salmon 282
Beer Battered Whitefish 283
Couscous Crusted Salmon 284
Easy One-Hour Salmon Dinner with Dill
   Sauce 285

Grilled Salmon with choice of three rubs 287
Honey Lime Tilapia 288
Little River Inn's Crab Pot Pie 289
Louisiana Barbecued Shrimp 290
Mendocino's First Place Crab Cakes 291
Mustard Crusted Tilapia 292
Pepper Jelly and Soy Glazed Salmon 293
Salmon Cakes with Ginger Sesame Sauce 294
Seared Scallops with Wine Sauce 295
Tilapia with Tomato and Artichoke Sauce 296

Main Dishes, Pork
Chili Pork Tenderloin 299
Panko Crusted Pork Tenderloin with Dijon Cream Sauce 297
Pulled Pork BBQ Sauce 301
Pulled Pork (Slow Cooker or Oven) 300

Main Dishes, Poultry
Baked Chicken with Honey Mustard Sauce 302
Cashew Chicken 303
Catalina Cranberry Chicken 304
Chicken Marengo 307
Chicken with Couscous Patties 305
Chicken with Quinoa and Vegetables 306
Perfect Moist & Tender Chicken Breasts Every Time 308
Pesto Chicken Florentine 309
Pickle Juice and Buttermilk Brined Fried Chicken 310
Slow Cooker Turkey Breast 311
Slow-Cooker Chicken and Potato Curry .. 312
Turkey Carving and Brining 313

Miscellaneous
Arthur Treacher's Fish and Chip Batter ... 441
Candied Flower Garnish 439
Colonel Sanders Cole Slaw 441
Everything Glazed Bacon 58, 228
How to Make Perfect Boiled Eggs 439
Kentucky Fried Chicken 441
Long John Silver's Fish Batter 441
McDonald's Big Mac Sauce 441
Sanders Hot Fudge Sauce 441
Substitutions 442
Tips for making Cake Mix Taste Closer to Homemade 440
Two Good Marinades 314
White Castle Sliders 442
Wonderful Imposters 440

Pies
Apple Cider Pie 316
Bumbleberry Pie 317
Caramel Pecan Pie 318
Dutch Apple Pie 319
Fresh Strawberry Pie (Version One) 320
Fresh Strawberry Pie with Whipped Cream 321
Great Meringue 337
Key Lime Pie 322
Lemon Meringue Pie 323
Mixed Berry Pie 324
Mud Pie 325
Pear-Butterscotch Pie 326
Pecan Pie with Brownie Crust and Vanilla Sauce 329
Pecan Pie without Corn Syrup 331
Pie Crust Five (Lard) 335
Pie Crust Four (Lard and Butter) 335
Pie Crust One (Basic) 334
Pie Crust Seven (Butter, shortening and vinegar) 336
Pie Crust Six (No Fail with Vinegar and Lard) 336
Pie Crust Three (Butter Crust) 335
Pie Crust Two (with Vinegar) 334
Pumpkin Praline Pie 327
Raspberry Pie with Crème de Cassis 332

Ryan's Easy Peanut Butter Pie 333
Streusel Topping 316

Salad Dressing

Basic oil/vinegar/lemon juice dressing: ... 411
Cilantro Vinaigrette 400
Creamy Blue Cheese Dressing 411
Creamy Brie Dressing: 411
Green Goddess Dressing 411
Julia Child's Lemon-Oil Dressing 411
Mustard Vinaigrette 391
Orange Vinaigrette 395
Raspberry Vinaigrette 411
Red Wine Vinaigrette 392
Sweet and Sour Dressing 386
Tomato-Miso Dressing 411

Salads, Sandwiches, Side Dishes, and Soups

Salads

April's Asian Salad 385
Bacon Potato Salad 386
Bread Salad (Panzanella) 387
Broccoli, Raisin, Bacon, and Almond Salad 388
Caprese Cookie Sheet Salad with Pasta and Roasted Tomato 390
Caprese Salad 389
Chopped Chicken Salad 391
Corn Salad 392
Creamy Coleslaw 393
Curry Chicken and Fruit Salad 393
Easy and Versatile Fruit Salad 394
Endive, Orange, and Roquefort Salad 395
Fig and Blue Cheese Salad 396
Freezer Cole Slaw 397
Fresh Zucchini and Corn Salad 398
German Potato Salad 398
Grilled Potatoes with Chevre and Cilantro Vinaigrette 400
Guest-Worthy Caesar Salad 399
Mandarin Chicken Salad 401
New Potato, Avocado, and Egg Salad 402
Pear, Gorgonzola, and Candied Walnut Salad 403
Potato Salad with Mayonnaise Dressing . 404
Salade Niçoise 405
Shrimp Cole Slaw 406
Shrimp Pasta Salad 407
Smoked Salmon Potato Salad with Dill ... 408
Sweet Potato Cakes with Kale Bean Salad 409
Tangy Two Potato Salad 410
Thai Cucumber and Tomato Salad with Lime/Peanut Dressing 410

Sandwiches

Black Bean Burgers 339
Chicken Curry Tea Sandwiches 341
Cucumber Tea Sandwiches 342
Egg Dipped Ultimate Grilled Cheese Sandwich 343
Fat Doug Burger 344
Grandma Bertha's Sloppy Joes 346
Greek Pork Gyros Souvlaki 347
Lum's Beer Steamed Hot Dogs 349
Marilyn's Favorite Sloppy Joes 350
Pulled Pork Biscuit Sliders 351
Putting on the Ritz Egg Salad Tea Sandwiches 352
Smoked Salmon Sandwich on Pumpernickel 354
Turkey Burgers 353
Upscale Philly Cheese Sandwiches 355

Side Dishes

Asparagus Made Foolproof 412

Asparagus with Lemon Zest, Goat Cheese, and Roasted Almonds 413
Asparagus with Pistachio Pesto 414
Boston Baked Beans 416
Brown Rice with Peppers and Onion 415
Butternut Squash and Mascarpone Bake 417
Corn Bread with Cream Style Corn 418
Corn Mushroom Bake 419
Cornbread Stuffing 420
Cranberry Sauce with Dried Cherries 421
Cranberry Sauce with Pineapple and Walnuts 421
Creamy Slow Cooker Mashed Potatoes .. 422
Everyday Recipe for Perfect Mashed Potatoes 423
Gingered Applesauce 423
Grand Marnier Cranberry Sauce 426
Grilled Chile-Lime Corn on the Cob 424
Hasselback Potatoes 425
Jacques Pepin's Pumpkin Gratin 427
Roasted Asparagus and Mushrooms 428
Roasted Mushrooms in Polenta with Goat Cheese, Caramelized Shallots and Sun-dried Tomatoes 429
Roasted New Potatoes 430
Roasted Vegetable Medley 431
Scalloped Potatoes 432
Simple Bread Stuffing 433
Twice Baked Potatoes 434
White House Traditional Bread Stuffing .. 435
White House Sweet Potatoes and Greens 436
Zucchini Boats (Stuffed) 437

Zucchini Sticks, Oven Roasted with Parmesan 438

Soups

Authentic Chicken and Andouille Sausage Gumbo 356
Barley Mushroom Soup 358
Bean Soup with Smoked Turkey 359
Butternut Squash with Apple Cider Soup 361
Butternut Squash, Corn, Potato, and Pea Soup 360
Chicken Chili with Black Beans 362
Chili with Pulled Pork and Beef 363
Cincinnati Skyline Chili 365
Cioppino (Fish Stew) 366
Clam Chowder 367
Crab and Corn Chowder 368
Cream Soup with Mushrooms 370
Curried Butternut Squash and Apple Bisque 371
Curry Sauce 371
Finch Bay Tomato Soup 373
French Onion Soup 374
Gazpacho 375
Hearty Chicken Soup with Noodles and Vegetables 376
Minestrone Soup 377
Potato Soup Chowder 378
Slow Cooker Bean and Vegetable Soup ... 379
Smoked Salmon Chowder 380
Smoked Turkey Split Pea Soup 381
Three Alarm Vegetarian Chili 382
Veggie Soup 383

www.ingramcontent.com/pod-product-compliance
Lightning Source LLC
Chambersburg PA
CBHW060453300426
44113CB00016B/2571